The Shelly Cashman Series®

Microsoft® Windows® 11

First Edition

Comprehensive

Steven M. Freund

Cengage

Australia • Brazil • Canada • Mexico • Singapore • United Kingdom • United States

The Shelly Cashman Series® Microsoft® Windows® 11 Comprehensive, First Edition
Steven M. Freund

SVP, Product: Cheryl Costantini

VP, Product: Thais Alencar

Portfolio Product Director: Rita Lombard

Senior Portfolio Product Manager: Amy Savino

Senior Product Assistant: Ciara Horne

Learning Designer: Zenya Molnar

Senior Content Manager: Anne Orgren

Digital Product Manager: Jim Vaughey

Developmental Editor: Lyn Markowicz

VP, Product Marketing: Jason Sakos

Senior Director, Product Marketing: Danaë April

Product Marketing Manager: Mackenzie Paine

Portfolio Specialist: Matt Schiesl

Content Acquisition Analyst: Ann Hoffman

Production Service: Lumina Datamatics Ltd.

Designer: Erin Griffin

Cover Image Source: PM Images/Getty Images

For product information and technology assistance, contact us at **Cengage Customer & Sales Support, 1-800-354-9706 or support.cengage.com.**

For permission to use material from this text or product, submit all requests online at **www.copyright.com.**

Library of Congress Control Number: 2023909197

Student Edition ISBN: 978-0-357-88177-4
Loose-leaf Edition: 978-0-357-88178-1*
*Loose-leaf available as part of a digital bundle

Cengage
5191 Natorp Boulevard
Mason, OH 45040
USA

Cengage is a leading provider of customized learning solutions with employees residing in nearly 40 different countries and sales in more than 125 countries around the world. Find your local representative at **www.cengage.com.**

To learn more about Cengage platforms and services, register or access your online learning solution, or purchase materials for your course, visit **www.cengage.com.**

Notice to the Reader

Printed at CLDPC, USA, 10-23

Brief Contents

Contents

Windows

Module 3: File and Folder Management ....WIN 3-1

Module 4: Personalizing Your Work Environment .... WIN 4-1

Module 5: Advanced Personalization and Customization .... WIN 5-1

Module 6: Advanced Searching Techniques .... WIN 6-1

Module 7: Microsoft Edge .... WIN 7-1

Module 8: Mastering Digital Media .... WIN 8-1

Module 9: Understanding Security, Networking, and Utilities .... WIN 9-1

Getting to Know Microsoft Office Versions

Cengage is proud to bring you the next edition of Microsoft Office. This edition was designed to provide a robust learning experience that is not dependent upon a specific version of Office.

Microsoft supports several versions of Office:

- **Office 365:** A cloud-based subscription service that delivers Microsoft's most up-to-date, feature-rich, modern productivity tools direct to your device. There are variations of Office 365 for business, educational, and personal use. Office 365 offers extra online storage and cloud-connected features, as well as updates with the latest features, fixes, and security updates.

- **Office 2021:** Microsoft's "on-premises" version of the Office apps, available for both PCs and Macs, offered as a static, one-time purchase and outside of the subscription model.

- **Office Online:** A free, simplified version of Office web applications (Word, Excel, PowerPoint, and OneNote) that facilitates creating and editing files collaboratively.

Office 365 (the subscription model) and Office 2021 (the one-time purchase model) had only slight differences between them at the time this content was developed. Over time, Office 365's cloud interface will continuously update, offering new application features and functions, while Office 2021 will remain static. Therefore, your onscreen experience may differ from what you see in this product. For example, the more advanced features and functionalities covered in this product may not be available in Office Online or may have updated from what you see in Office 2021.

For more information on the differences between Office 365, Office 2021, and Office Online, please visit the Microsoft Support site.

Cengage is committed to providing high-quality learning solutions for you to gain the knowledge and skills that will empower you throughout your educational and professional careers.

Thank you for using our product, and we look forward to exploring the future of Microsoft Office with you!

Introduction to Windows 11

Objectives

After completing this module, you will be able to:

- Describe Windows 11
- Explain the following terms: app, operating system, workstation, and server
- Differentiate among the various editions of Windows 11
- Use a touch screen and perform basic mouse operations
- Start Windows 11 and sign in to an account
- Identify the objects on the Windows 11 desktop
- Start an app
- Navigate within an app

- Start the File Explorer
- Switch between apps
- Customize the Start menu
- Search for an app or a file
- Install an app
- Use the Search box
- Add reminders
- Sign out of an account and shut down the computer

What Is Windows 11?

An **operating system** is a computer program that manages the complete operation of your computer or mobile device and lets you interact with it. The operating system coordinates all the activities of computer hardware, such as memory, storage devices, and printers, and provides the capability for you to communicate with the computer.

Windows 11 is the newest version of Microsoft Windows, which is a popular and widely used operating system. Windows 11 initially was released in 2021, but Microsoft releases updates to the operating system several times per year. The Windows operating system simplifies the process of working with documents and apps by organizing the manner in which you interact with the computer. Windows is used to start apps. An **app** (short for application), also called a program, is a computer program that performs specific tasks. Apps are designed to make users more productive and/or assist them with personal tasks, such as word processing or browsing the web.

Windows commonly is used on desktops, laptops and other mobile devices, and workstations. A **workstation** is a computer connected to a server. A **server** is a powerful, high-capacity computer you access using the Internet or other network; it stores files and "serves" them, that is, makes the files available to, users; usually grouped at a location called a data center. The server controls access to the hardware and software on a network and provides a centralized storage area for programs, data, and information. Figure 1–1 illustrates a simple computer network consisting of a server, three workstations, and a printer connected to the server.

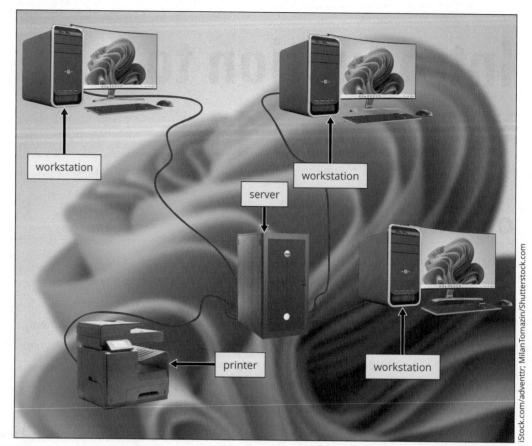

iStock.com/adventtr; MilanTomazin/Shutterstock.com

Figure 1–1

Windows is easy to use and can be customized to fit individual needs. The operating system simplifies working with documents and programs, transferring data between documents, interacting with the different components of the computer, and using the computer to access information on the Internet or an intranet. The **Internet** is a global collection of millions of computers linked together to share information, and gives users the ability to use this information, send messages, and obtain products and services. An **intranet** is an internal network site used by a group of people who work together that uses Internet technologies.

Windows 11 is designed to provide a similar user interface across multiple devices such as desktops, laptops, and tablets. The Windows 11 interface combines some of the most successful features of previous versions of Windows, such as the Start menu, an optimal interface for touch input, and enhanced search functionality. Several other improvements over previous versions of Windows make Windows 11 a suitable choice for all users.

This book demonstrates how to use Windows 11 to control the computer and communicate with other computers, both on a network and the Internet. In Module 1, you will learn about Windows and how to use some of its basic features.

Multiple Editions of Windows 11

Windows 11 is available in multiple editions. The first, **Windows 11 Home**, is simplified and designed primarily for home and small office users. **Windows 11 Pro** is designed for businesses and technical professionals. **Windows 11 Enterprise** has the same features as Windows 11 Pro but is designed for large enterprises where IT professionals need to manage and secure computers and mobile devices easily. **Windows 11 Education** contains many of the same features as Windows 11 Enterprise but is designed for faculty, staff, and students.

For a computer, minimum system requirements specify that the processor is 1 GHz or faster on a 64-bit architecture, random access memory (RAM) is at least 4 GB, the hard drive has at least 64 GB available space, and the video card supports DirectX 12 graphics with WDDM (Windows Display Driver Model) 2.0 or higher driver.

Windows can be customized using a Microsoft account. When you add a Microsoft account, you can sign in to the account and then sync (synchronize) your information with all of your Windows devices. This allows you to set your desktop background and color settings, for example, and then sync those settings with your other devices. When you sign in to your Microsoft account with another Windows device, your settings will appear the same as they do on your other Windows 11 devices.

Navigating Using Touch or a Mouse

Windows 11 provides touch support. With touch, you can use your fingers to control how Windows functions. For example, you can swipe your finger from the right to display the Action Center. (The Action Center is discussed in greater detail later in this book.) Touch also allows Windows 11 to more easily work on touch-enabled devices, such as laptops and tablets.

Using a Touch Screen

Windows users who have computers or devices with touch screen capability can interact with the screen using gestures. A **gesture** is a motion you make on a touch screen with the tip of one or more fingers or your hand. Touch screens are convenient because they do not require a separate device for input. Table 1–1 presents common ways to interact with a touch screen.

Table 1–1: Touch Screen Gestures

Motion	Description	Common Uses	Equivalent Mouse Operation
Tap	Quickly touch and release one finger one time.	Activate a link (built-in connection). Press a button. Start a program or an app.	Click
Double-tap	Quickly touch and release one finger two times.	Start a program or an app. Zoom in (show a smaller area on the screen so that contents appear larger) at the location of the double-tap.	Double-click
Press and hold	Press and hold one finger to cause an action to occur or until an action occurs.	Display a shortcut menu (immediate access to allowable actions). Activate a mode enabling you to move an item with one finger to a new location.	Right-click
Drag or slide	Press and hold one finger on an object and then move the finger to the new location.	Move an item around the screen. Scroll.	Drag

Table 1–1 (Continued)

Motion	Description	Common Uses	Equivalent Mouse Operation
Swipe	Press and hold one finger and then move the finger horizontally or vertically on the screen.	Select an object. Swipe from edge to display the Action Center.	Drag
Stretch	Move two fingers apart.	Zoom in (show a smaller area on the screen so that contents appear larger).	None
Pinch	Move two fingers together.	Zoom out (show a larger area on the screen so that contents appear smaller).	None

Using an On-Screen Keyboard

When using touch, you can access an on-screen keyboard that allows you to enter data using your fingers. To display the on-screen keyboard, click the Touch keyboard button on the taskbar. You tap a key on the keyboard to enter data or manipulate what you see on the screen. Figure 1–2 displays the on-screen keyboard.

on-screen keyboard

Figure 1–2

Using a Mouse

Windows users who do not have touch screen capabilities typically work with a mouse that has at least two buttons. For a right-handed user, the left button usually is the primary mouse button, and the right mouse button is the secondary mouse button. Left-handed people, however, can reverse the function of these buttons.

Table 1–2 explains how to perform a variety of mouse operations. Some apps also use keys in combination with the mouse to perform certain actions. For example, when you hold down CTRL while rolling the mouse wheel, text on the screen may become larger or smaller based on the direction you roll the wheel. The function of the mouse buttons and the wheel varies depending on the app.

Table 1–2: Mouse Operations

Operation	Mouse Action	Example*	Equivalent Touch Gesture
Point	Move the mouse until the pointer on the desktop is positioned on the item of choice.	Position the pointer on the screen.	None
Click	Press and release the primary mouse button, which usually is the left mouse button.	Select or deselect items on the screen or start an app or app feature.	Tap
Right-click	Press and release the secondary mouse button, which usually is the right mouse button.	Display a shortcut menu.	Press and hold
Double-click	Quickly press and release the primary mouse button twice without moving the mouse.	Start an app or app feature.	Double-tap
Triple-click	Quickly press and release the primary mouse button three times without moving the mouse.	Select a paragraph.	Triple-tap
Drag	Point to an item, hold down the primary mouse button, move the item to the desired location on the screen, and then release the mouse button.	Move an object from one location to another or draw pictures.	Drag or slide
Right-drag	Point to an item, hold down the right mouse button, move the item to the desired location on the screen, and then release the right mouse button.	Display a shortcut menu after moving an object from one location to another.	Press and hold, then drag
Rotate wheel	Roll the wheel forward or backward.	Scroll vertically (up and down).	Swipe
Free-spin wheel	Whirl the wheel forward or backward so that it spins freely on its own.	Scroll through many pages in seconds.	Swipe
Press wheel	Press the wheel button while moving the mouse.	Scroll continuously.	None
Tilt wheel	Press the wheel toward the right or left.	Scroll horizontally (left and right).	None
Press thumb button	Press the button on the side of the mouse with your thumb.	Move forward or backward through webpages and/or control media, games, etc.	None

*Note: The examples presented in this column are discussed as they are demonstrated in this module.

Scrolling

A **scroll bar** is a bar on the bottom edge (horizontal scroll bar) or right edge (vertical scroll bar) of a document window that lets you view a document that is too large to fit on the screen at once (Figure 1–3). A scroll bar contains scroll arrows and a scroll box. **Scroll arrows** are small triangular up and down arrows at each end of a scroll bar that you use to adjust your window view in small increments. A **scroll box** is a box in a scroll bar that you can drag, or click above and below, to display different parts of a window. Clicking the up and down scroll arrows moves the screen

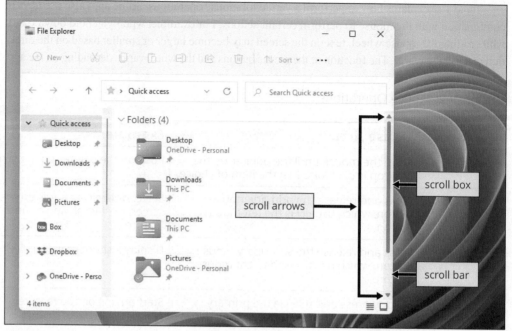

Figure 1–3

content up or down one line. You also can click above or below the scroll box to move up or down a section, or drag the scroll box up or down to move to a specific location.

Using Keyboard Shortcuts

In many cases, you can use the keyboard instead of the mouse to accomplish a task. To perform tasks using the keyboard, you can use a **keyboard shortcut**, which is a key or combination of keys that you press to access a feature or perform a command, instead of using a mouse or touch gestures. Some keyboard shortcuts consist of a single key, such as F3. Other keyboard shortcuts consist of multiple keys, in which case a plus sign separates the key names, such as CTRL+ESC. This notation means to press and hold down the first key listed, press one or more additional keys, and then release all keys. For example, another way to display the Start menu is by pressing CTRL+ESC; that is, hold down CTRL, press ESC, and then release both keys.

Starting Windows 11

It is not unusual for multiple people to use the same computer in a work, educational, recreational, or home setting. Windows enables each user to establish a **user account**, which identifies to Windows the resources, such as apps and storage locations, a user can access when working with the computer.

Each user account has a user name and may have a password and an icon, as well. A **user name** is a unique combination of letters or numbers that identifies a specific user to Windows. A **password** is a string of uppercase and lowercase letters, numbers, and symbols that, when entered correctly, allows you to open a password-protected database or to obtain access to a Windows user's account. A **picture password** is a replacement for a text password that gives you access to your device; instead of typing characters, you swipe across a picture using gestures you previously set for that image. Some devices support **Windows Hello**, which allows you to sign in to Windows when the computer or mobile device's camera recognizes your face. An icon is a small image that represents an object; thus, a **user icon** is a picture associated with a user name.

When you turn on a computer, Windows starts and displays a lock screen. A **lock screen**, which appears before you sign into Windows or after your computer has been idle for a certain

BTW
Microsoft Accounts
If you sign in to Windows using a Microsoft account, the email address associated with your Microsoft account will be displayed instead of a user name. The password you use to sign in to your Microsoft account will be the same password you will use to sign in to Windows.

BTW
PINs
In addition to passwords and picture passwords, you also can sign in to Windows using a PIN (personal identification number). If desired, Windows 11 also allows you to include letters and symbols in your PIN, making it more secure than using just numbers.

amount of time, displays the date and time and other information, such as network and battery status (shown in Figure 1–5). After tapping, sliding, or clicking anywhere on the lock screen, or pressing CTRL+ALT+DELETE, depending on your computer's settings, Windows may or may not display a sign-in screen that shows the user names and user icons for users who have accounts on the computer (Figure 1–4). This **sign-in screen**, sometimes called a log-in screen, enables you to sign in to your user account and makes the computer available for use. Clicking the user icon begins the process of signing in to, also called logging on to, your user account.

BTW
Strong Passwords
You should consider using a strong password with your Windows user account. A strong password is more secure because it is more difficult to guess. Strong passwords have at least eight characters and contain a combination of uppercase and lowercase letters, numbers, and special characters.

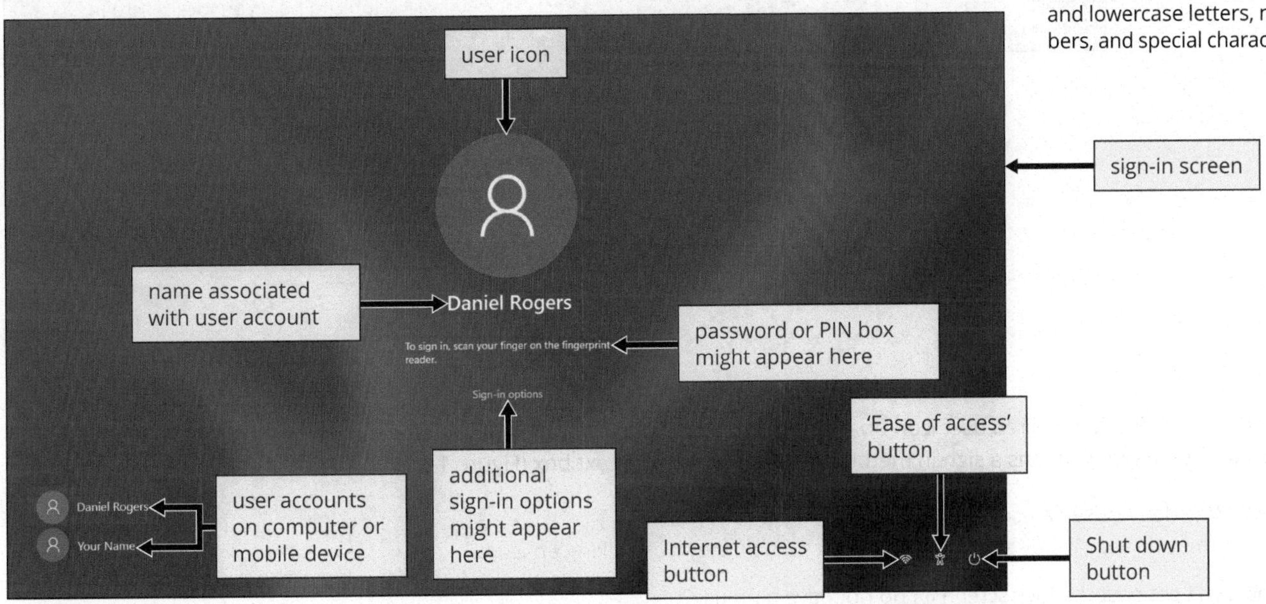

Figure 1–4

At the bottom of the sign-in screen are the Internet access button, the 'Ease of access' button, and a Shut down button. The Internet access button shows the current status of the network connection. Your Internet access button may look different, depending on the type of network connection you are using (wired or wireless). Clicking the 'Ease of access' button displays the Ease of access menu, which provides tools to optimize a computer to accommodate the needs of users with mobility, hearing, and vision impairments.

Clicking the Shut down button displays a menu containing commands related to restarting the computer, putting it in a low-power state, and shutting down the computer. The commands available on your computer may differ.

BTW
Shut Down Options
If you are walking away from your computer for only a brief period, you should put the computer in sleep mode instead of turning it off completely. Keeping the computer in sleep mode for this short period often uses less power than powering on the computer.

- The **Sleep command** saves your work, turns off the computer fans and hard drive, and places the computer in a lower-power state. To wake the computer from sleep mode, press the power button or lift a laptop's cover, and sign in to the computer.
- The **Shut down command** exits currently running apps, shuts down Windows, and then turns off the computer.
- The **Restart command** exits currently running apps, shuts down Windows, restarts the computer, and then restarts Windows.

To Sign In to an Account

The following steps, which use the user account for Daniel Rogers, sign in to an account based on a typical Windows installation. **Why?** After starting Windows, you might be required to sign in to access the computer's resources. You may need to ask your instructor how to sign in to your account.

1

- Click the lock screen (Figure 1–5) to display a sign-in screen.

lock screen

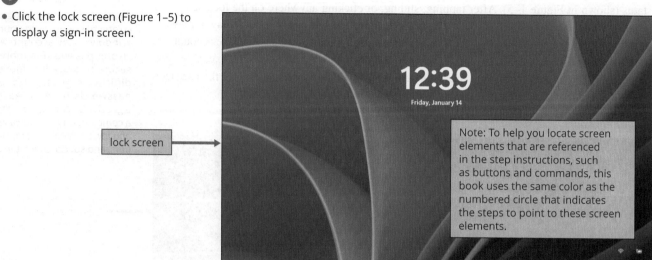

Note: To help you locate screen elements that are referenced in the step instructions, such as buttons and commands, this book uses the same color as the numbered circle that indicates the steps to point to these screen elements.

Figure 1–5

2

- If necessary, click the desired user icon on the sign-in screen, which, depending on settings, either will display a second sign-in screen that contains a sign-in method, such as a password text box (Figure 1–6), or will display the Windows desktop.

Q&A Why do I not see a user icon?
Your computer may require you to type a user name instead of clicking an icon.

How can I get past the lock screen if I do not have a mouse?
Swipe up on the lock screen to display the sign-in screen.

What is a text box?
A text box is a rectangular box in which you type text.

Why does my screen not show a password text box?
Your account does not require a password.

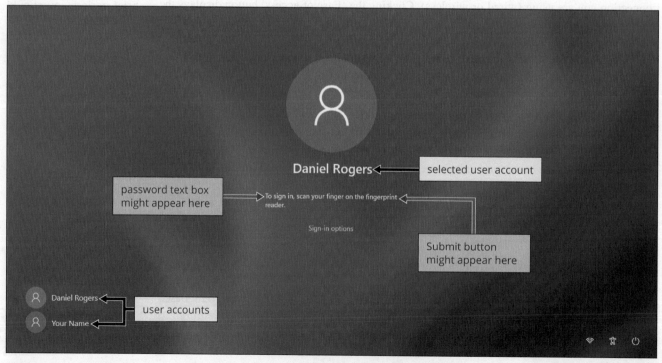

selected user account

password text box might appear here

Submit button might appear here

user accounts

Figure 1–6

● Depending on your sign-in options, type your password or PIN in the text box and then click the Submit button or scan your finger on the fingerprint reader to sign in to your account and display the Windows desktop (Figure 1–7).

Q&A Why does my desktop look different from the one shown in Figure 1–7?
The Windows 11 desktop is customizable, and your school or employer may have modified the screen to meet its needs. Also, your screen resolution, which affects the size of the elements on the screen, may differ from the screen resolution used in this book. Periodic updates released by Microsoft also may introduce differences between your screen and the figures associated with these steps.

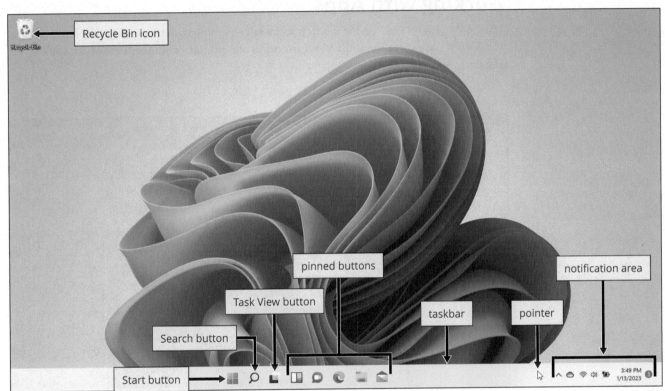

Figure 1–7

The Windows 11 Desktop

Think of the Windows desktop as an electronic version of the top of your desk. You can perform tasks such as placing objects on the desktop, moving the objects around the desktop, and removing items from the desktop.

When you start an app in Windows, it appears on the desktop. Some icons also may be displayed on the desktop. For instance, the icon for the **Recycle Bin**, the location of files and other objects that have been deleted, appears on the desktop by default. You can customize your desktop so that icons representing apps and files you use often appear on your desktop. When you start an app, that app's button appears on the taskbar. The **taskbar** is the horizontal bar at the bottom of the Windows 11 desktop; it displays icons representing apps, folders, and/or files on the left, and the notification area, containing the date and time and special program messages, on the right. Buttons for **Microsoft Edge** (Microsoft's browser) and the Widgets, Chat,

BTW
Pinned Buttons
If you use an app frequently, you should consider pinning that app button to the taskbar so that you can access it easily. Pinning and unpinning app buttons is discussed later in this module.

File Explorer, and Mail apps are pinned to the taskbar. Pinned app buttons always are displayed on the taskbar, regardless of whether the app is running or not. The right side of the taskbar contains the notification area, date, and time. The **notification area** is an area on the right side of the Windows 11 taskbar that displays the current time, as well as icons representing selected information; the Notifications button displays pop-up messages and, when selected, the Action Center. For example, the notification area can tell you if your virus protection is out of date, how much battery life you have remaining (if you are using a mobile device), and whether you are connected to a network. The taskbar also displays the **Search button** to the left of the app buttons, which allows you to type a term to locate files or folders containing that term in the location you are searching.

Working with Apps

Apps in Windows 11 run on the desktop and work smoothly with touch and other input devices. Windows 11 apps use the **Split View menu** as the primary command interface for the app (Figure 1–8).

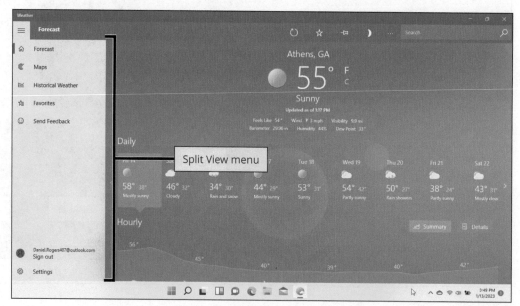

Figure 1–8

One way to start an app is by using the Start menu. The **Start menu** appears after you click the Start button and provides access to all programs, documents, and settings on the computer. It also can be used to display a list of apps, start apps, sign out of a user account, switch to a different user account, display computer or mobile device settings, put the computer in a low-power state, restart the computer or mobile device, and shut down the computer or mobile device. The Start menu also contains a Pinned section and a Recommended section. You can click an icon in either section to access an app or other resource. Click the All apps button to display an alphabetical list of all installed apps (Figure 1–9).

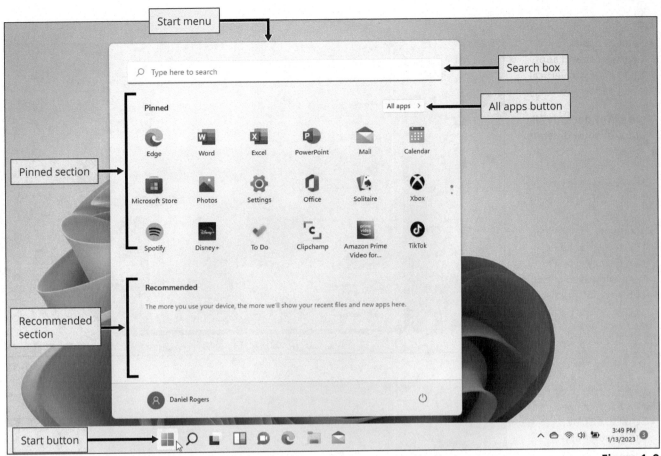

Figure 1–9

To Start an App Using the Start Menu

Why? When you install an app, one or more commands or icons are added to the Start menu so that you easily can start the app. The following steps, which assume Windows is running, use the Start menu to start the Weather app based on a typical installation. Although the steps illustrate starting the Weather app, the steps to start any app are similar.

1

- Click the Start button to display the Start menu shown in Figure 1–9.
- Click the All apps button to display the All apps list (Figure 1–10).

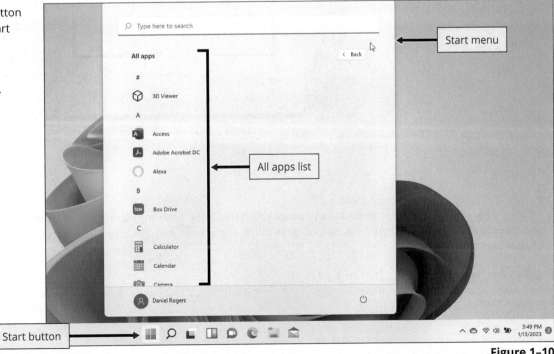

Figure 1–10

- Point to the right border of the All apps list to display a vertical scroll bar (Figure 1–11).

  Q&A Why does my All apps list show different apps?
  Your computer likely has different apps installed than the ones displayed. In addition, you might see a "Most Used" apps heading that displays your most frequently used apps at the top of your list.

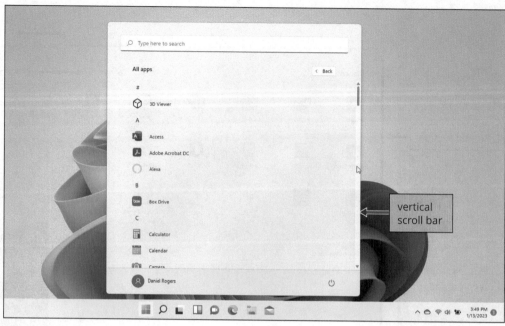

Figure 1–11

- Scroll to display the Weather app (Figure 1–12).

  Q&A What do the folders and arrows indicate?
  Folders in the All apps list contain additional commands. To view the commands, click the folder name.

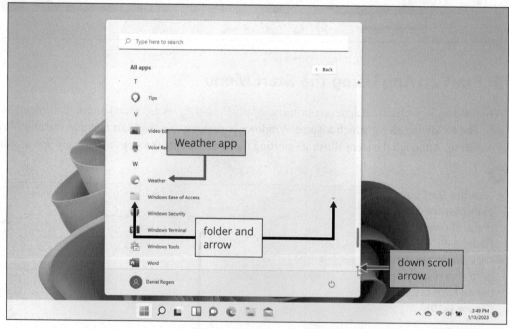

Figure 1–12

- Click Weather in the All apps list to start the Weather app. If this is the first time starting the Weather app on your computer, you first may have to specify your location and agree to the app's terms and conditions before the app displays as shown (Figure 1–13).

  Q&A What happens when you start an app?
  The Weather app starts in the desktop using a window. A **window** is a rectangular work area that displays an app or a collection of files, folders, and Windows tools. The top of a window has a **title bar**, which is a horizontal space that contains the window's name.

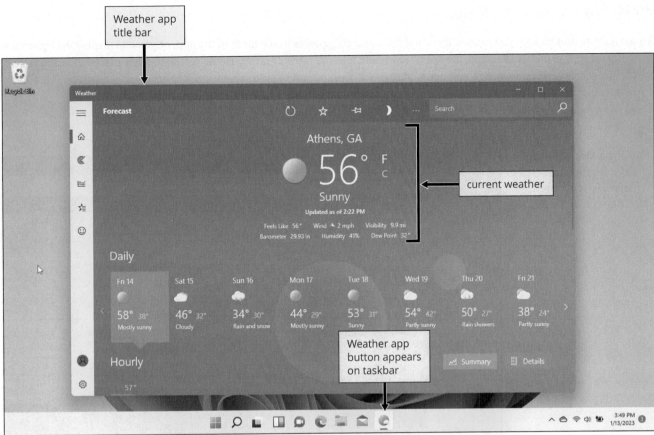

Weather app title bar

current weather

Weather app button appears on taskbar

Figure 1-13

5

- Type your current city in the Search text box and then click your city in the list that appears (Figure 1-14).

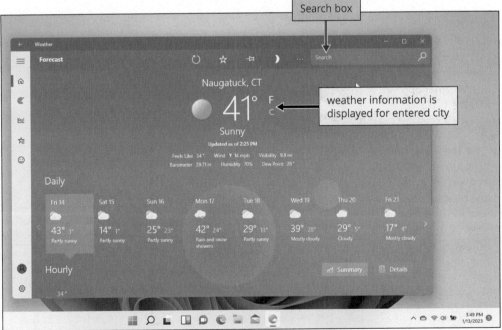

Search box

weather information is displayed for entered city

Figure 1-14

Other Ways

1. Click Start button or Search button, type **weather** in Search box, click Weather

2. Display Start menu, click Weather icon

To Navigate within an App

To navigate within an app, you can use the scroll bar or touch gestures to see more of the app, or you can display the Split View menu for an app. In the Weather app, the Split View menu lets you move from the Home screen to other places and even display maps, historical weather, favorites, and news. **Why?** You may intend to travel and see weather information in addition to the current temperature and forecast. The following steps display the current world weather information.

- Click the Maps button to display the radar imagery for the current location (Figure 1–15).

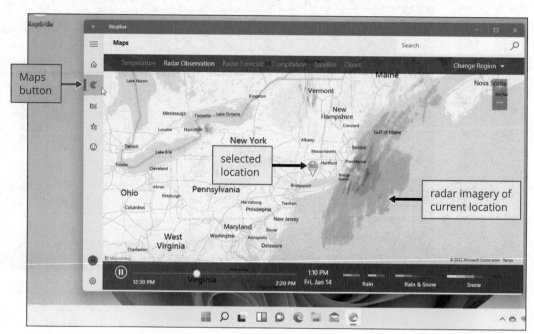

Figure 1–15

- Click the Settings button to display the settings for the Weather app (Figure 1–16).

- Click the Home button to return to the Home screen displaying the temperature and forecast for the selected location (shown in Figure 1–14).

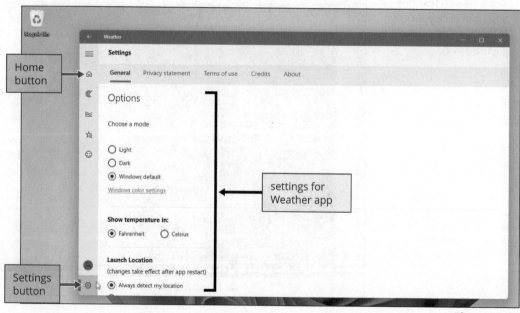

Figure 1–16

To Open and Maximize the File Explorer Window

In Windows, you can use the File Explorer to view your files and organize them into folders, as well as to access these files and folders. **Why?** If you want to move files and folders around on your hard drive, or copy or move files to or from a removable drive, such as a USB flash drive, the File Explorer can help you perform these operations. The following steps open and maximize the File Explorer window.

- Click the File Explorer button on the taskbar to start the File Explorer (Figure 1–17).

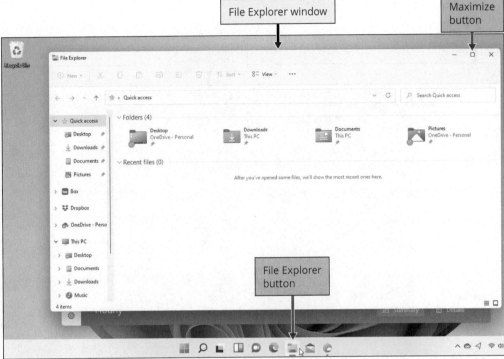

Figure 1–17

- Click the Maximize button (shown in Figure 1–17) on the title bar to maximize the File Explorer window (Figure 1–18).

Q&A What happens to the Maximize button after I click it?
When the window is maximized, the Maximize button turns into the Restore Down button. Clicking the Restore Down button will return the window to the size and position it was before you maximized it.

Figure 1–18

Other Ways

1. Drag title bar to top of screen
2. Right-click title bar, click Maximize on shortcut menu

To Switch between Apps

In Windows, you can switch between apps easily. **Why?** You may have several apps running and want to work with a different app than the one you currently are using. The following step switches from the File Explorer to the Weather app.

1

- Click the Weather app button on the taskbar to display the Weather app (Figure 1–19).

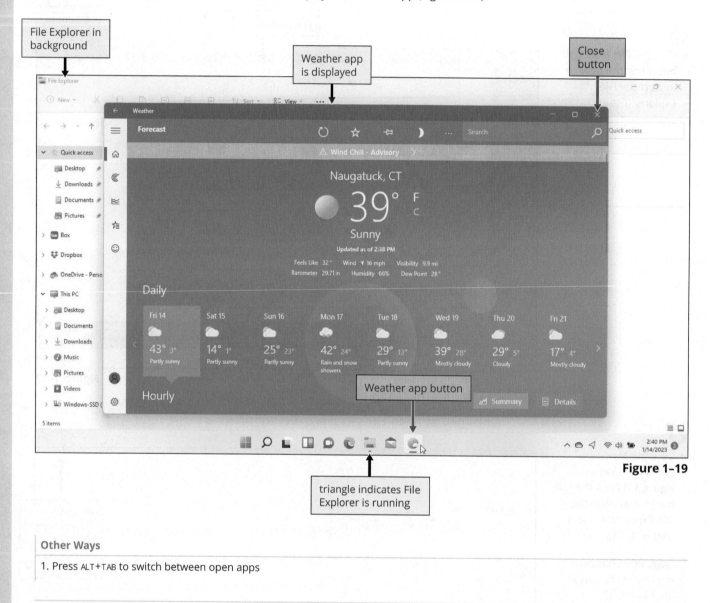

Figure 1–19

Other Ways

1. Press ALT+TAB to switch between open apps

To Exit an App

When you have finished using an app, you should exit the app. **Why?** When you exit an app, the system resources Windows requires to start the app can be released and made available to other apps running on your computer or mobile device. The following step exits the Weather app because you have finished using it.

- Click the Close button on the title bar (shown in Figure 1–19) to exit the Weather app and remove the Weather app button from the taskbar (Figure 1–20).

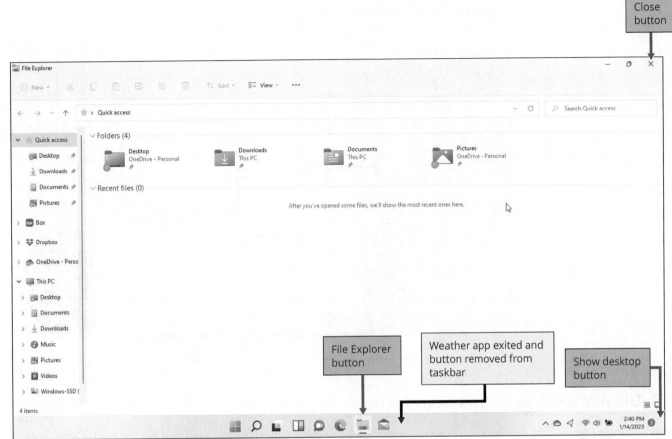

Figure 1–20

Other Ways

1. Right-click app button on taskbar, click 'Close all windows' on shortcut menu   2. Press ALT+F4

To Display the Windows Desktop

The Show desktop button to the right of the notification area on the taskbar will minimize all open windows and display the desktop. **Why?** The desktop provides many useful functions, and you may need to quickly minimize (or hide) all open windows. The following steps display the Windows desktop.

- Click the Show desktop button (shown in Figure 1–20) on the taskbar to minimize all open windows and show the desktop.

- Click the File Explorer button on the taskbar to redisplay the File Explorer window (shown in Figure 1–20).
- Click the Close button on the File Explorer window (shown in Figure 1–20) to close the File Explorer window.

Start Menu Folders

As you browse the list of apps on the Start menu, you will notice that in addition to icons that start apps, folder icons also are displayed. When expanded, these folder icons contain lists of related apps. For example, the Windows Ease of Access folder contains a list of related apps that are installed with Windows (Figure 1–21).

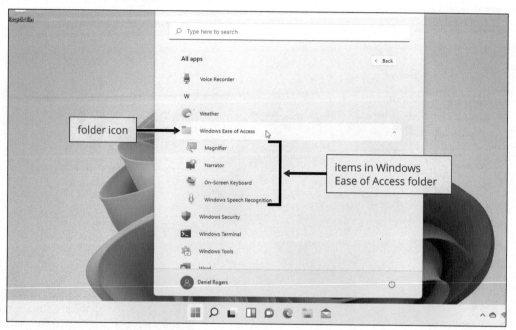

Figure 1–21

To Display a Folder on the Start Menu

As shown in Figure 1–21, the Windows Ease of Access folder contains a list of related apps that are installed with Windows. **Why?** Using folders makes it easier to organize apps and to find desired apps. If apps were not contained in folders, the All apps list would grow even longer. The following steps display the contents of the Windows Ease of Access folder.

1

- Click the Start button to display the Start menu (Figure 1–22).

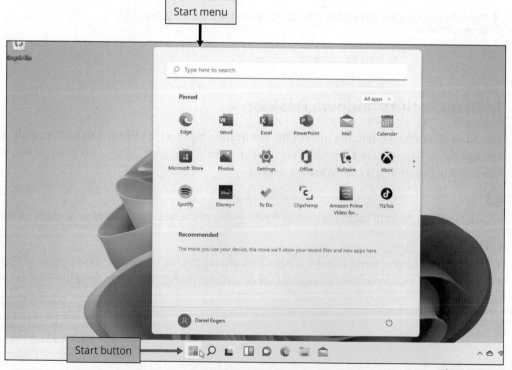

Figure 1–22

2

- Click the All apps button to display the All apps list.
- Scroll the list of apps until the Windows Ease of Access folder is displayed (Figure 1–23).

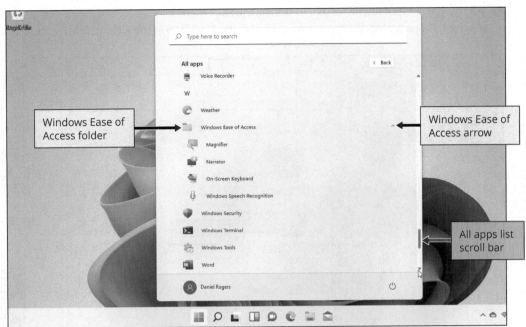

Windows Ease of Access folder

Windows Ease of Access arrow

All apps list scroll bar

Figure 1–23

3

- Click the Windows Ease of Access folder arrow to display the contents of the folder (Figure 1–24).

4

- Click the Start button to close the Start menu.

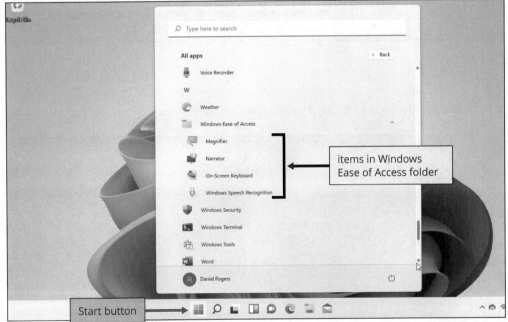

items in Windows Ease of Access folder

Start button

Figure 1–24

To Pin an App to the Start Menu

As mentioned previously, the Start menu contains commands and icons that you can click to perform an action, such as displaying a folder or starting an app. Clicking an icon on the Start menu is one of the fastest ways to start an app because you do not have to navigate the All apps list to locate the name of the app you want to start. **Why?** Pinning an app to the Start menu will add an icon for that app to the Start menu so that you easily can start the app. The following steps pin the Clock app to the Start menu.

1

- Click the Start button on the taskbar to display the Start menu.
- Click the All apps button and then scroll to display the Clock app in the All apps list (Figure 1–25).

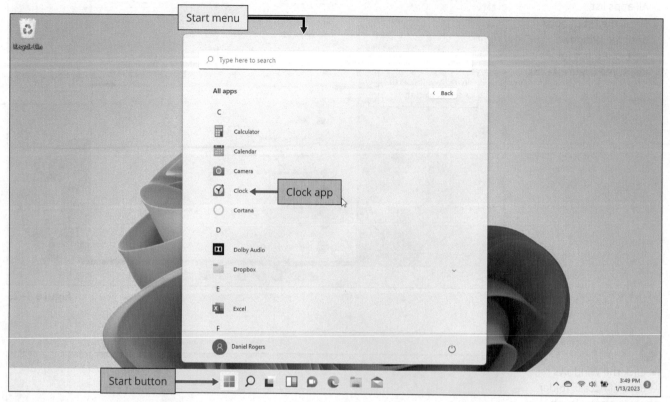

Figure 1–25

2

- Right-click the Clock app to display a shortcut menu (Figure 1–26).

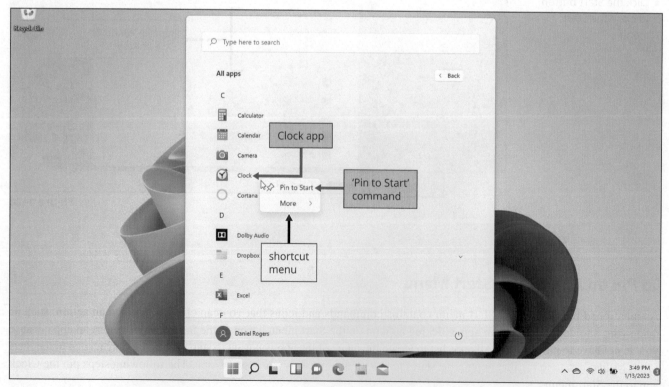

Figure 1–26

3

- Click 'Pin to Start' on the shortcut menu to pin the app to the Start menu.
- Click the Back button to display the Start menu.
- Scroll the Pinned section of the Start menu to display the pinned app (Figure 1–27).

Q&A Why is the 'Unpin from Start' command displayed on the shortcut menu instead of the 'Pin to Start' command?
If the Clock app already is pinned to the Start menu, Windows will instead display commands for unpinning the app.

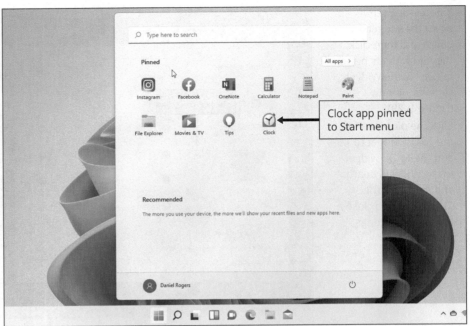

Clock app pinned to Start menu

Figure 1–27

Widgets

Besides starting an app on the Start menu, you can use widgets to access dynamic, up-to-the-minute information. A **widget** displays content from certain apps and services without requiring you to start the app. For example, the Weather app's widget shows current weather information. Other apps — such as the Photos app and Microsoft To Do app — also have widgets. Widgets for other apps display information relevant to their function. Widgets are displayed on the widgets board, not the Start menu.

To Add a Widget to the Widgets Board

Why? Widgets provide current information from apps and services at a glance. The following steps add the To Do widget to the widgets board.

- Click the Start button on the taskbar to close the Start menu.
- Click the Widgets button on the taskbar to display the widgets board (Figure 1–28).

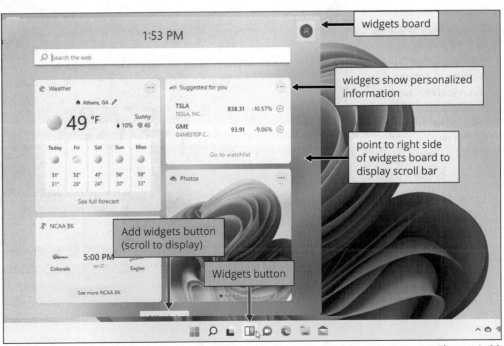

widgets board

widgets show personalized information

point to right side of widgets board to display scroll bar

Add widgets button (scroll to display)

Widgets button

Figure 1–28

2

- If necessary, scroll down the widgets board and then click the Add widgets button to display the Widget settings window (Figure 1–29).
- Click the plus icon for the To Do widget to add the To Do widget to the Widgets board and then click the Close button to close the Widget settings window.

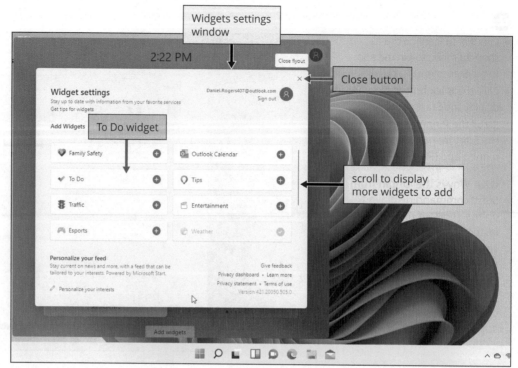

Figure 1–29

To Move a Widget on the Widgets Board

Why? You might choose to move a widget on the widgets board to display its information without scrolling. The following steps move the To Do widget so that it appears below the Weather widget.

1

- Drag the To Do widget to the desired location (in this case, below the Weather widget). Watch the widgets reposition as you drag, so that you can see a preview of where the widget will appear when you release the mouse button. Do not release the mouse button (Figure 1–30).

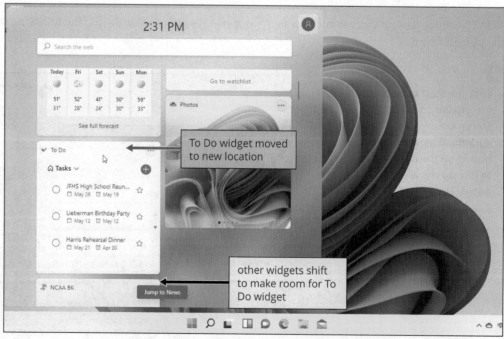

Figure 1–30

2

- Release the mouse button to move the widget to its new location and then scroll to the top of the widgets board (Figure 1–31).

Q&A What if the widgets on my widgets board do not match Figures 1–30 and 1–31?
Drag the To Do Widget to a location of your choosing on the widgets board and then release the mouse button.

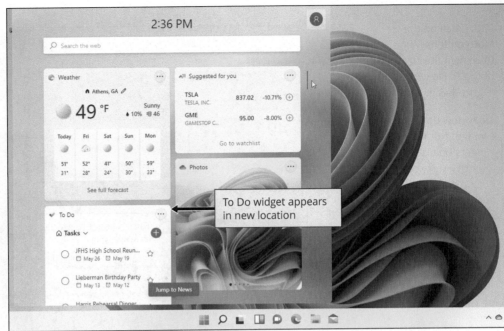

Figure 1–31

3

- Click the To Do widget and then click the Close button to display the To Do widget on the widgets board (shown in Figure 1–30).

To Resize a Widget on the Widgets Board

Widgets on the widgets board can be displayed in three sizes: small, medium, and large. **Why?** Resizing widgets on the widgets board will help you organize them in a way that makes the most sense for how you work. The following steps resize the To Do widget.

1

- If necessary, display the widgets board.
- Click the More options button on the To Do widget to display the More options menu, which lists the resizing options (Figure 1–32).

Q&A Can I resize any widget to be one of the three mentioned sizes?
No. Some widgets have only certain sizes available. For example, if you install an app on your computer, the app's widget may support fewer than three sizes.

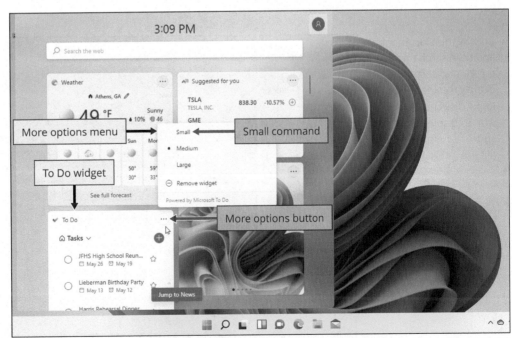

Figure 1–32

- Click Small on the More options menu to change the size of the To Do widget (Figure 1–33).

Q&A How do I remove a widget from the widgets board?
Click the More options button on the widget and then click Remove widget.

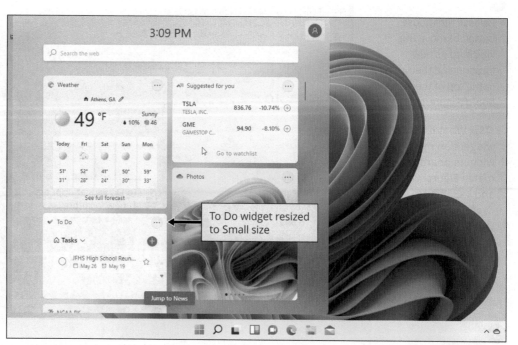

Figure 1–33

To Remove a Pinned App from the Start Menu

When you first buy a computer or mobile device or after using it for a while, you might notice pinned apps on the Start menu that you use infrequently. If you do not use these apps, you might want to unpin them from the Start menu. **Why?** Removing unused pinned apps from the Start menu will help you keep the Start menu organized so that you easily can locate apps you use the most. The following steps unpin the Clock app from the Start menu.

- Display the Start menu and then scroll through the Pinned section to display the Clock icon.
- Right-click the Clock icon to display a shortcut menu (Figure 1–34).

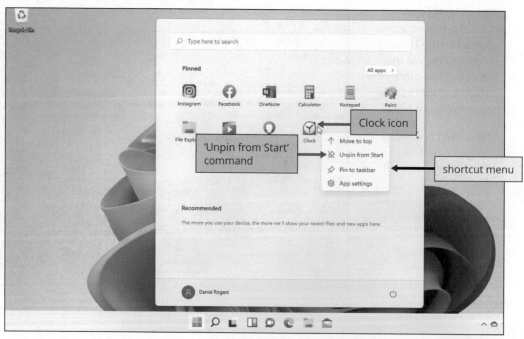

Figure 1–34

2

- Click 'Unpin from Start' on the shortcut menu to remove the pinned app from the Start menu and, if necessary, automatically reorganize the remaining icons (Figure 1–35).

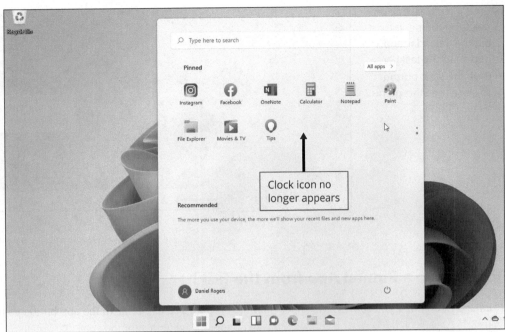

Figure 1–35

To Pin an App to the Taskbar

In addition to pinning apps to the Start menu, you also can pin frequently used apps to the Windows taskbar. As mentioned previously, the Task View, Microsoft Edge, Chat, File Explorer, and Mail buttons are pinned to the taskbar by default. The pinned apps on your taskbar may differ. **Why?** Pinning an app to the taskbar allows you to start the app by clicking only one button. If an app is pinned to the Start menu instead, you would have to click two times (one time to display the Start menu and one time when selecting the app to start). The following steps pin the Calendar app to the taskbar.

1

- If necessary, display the Start menu.
- Click the All apps button to display the All apps list.
- Right-click the Calendar app to display a shortcut menu and then point to More to display the More submenu (Figure 1–36).

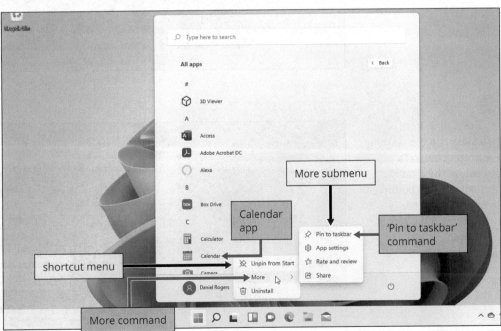

Figure 1–36

- Click 'Pin to taskbar' on the shortcut menu to pin the Calendar app button to the taskbar.
- Click the Start button to close the Start menu (Figure 1–37).

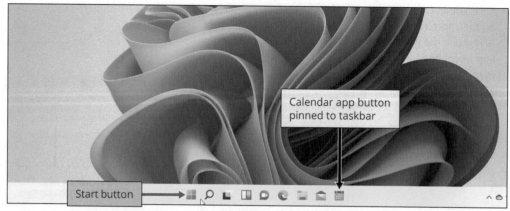

Calendar app button pinned to taskbar

Start button

Figure 1–37

To Remove a Pinned App from the Taskbar

If an app button that you seldom use appears on the taskbar, you can remove the app button so that it no longer is displayed. **Why?** The space on the taskbar is limited; consider pinning the buttons for the apps that you use most frequently. The following steps remove the pinned Calendar app button from the taskbar.

- Right-click the Calendar app button on the taskbar to display a shortcut menu (Figure 1–38).

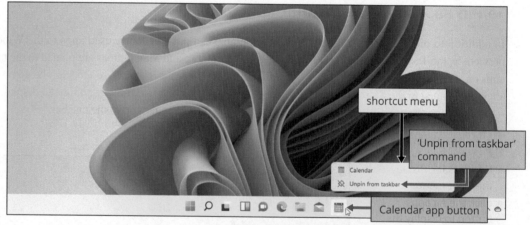

shortcut menu

'Unpin from taskbar' command

Calendar

Unpin from taskbar

Calendar app button

Figure 1–38

- Click 'Unpin from taskbar' on the shortcut menu to remove the pinned Calendar app button from the taskbar (Figure 1–39).

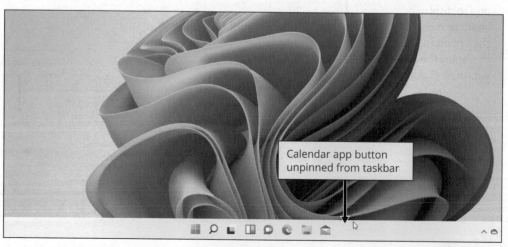

Calendar app button unpinned from taskbar

Figure 1–39

To Start an App Using the Search Box

In addition to starting apps using icons or commands on the Start menu or by using buttons on the taskbar, you also can start an app using the Search box. **Why?** If you want to start an app that is not pinned to the Start menu or taskbar, it might be faster to use the Search box to locate and start the app than by navigating the All apps list on the Start menu. The following steps use the Search box to start the WordPad app.

• Click the Start button on the taskbar.

• Type **WordPad** in the Search box to display the search results (Figure 1–40). Your search results might differ.

Q&A Does capitalization matter when you enter the search text?
No. Similar search results would appear if you type wordpad, WORDPAD, or WoRdPaD.

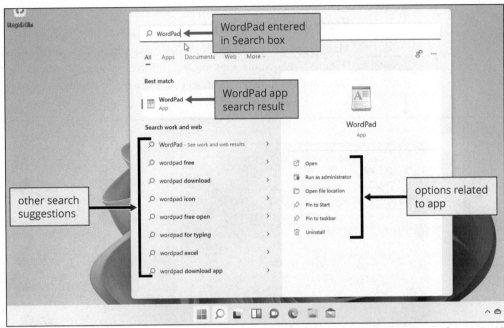

Figure 1–40

• Click WordPad at the top of the search results to start the WordPad app, display the WordPad app button on the taskbar, and close the Start menu (Figure 1–41).

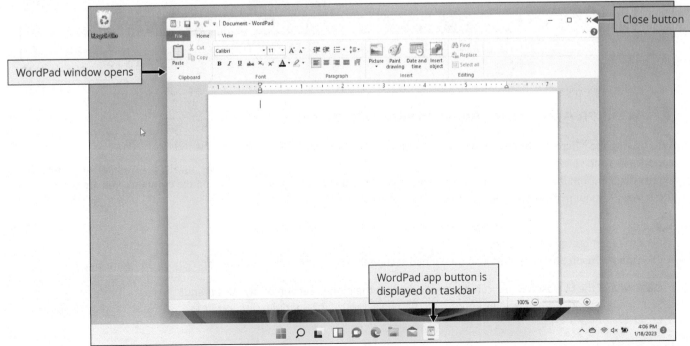

Figure 1–41

- Click the Close button on the WordPad title bar to exit WordPad.

Q&A Could I also use the Search button on the taskbar to search for an app?
Yes. You can click the Search button on the taskbar and then type search text in the Search box to search for an app.

Free and Paid Apps

Many apps are available for Windows, which you can find using the Microsoft Store app (Figure 1–42). Some apps are free, allowing you to download them without making a payment. Other apps require payment, so you will need to pay the fee before you can download them.

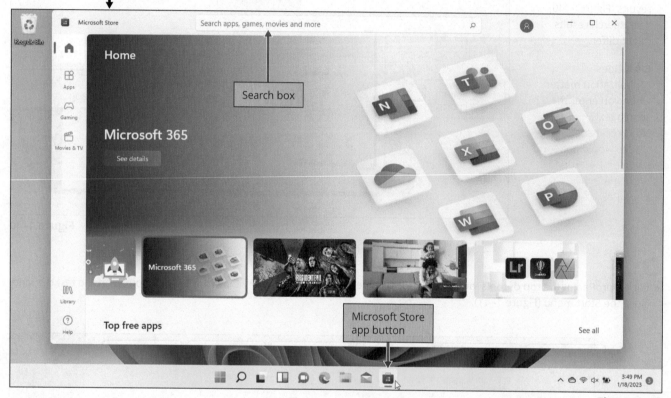

Figure 1–42

To Install an App Using the Microsoft Store App

When using the Microsoft Store app, you can install apps that are free or paid. **Why?** You find an app that you want to use and then download and install it so that it is on your computer or mobile device. The following steps download and install the Wikipedia app from the Microsoft Store. If you are not able to download and install apps on the computer you are using, read these steps without performing them.

- Click the Start button on the taskbar.
- Click the Microsoft Store app button in the Pinned section to display the Microsoft Store app (shown in Figure 1–42).

Q&A What if the Microsoft Store icon does not appear in the pinned section of my Start menu?
Start the Microsoft Store icon using another method presented in this module: click its name on the Start menu's All apps list or search for the Microsoft Store app using the Search box.

2

- Type **Wikipedia** in the Search box in the Microsoft Store window to display search results corresponding to the search text (Figure 1–43).

Q&A What if I do not know the exact name of the app I want to install?

You can scroll the Microsoft Store window to display various apps or click the category names to display apps in that category.

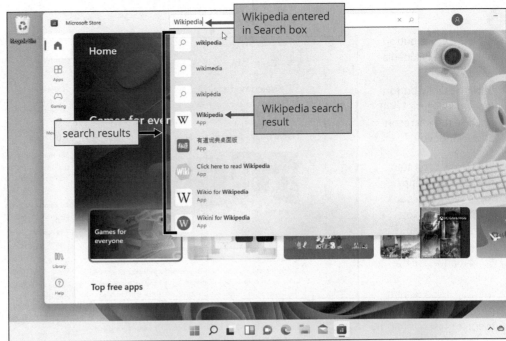

Figure 1–43

3

- Click the Wikipedia app search result to display information about the Wikipedia app (Figure 1–44).

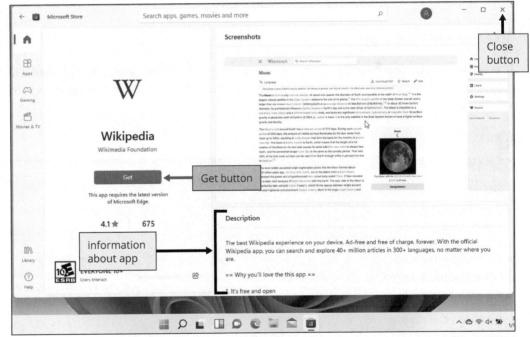

Figure 1–44

4

- Click the Get button to download and install the Wikipedia app. When the app has finished downloading and installing, click the Open button to start the Wikipedia app (Figure 1–45).

Q&A Where is the Open button?

The Open button replaces the Get button after the app has been installed and is ready to use.

5

- Click the Close button to close the Wikipedia window.
- Click the Close button (shown in Figure 1–44) to close the Microsoft Store window.

Q&A How can I start the Wikipedia app?

Apps you download from the Microsoft Store will appear in the All apps list on the Start menu. Use the skills presented in this module if you want to pin the app on the Start menu or taskbar for easier access. When you install the app, Windows may display a button for you to easily pin the app to the Start menu.

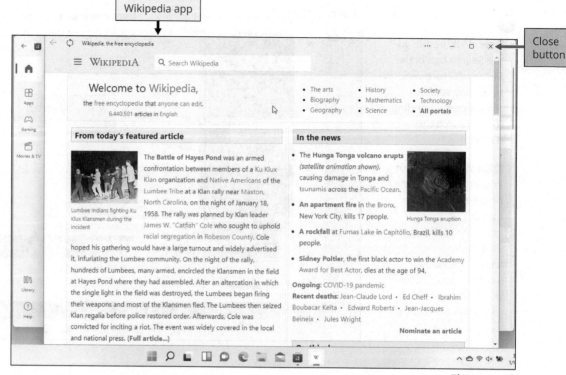

Wikipedia app

Close button

Figure 1–45

To Uninstall an App

If an app that you no longer use is on your computer or mobile device, you should consider uninstalling the app. **Why?** Uninstalling the app will increase the amount of available space on your hard drive. The following steps uninstall the Wikipedia app from your computer or mobile device.

1

- Click the Start button to display the Start menu.
- Click the All apps button to display the All apps list.
- Scroll to display the Wikipedia app in the All apps list (Figure 1–46).

Q&A How can I find an app in the All apps list without scrolling?

To find the Wikipedia app without scrolling, click a letter separating the alphabetic groups of apps, such as A, and then click W to display apps that have names starting with W.

Wikipedia app in All apps list

Start button

Figure 1–46

2

- Right-click the Wikipedia app to display a shortcut menu (Figure 1–47).

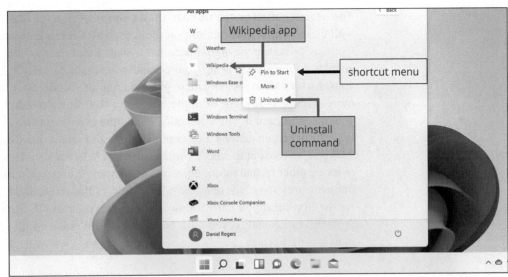

Figure 1–47

3

- Click Uninstall on the shortcut menu to display a confirmation message (Figure 1–48).

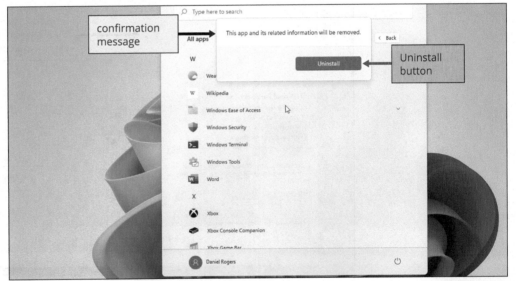

Figure 1–48

4

- Click the Uninstall button to uninstall the Wikipedia app from your computer or mobile device (Figure 1–49).
- Click the Start button to close the Start menu.

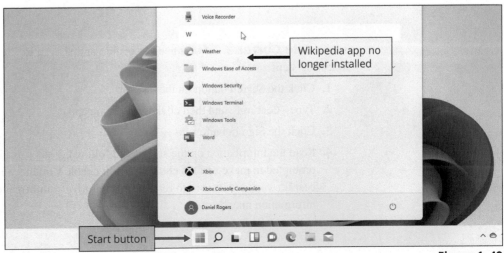

Figure 1–49

Search Button and Cortana

The Search button on the taskbar allows you to search for files and folders in Windows, as well as search for information on the web. The Search button is one way to interact with Cortana. **Cortana**, the digital personal assistant that comes with Windows 11, is an app that, enables you to search using your computer or mobile device's microphone and works with apps, such as Microsoft To Do, to give you reminders, alarms, directions, news, weather, and more (Figure 1–50). For example, you can ask Cortana to add a meeting with your boss to your calendar, and it will automatically add the event. You also can have Cortana remind you to perform certain actions. For example, you can request that Cortana remind you Tuesday at 7:00 p.m. to take out the trash. Cortana also can help track packages, gather flight information, or locate other factual information on the Internet. Cortana is intuitive; the more you use it, the more it learns about you and forms its search results accordingly. Before you can use Cortana for the first time, you must follow a brief setup process. To use Cortana and take advantage of its full functionality, you must be signed in to Windows with a Microsoft account, and you must enable Cortana.

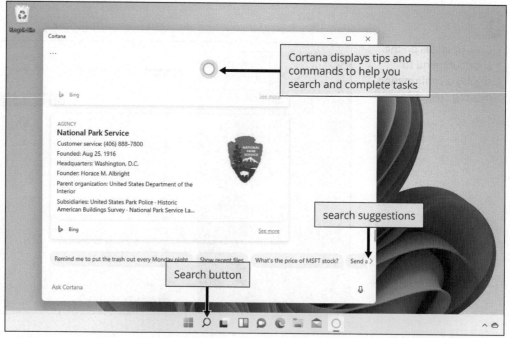

Figure 1–50

To Enable Cortana   If you need to enable and sign in to Cortana, you would perform the following steps.

1. Click the Search button on the taskbar.

2. Type   **Cortana**   and then click the Cortana app.

3. Click the Sign in button.

4. Read the information on the screen and follow the steps as indicated. You will be prompted to make various choices as you enable Cortana. Select the choices that work best for you, and be sure to read all related privacy information regarding how your information may be used.

To Search the Web Using the Search Button

In addition to searching for files and folders on your computer or mobile device, Windows also will search the Internet for the search text. **Why?** It may be faster to use the Search button to locate information on the Internet instead of starting a browser and using a search engine to locate information. The following steps search the web using the Search button.

1

- Click the Search button on the taskbar to display the Search screen (Figure 1–51).

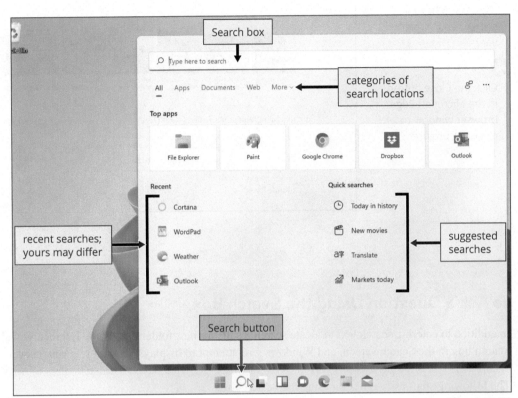

Figure 1–51

2

- Type **national parks** in the Search box to display search results and additional recommended search text (Figure 1–52).

Q&A Why do my search results and suggested search text differ from Figure 1–52?
Windows 11 uses the web and your previous search history to provide the most relevant search results. For this reason, your results might vary.

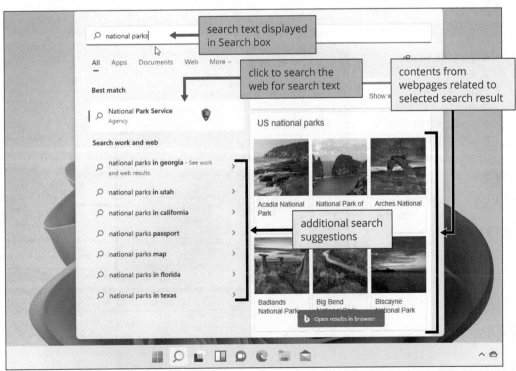

Figure 1–52

- Click 'National Park Service' to display the search results for the national parks search text in the Microsoft Edge browser (Figure 1–53). Your search results might vary.

- Click the Close button in the Microsoft Edge browser window to close the browser.

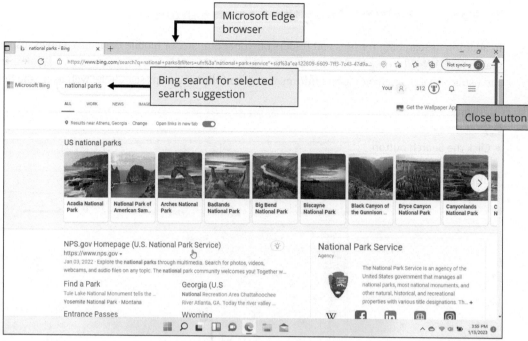

Figure 1–53

To Ask a Question Using the Search Box

In addition to entering search text to locate search results in files, folders, or on the Internet, you also can type questions in the Search box in the Search screen, and Windows will attempt to display the most relevant answer in the search results. **Why?** Windows can provide answers to many questions so that you do not have to search content on websites for the specific answer. The following steps ask a question using the Search box.

1

- Click the Search button on the taskbar to display the Search screen.
- Type **How many ounces are in a pound?** in the Search box to enter the question (Figure 1–54).

2

- Click outside the Search box to hide the search results.

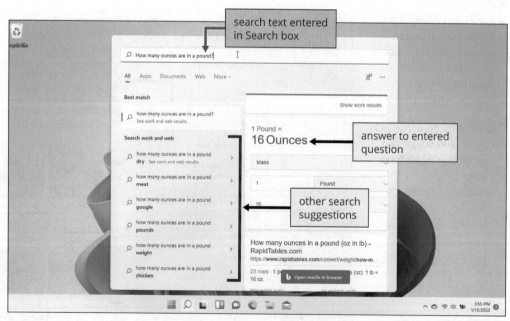

Figure 1–54

To Use Cortana to Create a To Do List

Cortana works with the Microsoft To Do app, which you use to create lists and reminders. For example, if you find it helpful to keep a list of tasks you need to complete, you can keep a to do list with Cortana to remind you of upcoming obligations. **Why?** Creating a list makes it easy to keep track of items that are important to you. The following steps use Cortana and the To Do app to create an item on your to do list.

- Click the Search button on the taskbar to display the Search screen.
- Click Cortana in the Recent list to start the app. If necessary, click the Sign in button to sign in to your account (Figure 1–55).

> **Q&A** Cortana does not appear in my Recent list. What should I do?
> Type **Cortana** in the Search box and then press ENTER.

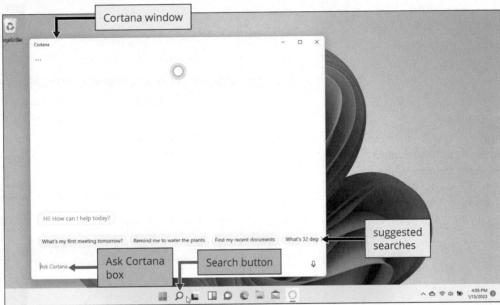

Figure 1–55

- Type Add **CIS 101 homework to To Do list** in the Ask Cortana box (Figure 1–56).

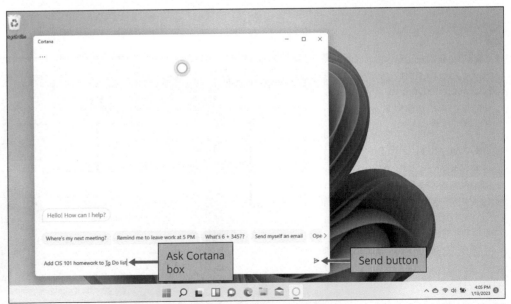

Figure 1–56

- Click the Send button to add the item to the Tasks list (Figure 1–57).

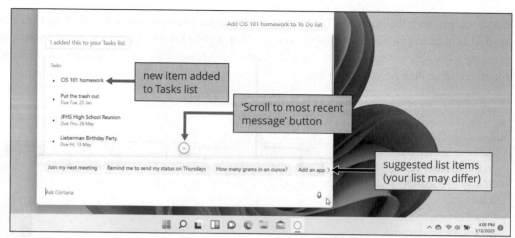

Figure 1–57

❹

- Click the 'Scroll to most recent message' button to display the complete message from Cortana (Figure 1–58).

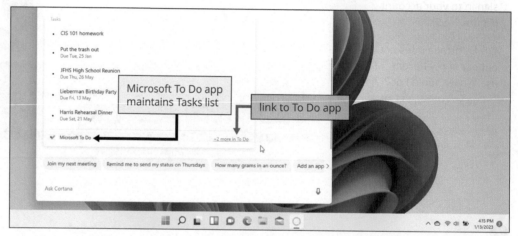

Figure 1–58

❺

- Click the link to the To Do app to start Microsoft To Do and display your Tasks list (Figure 1–59).

Q&A Why did the To Do app start?
Cortana works with the To Do app to create tasks, set reminders, and perform other related functions.

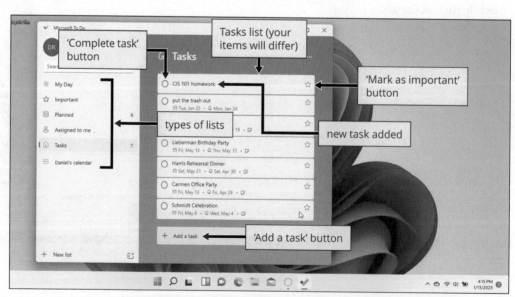

Figure 1–59

- Click the CIS 101 homework task to display its details (Figure 1–60).

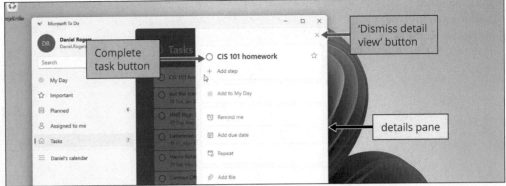

Figure 1–60

- Click the Complete task button next to the CIS 101 homework task title to remove the item from the Tasks list.
- Click the 'Dismiss detail view' button to close the details pane (Figure 1–61).
- Click the Close button to exit the To Do app.
- Click the Close button to exit the Cortana app.

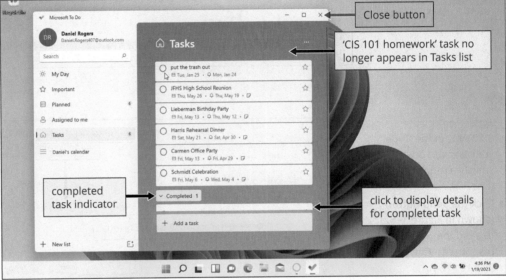

Figure 1–61

To Set a Reminder Using Cortana

You also can use Cortana and the To Do app to set reminders. **Why?** If you use your computer or mobile device frequently and need to be reminded of an event at a future date and time, you can set a reminder to display at the desired time. The following steps set a reminder using Cortana.

- Start Cortana again.
- Type **Remind me to submit Assignment 4** in the Ask Cortana box (Figure 1–62).

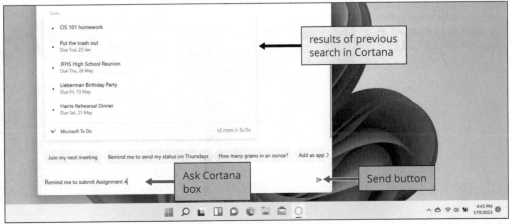

Figure 1–62

2

- Click the Send button to submit the request to Cortana (Figure 1–63).

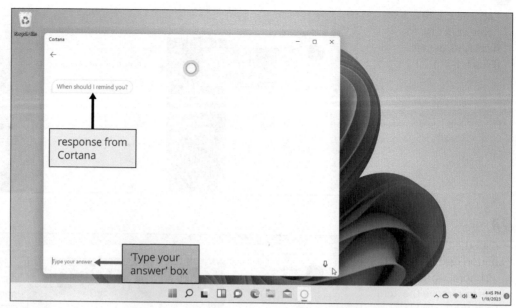

Figure 1–63

3

- Type **Today at 8:00 PM** in the 'Type your answer' box to specify a reminder time.
- Click the Send button (shown in Figure 1–62) to send the response to Cortana (Figure 1–64).

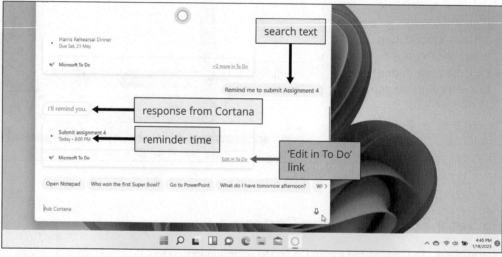

Figure 1–64

4

- Click the 'Edit in To Do' link for the reminder to start the To Do app and display the reminder as an item in the Tasks list (Figure 1–65).

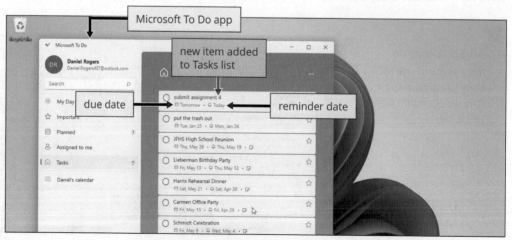

Figure 1–65

5

- Click the 'submit assignment 4' item in the Tasks list to display its details in the details pane.
- Click 'Remind me at 8:00 PM' to display other reminder times (Figure 1–66).

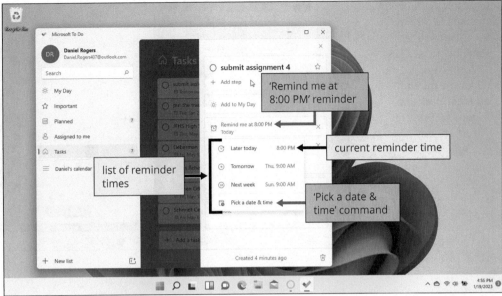

Figure 1–66

6

- Click 'Pick a date & time' to display a calendar for selecting a different date (Figure 1–67).

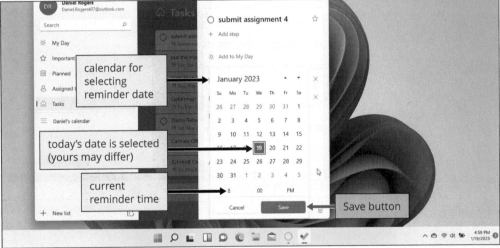

Figure 1–67

7

- Choose a month, day, and year in the future on the calendar to change the reminder date (Figure 1–68).

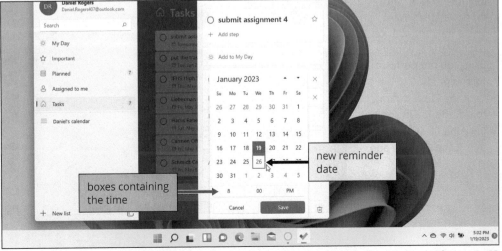

Figure 1–68

8

- Click a box containing the time to display the options to set the reminder time. Click 12 for the hour, click 00 for the minute, and then click PM (Figure 1–69).

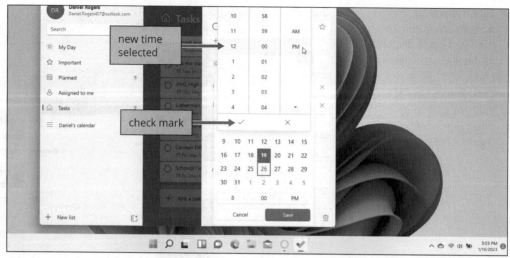

Figure 1–69

9

- Click the check mark to set the time (Figure 1–70).

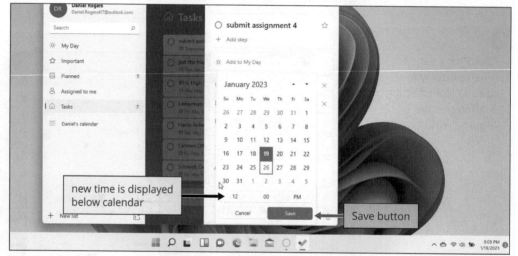

Figure 1–70

10

- Click the Save button to set the reminder (Figure 1–71). If you do not actually want to set the reminder on the computer you are using, do not perform this step.
- Click the Close button to exit the To Do app.
- Click the Close button to exit the Cortana app.

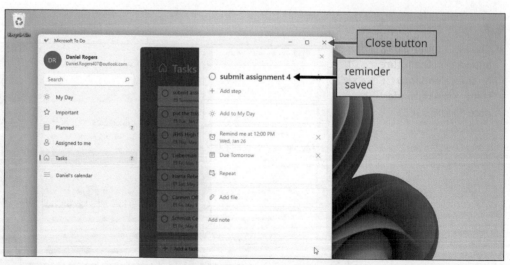

Figure 1–71

Getting Help

In versions of Windows prior to Windows 10, you would use Windows Help and Support to locate help information. In Windows 11, you search for help using the Search box that you access from the Search button or Start button on the taskbar. If you need help performing a task, type a description of the task in the Search box, and Windows will provide search results linking to the proper window and setting that will help you accomplish that task. For example, if you type "change the background" in the Search box, the search results will include a link to the Settings app, which includes the settings to change the background image.

To Get Help Using the Search Box

Why? If you are having trouble locating where to find a particular feature in Windows, you can use the Search box to locate that feature. The following steps use the Search box to locate where to change the desktop background.

1

- Click the Start button on the taskbar to display the search box.
- Click the Search box to activate it.
- Type **change desktop background** in the Search box to display the search results (Figure 1–72).

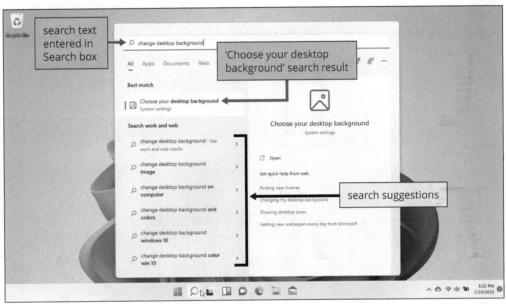

Figure 1–72

2

- Click 'Choose your desktop background' in the search results to open the Settings window, where you can personalize and adjust the desktop background (Figure 1–73).
- Click the Close button to close the Settings window.

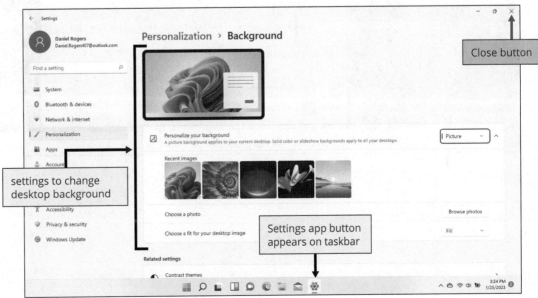

Figure 1–73

Shutting Down Windows

After completing your work with Windows, you should end your session by signing out of your account. In addition to signing out, several options are available for ending your Windows session. You can choose to sign out only, to lock the computer until you come back, to put the computer in sleep mode that saves power, or to shut down the computer as well as sign out of your account.

To Sign Out of an Account

If you are leaving the computer but do not want to turn it off, you can choose to sign out of your account. **Why?** You might be using a computer in the school lab and need to leave the class. The computer does not need to be shut down because a student in the following class will need to use the computer. **The following steps sign out of an account.**

1
- Click the Start button to display the Start menu.
- Click the name associated with your user account to display a menu of options (Figure 1–74).

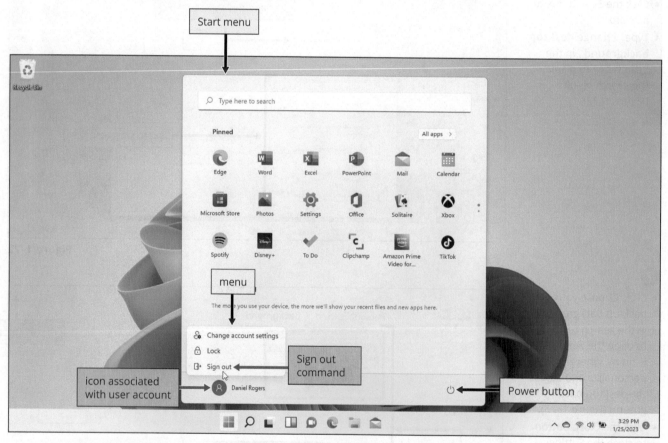

Figure 1–74

2

- Click Sign out on the menu of options to sign out of Windows and return to the lock screen (Figure 1–75).

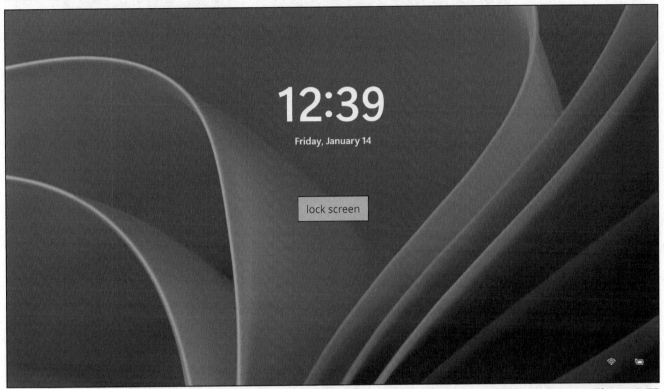

Figure 1–75

To Shut Down the Computer

When you have finished using the computer, you should shut it down. **Why?** You are finished using the computer and want to shut it down to conserve power. The following steps shut down the computer.

- Click the lock screen to display the sign-in screen (Figure 1–76).

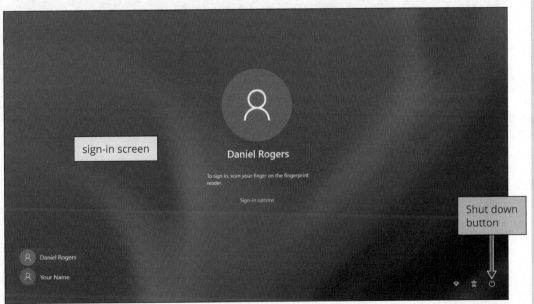

Figure 1–76

2

- Click the Shut down button on the sign-in screen to display the Shut down menu (Figure 1–77).

Figure 1–77

3

- Click Shut down on the Shut down menu to shut down the computer (Figure 1–78).

Q&A Can I just shut down the computer without first signing out?
Yes. Click the Power button on the Start menu (shown in Figure 1–74). Next, click Shut down on the Power menu to shut down the computer.

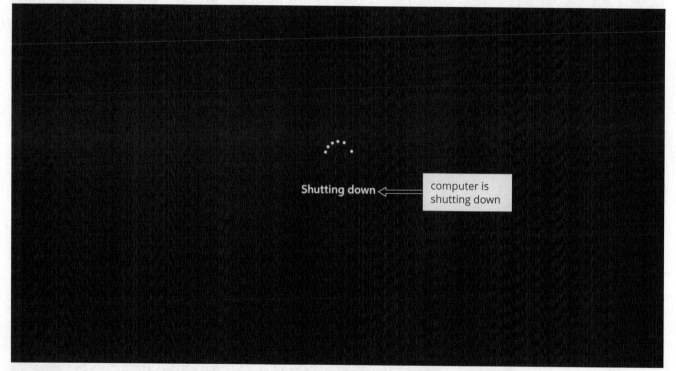

Figure 1–78

Summary

In this module, you learned how to work with the Windows 11 interface and some of its basic features. Topics covered included describing Windows 11 and elements of the Windows 11 interface, differentiating among the various editions of Windows 11, using a touch screen and performing basic mouse operations, starting Windows 11 and signing in to an account, starting an app and navigating within an app, starting the File Explorer, switching between apps, customizing the Start menu, searching for an app or file, installing an app, using the Search box, and adding to do list items and reminders. Finally, you learned to sign out of an account and shut down the computer.

Student Assignments

Apply Your Knowledge

Reinforce the skills and apply the concepts you learned in this module.

Exploring Windows 11

Instructions: You will use Windows 11 to perform the following tasks. For each task, record the exact steps you take and submit them in the format required by your instructor.

Perform the following tasks:

1. Pin the Photos app to the taskbar.
2. Unpin the Photos app from the taskbar.
3. Pin the File Explorer to the Start menu.
4. Unpin the File Explorer from the Start menu.
5. Change the size of a widget on the widgets board (choose from any available size).
6. Add the Tips widget to the widgets board.
7. Remove the Tips widget from the widgets board.
8. Move a widget to a different area on the widgets board.
9. Search for an app.
10. Start the Microsoft Store app (Figure 1–79).
11. Exit the Microsoft Store app.

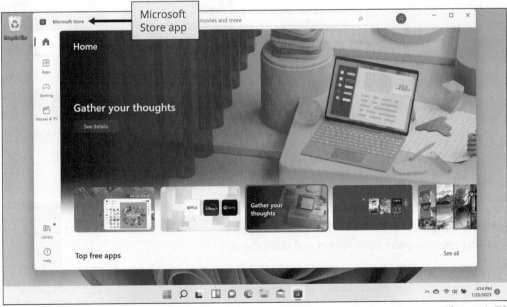

Figure 1–79

Extend Your Knowledge

Extend the skills you learned in this module and experiment with new skills. You will use the Search box to complete the assignment.

Obtaining Help

Instructions: Use the Search box to search for the answers to the following questions.

1. Find information about Windows shortcuts by typing **Windows shortcuts** in the Search box
   (Figure 1–80). Browse the search results to locate websites that can help you answer the following questions:

   a. What keyboard shortcut is used to copy a file?

   b. What keyboard shortcut is used to paste a file?

   c. How do you display a shortcut menu?

Figure 1–80

2. Determine the appropriate search text to use in the Search box and then use the Search box to locate information to answer the following questions:

   a. What is Windows Defender Antivirus?

   b. What is Windows Defender Firewall?

   c. What settings can you control for kids who use your computer?

   d. What are five ways to protect your computer from viruses and other threats?

   e. What is a user account?

   f. What is the difference between a local user account and a Microsoft account?

3. Use the Search box or other available method in Windows to obtain answers to the following questions:

   a. How do you turn on Windows Defender Firewall?

   b. How do you perform a full scan of your computer or mobile device using Microsoft Defender Antivirus?

   c. How do you add a printer?

   d. How do you display the Control Panel?

   e. How do you change the screen saver?

   f. How do you change the date and time?

   g. How do you connect to a wireless network?

Expand Your World

Using Microsoft Edge

Create a solution that uses cloud or web technologies by learning and investigating on your own from general guidance.

Part 1 Instructions: Starting Microsoft Edge

1. If necessary, connect to the Internet.

2. If necessary, display the desktop and then start Microsoft Edge.

Part 2 Instructions: Exploring the Cengage Website

1. Type **cengage.com** in the 'Search or enter web address' text box and then press ENTER (Figure 1–81).

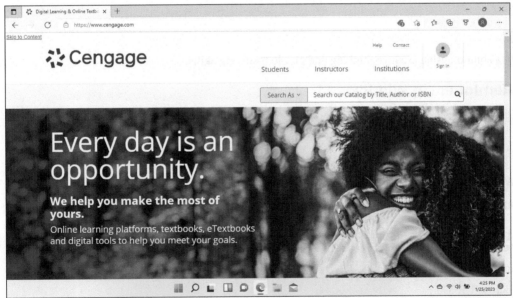

Figure 1–81

Continued on next page

2. Answer the following questions:

   a. What web address is displayed on the address bar?

   b. What content is displayed on the cengage.com webpage?

3. If necessary, scroll to view the contents of the webpage. List three links shown on this webpage.

4. Click any link on the webpage. Which link did you click?

5. Describe the webpage that was displayed when you clicked the link.

6. If requested by your instructor, click the More actions button and then click the Print button to print the webpage.

Part 3 Instructions: Exploring the National Park Service Website

1. Click the web address in the address bar to select it.

2. Type **nps.gov** in the address bar and then press ENTER.

3. What title is displayed on the browser tab?

4. Scroll the webpage to view its contents. Do any graphic images appear on the webpage?

5. Does the webpage include an image that is a link? (Pointing to an image on a webpage and having the pointer change to a hand indicates the image is a link.) If so, describe the image.

6. Click the image to display another webpage. What title is displayed on the browser tab?

7. If requested by your instructor, print the webpage.

Part 4 Instructions: Displaying Previously Displayed Webpages

1. Click the Back button. What webpage is displayed?

2. Click the Back button two times. What webpage is displayed?

3. If requested by your instructor, print the webpage.

4. Click the Close button on the Microsoft Edge title bar to exit Microsoft Edge.

In the Labs

Design and implement a solution using creative thinking and problem-solving skills.

Lab 1: Setting Reminders in Windows 11

Problem: You have just started a new job and want to be sure that you meet all project deadlines and attend required meetings. You have added these events to your calendar but also want to set reminders for these events in Windows 11 (Figure 1–82).

Perform the following steps:

1. Click the Start button or the Search button on the taskbar.

2. Start Cortana.

3. Type   **Remind me about the weekly project team meeting**   in the Ask Cortana box.

4. Select 2:00 PM for the reminder time.

5. Edit the task in Microsoft To Do.

6. Set the meeting to occur every Wednesday. (**Hint:** Select the task, click Repeat in the details pane, and then click Weekly.)

7. Click the 'Add a task' button.

8. Add the following tasks with reminders. Choose descriptive text to identify each task:

   a. Accounting report due every Tuesday at 3:00 p.m.

   b. Meeting with IT Department on March 19 of this year, at 9:00 a.m.

   c. Complete system backup every Wednesday at 4:00 p.m.

   d. Attend team lunch every Friday at 12:00 p.m.

   e. Financial system training on April 12 of this year, at 11:00 a.m.

9. Record the steps you took to perform these actions, and submit them in a format required by your instructor.

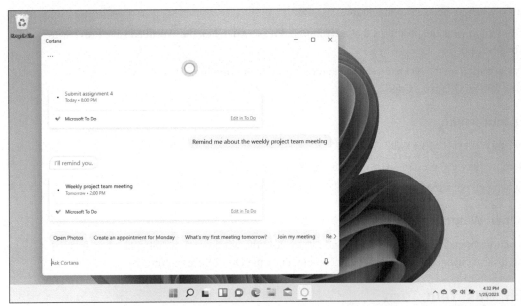

Figure 1–82

Lab 2: Working with Multiple Apps

Problem: You have learned that Windows supports multitasking, which is the ability to have multiple apps open at once and switch between them (Figure 1–83). You would like to experiment with the different methods by which you can switch between apps.

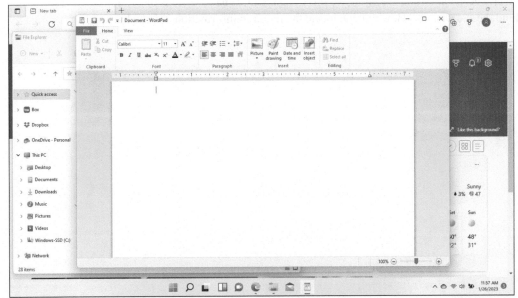

Figure 1–83

Continued on next page

Perform the following steps:

Part 1: Starting Microsoft Edge, the File Explorer, and WordPad

1. Display the desktop and then click the Microsoft Edge app button on the taskbar to start Microsoft Edge.

2. Click the File Explorer button to open the File Explorer window.

3. Type **WordPad** in the Search box and then click the WordPad Desktop app search result to start the WordPad app.

Part 2: Switching among the Windows

1. Press ALT+TAB to switch to the next open window.

2. Press CTRL+ALT+TAB to view the programs that are running. Press TAB. Click the WordPad Live Preview to switch to the WordPad app.

3. Click the Task View button on the taskbar to view the programs that are running. Click the Microsoft Edge Live Preview to switch to Microsoft Edge.

Part 3: Reporting Your Findings

1. What happens when you press ALT+TAB?

2. What is the difference between pressing ALT+TAB and CTRL+ALT+TAB?

3. What happens when you click the Task View button?

Part 4: Close All Open Windows

1. Click the Close button for each of the three open windows to close the windows. If a dialog box is displayed that prompts you to save changes to the WordPad document, click the Don't Save button.

Lab 3: Consider This: Your Turn
Reviewing Installed Apps

Problem: You have been hired at a local accounting company to oversee the delivery, installation, and configuration of new computers for each of the company's 20 employees. The company's president has asked you to remove apps that might be a distraction to the employees and prevent them from working efficiently.

Part 1:   Review the apps preinstalled on your computer and prepare a list of apps you might remove. In addition, prepare a list of apps you might keep that would help employees perform their job functions.

Part 2:   You made several decisions while searching for this assignment. What decisions did you make? What was the rationale behind these decisions? How did you locate the required information about which apps to keep or remove?

Working with the Windows 11 Desktop

Objectives

You will have mastered the material in this module when you can:

- Create, name, and save a document directly in the Documents folder
- Use WordPad to print and edit a document
- Change the view and arrange objects in groups in the Documents folder
- Create and name a folder in the Documents folder
- Move documents into a folder

- Add and remove a shortcut on the Start menu
- Open a document using a shortcut on the Start menu
- Open a folder using a desktop shortcut
- Open, modify, and print multiple documents in a folder
- Delete multiple files and folders
- Work with the Recycle Bin

Introduction

In Module 2, you will learn about the Windows 11 desktop. With thousands of hardware devices and software products available for computers and mobile devices, users need to manage these resources quickly and easily. One of Windows 11's impressive features is the ease with which users can create and access documents and files.

Mastering the desktop will help you take advantage of user-interface enhancements and innovations that make computing faster, easier, and more reliable and that offer seamless integration with the Internet. Working with the Windows 11 desktop in this module, you will find out how these features can save time, organize files and folders, and ultimately help you work more efficiently.

Creating a Document in WordPad

An app, sometimes referred to as a program, is a set of computer instructions that carries out a task on the computer. For example, you create written documents with a word processing app, spreadsheets and charts with a spreadsheet app, and presentations with a presentation app.

To learn how to work with the Windows 11 desktop, you will create two daily reminders lists, one for Ms. Estes and one for Mr. Raymond. Because they will be reviewing their lists throughout the day, you will need to update the lists with new reminders as necessary. You decide to use WordPad, a word processing program available with Windows 11, to create the daily reminders lists. The finished documents are shown in Figure 2–1.

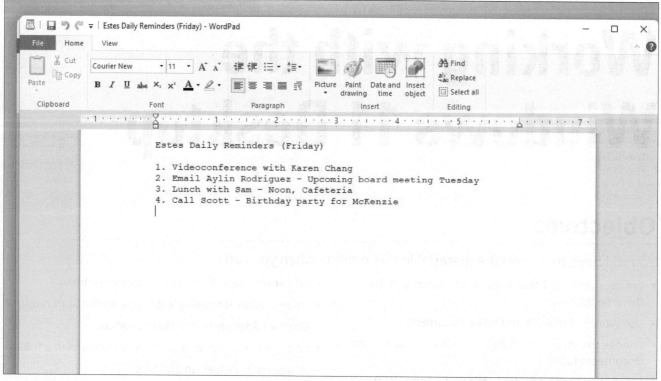

Figure 2–1(a): Estes Daily Reminders

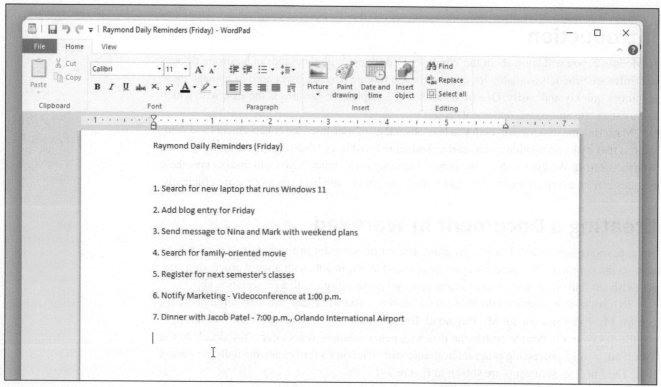

Figure 2–1(b): Raymond Daily Reminders

To Start an App and Create a Document

Why? You first will create the daily reminders document for Mr. Raymond using WordPad by starting the WordPad app, typing the reminders, and then saving the document in the Documents folder. The following steps start WordPad and create a daily reminders document for Mr. Raymond.

1

- Click the Start button on the taskbar to display the Start menu.
- Type **wordpad** in the Search box to prompt Windows 11 to search for the WordPad app.
- Click the WordPad app search result to start WordPad and open the Document - WordPad window (Figure 2–2).

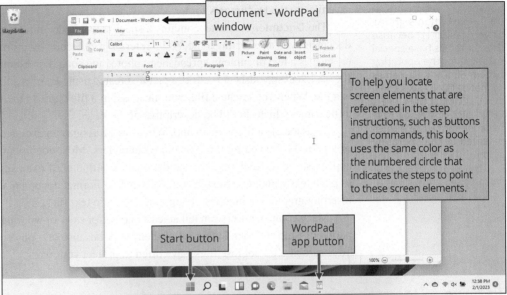

Figure 2–2

2

- Type **Raymond Daily Reminders (Friday)** and then press ENTER two times.
- Type **1. Search for new laptop that runs Windows 11** and then press ENTER.
- Type **2. Add blog entry for Friday** and then press ENTER.
- Type **3. Send message to Nina and Mark with weekend plans** and then press ENTER.
- Type **4. Search for family-oriented movie** and then press ENTER (Figure 2–3).

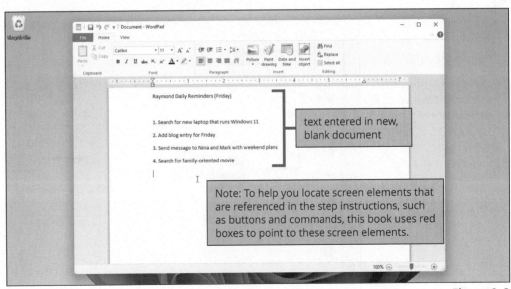

Figure 2–3

Other Ways

1. Click Search button, type **wordpad,** click WordPad

BTW
File Names
A file name can contain up to 255 characters, including spaces. Any uppercase or lowercase character is valid when creating a file name, except a backslash (\), slash (/), colon (:), asterisk (*), question mark (?), quotation mark (' '), less-than sign (<), greater-than sign (>), or vertical bar (|) because these symbols have special meaning for the operating system. Similarly, file names cannot be CON, AUX, COM1, COM2, COM3, COM4, LPT1, LPT2, LPT3, PRN, or NUL because those are names reserved by the operating system.

Saving Documents

When you create a document using an app, such as WordPad, the document is stored in the main memory (RAM) of the computer. If you exit the app without saving the document or if the computer accidentally loses electrical power, the document will be lost. To protect against the accidental loss of a document and to allow you to modify the document easily in the future, you should save the document. Although you can save a file on the desktop, it is recommended that you save the document in a different location to keep the desktop free from clutter. For example, you can save files to the Documents folder.

The **Documents folder** contains a specific user's documents and folders. When you save a document, you are creating a file. A **file** refers to a collection of information stored on your computer, such as a text document, spreadsheet, photo, and song. For example, a WordPad document is a file, an Excel spreadsheet is a file, a picture created using Paint is a file, and a saved email message is a file. When you create a file, you must assign a file name to the file. All files are identified by a file name, which should be descriptive of the saved file.

To associate a file with an app, Windows 11 assigns an extension to the file name, consisting of a period followed by three or more characters. Most documents created using the WordPad app are saved as Rich Text Format documents with the .rtf extension, but they also can be saved as plain text with the .txt extension. A Rich Text Format document allows for formatting text and inserting graphics, which is not supported in plain text files.

Many computer users can tell at least one horror story of working on their computers for a long period of time and then losing all of their work because of a power failure or software problem. To ensure you do not lose files, save often to protect your work.

To Save a Document in the Documents Folder

Why? You want to save the file with a meaningful file name so that you easily can retrieve it later. The following steps save the document you created using WordPad to the Documents folder using the file name, Raymond Daily Reminders (Friday).

1

- Click the File tab to display the File menu (Figure 2–4).

    Q&A What is the arrow next to the Save as command?
The arrow indicates that several preset ways to save the file are available, which can be accessed by clicking the arrow.

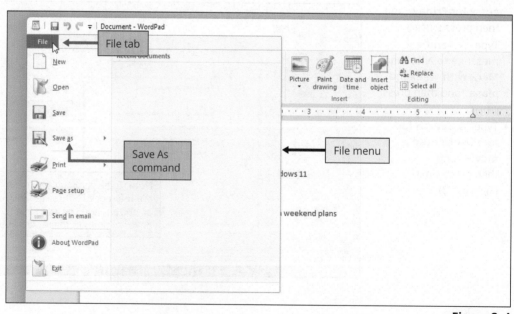

Figure 2–4

- Click Save as on the File menu to display the Save As dialog box.
- Type **Raymond Daily Reminders (Friday)** in the File name box (Figure 2–5).

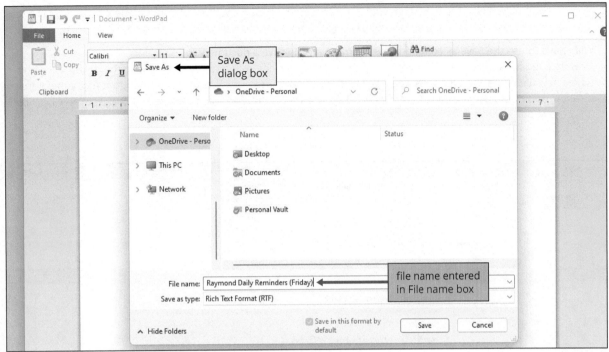

Figure 2–5

- Click Documents in the Navigation pane to specify that you want to save the file in the Documents folder (Figure 2–6).

Q&A Why do the contents of my Documents folder look different?
Depending on the files and folders you have saved on your computer, your Documents folder's contents may differ.

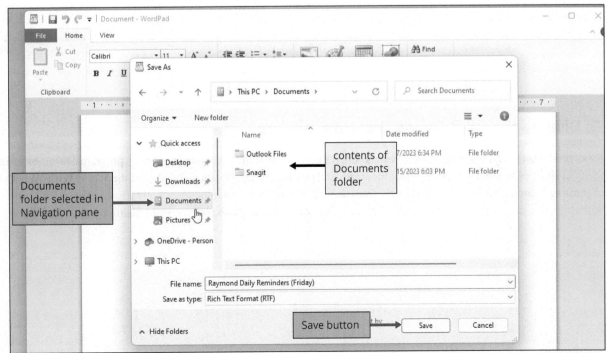

Figure 2–6

- Click the Save button (Save As dialog box) to save the document and close the Save As dialog box (Figure 2–7).

Q&A Why did the WordPad title bar change?
Now that you have saved the document with a file name, the file name will appear on the title bar. To display a preview of the Raymond Daily Reminders (Friday) - WordPad window, point to the WordPad app button on the taskbar.

Will I have to use the Save as command every time I want to save a document?
Now that you have saved the document, you can use the Save command to save changes to the document without having to type a new file name or select a new storage location. If you want to save the file with a different file name or in a different location, you would use the Save as command. By changing the location using the address bar, you can save a file in a different folder or drive.

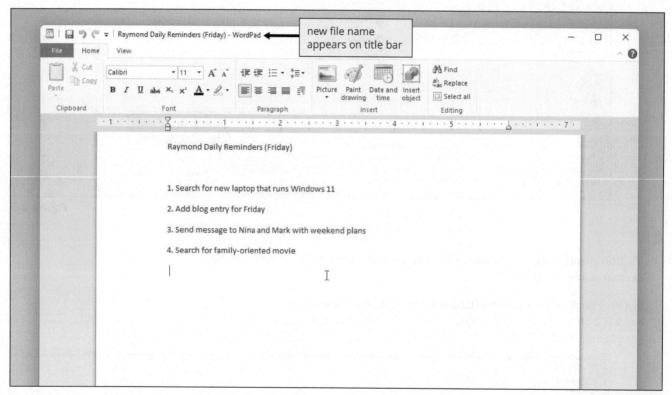

Figure 2–7

To Display the Print Dialog Box from an App

Paper printouts are and will remain an important form of output for electronic documents. Many programs, however, are expanding their capabilities to include sending email messages and posting documents on webpages on the World Wide Web. One method of printing a document is to print it directly from an app. **Why?** Displaying the Print dialog box before printing the document will allow you to specify your printing preferences. The following steps display the Print dialog box in WordPad.

- Click the File tab to display the File menu (Figure 2–8).

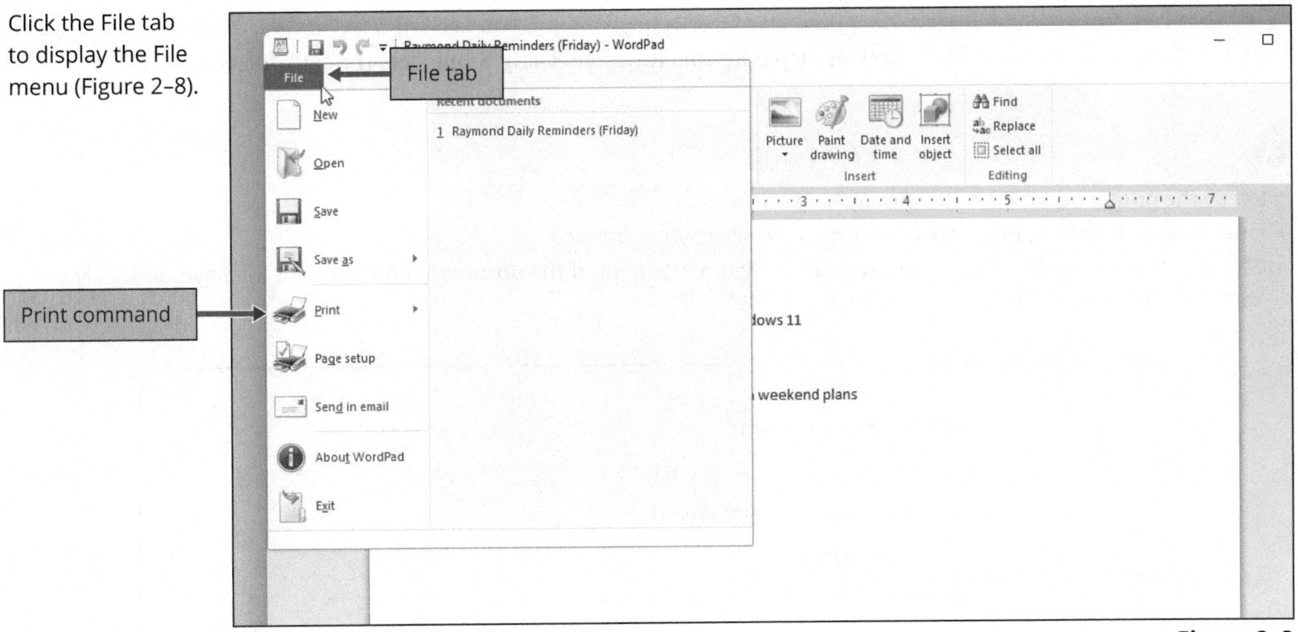

Print command

File tab

Figure 2–8

2

- Click Print on the File menu to display the Print dialog box (Figure 2–9).

Q&A What do the four options in the Page Range area represent?

The option buttons give you the choice of printing all pages of a document (All), selected parts of a document (Selection), current page (Current Page), or selected pages of a document (Pages). The selected All option button indicates all pages of a document will print.

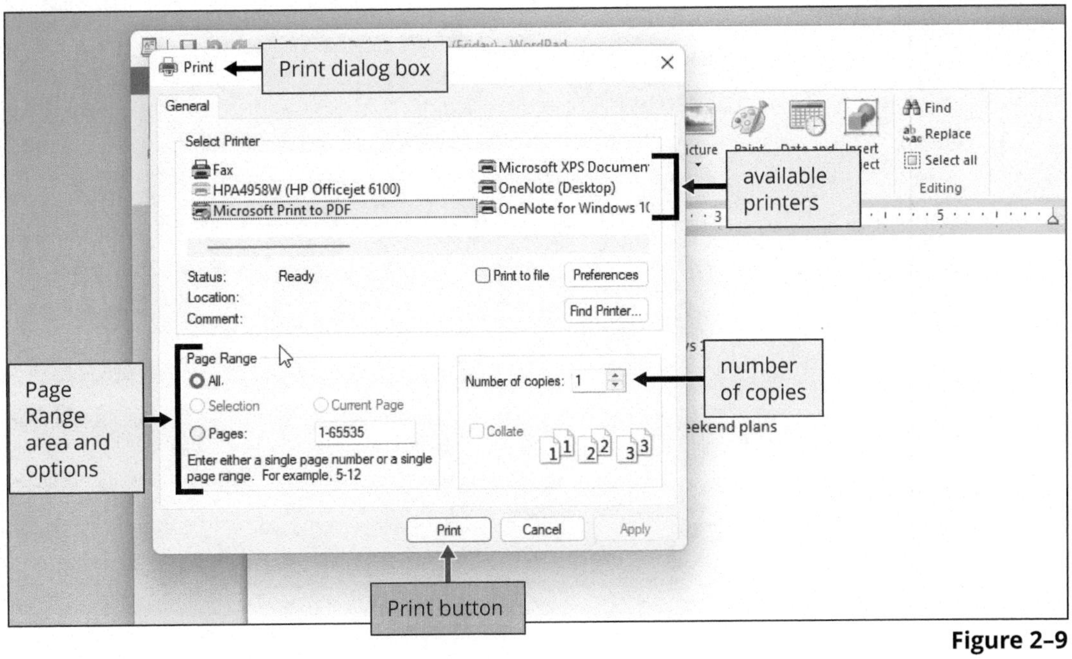

Print dialog box

available printers

Page Range area and options

number of copies

Print button

Figure 2–9

Other Ways

1. Press ALT+F, press P

To Print a Document

Why? It sometimes is important to have a printout of a document in case you need to reference the information when you do not have access to a computer. The following step prints the Raymond Daily Reminders (Friday) document.

- Ready the printer according to the printer's instructions.
- If necessary, click the appropriate printer name to select your printer.
- Click the Print button (Print dialog box) (shown in Figure 2–9) to print the document and return to the Raymond Daily Reminders (Friday) - WordPad window (Figure 2–10).

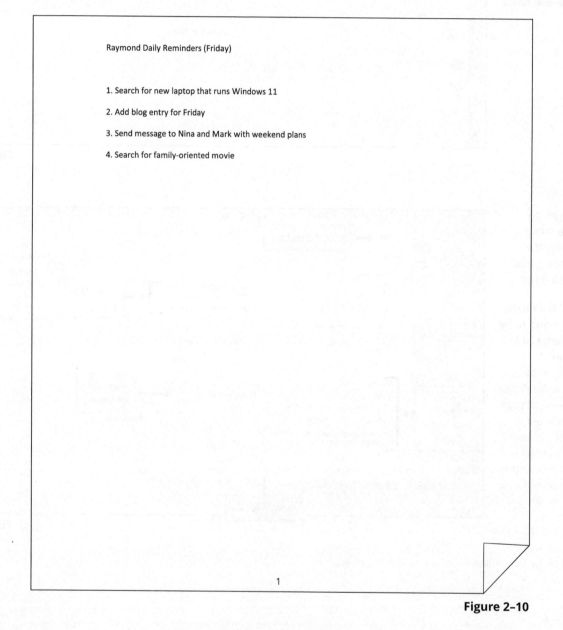

Raymond Daily Reminders (Friday)

1. Search for new laptop that runs Windows 11

2. Add blog entry for Friday

3. Send message to Nina and Mark with weekend plans

4. Search for family-oriented movie

1

Figure 2–10

Other Ways

1. Click appropriate printer name, press ENTER

To Edit a Document

For any document, edits can be as simple as correcting a spelling mistake or as complex as rewriting the entire document. **Why?** Undoubtedly, you will want to make changes to a document after you have created it and saved it. The following step edits the Raymond Daily Reminders (Friday) document by adding a new reminder.

- Click the blank line following the fourth daily reminder.
- Type **5. Register for next semester's classes** and then press ENTER (Figure 2–11).

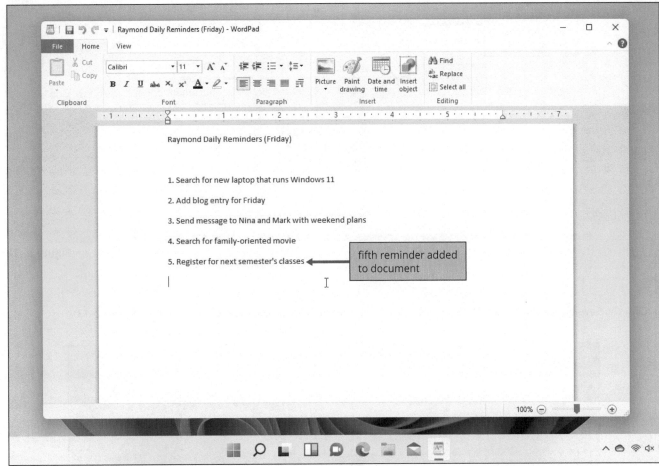

Figure 2–11

To Save and Close a Document

If you forget to save a document after you have edited it, a dialog box will be displayed asking if you want to save the changes. This is how many programs help protect you from losing your work. If you choose to not save the changes, then all edits you made since the last time you saved will be lost. If you click the Cancel button, the changes are not saved, but the document remains open and you can continue working. **Why?** You have made several changes to the document since the last time you have saved it, so you want to save it again. The following steps close and save the Raymond Daily Reminders (Friday) document.

- Click the Close button on the title bar to display the WordPad dialog box (Figure 2-12).

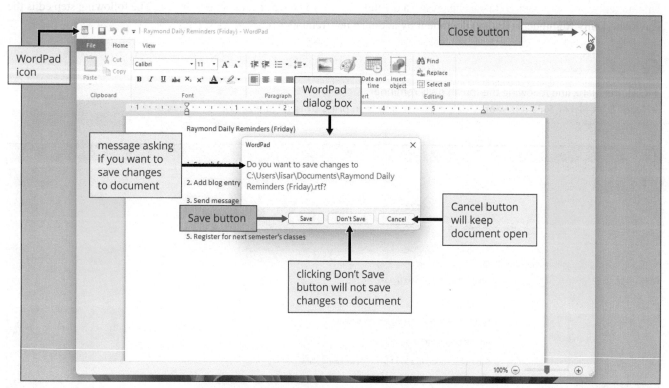

Figure 2-12

- Click the Save button (WordPad dialog box) to save the changes to the document and exit WordPad (Figure 2-13).

Figure 2-13

Other Ways

1. On title bar, double-click WordPad icon, click Save button
2. On title bar, click WordPad icon, click Close on menu, click Save button
3. On File menu, click Exit, click Save (WordPad dialog box)
4. Press CTRL+S, press ALT+F, press X; or press ALT+F4, press ENTER

Creating a Document in the Documents Folder

After completing the reminders list for Mr. Raymond, the next step is to create a similar list for Ms. Estes. Starting an app and then creating a document (the application-centric approach) was the method used to create the first document. Although the same method could be used to create the document for Ms. Estes, another method is to create the new document in the Documents folder without first starting an app. Instead of starting an app to create and modify a document, you first create a blank document directly in the Documents folder and then use the WordPad app to enter data into the document. This method, called the **document-centric approach**, will be used to create the document that contains the reminders for Ms. Estes.

To Open the Documents Folder

Why? You first must open the Documents folder so that you can create a new file in that location. The following step opens the Documents folder.

- Click the File Explorer button on the taskbar to open a File Explorer window.
- If necessary, click Documents in the Quick access list in the Navigation pane (Figure 2–14).

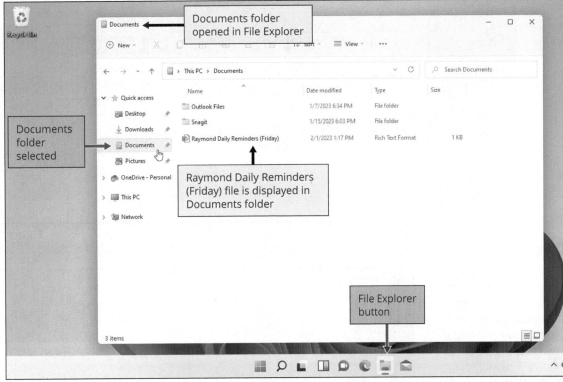

Figure 2–14

Other Ways

1. Right-click File Explorer button on taskbar, click Documents on shortcut menu

To Create a Blank Document in the Documents Folder

When you create a document using the shortcut menu in the Documents folder, the document you actually create contains no data; it is blank. You can think of it as placing a blank piece of paper with a name inside the Documents folder. The document has little value until you add text or other data to it. **Why?** You need to instruct Windows to create the document so that you can prepare to enter content in the document. The following steps create a blank document in the Documents folder to contain the daily reminders for Ms. Estes.

1

- Right-click an open area of the Documents folder to display the shortcut menu.
- Point to New on the shortcut menu to display the New submenu (Figure 2–15).

Q&A Why does my shortcut menu look different?
Depending on the apps you have installed on your computer, the list of commands on the shortcut menu might differ.

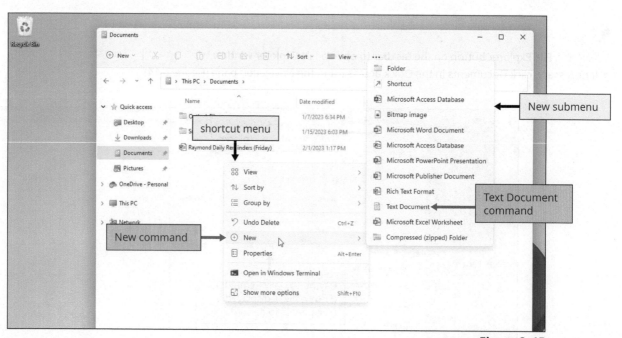

Figure 2–15

2

- Click Text Document on the New submenu to display an entry for a new text document in the Documents folder window (Figure 2–16).

Q&A Why does my file name have .txt at the end?
If Windows is configured to show file name extensions, .txt will appear at the end of this file name. You will learn more about file name extensions later in this module.

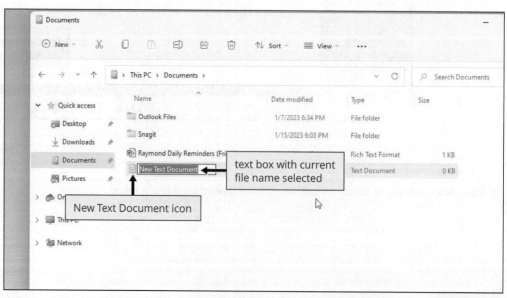

Figure 2–16

To Name a Document in the Documents Folder

In Figure 2–16, the default file name (New Text Document) is highlighted, and on your screen, the insertion point would be blinking, indicating that you can type a new file name. **Why?** After you create a blank document, you need to name the document so that it is easily identifiable. The following step assigns the file name, Estes Daily Reminders (Friday), to the blank document you just created.

- Type **Estes Daily Reminders (Friday)** in the title text box and then press ENTER to assign a name to the new file in the Documents folder (Figure 2–17).

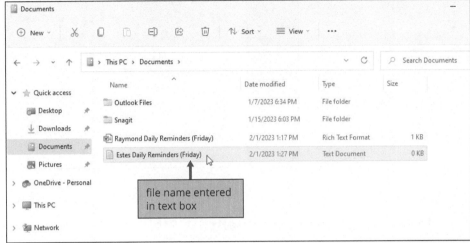

Figure 2–17

Other Ways

1. Right-click icon, click Rename button on shortcut menu, type file name, press ENTER
2. Click icon to select icon, press F2, type file name, press ENTER
3. Click file name, pause, click file name, type new file name, press ENTER
4. Click file name, click Rename button on toolbar, type file name, press ENTER

To Open a Document with WordPad

Although you have created the Estes Daily Reminders (Friday) document, the document contains no text. To add text to the blank document, you must open the document. **Why?** Because text files open with Notepad by default, you need to use the shortcut menu to open the file using WordPad. The following steps open a document in WordPad.

- Right-click the Estes Daily Reminders (Friday) document icon to display the shortcut menu.
- Point to Open with on the shortcut menu to display the Open with submenu (Figure 2–18).

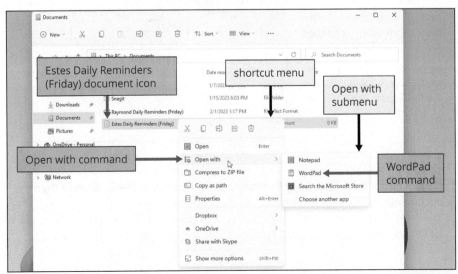

Figure 2–18

2

- Click WordPad on the Open with submenu to open the Estes Daily Reminders (Friday) document in WordPad (Figure 2–19).

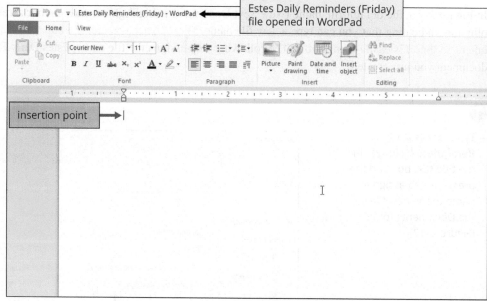

Estes Daily Reminders (Friday) file opened in WordPad

insertion point

Figure 2–19

To Add Text to a Blank Document

Why? After the document is open, you can add text by typing in the document. The following step adds text to the Estes Daily Reminders (Friday) document and then saves the document.

1

- Type **Estes Daily Reminders (Friday)** and then press ENTER twice.
- Type **1. Videoconference with Karen Chang** and then press ENTER.
- Type **2. Email Aylin Rodriguez – Upcoming board meeting Tuesday** and then press ENTER.
- Type **3. Lunch with Sam – Noon, Cafeteria** and then press ENTER.
- Click the Save button on the Quick Access Toolbar to save the file (Figure 2–20).

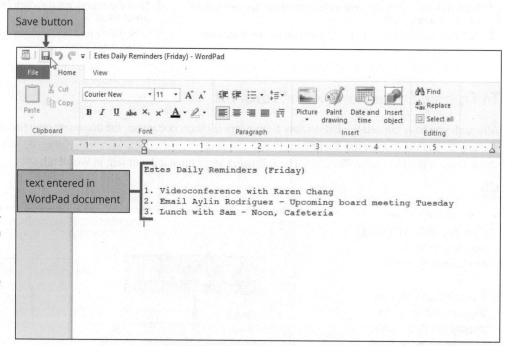

Save button

text entered in WordPad document

Estes Daily Reminders (Friday)

1. Videoconference with Karen Chang
2. Email Aylin Rodriguez – Upcoming board meeting Tuesday
3. Lunch with Sam – Noon, Cafeteria

Figure 2–20

Q&A Why does the Estes Daily Reminders (Friday) document look different than the Raymond Daily Reminders (Friday) document?

The Estes Daily Reminders (Friday) file was first created and saved as a text file, which is different in appearance than the Raymond Daily Reminders (Friday) file, which first was saved in Rich Text Format (.rtf).

To Save a Text Document in Rich Text Format (.rtf)

Typing text in the Estes Daily Reminders (Friday) document modifies the document, which results in the need to save the document. If you make many changes to a document, you should save the document as you work. **Why?** When you created the blank text document, Windows 11 assigned it the .txt file name extension, so you will need to use the Save as command to save it in Rich Text Format, which is WordPad's default format. Using the Rich Text Format will allow you to use all of WordPad's features, including formatting options. The following steps save the document in Rich Text Format.

- Click the File tab to display the File menu.
- Point to the Save as arrow to display a list of available file types (Figure 2–21).

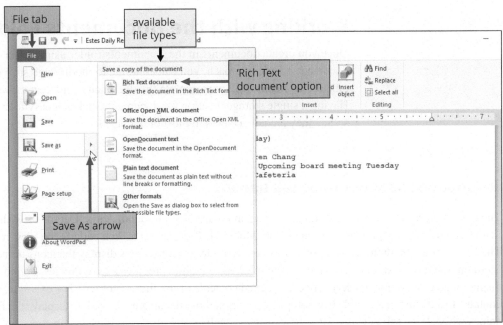

Figure 2–21

- Click 'Rich Text document' to display the Save As dialog box.
- If necessary, type **Estes Daily Reminders (Friday)** in the File name box to change the file name (Figure 2–22).
- Click the Save button (Save As dialog box) to save the document in Rich Text Format.

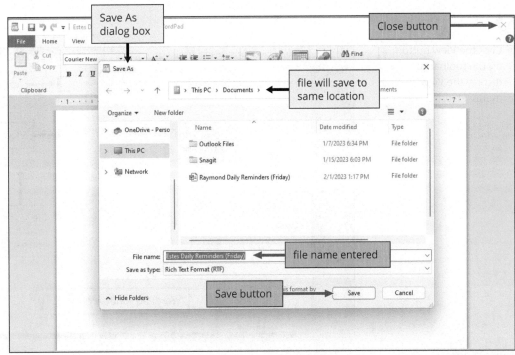

Figure 2–22

To Close the Document

You have saved your changes to Estes Daily Reminders (Friday), and now you can close the document. The following step closes the Estes Daily Reminders (Friday) document.

 Click the Close button on the WordPad title bar (shown in Figure 2–22) to close the document and exit WordPad.

Working with the Documents Folder

Once you create documents in the Documents folder using either the application-centric or the document-centric approach, you can continue to modify and save the documents, print the documents, or create a folder to contain the documents and then move the documents to the folder. Having a single storage location for documents makes it easy to create a copy of the documents so that they are not accidentally lost or damaged.

To Change the View to Small Icons

The default view in the Documents folder (shown in Figure 2–23) is Details view. Details view shows a list of files and folders, in addition to common properties, such as Date Modified, Type, and Size. You can use the View menu to change to other views. The Small icons, Medium icons, Large icons, and Extra large icons views display the icons in increasingly larger sizes. When Medium, Large, or Extra large icon views are selected, Windows provides a Live Preview option. With Live Preview, the icons display images that more closely reflect the actual contents of the files or folders. For example, a folder icon for a folder that contains text documents would show sample pages from those documents. List view displays the files and folders as a list of file names without any extra details. Tiles view displays the files and folders as tiles, which consist of an icon and icon description. With all of these views, the default arrangement for the icons is to be alphabetical by file name. **Why?** You want to change the layout of the icons in the Documents folder to one that suits your desires. The following steps change the view from the Details view to the Small icons view.

- Click the View button on the toolbar to display the View menu (Figure 2–23).

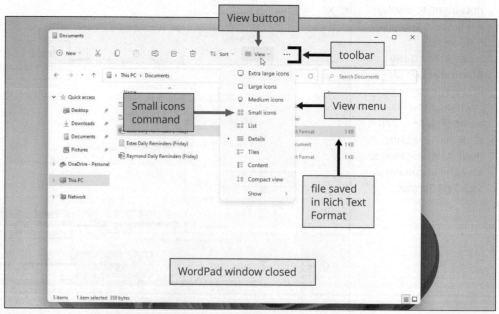

Figure 2–23

- Click the Small icons command to change the view to display small icons (Figure 2–24).
- **Experiment:** Click each of the first eight commands on the View menu to see the various ways that Windows can display folder contents. After you have finished, select the Small icons view.

Q&A What is Compact view?
In Compact view, Windows decreases the space between items listed in the Documents window. To turn Compact view on or off, click the View button on the toolbar and then click Compact view.

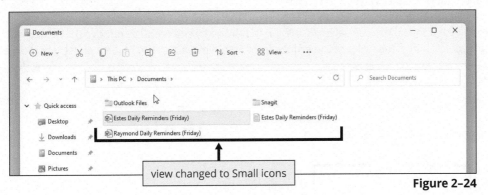

Figure 2–24

Other Ways

1. Right-click open space in Documents folder, point to View on shortcut menu, click Small icons on View submenu

To Arrange Items in Groups by File Type

Other methods are available for arranging the icons in the Documents folder. One practical arrangement is to display the icons in groups based on file type. This arrangement places files of the same type (File Folder, Text Documents, Microsoft Word Documents, Microsoft PowerPoint Presentations, and so on) in separate groups. **Why?** When a window contains many files and folders, this layout makes it easier to find a particular file or folder quickly. The following steps group the icons in the Documents folder by file type.

- Click the Sort button on the toolbar to display the Sort menu.
- Point to Group by on the Sort menu to display the Group by submenu (Figure 2–25).

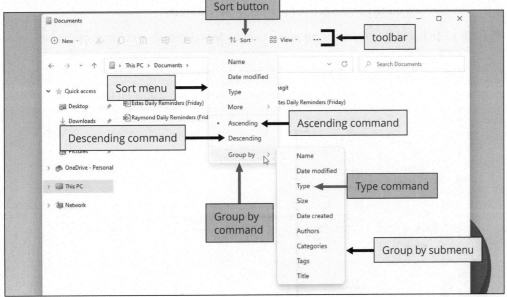

Figure 2–25

Q&A What if the Sort button does not appear on the toolbar?

If your computer's screen resolution is low or the window is not large enough, the commands on the toolbar might be displayed differently. Point to the left or right border of the Documents window, press and hold the mouse button, and then drag to widen the window.

• Click Type on the Group by submenu to display the files and folders grouped by type (Figure 2–26).

Q&A Can I group the files and folders in other ways?

You can group the files by any of the options on the Group by sub menu. This includes options such as Name, Date modified, Type, and Size. If a grouping is applied, you can select (None) on the Group by sub menu to remove the grouping. The Ascending and Descending options change the order of the groups from alphabetical order to reverse alphabetical order.

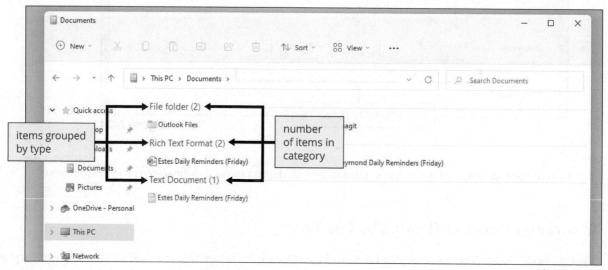

Figure 2–26

Other Ways

1. Right-click empty area of Documents folder, point to Group by on shortcut menu, click Type on Group by submenu

To Change to Medium Icons View

The following steps change the view to Medium icons.

1 Click the View button on the toolbar to display the View menu.

2 Click Medium icons on the View menu to change the view to Medium icons view (Figure 2–27).

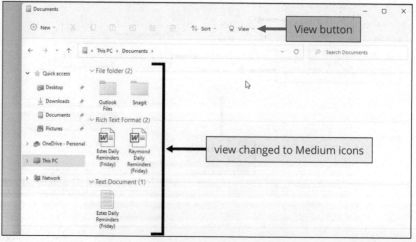

Figure 2–27

To Create and Name a Folder in the Documents Folder

Windows 11 allows you to place one or more documents into a folder in much the same manner as you might take a document written on a piece of paper and place it in a file folder. You want to keep the Raymond and Estes documents together so that you can find and easily distinguish them from other documents stored in the Documents folder. **Why?** To keep multiple documents together in one place, you first must create a folder in which to store them. The following steps create and name a folder titled Daily Reminders in the Documents folder to store the Raymond Daily Reminders (Friday) and Estes Daily Reminders (Friday) documents.

- Click the New button on the toolbar to display the New menu.
- Click Folder on the New menu to create a new folder (Figure 2–28).

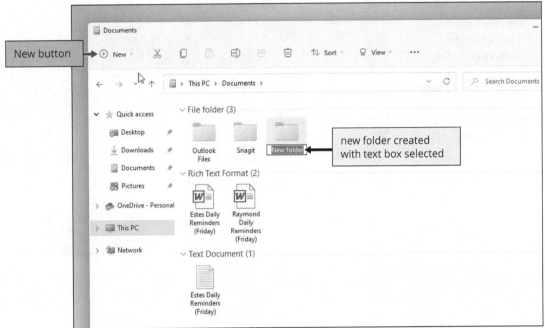

Figure 2–28

- Type **Daily Reminders** in the icon title text box and then press ENTER to name the folder and store the folder in the Documents folder (Figure 2–29).

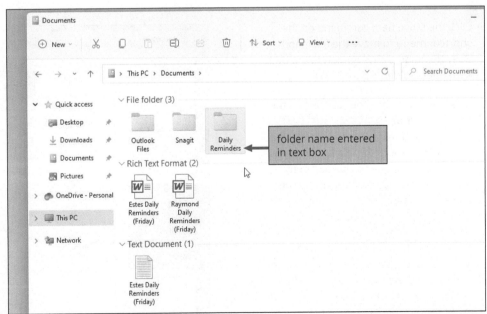

Figure 2–29

Other Ways
1. Right-click open space in Documents folder, point to New on shortcut menu, click Folder on New submenu, type file name, press ENTER   2. Press CTRL+SHIFT+N

To Move a Document into a Folder

The ability to organize documents and files within folders allows you to keep the Documents folder organized when using Windows 11. **Why?** After you create a folder in the Documents folder, the next step is to move documents into the folder. The following steps move the Raymond Daily Reminders (Friday) and the Estes Daily Reminders (Friday) documents into the Daily Reminders folder.

1

- Right-click and drag (also known as right-drag) the Raymond Daily Reminders (Friday) icon to the Daily Reminders folder icon and then release the mouse button to display the shortcut menu (Figure 2–30).

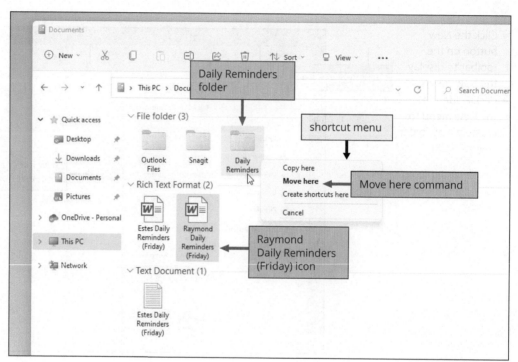

Figure 2–30

2

- Click the Move here command on the shortcut menu to move the Raymond Daily Reminders (Friday) icon to the Daily Reminders folder (Figure 2–31).

Q&A What are the other options on the shortcut menu?

When you right-drag, a shortcut menu is displayed that lists the available options. In this case, the options include Copy here, Move here, Create shortcuts here, and Cancel. Selecting Copy here creates a copy of the Raymond document in the Daily Reminders folder, Create shortcuts here puts a link to the Raymond document (not the file or a copy of the file) in the Daily Reminders folder, and Cancel terminates the right-drag process. The options on the shortcut menu might change, depending on the type of file and where you are dragging it.

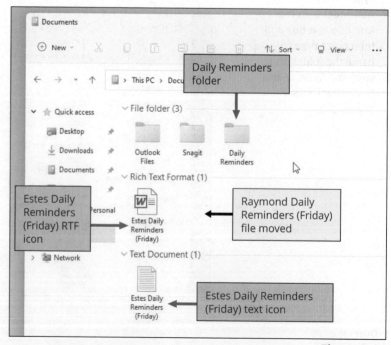

Figure 2–31

3

- Right-drag the Estes Daily Reminders (Friday) RTF icon to the Daily Reminders icon and move it to the Daily Reminders folder.
- Right-drag the Estes Daily Reminders (Friday) text icon to the Daily Reminders icon and move it to the Daily Reminders folder (Figure 2–32).

Q&A What happened to the Rich Text Document and Text Document groups?
The documents have been moved to the Daily Reminders folder, so the groups no longer were needed. Only if other RTF and text documents were contained in the Documents folder would the groupings remain.

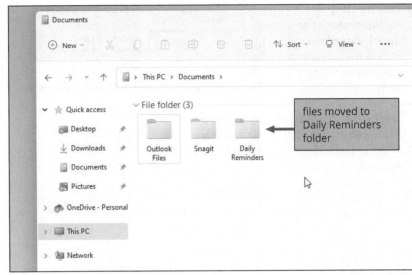

Figure 2–32

Other Ways

1. Drag document icon to folder icon

2. Right-click document icon, click Cut on shortcut menu, right-click folder icon, click Paste on shortcut menu

---

To Change Location Using the Address Bar

If you would like to navigate to the folder to see if your files are there, you have several ways to do this. One way in Windows 11 is to use the address bar. The address bar appears at the top of the Documents folder window and displays your current location as a series of links separated by arrows. By clicking the arrows, you can change your location. The Forward and Back buttons can be used to navigate through the locations you have visited, just like the Forward and Back buttons in a browser. **Why?** You would like to view the contents of the Daily Reminders folder by changing the location in the address bar. The following steps change your location to the Daily Reminders folder.

1

- Click the Documents arrow on the address bar to display a location menu that contains a list of folders in the Documents folder (Figure 2–33).

Q&A What if the Documents arrow is not displayed?
Click the Documents button on the address bar and then the Documents arrow should be displayed.

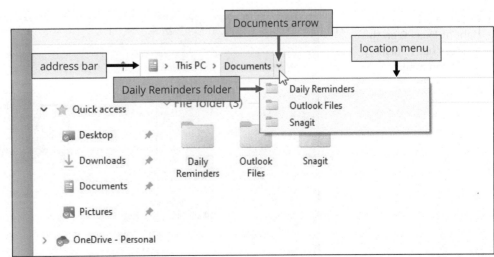

Figure 2–33

2

- Click the Daily Reminders folder on the location menu to display the contents of the Daily Reminders folder (Figure 2–34).

> **Q&A** What should I do if the arrow to the right of Documents does not appear?
> If the arrow did not appear, double-click the Daily Reminders folder in the Documents folder to display the contents of the Daily Reminders folder.

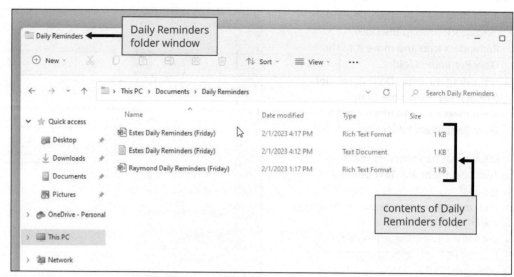

Figure 2–34

3

- Click the This PC button on the address bar to switch to the This PC window (Figure 2–35).

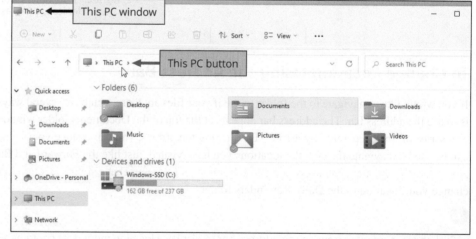

Figure 2–35

4

- Click the arrow to the right of This PC on the address bar to display a location menu (Figure 2–36).

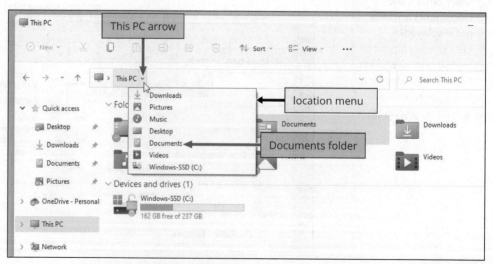

Figure 2–36

- Click Documents on the location menu to move to the Documents folder.
- Click the Documents arrow to display a location menu.
- Click the Daily Reminders folder on the location menu to move to the Daily Reminders folder.

To Display and Use the Preview Pane

Now that you are viewing the contents of the Daily Reminders folder, you can add a Preview pane to the layout, which will provide you with an enhanced Live Preview of your documents. **Why?** When you select a document, the Preview pane displays a Live Preview of the document to the right of the list of files in the folder window. The following steps add the Preview pane to the layout of the Daily Reminders folder and then display a Live Preview of the Raymond document.

- Click the View button on the toolbar to display the View menu.
- Point to the Show command to display the Show submenu (Figure 2–37).
- Click Preview pane on the Show submenu to display the Preview pane.

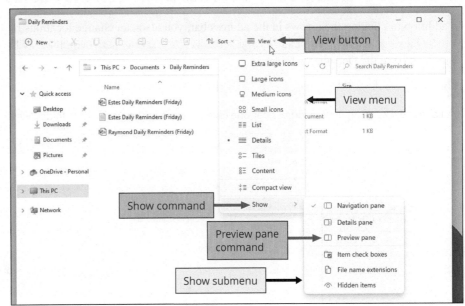

Figure 2–37

- Click the Raymond Daily Reminders (Friday) document icon to display a preview of the document in the Preview pane (Figure 2–38).
- **Experiment:** Select different documents to display their preview in the Preview pane. When you have finished, select the Raymond Daily Reminders (Friday) document.

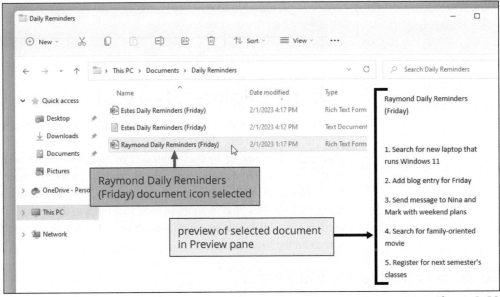

Figure 2–38

Other Ways

1. Press ALT+P

To Close the Preview Pane

After verifying that your files are in the Daily Reminders folder, you can close the Preview pane and then use the address bar to return to the Documents folder. The following steps close the Preview pane.

1 Click the View button on the toolbar and then point to Show.

2 Click Preview pane on the Show submenu to close the Preview pane.

Other Ways

1. Press ALT+P

To Change Location Using the Back Button on the Address Bar

In addition to clicking the arrows in the address bar, you also can change locations by using the Back and Forward buttons. **Why?** Clicking the Back button allows you to return to a location that you previously have visited. The following step changes your location to the Documents folder.

• Click the Back button on the address bar one time to return to the Documents folder (Figure 2–39).

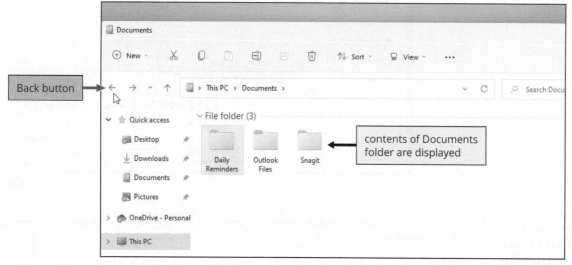

Figure 2–39

Creating Folder Shortcuts

One way to customize Windows 11 is to use shortcuts to start apps and open files or folders. A shortcut is a link to any object on the computer or on a network, such as an app, a file, a folder, a webpage, a printer, or another computer or mobile device. Placing a shortcut to a folder on the Start menu or on the desktop can make it easier to locate and open the folder.

A shortcut icon is not the actual document or app. You do not actually place the folder on the menu; instead, you place a shortcut icon that links to the folder on the menu. When you delete a shortcut, you delete the shortcut icon but do not delete the actual folder, document, or app; they remain on the hard drive.

To Pin a Folder to the Start Menu

Why? Pinning the Daily Reminders folder to the Start menu will enable easier access to the folder, instead of having to open the File Explorer window and navigate to the folder each time. The following steps pin the Daily Reminders folder to the Start menu.

• Right-click the Daily Reminders folder to display a shortcut menu (Figure 2–40).

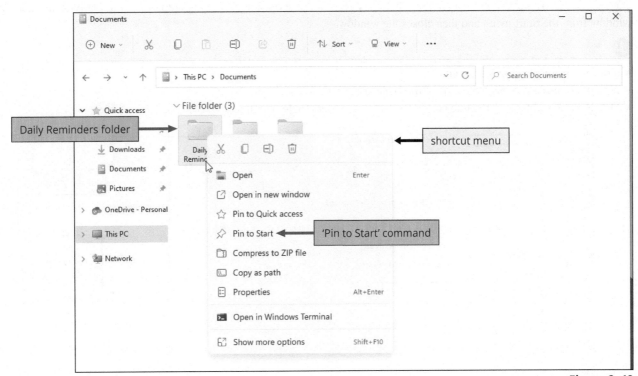

Figure 2–40

• Click 'Pin to Start' on the shortcut menu to pin the Daily Reminders folder to the Start menu.
• Click the Start button to display the Start menu so that you can see the Daily Reminders folder icon pinned to the Start menu. You might have to scroll or click the More button to see the pinned folder (Figure 2–41).

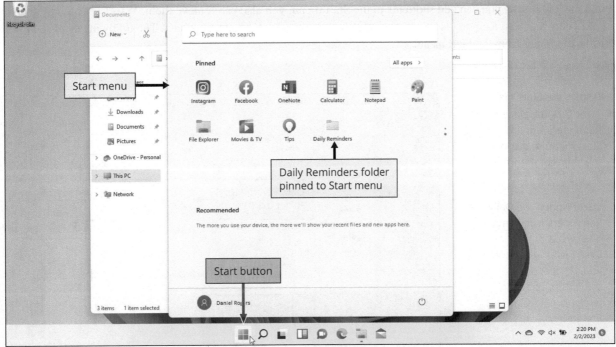

Figure 2–41

To Open a Folder Using a Pinned Icon on the Start Menu

Why? After placing a shortcut to the Daily Reminders folder on the Start menu, you can open the Daily Reminders folder by clicking the Start button and then clicking the Daily Reminders icon. The following step opens the Daily Reminders folder window from the Start menu and then closes the window.

- If necessary, display the Start menu.
- Click the Daily Reminders icon to open the Daily Reminders folder (Figure 2–42).
- Click the Close button on the title bar of the Daily Reminders folder window.

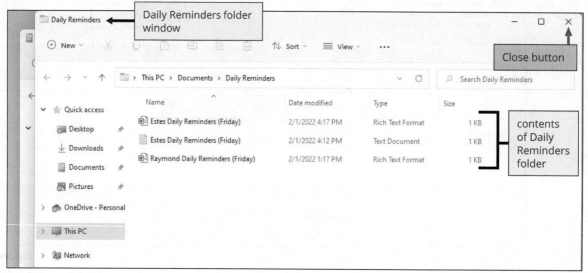

Figure 2–42

To Remove a Pinned Folder Icon from the Start Menu

The capability of adding shortcuts to and removing them from the Start menu provides great flexibility when customizing Windows 11. Just as you can add shortcuts to the Start menu, you also can remove them. **Why?** If you find that you are no longer using a pinned icon on the Start menu, you should remove it to minimize clutter. The following steps remove the Daily Reminders folder from the Start menu.

- Display the Start menu.
- Right-click the Daily Reminders icon on the Start menu to display the shortcut menu (Figure 2–43).

Q&A What if the Daily Reminders icon is not displayed?
Click the More button and, if necessary, scroll through the list to display the Daily Reminders icon.

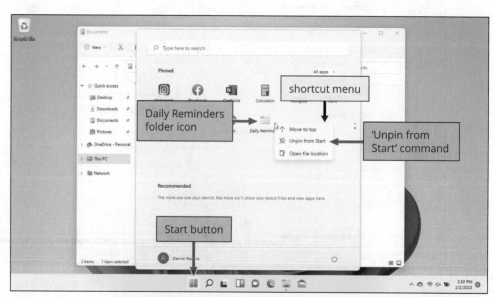

Figure 2–43

2

- Click 'Unpin from Start' on the shortcut menu to remove the Daily Reminders shortcut from the Start menu (Figure 2–44).

Q&A What if 'Unpin from Start' does not appear on the shortcut menu?
If 'Unpin from Start' does not appear, click 'Remove from list.'

- Click somewhere on the desktop to close the Start menu.

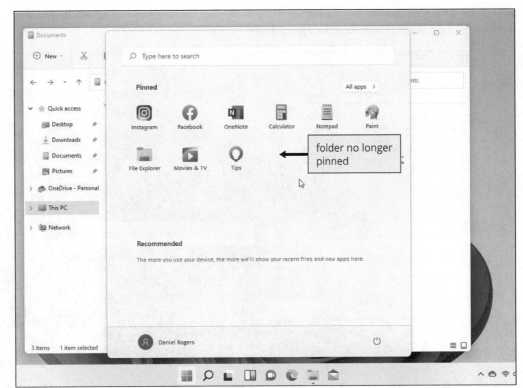

Figure 2–44

To Create a Shortcut on the Desktop

You also can create shortcuts directly on the desktop. It is best that only shortcuts be placed on the desktop rather than actual folders and files. **Why?** You want to be able to open a folder quickly without using File Explorer, which might take additional time. The following steps create a shortcut for the Daily Reminders folder on the desktop.

1

- Right-click the Daily Reminders folder to display the shortcut menu.
- Click 'Show more options' on the shortcut menu to display more options.
- Point to Send to on the shortcut menu to display the Send to submenu (Figure 2–45).

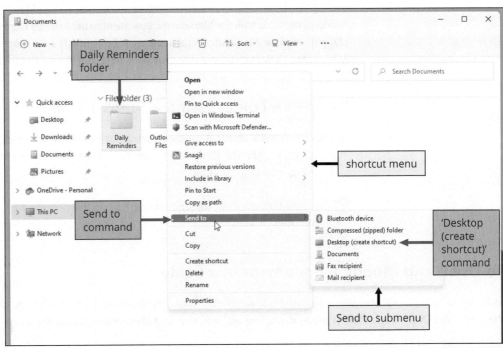

Figure 2–45

2

- Click 'Desktop (create shortcut)' on the Send to submenu to create a shortcut on the desktop.
- Close the Documents folder window (Figure 2–46).

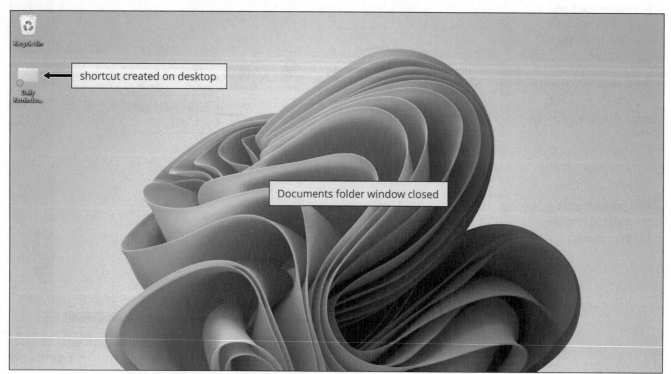

shortcut created on desktop

Documents folder window closed

Figure 2–46

Opening and Modifying Documents within a Folder

When editing a document, you can open the document directly instead of first starting the app and then opening the document. You have received new information to add to Mr. Raymond's daily reminders. A videoconference with the Marketing Department in the western United States has been scheduled for 1:00 p.m., and the Marketing Department must be notified of the meeting. To add this new item to the daily reminders document, you first must open the Daily Reminders folder that contains the document.

To Open a Folder Using a Shortcut on the Desktop

You have created a shortcut on the desktop for the Daily Reminders folder, so you can use the shortcut icon to open the Daily Reminders folder. The following step opens the Daily Reminders folder using a desktop shortcut.

1 Double-click the Daily Reminders shortcut on the desktop to open the Daily Reminders folder.

To Open and Modify a Document in a Folder

Why? You want to perform additional modifications to the Raymond Daily Reminders (Friday) file. The following steps open the Raymond Daily Reminders (Friday) document and add new text about the videoconference.

- Open the Raymond Daily Reminders (Friday) document in WordPad.

Q&A I have two Estes Daily Reminders (Friday) documents. Which one should I open?

Open the Rich Text Format document.

- Move the insertion point to the blank line below item 5 in the document.
- Type **6. Notify Marketing – Videoconference at 1:00 p.m.** and then press ENTER to modify the Raymond Daily Reminders (Friday) document (Figure 2–47).

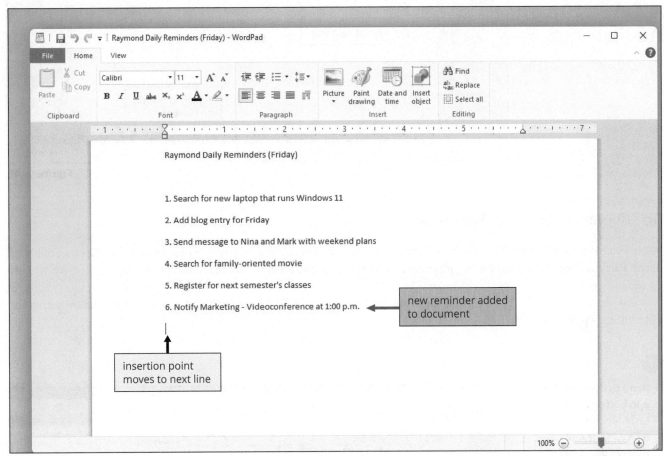

Figure 2–47

To Open and Modify Multiple Documents

Windows 11 allows you to have more than one document open and one app running at the same time so that you can work on multiple documents. The concept of multiple apps running at the same time is called **multitasking**. To illustrate how you can work with multiple windows open at the same time, you now will edit the Estes Daily Reminders (Friday) document. **Why?** You want to include a reminder to talk to Scott about McKenzie's birthday party. You will not have to close the Raymond Daily Reminders (Friday) document. The following steps open the Estes Daily Reminders (Friday) document and add the new reminder.

- Open the Estes Daily Reminders (Friday) document in WordPad.

Q&A Why did the WordPad icon on the taskbar change?

When only one document is open in WordPad, the WordPad icon appears like a single button. If multiple documents are open, the icon changes to appear as a stacked button to indicate more than one document is open.

2

- Move the insertion point to the end of the document in the WordPad window.
- Type **4. Call Scott – Birthday party for McKenzie** and then press ENTER (Figure 2–48).

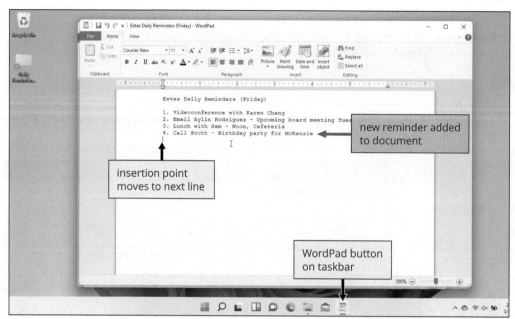

new reminder added to document

insertion point moves to next line

WordPad button on taskbar

Figure 2–48

To Display an Inactive Window

After you have modified the Estes Daily Reminders (Friday) document, you receive information that a dinner meeting with Jacob Patel has been scheduled for Mr. Raymond for 7:00 p.m. in the Orlando International Airport. **Why?** You are directed to add this entry to Mr. Raymond's reminders. To do this, you must make the Raymond Daily Reminders (Friday) - WordPad window the active window. The following steps make the Raymond Daily Reminders (Friday) - WordPad window active and enter the new reminder.

1

- Point to the WordPad app button on the taskbar to display a Live Preview of the two documents (Figure 2–49).

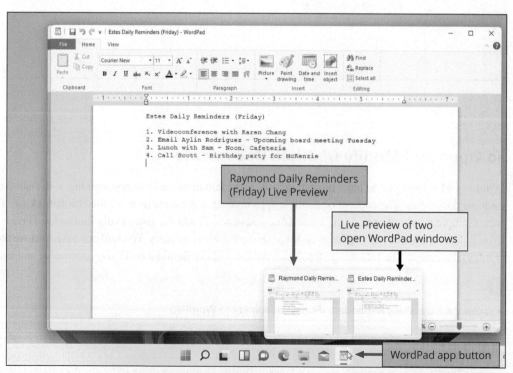

Raymond Daily Reminders (Friday) Live Preview

Live Preview of two open WordPad windows

WordPad app button

Figure 2–49

● Click the Raymond Daily Reminders (Friday) Live Preview to make it the active window (Figure 2–50).

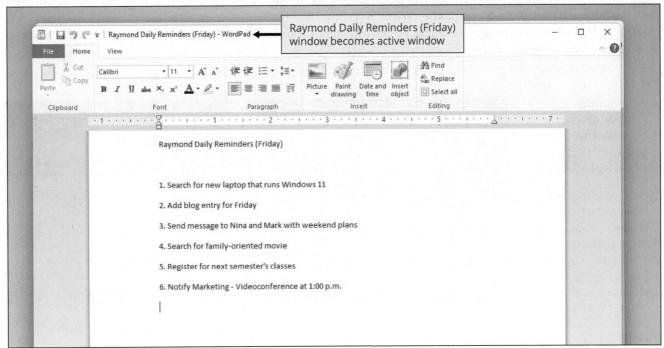

Figure 2–50

● When the window opens, position the insertion point at the end of the document, type   **7. Dinner with Jacob Patel – 7:00 p.m., Orlando International Airport**   and then press ENTER to update the document (Figure 2–51).

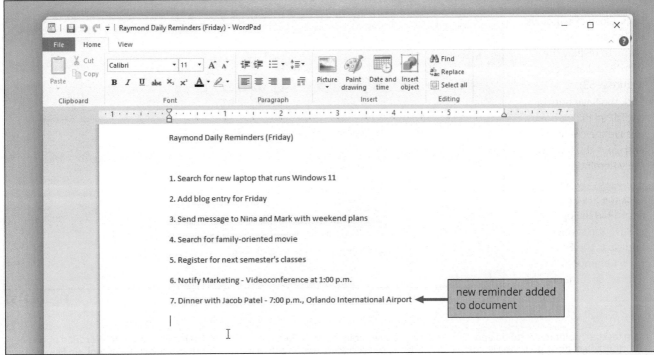

Figure 2–51

To Close Multiple Open Windows and Save Changes Using the Taskbar

If the windows are open on the desktop, you can click the Close button on the title bar of each open window to close them. Regardless of whether the windows are open on the desktop or are minimized using the Show desktop button, you can close the windows using the buttons on the taskbar. **Why?** When you have finished working with multiple windows, you should close them. The following steps close the Raymond Daily Reminders (Friday) - WordPad and Estes Daily Reminders (Friday) - WordPad windows using the taskbar.

1

- Right-click the WordPad app button on the taskbar to display a shortcut menu (Figure 2–52).

Q&A Why do multiple instances of the documents appear in the Recent list?
The list shows the files you recently have edited and does not remove duplicate listings. As a result, a document might appear in the list multiple times.

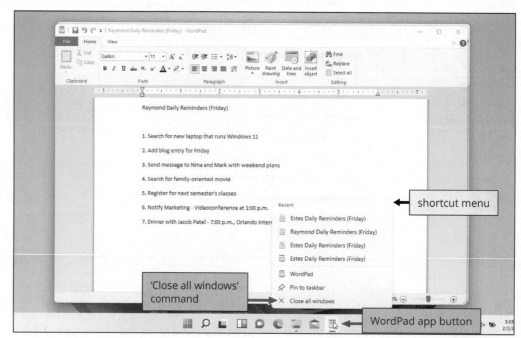

Figure 2–52

2

- Click 'Close all windows' on the shortcut menu to display the WordPad dialog box (Figure 2–53).
- Click the Save button (WordPad dialog box) to save the changes and close the Raymond Daily Reminders (Friday) document.
- Click the Save button (WordPad dialog box) to save the changes and close the Estes Daily Reminders (Friday) document.

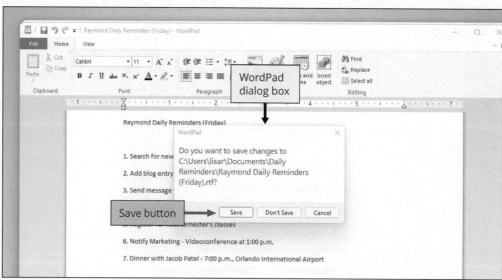

Figure 2–53

Other Ways

1. On taskbar, point to WordPad app button, select document, on File menu click Save (WordPad dialog box), click Close button on title bar

2. On taskbar, point to WordPad app button, select document, on title bar click Close button, click Save button (WordPad dialog box)

3. On taskbar, point to WordPad app button, select document, on File menu click Exit, click Save button (WordPad dialog box)

The Recycle Bin

Occasionally, you will want to delete files and folders from the Documents folder. Windows 11 offers three different techniques to perform this operation: (1) drag the object to the Recycle Bin, (2) right-drag the object to the Recycle Bin, and (3) right-click the object and then click Delete on the shortcut menu.

It is important to understand what you are doing when you delete a file or folder. When you delete a shortcut from the desktop, you delete only the shortcut icon and its reference to the file or folder. The file or folder itself is stored elsewhere on the hard drive or storage device and is not deleted. When you delete the icon for a file or folder (not a shortcut), the actual file or folder is deleted. A shortcut icon includes an arrow to indicate that it is a shortcut, whereas a file or folder does not have the arrow as part of its icon.

When you delete a file or folder, Windows 11 places these items in the Recycle Bin, which is an area on the hard drive that contains all the items you have deleted. If you are running low on hard drive space, one way to gain additional space is to empty the Recycle Bin. Up until the time you empty the Recycle Bin, you can recover deleted files. Even though you have this safety net, you should be careful whenever you delete anything from your computer.

To Move a Text File to the Recycle Bin

The following steps move the file to the Recycle Bin. **Why?** You will not be using the Estes Daily Reminders (Friday) text file, so you will move it to the Recycle Bin.

1

- If necessary, display the contents of the Daily Reminders folder.
- Drag the Estes Daily Reminders (Friday) text icon to the Recycle Bin. Do not release the mouse button (Figure 2–54).

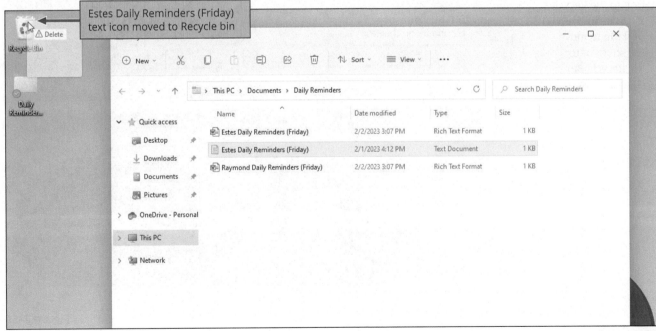

Figure 2–54

2

- Release the mouse button to move the Estes Daily Reminders (Friday) text file to the Recycle Bin (Figure 2–55).
- Click the Close button on the Daily Reminders window's title bar to close the Daily Reminders folder window.

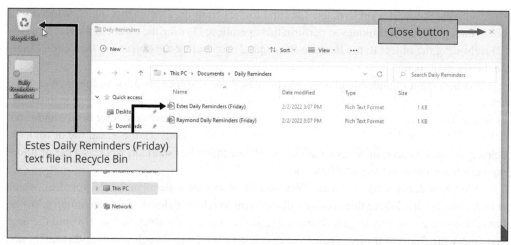

Figure 2–55

Other Ways

1. Select file, press DELETE

To Delete a Shortcut from the Desktop

Why? You have finished working with the files in the Daily Reminders folder, so you can remove the shortcut from the desktop. The following step removes the Daily Reminder folder shortcut from the desktop.

1

- Drag the Daily Reminders - Shortcut icon to the Recycle Bin icon on the desktop to move the shortcut to the Recycle Bin (Figure 2–56).

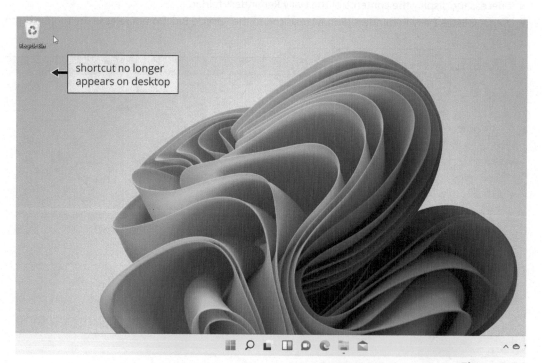

Figure 2–56

To Restore an Item from the Recycle Bin

The following steps restore the Daily Reminders - Shortcut icon to the desktop. **Why?** At some point, you might discover that you accidentally deleted a shortcut, file, or folder that you did not want to delete. As long as you have not emptied the Recycle Bin, you can restore deleted files.

- Double-click the Recycle Bin icon to open the Recycle Bin window.
- Click the Daily Reminders - Shortcut icon to select it (Figure 2–57).

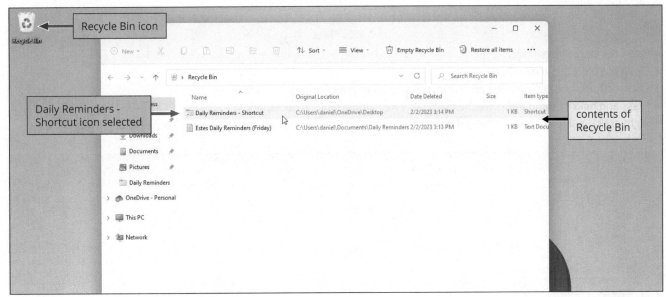

Figure 2–57

2

- Click the See more button on the toolbar to display the See more menu (Figure 2–58).
- Click 'Restore the selected items' on the See more menu to restore the Daily Reminders - Shortcut icon to its previous location. In this case, the icon is restored to the desktop.
- Close the Recycle Bin window.

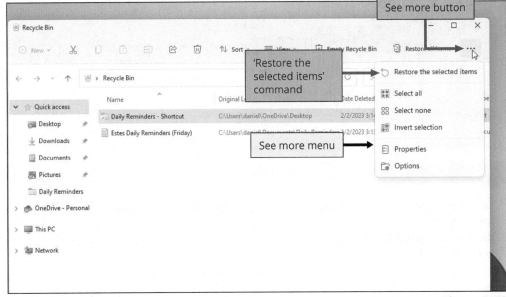

Figure 2–58

To Delete a Shortcut from the Desktop

The following step deletes the Daily Reminders shortcut icon again so that you can leave the desktop how you found it.

 Drag the Daily Reminders - Shortcut icon to the Recycle Bin icon.

To Delete Multiple Files from a Folder

You can delete several files at one time. **Why?** If you have several objects you want to delete in the same location, you can delete them all at one time. The following steps delete both the Raymond Daily Reminders (Friday) and the Estes Daily Reminders (Friday) documents.

- Open the Documents folder.
- Open the Daily Reminders folder.
- Click the Raymond Daily Reminders (Friday) document to select it.
- Press and hold CTRL and then click the Estes Daily Reminders (Friday) document.
- Right-click the documents to display the shortcut menu and then click 'Show more options' (Figure 2–59).

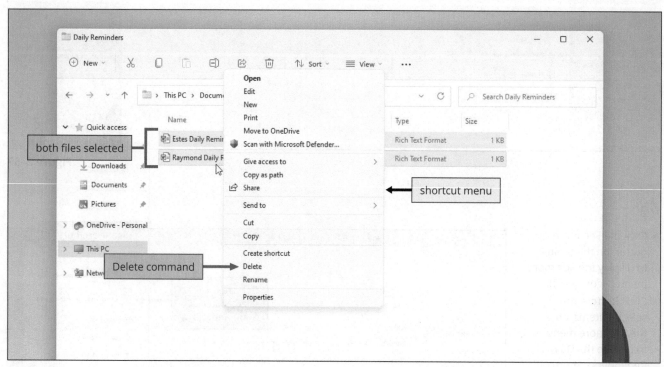

Figure 2–59

- Click the Delete button on the toolbar to delete the selected items (Figure 2–60).

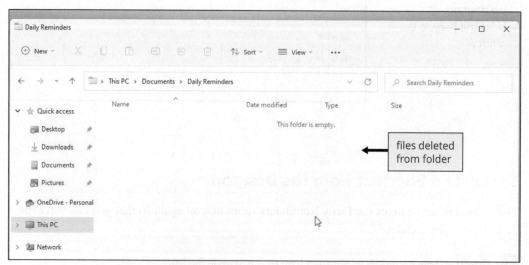

Figure 2–60

To Delete a Folder from the Documents Folder and Empty the Recycle Bin

You also can delete folders from the Documents folder using the same method. The following steps delete the Daily Reminders folder and empty the Recycle Bin.

1 Click Documents in the Navigation pane.

2 Delete the Daily Reminders folder.

3 Close the Documents folder.

4 Right-click the Recycle Bin to display the shortcut menu.

5 Click 'Empty Recycle Bin' on the shortcut menu.

6 Click the Yes button (Delete Multiple Items dialog box) to delete the contents of the Recycle Bin permanently.

To Sign Out of an Account and Shut Down the Computer

You have completed the work with Windows. The following steps end the session by signing out of your account and then shutting down the computer.

1 Display the Start menu.

2 Click the name identifying your user account and then click Sign out.

3 Click the lock screen to display the sign-in screen.

4 Click the Shut down button.

5 Click the Shut down command on the Shut down menu to shut down the computer.

Summary

In this module, you learned how to create WordPad documents using both the application-centric approach and the document-centric approach. You moved these documents to the Documents folder and then modified and printed them. You created a new folder in the Documents folder and placed documents in the folder. You worked with multiple documents open at the same time. You pinned a folder to the Start menu and added a shortcut on the desktop. Using various methods, you deleted shortcuts, documents, and a folder. Finally, you learned how to work with the Recycle Bin and restore items that have been deleted.

Student Assignments

Apply Your Knowledge

Reinforce the skills and apply the concepts you learned in this module.

Creating a Document with WordPad

Instructions: Use WordPad to create the shopping list shown in Figure 2–61.

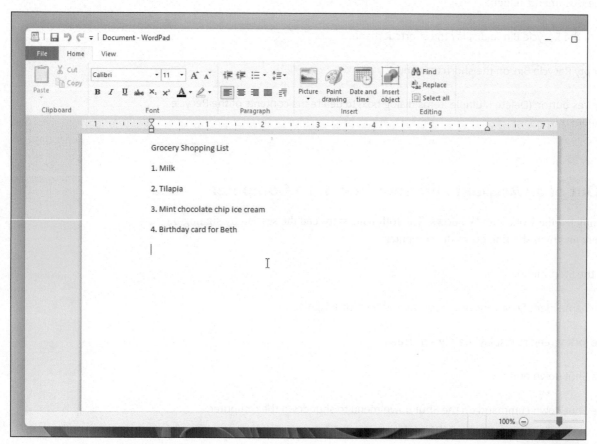

Figure 2–61

Perform the following tasks:

1. Start WordPad.

2. Type   **Grocery Shopping List**   and then press ENTER.

3. Type   **1. Milk**   and then press ENTER.

4. Type   **2. Tilapia**   and then press ENTER.

5. Type   **3. Mint chocolate chip ice cream**   and then press ENTER.

6. Type   **4. Birthday card for Beth**   and then press ENTER.

7. Click the File tab and then click Print to display the Print dialog box. Click the Print button (Print dialog box) to print the document.

8. Click the File tab and then save the file in Rich Text Format.

9. Save the document in the Documents folder with the file name, Shopping List.

10. Exit WordPad, and close any open windows.

In the Labs

Design and implement a solution using creative thinking and problem-solving skills.

Lab 1: Creating a To Do List

Problem: You have a schedule of tasks to complete today. You decide to use WordPad to create a to do list.

Perform the following tasks.

1. Open a new WordPad document. Save the document on the desktop using the file name, To-Do List. (**Hint:** When saving, save on the desktop.)

2. Type the text shown in Figure 2–64.

3. Save changes to the document.

4. Print the document.

5. Close the document.

6. Create a folder in the Documents folder named Important Documents.

7. Place the To-Do List document in the Important Documents folder.

8. Place a shortcut on the desktop that opens the Important Documents folder.

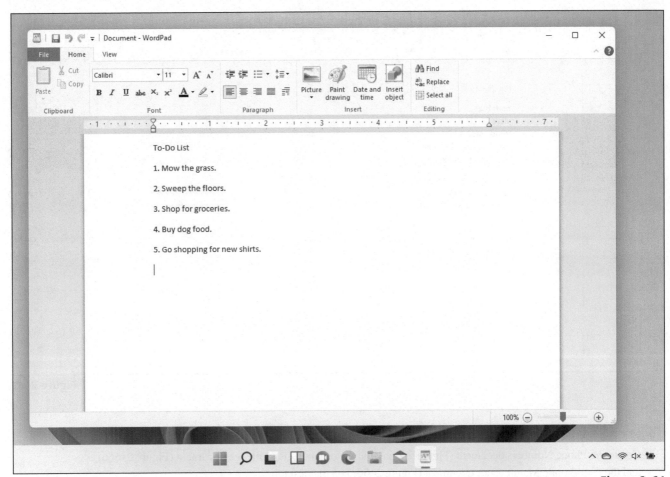

Figure 2–64

Lab 2: Creating, Saving, and Printing Automobile Information Documents

Problem: For eight months, you have accumulated data about your automobile. Some of the information is written on pieces of paper, while the rest is in the form of receipts. You have decided to organize this information using your computer or mobile device. You create the document shown in Figures 2–65 and 2–66 using the application-centric approach and WordPad.

Perform the following tasks:

1. Create a new WordPad document. Save the document in the Documents folder with the file name, Automobile Information.
2. Enter the text shown in Figure 2–65. (**Hint:** If the line spacing is too great, try pressing SHIFT+ENTER (instead of ENTER) at the end of each line.)
3. Save the document.
4. Print the document.
5. Create a folder in the Documents folder called Automobile Documents.

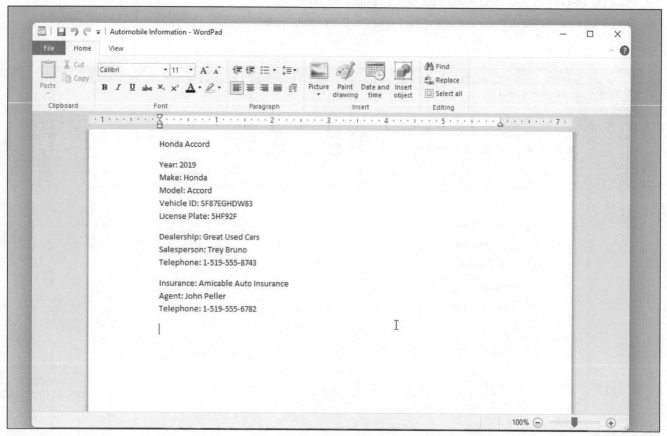

Figure 2–65

6. Move the Automobile Information document to the Automobile Documents folder.
7. Create the Phone Numbers document (Figure 2–66a), the Automobile Gas Mileage document (Figure 2–66b), and the Automobile Maintenance document (Figure 2–66c) on the desktop.
8. Save each document into the Documents folder.
9. Print each document.
10. Place each document in the Automobile Documents folder.

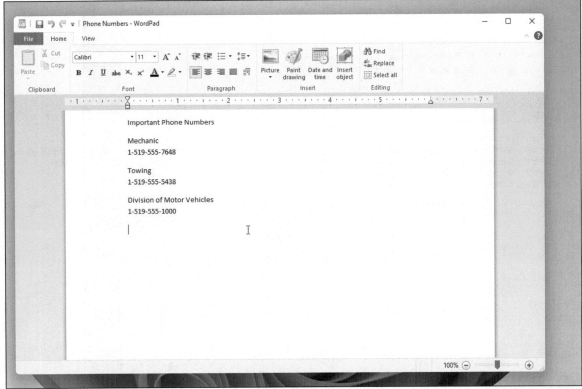

Figure 2–66a

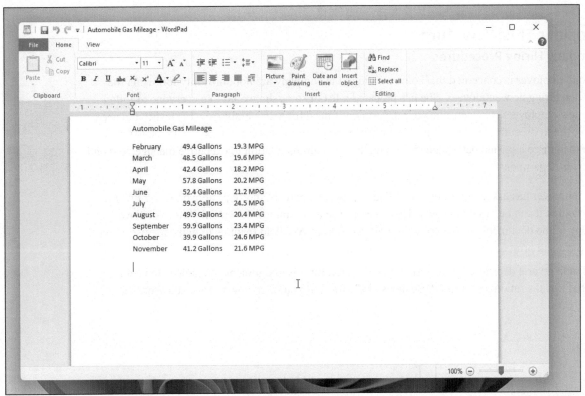

Figure 2–66b

Continued on next page

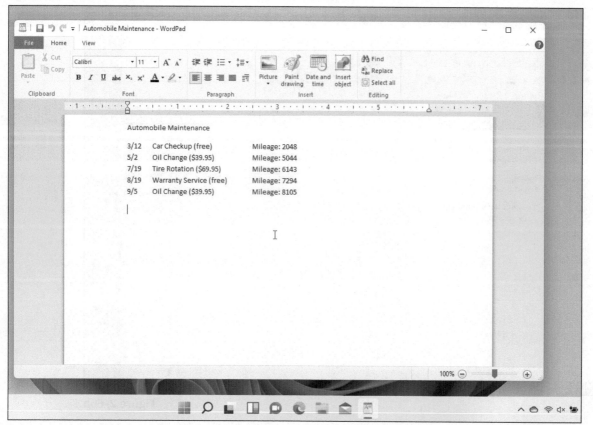

Figure 2–66c

Lab 3: Consider This: Your Turn

Posting Company Hiring Procedures

Problem: Your employer is concerned that some people in the company are not uniformly following the same policy when hiring new employees. She has prepared a list of steps she would like everyone to follow when hiring a new employee: (1) determine your department's need for a new employee, (2) justify the need for a new employee to executive management, (3) advertise the position in at least three locations, (4) interview no fewer than three top candidates, and (5) submit hiring recommendation to executive management and Human Resources department.

Part 1: Your employer has asked you to use WordPad to prepare a copy of the steps above that outline the hiring process so that it can be posted in every department. Save and print the document. After you have printed one copy of the document, try experimenting with different WordPad features to make the list more eye-catching. Save and print a revised copy of the document.

Part 2: You made several decisions while performing research for this assignment. What decisions did you make? What was the rationale behind these decisions? How did you learn how to format a WordPad document?

File and Folder Management

Objectives

After completing this module, you will be able to:

- View the contents of a drive and folder using the This PC window
- View the properties of files and folders
- Find files and folders from a folder window
- Use Shake and Snap to manipulate windows
- View, copy, and move contents of the Pictures folder

- View and change the properties of a picture
- Start and use the Photos app
- View pictures as a slide show
- Compress a folder and view the contents of a compressed folder
- Back up files and folders using OneDrive

Introduction

In addition to creating documents on the desktop and working with documents and folders in the Documents folder, Windows also allows you to examine the files and folders on the computer in a variety of other ways, enabling you to choose the easiest and most accessible manner when working with a computer or mobile device. The This PC window and the Documents folder provide two ways for you to work with files and folders. In addition, the Pictures folder allows you to organize and share picture files, and the Music folder allows you to organize and share your music files.

This PC Window

Clicking the File Explorer button opens the File Explorer window. Using the navigation bar, you can navigate to the This PC window that contains the storage devices that are installed on the computer. Windows uses folder windows to display the contents of the computer. A **folder window** consists of a toolbar at the top that displays the ribbon with multiple commands, an address bar below the toolbar, a small toolbar to the left of the address bar that contains buttons to help you navigate your computer's folder structure, a navigation pane on the left, a headings bar and list area on the right below the address bar, and a status bar at the bottom of the window. Depending upon which folder you are viewing — This PC, Documents, Pictures, and so on — the folder window will display the toolbar options that are most appropriate for working with the contents.

BTW
Managing Windows
Having multiple windows open on the desktop can intimidate some users. Consider working in a maximized window, and when you want to switch to another open window, display that window instead.

To Open and Maximize the This PC Window

The list area of the This PC window groups objects based upon their type. The Folders group lists folders you might access frequently, such as the Desktop, Documents, Downloads, Music, Pictures, and Videos folders. The Devices and drives group contains the icon that represents the hard drive on the computer. The **hard drive** is where you can store files and folders. Storing data on a hard drive is more convenient than storing data on a removable drive, such as an optical drive or USB flash drive, because the hard drive is readily available and generally has more available storage space. A computer always will have at least one hard drive, which normally is designated as drive C. On the computer represented by the This PC window in Figure 3–1, the icon consists of an image of a hard drive and a **drive label**, or title, Windows-SSD, and a drive letter (C:). The drive label can change and may differ depending upon the name assigned to the hard drive. For example, some people label their hard drive based upon usage; therefore, it could be called PRIMARY (C:), where PRIMARY is the label given to the hard drive, as it is the drive that houses the operating system and main apps. If you have another type of drive, such as an optical drive, installed in or connected to your computer, the drive also will appear in the 'Devices and drives' group. The Network locations group will appear if you are connected remotely to drives on computers in another location. The following step opens and maximizes the This PC window. **Why?** This will allow you to view the computer's content in its entirety.

- If necessary, sign in to your Windows account.
- Click the File Explorer button to open a File Explorer window.
- Click This PC in the navigation pane to open the This PC window. If necessary, maximize the This PC window (Figure 3–1).

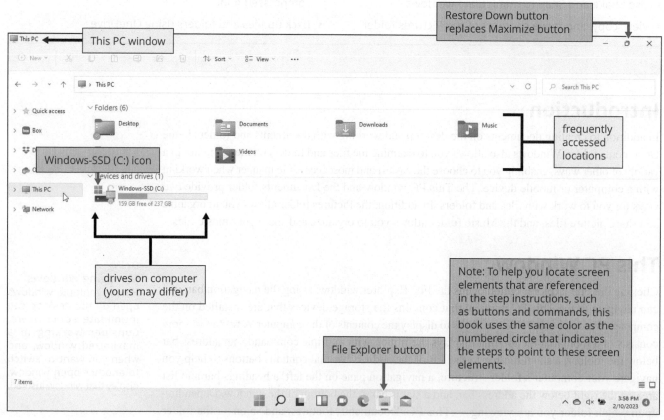

Figure 3–1

Extend Your Knowledge

Extend the skills you learned in this module and experiment with new skills.

Using Help

Instructions: Use WordPad to perform the following tasks. Write the steps you take to perform each of these skills. Use Help resources if you need assistance with performing any of these skills. Figures 2–62a and 2–62b show the WordPad ribbon containing the commands necessary to perform some of the functions listed below.

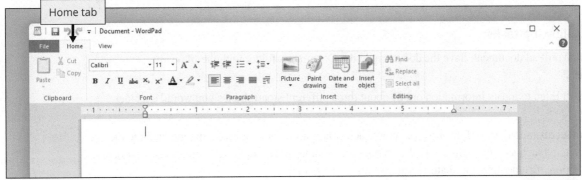

Figure 2–62a

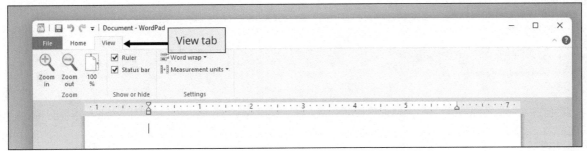

Figure 2–62b

Perform the following tasks:

1. Apply bold formatting to text.
2. Change the font color of text.
3. Right-align text.
4. Insert a picture.
5. Enable and disable wordwrap.
6. Change the font size.
7. Create a bulleted list.
8. Create a numbered list.
9. Insert the date and time.
10. Change the font size of text.
11. Undo the last action.
12. Zoom in.
13. Zoom out.
14. Display information about WordPad.
15. Obtain Help about WordPad.

Expand Your World

Create a solution that uses cloud or web technologies by learning and investigating on your own from general guidance.

Selecting a Smartphone

Instructions: You want to purchase a new smartphone and decide to research them online. You decide to create a WordPad document that contains information about the smartphones you are researching (Figure 2–63).

Perform the following tasks:

1. Open a new WordPad document. Save the document in the Documents folder with the file name, Smartphones.

2. Use Microsoft Edge to locate information online about three different smartphones you would consider purchasing.

3. In the WordPad document, record information about each smartphone. For each smartphone, include the operating system (such as iOS or Android), the screen size, storage space, supported wireless carrier(s), and price. In addition, include three top features you like about the phone.

4. Save the changes to the document.

5. Print the document.

6. Close the document.

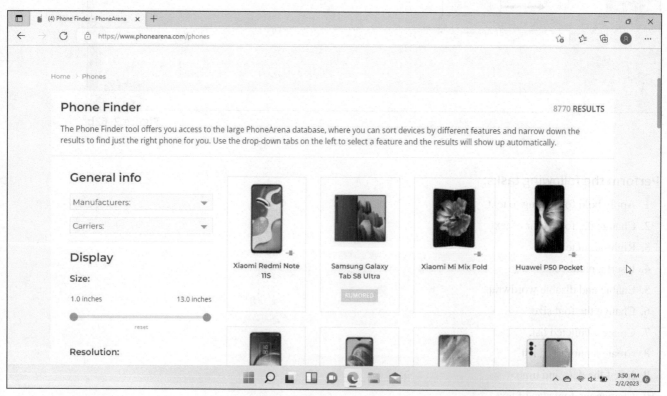

Figure 2–63

To Display Properties for the Hard Drive in the Details Pane

The details pane of a folder window displays the properties of devices, apps, files, and folders, which all are considered to be objects by Windows. Every object in Windows has properties that describe the object. A **property** is a characteristic of an object, such as the amount of storage space on a storage device or the number of items in a folder. The properties of each object will differ, and in some cases, you can change the properties of an object. **Why?** For example, in the Windows-SSD (C:) properties, you could check the file system being used on the drive using the File system property. To determine the drive's capacity, you would view the Total size property. The following steps display the properties for the Windows-SSD (C:) in the details pane of the This PC window.

- Click the Windows-SSD (C:) icon to select the hard drive (Figure 3–2).

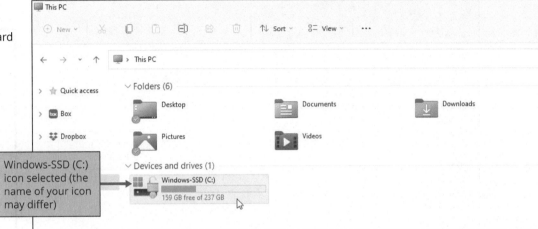

Figure 3–2

- Click the View button on the toolbar to display the View menu.
- Point to Show to display the Show submenu (Figure 3–3).

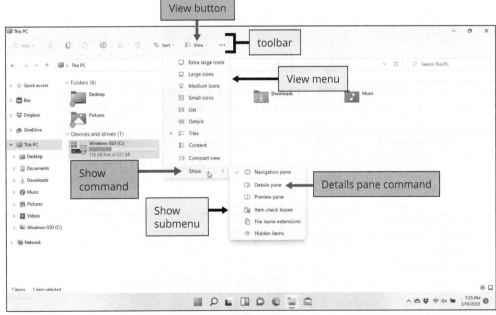

Figure 3–3

- Click Details pane on the Show submenu to open the details pane (Figure 3–4).

- **Experiment:** See what properties are displayed for the other drives and devices shown. Click each one and note what properties appear in the details pane. Click the icon for your hard drive when you are done.

Q&A Why do the properties of my drive differ from those in the figure?
The size and contents of your drive will be different from the one in the figure. As a result, the properties of the drive also will be different. Depending upon what has been installed on the drive and how it is formatted, the Space used, Space free, Total size, File system, and BitLocker status properties will vary.

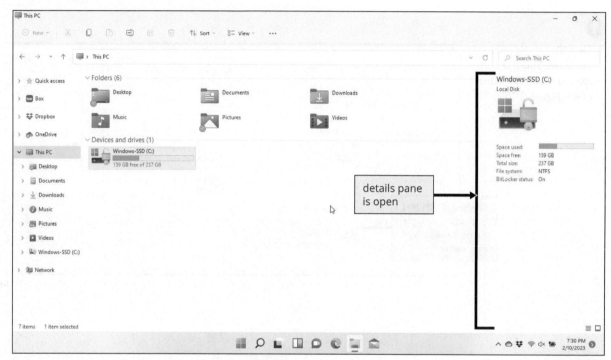

Figure 3–4

To Display the Properties Dialog Box for the Hard Drive

The properties shown in the details pane are just a few of the properties of drive C. In fact, the details pane is used to highlight the most popular properties of a hard drive: how much space is used, how much space is free, the size of the drive, and how the drive is formatted. You also can display more detailed information about the hard drive.

The following steps display the Properties dialog box for the Windows-SSD (C:) drive. **Why?** You would like to view information about the hard drive, such as the drive capacity, and perform other actions to help increase the drive's performance.

- Right-click the Windows-SSD (C:) drive to display its shortcut menu (Figure 3–5).

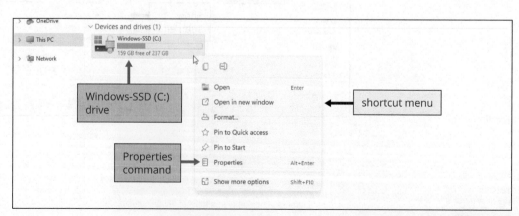

Figure 3–5

● Click Properties on the shortcut menu to display the Windows-SSD (C:) Properties dialog box (Figure 3–6).

Q&A What sheets are in the Windows-SSD (C:) Properties dialog box?
The Tools sheet in the Windows-SSD (C:) Properties dialog box, accessible by clicking the Tools tab, allows you to check for errors on the hard drive or defragment the hard drive. The Hardware sheet allows you to view a list of all drives, troubleshoot drives that are not working properly, and display the properties for each drive. The Sharing sheet allows you to share the contents of a hard drive with other computer users. To protect a computer from unauthorized access, however, sharing the hard drive is not recommended. The Security sheet displays the security settings for the drive, such as user permissions. The Previous Versions sheet allows you to work with previous versions of files and folders on your hard drive if you have File History enabled or have created restore points. Finally, the Quota sheet can be used to see how much space is being used by various user accounts. Other tabs might be displayed in the Windows-SSD (C:) Properties dialog box on your computer.

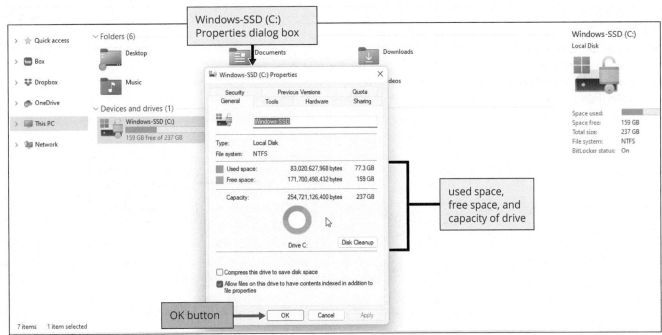

Figure 3–6

● Click OK (Windows-SSD (C:) Properties dialog box) to close the dialog box.

Other Ways

1. Select drive icon in right pane, press ALT+ENTER

To Switch Folders Using the Address Bar

Why? Folder windows contain the address bar, which indicates which folder you are viewing. A useful feature of the address bar is its capability to allow you to switch to different folder windows by clicking the arrows preceding or following the folder names. Clicking the arrow to the right of the This PC label, for example, displays a menu containing options for showing other drives, as well as other locations and folders, such as the Downloads, Pictures, Music, Desktop, Documents, and Videos folders. The drives and folders that are displayed can vary from computer to computer. The following steps use the address bar to change the folder window from displaying the This PC folder to displaying the desktop and then return to the This PC folder.

①

- Click the This PC arrow on the address bar to display a menu that contains locations in This PC (Figure 3–7). Depending upon your computer's configuration, the list of locations might differ.

Q&A What if the This PC arrow is not displayed?
Click the This PC button to get the This PC arrow to appear.

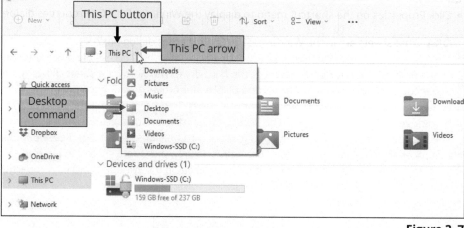

Figure 3–7

②

- Click Desktop on the menu to switch to viewing the contents of the desktop in the folder window (Figure 3–8).

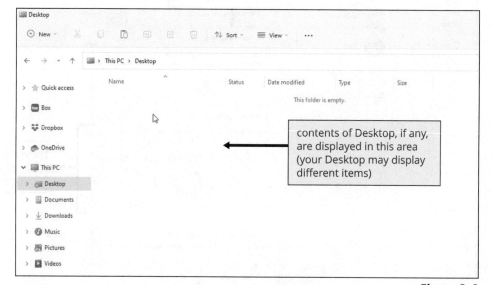

Figure 3–8

③

- Click the Back button to the This PC window (Figure 3–9).

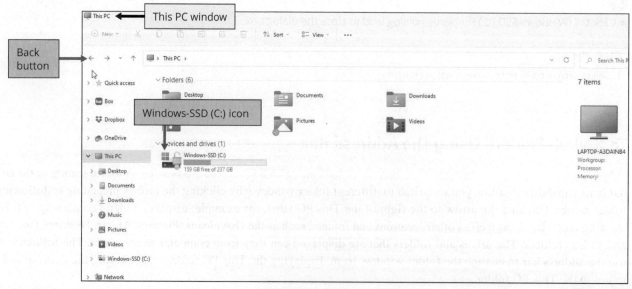

Figure 3–9

To View the Contents of a Drive

In addition to viewing the contents of the Desktop folder, you can view the contents of drives and other folders. In fact, the contents of any folder or drive on the computer will be displayed in a folder window. By default, Windows uses the active window to display the contents of a newly opened drive or folder. The following step displays the contents of drive C in the active window. **Why?** You should know the contents of the drive so that you can see where your information is stored.

- Double-click the Windows-SSD (C:) icon in the This PC window to display the contents of the Windows-SSD (C:) drive (Figure 3–10).

  Q&A Why do I see different folders?
  The contents of the drive window that appear on your computer can differ from the contents shown in Figure 3–10 because each computer has its own folders, apps, and documents.

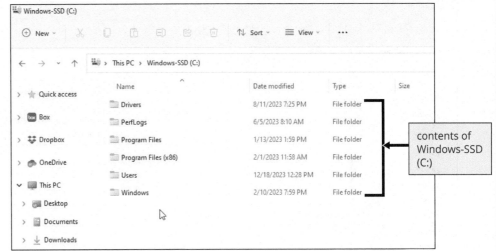

Figure 3–10

Other Ways

1. Right-click Windows-SSD (C:), click Open on shortcut menu   2. Click Windows-SSD (C:), press ENTER

To Preview the Properties of a Folder

Why? When you move the pointer over a folder icon, a preview of the folder properties is displayed in a ScreenTip so that you can see information about the folder. A **ScreenTip** is a brief description that appears when you position the pointer over an object on the screen. ScreenTips do not appear for every object, but when they do, they provide useful information. The properties typically consist of the date and time created, the folder size, and the name of the folder. The Windows folder in the Windows-SSD (C:) window contains apps and files necessary for the operation of the Windows operating system. As such, you should exercise caution when working with the contents of the Windows folder, because changing the contents of the folder might cause the operating system to stop working correctly. The following step shows a ScreenTip displaying the properties of the Windows folder.

- Point to the Windows folder icon to display a ScreenTip displaying the properties of the Windows folder (Figure 3–11).

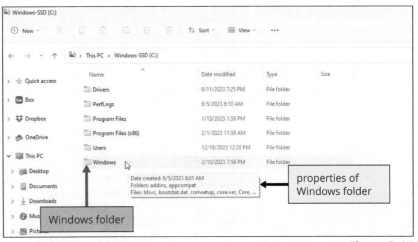

Figure 3–11

To Display Properties for the Windows Folder in the Details Pane

Just like with drives, some properties of folders can be displayed in the details pane. **Why?** You want to view the properties of the Windows folder so that you can see the date it was last modified. The following step displays the properties for the Windows folder in the details pane of the Windows-SSD (C:) window.

1

• Click the Windows folder icon to display the properties in the details pane (Figure 3–12).

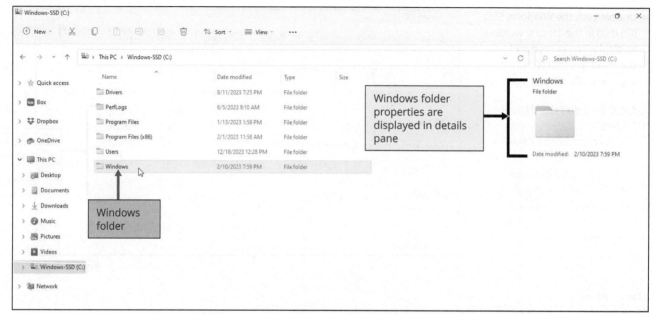

Figure 3–12

To Use the Shortcut Menu to Display the Properties for the Windows Folder

Why? If you want to see all of the properties for the Windows folder, you will need to display the Properties dialog box. The following steps display the Properties dialog box for the Windows folder.

1

• Right-click the Windows folder icon to display a shortcut menu (Figure 3–13). (The commands on your shortcut menu might differ.)

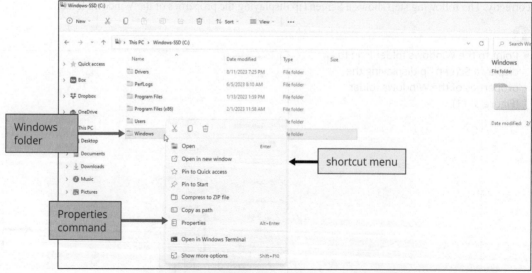

Figure 3–13

● Click Properties on the shortcut menu to display the Windows Properties dialog box (Figure 3–14).

● **Experiment:** Click the various tabs in the Windows Properties dialog box to see the different properties available for a folder.

Q&A Why might I want to look at the properties of a folder?
When you are working with folders, you might need to look at folders' properties to make changes, such as configuring a folder for sharing over a network or hiding folders from users who do not need access to them.

Why are the tabs of the Windows folder properties different from the Windows-SSD (C:) properties?
Drives, folders, and files have different properties and, therefore, need different tabs. A folder's Properties dialog box typically shows the General, Sharing, Security, and Previous Versions tabs; however, depending upon your Windows edition and installed apps, the tabs may differ. The Properties dialog box always will have the General tab, although what it displays also may differ.

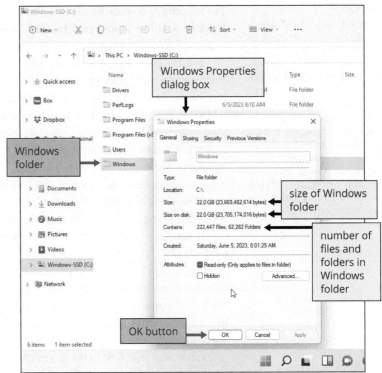

Figure 3–14

● Click OK (Windows Properties dialog box) to close it.

To View the Contents of a Folder

The following step opens the Windows folder so that you can view its contents. **Why?** You will be able to see what sort of files your operating system installed.

● Double-click the Windows folder icon to display the contents of the Windows folder (Figure 3–15).

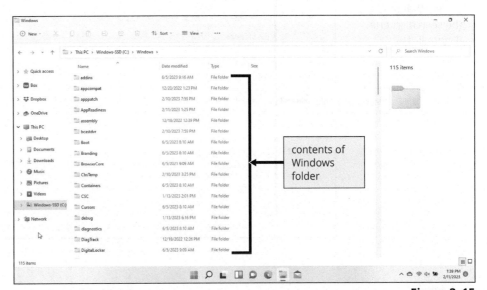

Figure 3–15

Other Ways

1. Right-click Windows folder, click Open on shortcut menu   2. Click Windows folder, press ENTER

BTW
Hidden Files and Folders
Hidden files and folders usually are placed on your computer's hard drive by software vendors (such as Microsoft) and often are critical to the operation of their apps. Rarely will you need to designate a file or folder as hidden. You should not delete a hidden file or folder, as doing so might interrupt how or whether an app works. By default, hidden files and folders are not displayed in a file listing.

Searching for Files and Folders

The majority of objects displayed in the Windows folder, as shown in Figure 3–15, are folder icons. By default, folder icons are displayed in alphabetical order at the top of the file list in a folder window, before the icons for apps or files.

Folders, such as the Windows folder, can contain many files and folders. When you want to find a particular file or folder in the currently displayed folder but do not know where it is located, you can use the **Search box** in the folder window to find the file or folder quickly. When you are in a folder, the Search box displays the word, Search, plus the folder name. For example, in the Windows folder, the Search box contains the text, Search Windows. As soon as you start typing, the window updates to show search results that match what you are typing. As Windows is searching for files or folders that match your search criteria, you will see a searching message displayed in the list area, an animated circle attached to the pointer, and an animated progress bar on the address bar, which provides live feedback as to how much of the search has been completed. When searching is complete, you will see a list of all the items that match your search criteria.

If you know only a portion of a file's name and can specify where the known portion of the name should appear, you can use an asterisk in the name to represent the unknown characters. For example, if you know a file starts with the letters MSP, you can type msp* in the Search box. All files that begin with the letters, msp, regardless of what characters follow, will be displayed. With Windows' powerful search capabilities, however, you would get the same results if you did not include the asterisk. If you want to search for all files with a particular extension, you can use the asterisk to substitute for the name of the files. For example, to find all the text files with the extension .rtf, you would type *.rtf in the Search box. Windows will find all the files with the .rtf extension.

To Search for a File and Folder in a Folder Window

The following step uses the Search box to search the Windows folder for all the objects that contain the letters, system, in the file name. **Why?** Sometimes you may forget where a file is stored. Knowing how to search can help you find files faster.

1

- Type **system** in the Search box and then press ENTER to search for all files and folders that match the search criteria (Figure 3–16).

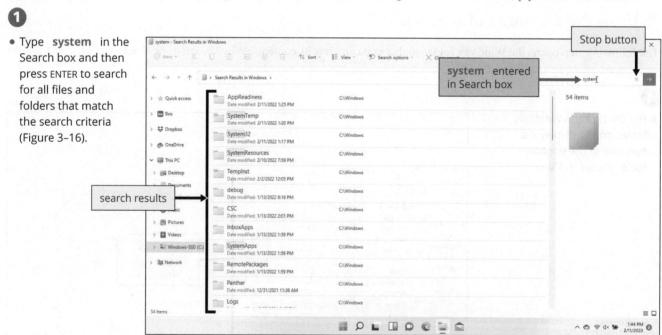

Figure 3–16

To Refine the Search Results

You can refine your search results by specifying properties by which you want to refine them. For example, you can refine search results to display files that were modified within a certain timeframe, certain kinds of files (for example, documents, email messages, or videos), file size, or other properties, such as type, name, folder path, or tags. **Why?** If your search returns too many results, you can refine the results to display fewer files and folders. The following steps refine the search results by file size so that only files between 16 KB (kilobytes) and 1 MB (megabyte) are displayed.

- Click the Search options button on the toolbar to display the Search options menu.
- Point to Size to display a list of options by which to refine the search by size (Figure 3–17).

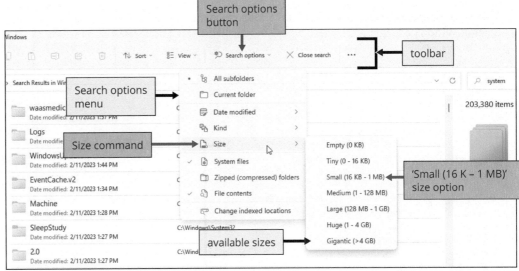

Figure 3–17

❷

- Click 'Small (16 KB – 1 MB)' to refine the search results by size (Figure 3–18).

Q&A Can I refine the search results by more than one property?
Yes.

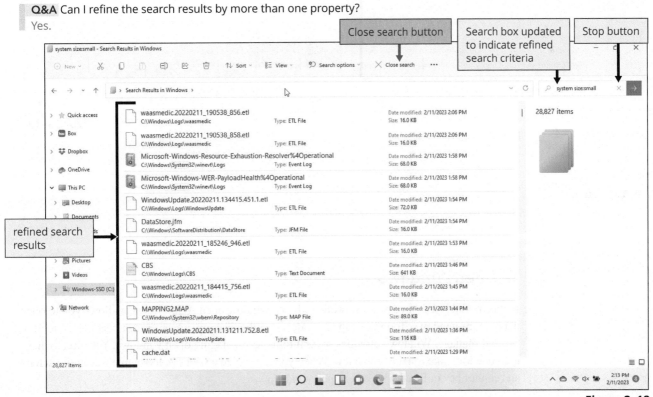

Figure 3–18

Other Ways

1. Type **system size: small** in Search box, press ENTER

To Clear the Search Box

When you finish searching, you can end the search by clearing the Search box. The following step clears the Search box. **Why?** You clear the Search box so that you can resume normal navigation of the folder you are viewing.

1

- Click the Close search button on the toolbar (shown in Figure 3-18) to clear the Search box and redisplay all files and folders in the Windows folder (Figure 3-19).

Q&A What happened to the Stop button in the Search box?
The Stop button no longer is displayed when you clear the Search box and search results.

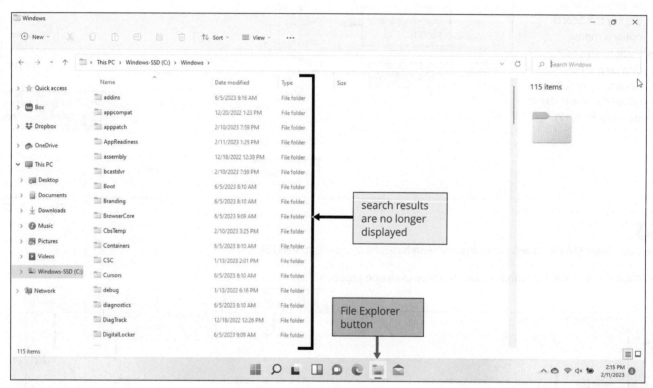

Figure 3-19

Other Ways

1. Click Back button

To Open Windows

In this module, you have been working with one window open. Windows also allows you to open many more windows. Too many open windows on the desktop, however, can become difficult to use and manage. Windows provides several tools for managing open windows. You already have used one tool, maximizing a window. When you maximize a window, it occupies the entire screen and cannot be confused with other open windows.

Sometimes, it is important to have multiple windows appear on the desktop simultaneously. Windows offers simple commands that allow you to arrange multiple windows in specific ways. The following sections describe the ways that you can manage multiple open windows. The following steps open another File Explorer window.

1 Right-click the File Explorer button on the taskbar.

2 Click File Explorer on the shortcut menu to open another File Explorer window.

3 Double-click the Pictures folder to display its contents.

To Use Shake to Minimize All Background Windows

Shake lets you minimize all windows except the active window and then restore all those windows by shaking the title bar of the active window. **Why?** To reduce clutter on the desktop, you want to quickly minimize all windows other than the window you currently are viewing. The following steps use Shake to minimize all windows and then restore those windows.

- Click the title bar of the Pictures folder window and then shake the title bar (drag the title bar back and forth in short, swift motions several times) to minimize all windows except the Pictures folder (Figure 3–20).

Q&A Shaking did not minimize any windows. What should I do?
Most likely, you need to enable the Shake feature. Click the Start button and then click Settings. In the right pane of the System window, click Multitasking. Click the Off button for 'Title bar window shake' to change the setting to On and enable the Shake feature. Close the Settings window.

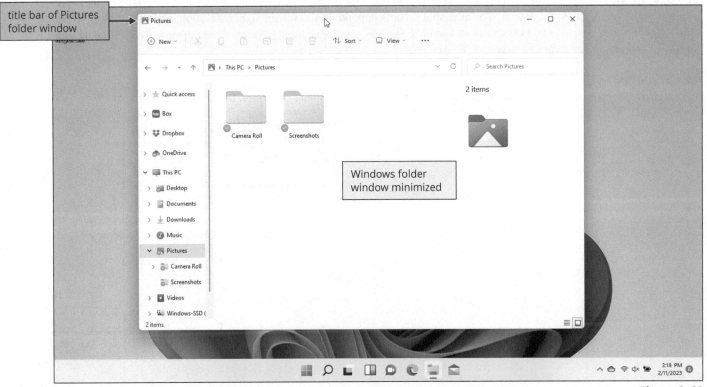

Figure 3–20

- Point to the File Explorer button on the taskbar and then click the Windows thumbnail to restore the minimized window (Figure 3–21).

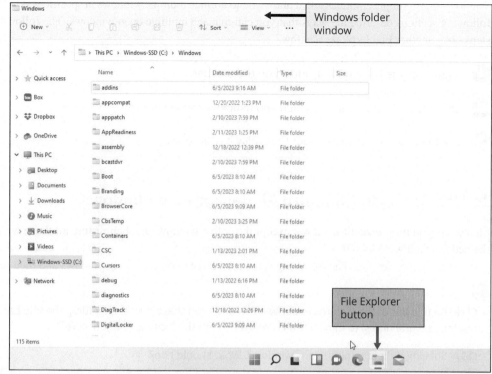

Figure 3–21

To Apply a Snap Layout

One way to organize windows on the desktop is to apply a **snap layout**, which is an arrangement of open windows that displays their contents without overlapping. All open windows, including minimized windows, can be displayed in snap layout; closed windows will not appear in the layout. The available layouts depend on the screen size, resolution, and orientation. **Why?** Applying a snap layout will help you identify all open windows and easily choose the one you want to view. The following steps apply a snap layout to all open windows.

- Point to the Restore Down button on the Windows title bar to display a gallery of window layouts (Figure 3–22).

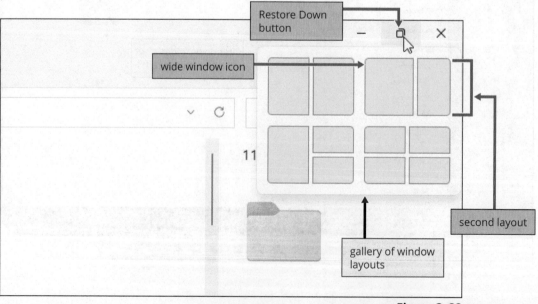

Figure 3–22

- In the second layout, click the wide window icon to snap the Windows window to the left side of the desktop.
- Click the Pictures window thumbnail to snap the window to the right side of the desktop (Figure 3–23).

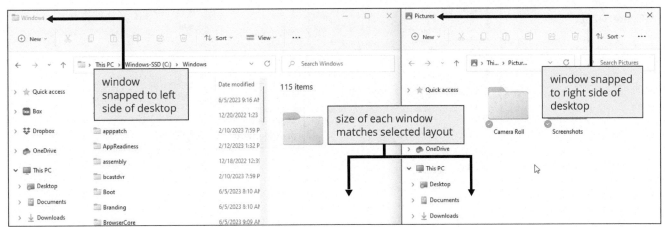

Figure 3–23

To Display a Snap Group

After you display windows in a snap layout, they form a **snap group**, which appears with the other window thumbnails on the taskbar button. **Why?** If you open another window or minimize the snapped windows, you can select a snap group to redisplay the windows in their original layout. The following steps display a snap group.

1

- Click the Minimize button on each window to minimize both windows.
- Point to the File Explorer button on the taskbar to display thumbnails of the windows and the snap group (Figure 3–24).

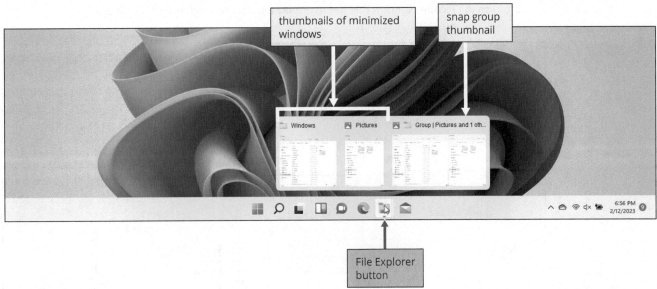

Figure 3–24

2

- Click the 'Group | Pictures and 1 other window' thumbnail to restore the snap layout (Figure 3–25).

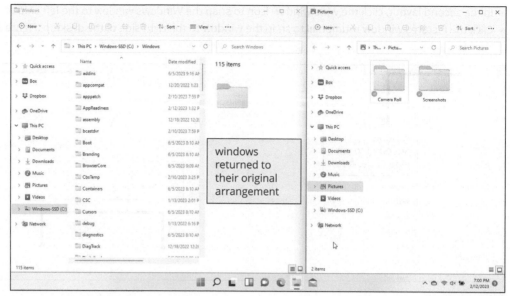

windows returned to their original arrangement

Figure 3–25

Other Ways

1. Press WIN+Z

To Stack Open Windows

Another snap layout arranges four windows in a grid, with each window displayed in a quarter of the desktop. You can use this layout to stack two windows, one of top of the other, on the left or right side of the desktop. **Why?** You can access the contents of two open windows while displaying half of the desktop. When using the grid layout with two windows, the windows do not have to be stacked. They can be arranged in any of the four corners of the desktop. The following steps stack the open windows.

1

- Point to the Maximize button on the Pictures window title bar to display a gallery of window layouts (Figure 3–26).

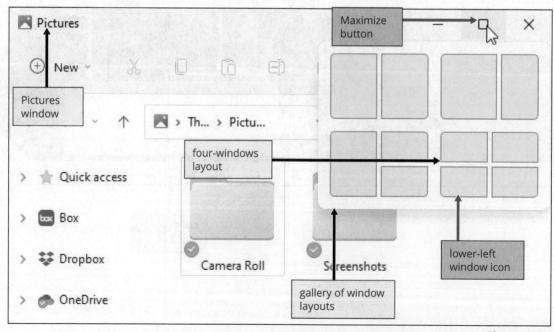

Figure 3–26

- Click the lower-left window icon in the four-windows layout to display the Pictures window in the lower-left quarter of the desktop.
- Click the thumbnail of the Windows window to stack the open windows on the left side of the desktop (Figure 3–27).

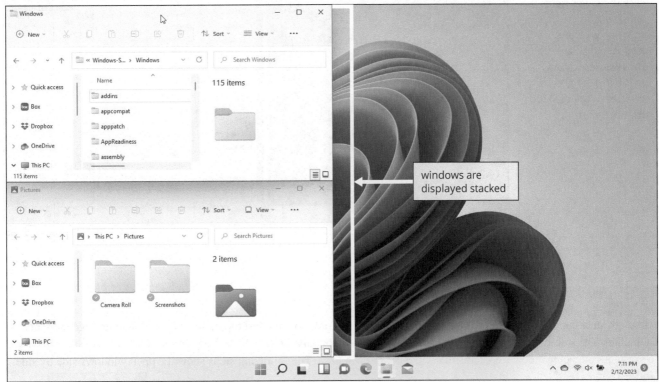

Figure 3–27

To Change a Snap Layout

You use the layouts gallery to change a snap layout. In this case, you will change the layout so that the windows are stacked on the right side of the desktop. **Why?** If you drag the windows to change the layout, they are no longer snapped and you lose the snap group on the taskbar. The following steps change the snap layout.

- Point to the Maximize button on the Windows folder window title bar to display a gallery of window layouts.
- Click the upper-right window icon in the four-windows layout to display the Windows folder window in the upper-right quarter of the desktop (Figure 3–28).

Q&A Do the windows remain snapped even when I minimize them?
A snap layout keeps windows snapped in place until you move a window or select a different layout from the layouts gallery. If you minimize and then restore the windows, they return to their snapped sizes and positions.

Figure 3–28

2

- Point to the Maximize button on the Pictures window title bar and then click the lower-right window icon in the four-windows layout to display the Pictures window in the lower-right quarter of the desktop (Figure 3–29).

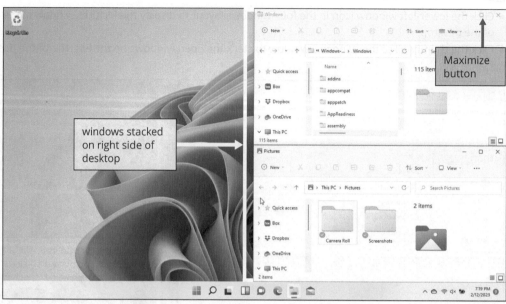

Figure 3–29

To Show Windows Side by Side

Although stacking arranges the windows vertically above each other on the desktop, it also is possible to arrange them next to each other. The side-by-side layout displays each window horizontally. **Why?** Displaying windows side by side may allow you to see more of each window's contents than stacking the windows. The following steps show the open windows side by side.

1

- Point to the Maximize button on the Windows window title bar to display a gallery of window layouts (Figure 3–30).

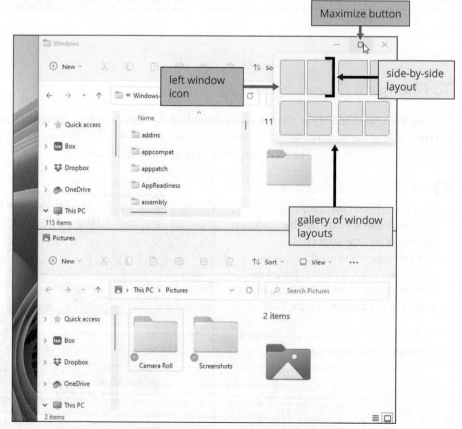

Figure 3–30

• Click the left window icon in the side-by-side layout to display the Windows window on the left half of the desktop.

• Click the thumbnail of the Pictures window to display the open windows side by side (Figure 3–31).

Q&A What happens if I have more than two windows open?

When you are working with more than two open windows, you select the position of the first window. Windows shows thumbnails for the other open windows. Click the thumbnail of the window you want to add to the snap layout.

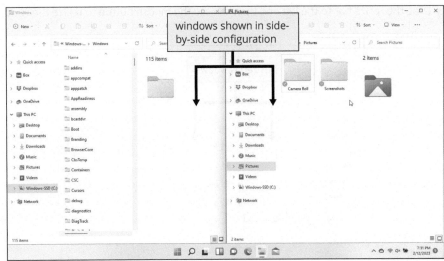

windows shown in side-by-side configuration

Figure 3–31

To Resize Snapped Windows

Why? You want to adjust the size of the snapped windows without unsnapping them. The following steps change the width of the side-by-side snapped windows.

• Point to the border separating the two windows to display a resize bar (Figure 3–32).

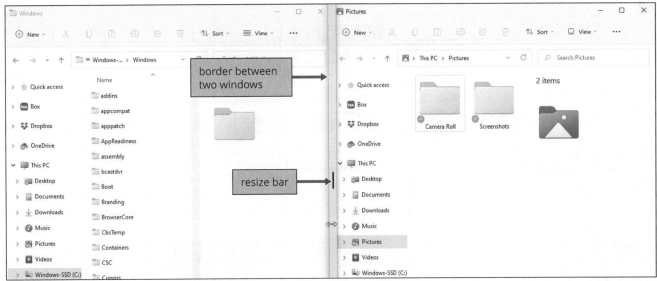

border between two windows

resize bar

Figure 3–32

- Drag the resize bar to the left and then release the mouse button to resize the windows (Figure 3–33).

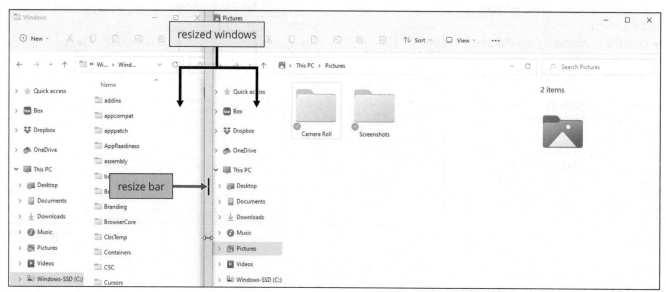

Figure 3–33

To Use Snap to Maximize Windows

Why? Sometimes you want to see a larger portion of a window. Snap allows you to maximize a window by dragging its title bar to the top of the screen. The following step maximizes the Pictures folder window.

1

- Point to the top border of the Pictures window and then drag down to change the height of the window.
- Drag the Pictures folder window to the top of the screen to maximize the Pictures folder window (Figure 3–34).

Q&A Is Snap used only to maximize windows?

No. If you drag a window's title bar to the right side of the screen, the window will resize to fill the right half of the screen. If you drag the title bar to the left side of the screen, the window will resize to fill only the left half of the screen. When you snap a window to one side of the screen, Windows will display thumbnail images of the remaining open windows on the other side of the screen. Click the thumbnail for the window you want to fill the other side of the screen.

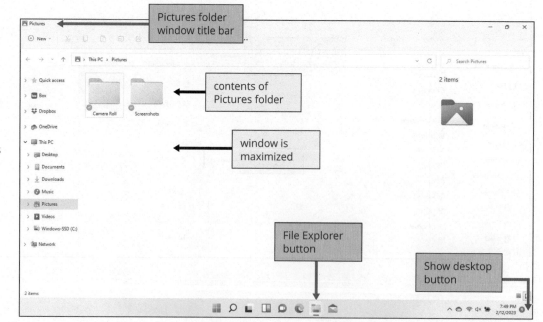

Figure 3–34

To Use the Show Desktop Button to Minimize All Windows

Why? You need to access an app or file that is on the desktop, so you minimize all open windows so that you can access it. The following step minimizes all windows to show the desktop.

- Click the Show desktop button (shown in Figure 3–34) on the taskbar to minimize all windows.

To Restore a Window

Why? To work with one of the windows you previously minimized, you first must restore it. The following steps switch to the Pictures folder window; however, the steps are the same for any app or folder window currently displayed as a button on the taskbar.

- Point to the File Explorer button on the taskbar to see a Live Preview of the open File Explorer windows or the window title(s) of the open window(s), depending on your computer's configuration (Figure 3–35).

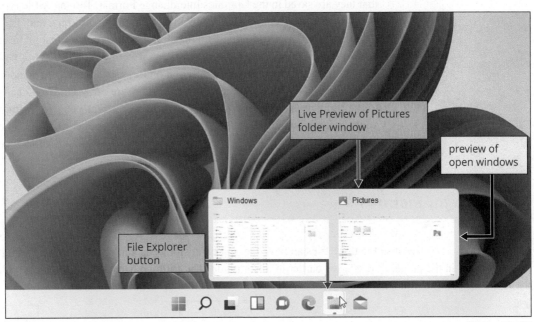

Figure 3–35

- Click the Live Preview of the Pictures folder window to restore the window (Figure 3–36).

Q&A What happens if I click the wrong window? Click the remaining windows until the Pictures window is displayed in the foreground.

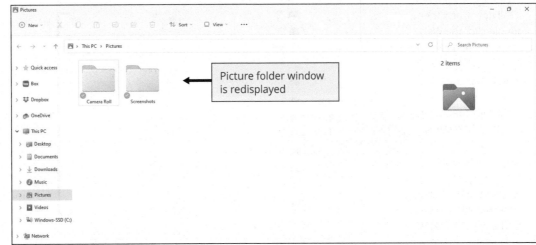

Figure 3–36

Other Ways

1. Press ALT+TAB until Pictures folder window is selected, release ALT

The Pictures Folder

You can organize your pictures and share them with others using the Pictures folder. By putting all your pictures in the Pictures folder, you always will know where to find them. When you save pictures from a digital camera, scanner, smartphone, or the Internet, they are saved to the Pictures folder by default.

Windows also includes the Photos app. The **Photos app** is used to view the pictures on your computer. You can use the Photos app to work with your pictures no matter where they are stored on your hard drive.

Using the Pictures folder allows you to organize pictures, preview pictures, share your pictures with others, display your pictures as a slide show, print your pictures, attach your pictures to email messages, or save your pictures on an optical disc.

Many different formats are available for picture files. Some pictures have an extension of .bmp to indicate that they are bitmap files. Other pictures may have the .gif extension, which indicates that they are saved in the Graphics Interchange Format. Too many file types exist to mention them all; however, some common types include .bmp, .jpg, .gif, .png, and .tif.

When working with pictures, you should be aware that most pictures that you did not create yourself, including other multimedia files, are copyrighted. A **copyright** means that a picture belongs to the person who created it. The pictures that come with Windows are part of Windows, and you are allowed to use them; however, they are not yours. You can use them only according to the rights granted to you by Microsoft. Pictures that you take using your digital camera are yours because you created them. Before using pictures and other multimedia files, you should be aware of any copyrights associated with them, and you should know whether you are allowed to use them for your intended purpose.

To Search for Pictures

Why? You want to copy three files (img101, img102, and img103) from the Web folder to the Pictures folder, but you have to find these files first. Because the three files all have the .jpg extension, you can search for them using an asterisk (*) in place of the number in the name, as discussed earlier in this module. The following step opens the Web folder window and displays the icons for the files you want to copy.

- Restore the Windows folder window, and, if necessary, maximize it, scroll down, and then double-click the Web folder to open it.
- Type **img*.jpg** in the Search box and then press ENTER to search for all files that begin with the characters, img, and that have a .jpg file extension.
- If necessary, scroll down in the Web folder window until the icons for the img101, img102, and img103 files are visible (Figure 3–37). If one or more of these files are not available, select any of the other picture files.

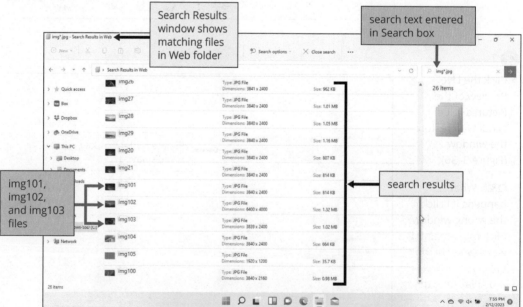

Figure 3–37

Item Check Boxes

When an item is selected, you can see the item check box for that item. By clicking the item check box for several items, you can select them for your use. For example, you can copy multiple files or folders from one location to another. Using item check boxes to select items works well if you are using a touch screen or are selecting nonadjacent files and folders. To select adjacent files from a list, click the first file, hold SHIFT, and click the last file. Windows will then select all files in between.

To Copy Files to the Pictures Folder

A method you can use to copy a file or folder is the **copy and paste method**. When you **copy** a file, you place a copy of the file in a temporary storage area of the computer called the **Clipboard**. When you **paste** the file, Windows copies it from the Clipboard to the location you specify, giving you two copies of the same file.

Why? Because the search results include the pictures you were looking for, you now can select the files and then copy them to the Pictures folder. Once the three files have been copied to the Pictures folder, the files will be stored in both the Pictures folder and Web folder on drive C. Copying and moving files are common tasks when working with Windows. If you want to move a file instead of copy a file, you use the Cut button on the toolbar to move the file to the Clipboard and the Paste command to copy the file from the Clipboard to the new location. When the paste is complete, the files are moved into the new folder and no longer are stored in the original folder. You also can move folders to different locations using the Cut and Paste buttons. The following steps copy the img101, img102, and img103 files from the Web folder to the Pictures folder.

- Click the View button on the toolbar to display the View menu.
- Point to Show on the View menu to display the Show submenu (Figure 3–38).

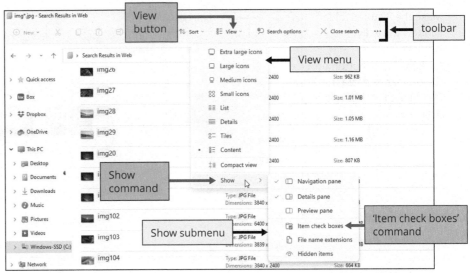

Figure 3–38

- Click 'Item check boxes' to display check boxes for the files in the search results.
- Click the item check boxes for the img101, img102, and img103 pictures to select the files (Figure 3–39).

Q&A Are copying and moving the same?
No. When you copy a file, it is located in both the place to which it was copied and in the place from which it was copied. When you move a file, it is located only in the location to which it was moved.

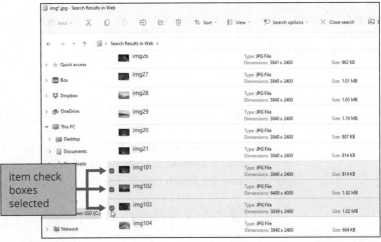

Figure 3–39

3

- Click the Copy button on the toolbar to copy the files to the Clipboard (Figure 3–40).

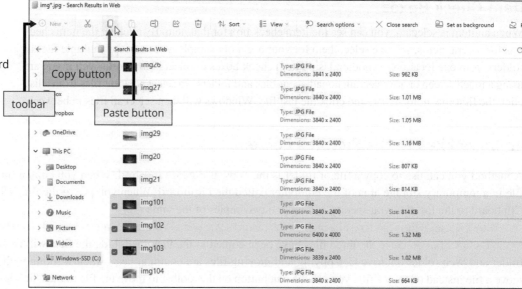

Figure 3–40

4

- Make the Pictures folder window the active window.
- Click the Paste button on the toolbar to paste the files in the Pictures folder (Figure 3–41).

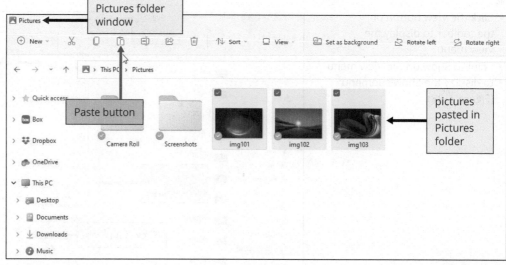

Figure 3–41

Other Ways

1. Select file icons, right-click, click 'Show more options' on shortcut menu, click Copy; display where you want to store files, right-click selected icons, click 'Show more options' on shortcut menu, click Paste

2. Select file icons, press CTRL+C, display window where you want to store files, press CTRL+V

To Close the Search Results Window

You no longer need the Search Results window open, so you can close it. Whenever you are not using a window, it is a good idea to close it so as not to clutter your desktop. The following steps close the Search Results window.

1 Display the Search Results window.

2 Click the Close button on the Search Results window's title bar to close the window.

To Create a Folder in the Pictures Folder

Why? When you have several related files stored in a folder with a number of unrelated files, you might want to create a folder to contain the related files so that you can find and reference them easily. To reduce clutter and improve the organization of files in the Pictures folder, you will create a new folder in the Pictures folder and then move the pictures you copied into the new folder. The following step creates the Backgrounds folder in the Pictures folder.

- Click the New button on the toolbar to display the New menu.
- Click Folder to create a new folder.
- Type **Backgrounds** in the new folder's text box and then press ENTER to assign the name to the new folder (Figure 3–42).

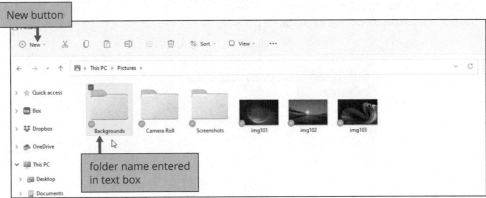

Figure 3–42

Other Ways

1. Right-click empty area of folder window, point to New, click Folder on shortcut menu

2. Press CTRL+SHIFT+N

To Move Multiple Files into a Folder

Why? After you create the Backgrounds folder in the Pictures folder, the next step is to move the three picture files into the folder. The following steps move the img101, img102, and img103 files into the Backgrounds folder.

- If necessary, click the check box for the Backgrounds folder to deselect the folder.
- Click the item check boxes for the img101, img102, and img103 pictures to select the files (Figure 3–43).

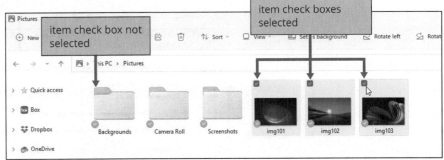

Figure 3–43

- Drag the selected icons to the Backgrounds folder and then release the mouse button to move the files to the Backgrounds folder (Figure 3–44).

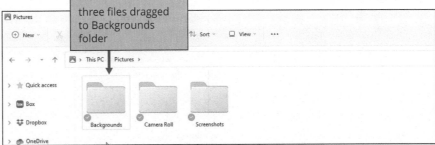

Figure 3–44

Other Ways

1. Drag files individually to folder icon

2. Right-click icon, click 'Show more options' on shortcut menu, click Cut; right-click folder icon, click 'Show more options' on shortcut menu, click Paste

To Optimize the Folder for Pictures

Why? When you optimize a folder for pictures, Windows provides tools for working with pictures in the folder. To rotate an image file, for example, the folder containing the files must be optimized for pictures. You set this option using the Customize sheet in the folder's Properties dialog box. The following steps optimize the Backgrounds folder for pictures.

1

- Right-click the Backgrounds folder to display a shortcut menu (Figure 3–45).

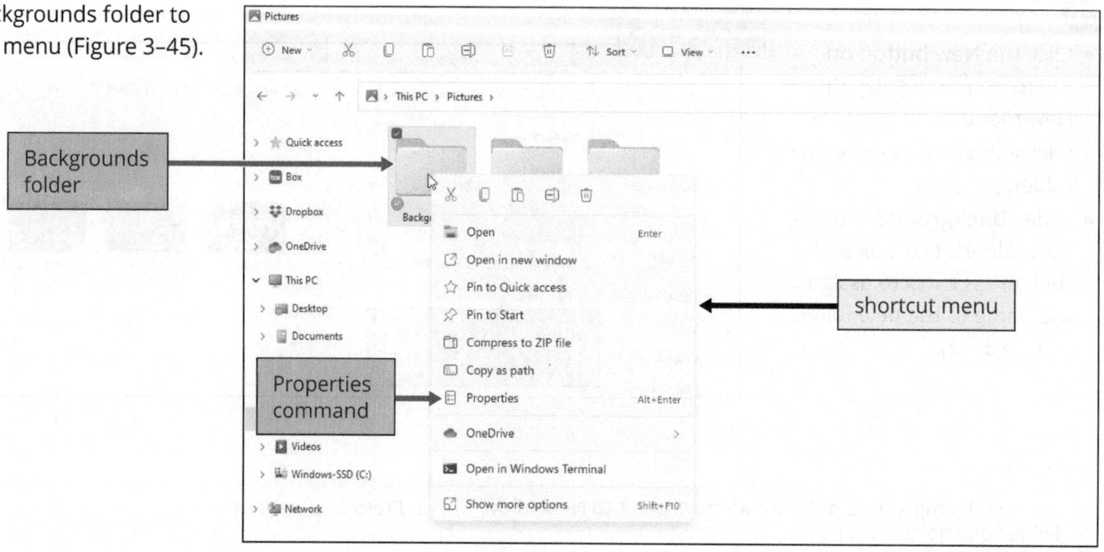

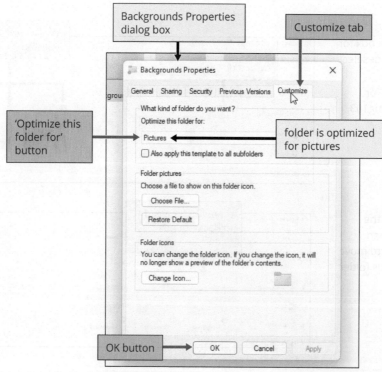

Figure 3–45

2

- Click Properties on the shortcut menu to display the Backgrounds dialog box.
- Click the Customize tab to display the settings on the Customize sheet (Figure 3–46).
- If necessary, click the 'Optimize this folder for' button (Backgrounds Properties dialog box) and then click Pictures.
- Click OK (Backgrounds Properties dialog box) to close the dialog box.

Figure 3–46

Other Ways

1. Click See more on toolbar, click Properties, click Customize tab

To View and Change the Properties of a Picture

As mentioned earlier in the module, in Windows, all objects have properties. You already have explored the properties of a drive and a folder, and now you will review the properties of a picture. Picture properties include the Size, Title, Authors, Date taken, Tags, Rating, and Dimensions. **Why?** Tags are keywords you associate with a picture file to aid in its classification. For example, you could tag a family photo with the names of the people in the photo so that you easily can perform a search for photos with certain tags. When you create a tag, it should be meaningful. For example, if you have pictures from a family vacation at the beach and you add the title, vacation, you later will be able to find the file using the tag, vacation, in a search. Be aware that you can search only for tags that you already have created. If your family vacation photo was saved as photo1.jpg and tagged with the tag, vacation, you will not find it by searching for the word, beach, as it is not part of the name or tag. Rating refers to the ranking, in stars, that you assign to a picture. You can rate a picture from zero to five stars. Date taken, Tags, and Rating all can be changed using the details pane. Because you do not know when the Background pictures were created, you will change only the Tags and Rating properties. Windows will allow you to set properties, such as Tags and Rating, only for certain image types. These properties might not be available for other image types. The following steps display and change the Tags property of the img101 image in the Backgrounds folder.

- Display the contents of the Backgrounds folder.
- Click the img101 icon to select it.
- Click the 'Add a tag' text box in the details pane to activate it (Figure 3–47).

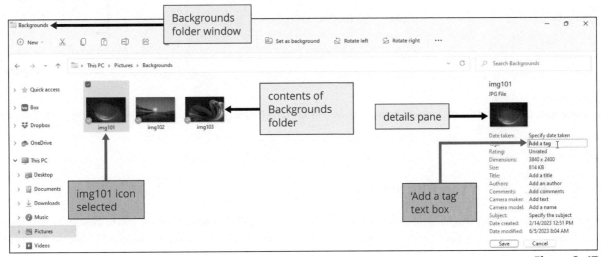

Figure 3–47

- Type **Moon** in the text box and then press ENTER to create a tag for the picture (Figure 3–48).

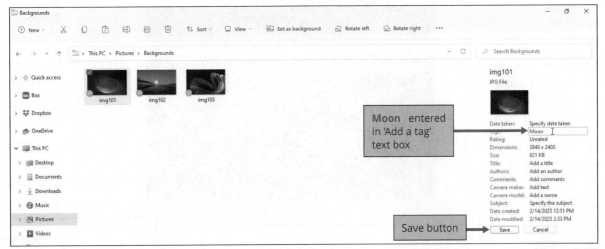

Figure 3–48

Q&A Can I add more than one tag to a picture?
Yes. After typing the first tag, click to the right of the semicolon and add an additional tag. Repeat this step to add additional tags.

3

- Click the Save button in the details pane to save the change to the Tags property (Figure 3–49).

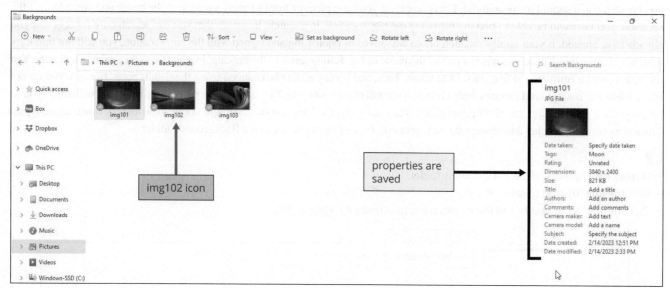

Figure 3–49

Other Ways

1. Right-click icon, click Properties on shortcut menu, click Details tab (img Properties dialog box), enter desired tag(s), click OK

To View a Picture in the Photos App

Why? You can view the images in a folder in the Photos app or as a slide show. The Photos app allows you to view, print, edit, share, and open the pictures in your Pictures folder. The following steps display the img102 picture in the Backgrounds folder in the Photos app.

1

- Double-click the img102 icon (shown in Figure 3–49) to display the picture in the Photos app (Figure 3–50).

Q&A What should I do if the How do you want to open this file? dialog box is displayed?
This dialog box allows you to select the program you wish to use to open the selected type of file. In this case, click Photos and then click OK.

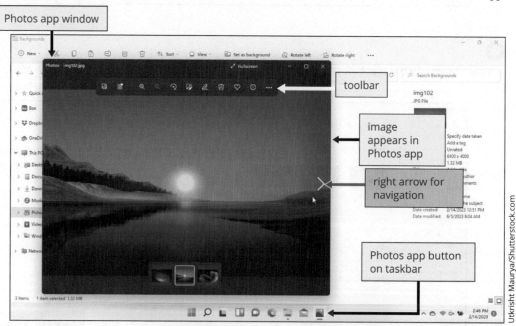

Figure 3–50

Utkrisht Maurya/Shutterstock.com

2

● Click the right arrow (shown in Figure 3–50) to navigate to the next picture in the folder (Figure 3–51).

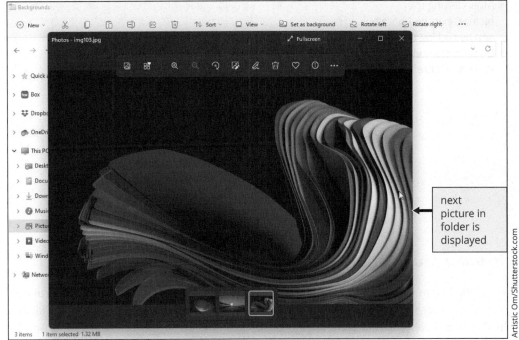

next picture in folder is displayed

Figure 3–51

Artistic Om/Shutterstock.com

3

● Click the left arrow two times to navigate back two pictures in the folder (Figure 3–52).

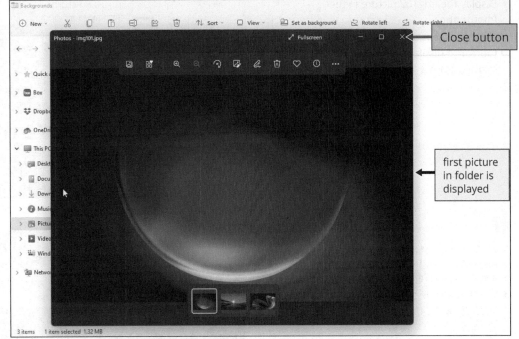

Close button

first picture in folder is displayed

Figure 3–52

4

- After viewing the picture, exit the Photos app by clicking the Close button on the title bar (Figure 3–53).

Photos app has been exited

Figure 3–53

To View Your Pictures as a Slide Show

Using the Photos app, you can view pictures as a **slide show**, which displays each image in the folder in a presentation format on the computer screen. The slide show automatically will display one picture at a time while everything else on the desktop is hidden from sight. The slide show allows you to select whether the pictures will loop in order or will be shuffled to appear in random order. You also can select the speed at which the pictures are displayed, pause the slide show, and exit the slide show. The following steps view the images in the Backgrounds folder as a slide show. **Why?** Viewing pictures as a slide show makes it easy to display pictures on the full screen so that you can show them to others.

1

- Display the img102 picture in the Photos app.
- Click the See more button on the toolbar to display the See more menu (Figure 3–54).

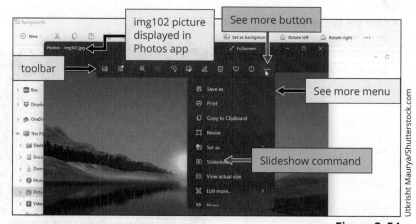

img102 picture displayed in Photos app

See more button

toolbar

See more menu

Slideshow command

Figure 3–54

Utkrisht Maurya/Shutterstock.com

2

- Click Slideshow on the See more menu to view the selected files as a slide show (Figure 3–55).
- Watch the slide show for a few seconds while the pictures change.

pictures are displayed as slide show

Figure 3–55

Artistic Om/Shutterstock.com

To End a Slide Show

When you are done viewing the slide show, the next step is to end it. The following step ends the slide show.

 Press ESC to end the slide show and then exit the Photos app.

Compressing Files and Folders

Sometimes when working with files, you may need to send them via email, post them online, or even transfer them to another computer. If the files are large or numerous, you can make them easier to manage by compressing the files. Compressing (zipping) a file or files creates a **zipped file** that will contain compressed copies of the files. You also can compress folders so that your compressed file has a copy of your folder in it.

To Compress (Zip) a Folder

Why? You want to send the pictures to a friend via an email message, but you want to attach only one file, not three separate ones. The following step compresses the Backgrounds folder.

- Navigate to the Pictures folder.
- If necessary, select the Backgrounds folder.
- Click the See more button on the toolbar to display the See more menu.
- Click 'Compress to ZIP file' on the See more menu to create a zipped file (Figure 3–56). Press ENTER to accept the file name Windows assigned to the file.

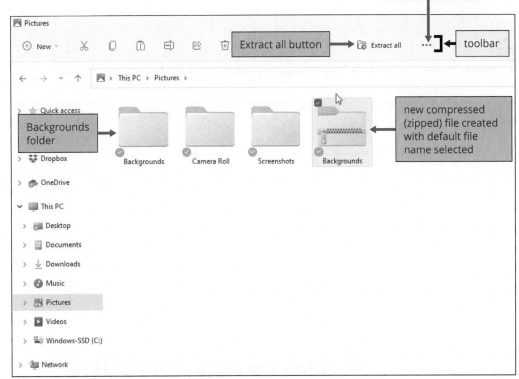

Figure 3–56

Other Ways

1. Right-click folder, click 'Compress to ZIP file' on shortcut menu

To View the Contents of a Compressed Folder

Why? You want to verify that the files are in the compressed folder before you share it. You can open a compressed folder and then view the contents as if you were browsing a regular folder. The following steps display the contents of the Backgrounds compressed folder.

- Double-click the Backgrounds compressed (zipped) folder icon to display the contents of the folder (Figure 3–57).

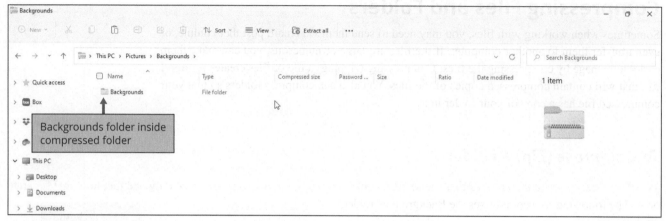

Figure 3–57

- Double-click the Backgrounds folder to display the contents of the folder (Figure 3–58).

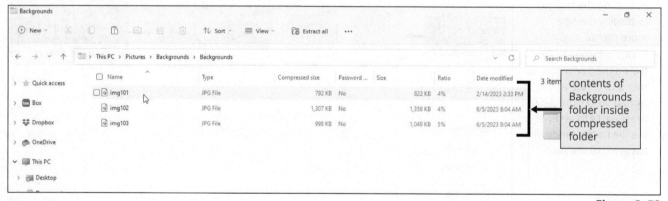

Figure 3–58

Backing Up Files and Folders

It is very important that you make backups of your important files and folders. A **backup** is a copy of files and folders that are stored at a different location than the originals. Backing up files and folders is a security aid; if something happens to the primary copy of a file or folder, you can restore it from the backup.

Although you can back up files and folders on the same drive where they were created, it is not considered as safe as backing them up to a separate drive. For example, you should not back up the files and folders on your primary hard drive to the same hard drive. If something goes wrong with this drive, it would affect any backups stored there, as well. Depending upon the size of the files and folders you are backing up, you might use a USB flash drive, an optical disc, an external hard

drive, cloud storage, or any other available storage device to back up your files. You might even consider creating a scheduled backup. A **scheduled backup** is a backup that is made according to predetermined dates and times.

After you have created a backup, you should store your backup away from the computer. Many people store their backups right by their computer, which is not a good practice. If a mishap occurs in which the computer area is damaged, someone steals the computer, or any other number of events occurs, the backup still will be safe if it is stored in a different location. Most corporations make regular backups of their data and store the backups off site.

When you **restore** files or folders from a backup, you copy the files or folders from the backup location to the original location. If your hard drive crashes, a virus infects your computer, or an electrical surge damages your computer, you can restore the files and folders that you have stored on the backup. Before restoring files or folders, make sure that the location where you are restoring the files is now secure. For example, before restoring files on a hard drive that has been infected by a virus, first make sure the virus is gone.

You will copy the compressed (zipped) Backgrounds folder to OneDrive so that the files are stored somewhere other than your primary hard drive. **OneDrive** is a cloud storage location used for storing files on the Internet and for sharing files with other users. Storing these files on OneDrive also will allow you to access these files from any computer or mobile device you use to sign in to your OneDrive account. Similar to previous steps in this text, these steps assume you are signed in to Windows using a Microsoft account. If you are not signed in with a Microsoft account, read the steps in this section without performing them.

To Copy a File to OneDrive

Why? You want to create a backup of your Backgrounds folder on OneDrive so that you have an extra copy of the files in case you lose the files on your hard drive. The following steps copy the compressed (zipped) Backgrounds folder to OneDrive.

1
- If necessary, display the Pictures folder.
- Click to select the compressed (zipped) Backgrounds folder.
- Click the Copy button on the toolbar to copy the compressed (zipped) folder to the Clipboard (Figure 3–59).

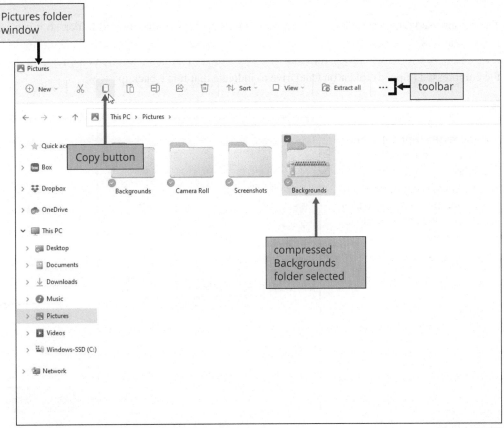

Figure 3–59

- Click OneDrive in the Navigation pane to display the files and folders you currently have stored on OneDrive.
- Click the Paste button on the toolbar to copy the compressed (zipped) file to OneDrive (Figure 3–60).

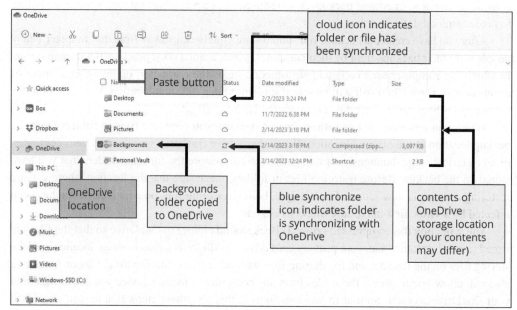

Figure 3–60

Other Ways

1. Select files to copy, right-click, click 'Show more options' on shortcut menu, click Copy; navigate to OneDrive folder, right-click empty area of folder window, click 'Show more options' on shortcut menu, click Paste

2. Select files to copy, press CTRL+C, navigate to OneDrive folder, press CTRL+V

To Rename a Folder

The compressed (zipped) folder on OneDrive is a backup copy of the original folder, so it is a good idea to change its name to reflect that it is a backup. **Why?** It is a good idea to assign a unique name to the backup file so that if you have to restore it, it does not try to overwrite existing files that might be stored in the same location on your hard drive. The following steps rename the compressed (zipped) folder on OneDrive to indicate that it is a backup.

- Right-click the Backgrounds compressed (zipped) folder (shown in Figure 3–60) to display a shortcut menu.
- Click 'Show more options' on the shortcut menu to display an expanded shortcut menu (Figure 3–61).

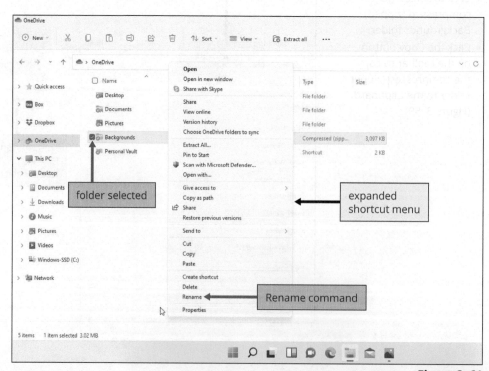

Figure 3–61

- Click Rename on the shortcut menu to open the name of the folder in a text box (Figure 3–62).

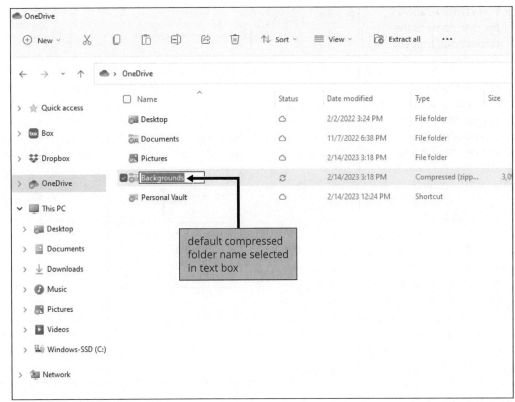

Figure 3–62

- Type **Backgrounds - Backup** as the new compressed folder name (Figure 3–63).

Q&A What if the extension (.zip) is displayed in the text box as I rename the compressed folder? This might happen if your computer is configured to display file name extensions. If the extension (.zip) is displayed, do not remove it. If you do, you might not be able to access the compressed folder until you restore the extension. To display or hide file name extensions, click the 'File name extensions' check box (View tab | Show/hide group).

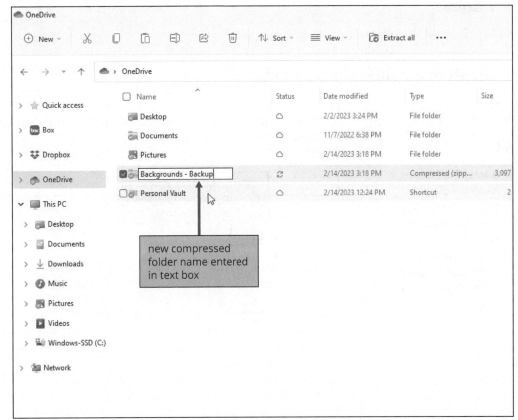

Figure 3–63

4

- Press ENTER to apply the new name to the compressed (zipped) folder (Figure 3–64).

Q&A Why does the Personal Vault shortcut appear when I copy and rename the compressed folder? The Personal Vault shortcut appears when you copy files or folders to OneDrive. The Personal Vault has additional security to protect sensitive information, such as your driver's license information.

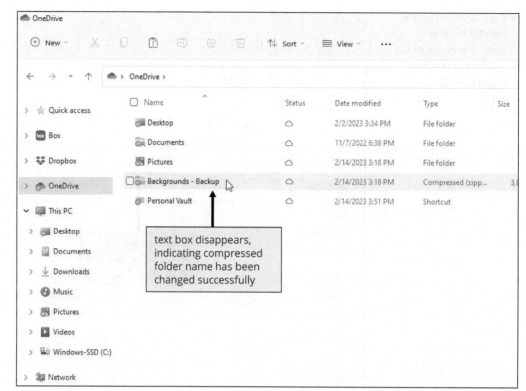

text box disappears, indicating compressed folder name has been changed successfully

Figure 3–64

Other Ways

1. Select folder to rename, press F2, type new name in text box, press ENTER

2. Click folder name two times (do not double-click), type new name, press ENTER

To Restore a Folder from a Backup

Why? If something happens to the original files on your hard drive, you can restore the files or folders from the backup. The following steps simulate a loss of data and then restore the data using the backup on OneDrive.

1

- Display the Pictures folder window.
- Click the item check boxes to select the Backgrounds folder and the Backgrounds compressed (zipped) folder (Figure 3–65).

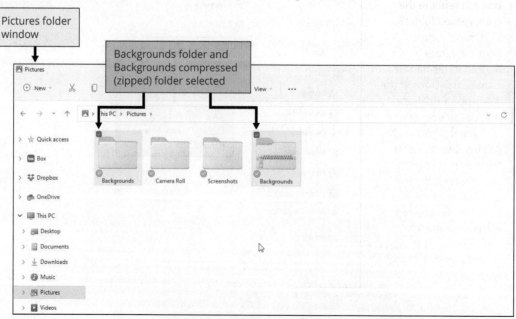

Pictures folder window

Backgrounds folder and Backgrounds compressed (zipped) folder selected

Figure 3–65

2

- Press DELETE to move the items to the Recycle Bin (Figure 3–66).

Q&A After I press DELETE, a dialog box is displayed asking for confirmation for deleting the folders. What should I do?
Click Yes to move the folders to the Recycle Bin.

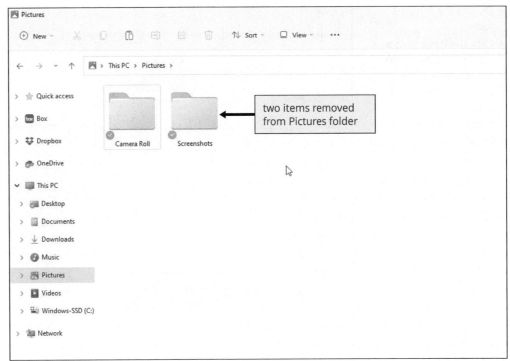

Figure 3–66

3

- Click OneDrive in the Navigation pane to display the contents of the OneDrive folder.
- Click the Backgrounds - Backup compressed (zipped) folder to select it.
- Click the Copy button on the toolbar to copy the backup file to the Clipboard (Figure 3–67).

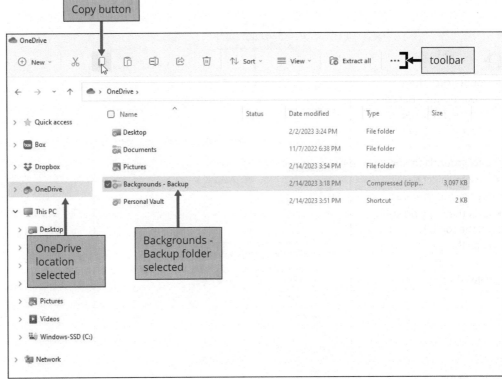

Figure 3–67

- Display the Pictures folder.
- Click the Paste button on the toolbar to copy the Backgrounds - Backup compressed (zipped) folder to the Pictures folder (Figure 3–68).

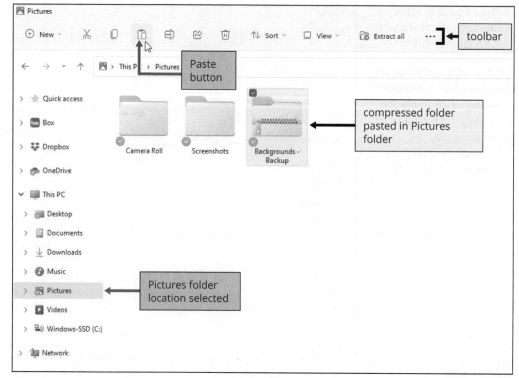

Figure 3–68

- Double-click the Backgrounds - Backup compressed (zipped) folder to display its contents (the Backgrounds folder).
- Click to select the Backgrounds folder.
- Click the Copy button on the toolbar to copy the Backgrounds folder to the Clipboard (Figure 3–69).

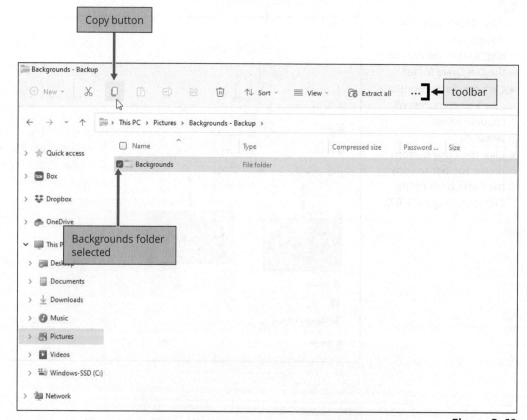

Figure 3–69

- Display the Pictures folder.
- Click the Paste button on the toolbar to copy the Backgrounds folder to the Pictures folder (Figure 3–70).

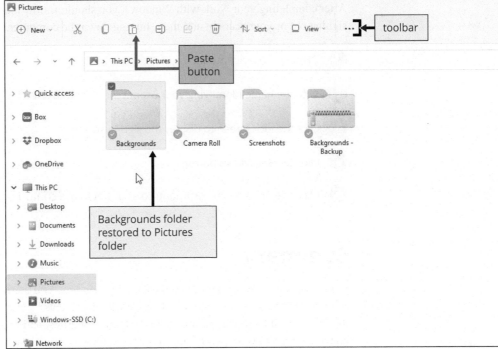

Figure 3–70

Other Ways

1. Select files to copy, right-click selected files, click 'Show more options' on shortcut menu, click Copy; navigate to original folder, right-click empty area of folder window, click 'Show more options' on shortcut menu, click Paste

2. Select files to restore, press CTRL+C, navigate to original folder, press CTRL+V

To Delete Folders from the Pictures Folder and from OneDrive

To return the Pictures folder to its original state, you will delete the Backgrounds folder and the Backgrounds - Backup compressed (zipped) folder. The following steps delete the Backgrounds folder and the Backgrounds - Backup compressed (zipped) folder.

1 If necessary, navigate to the Pictures folder.

2 Select the Backgrounds folder, and then click the Delete button on the toolbar to delete the Backgrounds folder.

3 Select the Backgrounds - Backup compressed (zipped) folder, and then click the Delete button on the toolbar to delete the Backgrounds - Backup compressed (zipped) folder.

4 Click OneDrive in the Navigation pane to display the contents of your OneDrive folder.

5 Select the Backgrounds - Backup compressed (zipped) folder, and then click the Delete button on the toolbar to delete the Backgrounds - Backup compressed (zipped) folder.

6 Close the OneDrive folder window.

To Sign Out of Your Account and Shut Down the Computer

After completing your work with Windows, you should follow these steps to end your session by signing out of your account and then shutting down the computer.

1 Display the Start menu.

2 Click the name identifying your user account, and then click Sign out.

3 Click the lock screen to display the sign-in screen.

4 Click the Shut down button.

5 Click the Shut down command to shut down the computer.

Summary

In this module, you learned about the This PC window. You learned how to view the properties of drives and folders, as well as how to view their contents. You worked with files and folders in the Pictures folder, reviewed and changed their properties, and viewed images in the Photos app and as a slide show. As part of this process, you also learned how to copy and move files, as well as how to create folders. You gained knowledge of how to compress folders so that you can share them. You also learned how to back up files and folders and then restore them using OneDrive.

Student Assignments

Apply Your Knowledge

Reinforce the skills and apply the concepts you learned in this module.

Working with File Properties

Instructions: You want to demonstrate to a friend how to display the properties of an image, display the image using the Paint app instead of the Photos app, and print the image. You also want to demonstrate how to display the properties of the folder containing the image.

Part 1: Displaying File Properties

1. Display the desktop and then click the File Explorer button to open the File Explorer window.
2. Click This PC in the navigation pane to display its contents.
3. Double-click the Windows-SSD (C:) icon (or the icon representing your hard drive).
4. Double-click the Windows folder and then double-click the Web folder.
5. Search for the img104 picture file. If the img104 file is not available on your computer, find another image file.
6. Right-click the img104 icon. Click Properties on the shortcut menu (Figure 3–71). Answer the following questions about the img104 file:
   a. What type of file is img104?
   b. What app is used to open the img104 image?
   c. What is the path for the location of the img104 file?
   d. What is the size (in bytes) of the img104 file?
   e. When was the file created?
   f. When was the file last modified?
   g. When was the file last accessed?

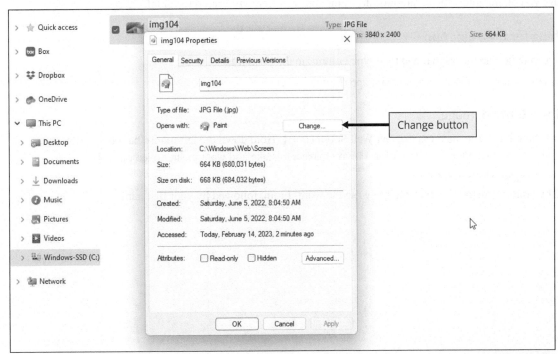

Figure 3–71

Continued on next page

7. Search for another image file in the Web folder and answer the following questions:

   a. What is the name of the image file you selected?

   b. What is the size (in bytes) of the image file you selected?

Part 2: Using the Paint App to Display an Image

1. Click the Change button in the img104 Properties dialog box. Answer the following question:

   a. Which app(s) can you use to open the file?

2. Click the Paint icon and then click OK.

3. Click OK in the img104 Properties dialog box.

4. Double-click the img104 icon to start the Paint app and open the img104 file in the img104 - Paint window.

5. Print the image by clicking the File tab on the ribbon, clicking Print, and then clicking the Print button (Print dialog box).

6. Exit the Paint app. Do not save any changes.

Part 3: Resetting the App Selection

1. Right-click the img104 icon. Click Properties on the shortcut menu.

2. Click the Change button (img104 Properties dialog box).

3. If necessary, click the Photos app icon in the dialog box to select the app icon and then click OK.

4. Click OK in the img104 Properties dialog box.

Extend Your Knowledge

Extend the skills you learned in this module and experiment with new skills.

Creating a Picture

Instructions: You want to use Paint to design a get well soon greeting for a friend and then print the message. Because you do not know the location of the Paint app, you first will search to find it.

Part 1: Searching for the Paint App

1. Click the Search button on the taskbar and then type **paint** in the Search box.

2. Click Paint in the search results to start the Paint app (Figure 3–72).

Part 2: Creating a Bitmap Image

1. Use the Pencil button to write the message, Get Well Soon! (**Hint:** Hold down the left mouse button to write and release the left mouse button to stop writing.) If you make a mistake and want to start over, click the Undo button on the Quick Access Toolbar.

2. If requested by your instructor, use the Pencil to write the word, From, followed by your first name.

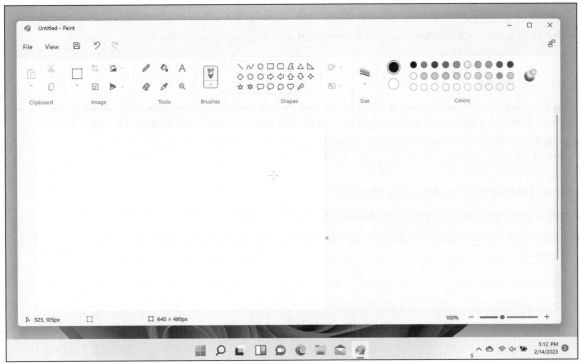

Figure 3–72

3. Click the File tab on the ribbon and then click Save in Backstage view. When the Save As dialog box is displayed, type **Get Well Soon** in the File name text box, if necessary click the Pictures folder in the navigation pane, and then click the Save button (Save As dialog box) to save the file in the Pictures folder.

4. Exit Paint.

Part 3: Viewing and Printing the Get Well Soon Image

1. Open the Pictures folder.

2. Double-click the 'Get Well Soon' icon in the Pictures folder window to open the picture in the Photos app.

3. After viewing the image in the Photos app, exit the Photos app and return to the Pictures folder window.

4. Right-click the 'Get Well Soon' icon, click 'Show more options' on the shortcut menu, and then click Print to display the Print dialog box.

5. Click the Print button (Print dialog box) to print the image.

6. Close the Print dialog box.

Part 4: Deleting the Get Well Soon Image

1. Click the Get Well Soon icon to select the file.

2. Click the Delete button on the toolbar.

3. Close the Pictures folder window.

Expand Your World

Create a solution that uses cloud or web technologies by learning and investigating on your own from general guidance.

Finding Pictures Online

Instructions: You have learned that the Internet is a great source of photos, pictures, and images. You decide to start Microsoft Edge, search for well-known company logos on the Internet, and then save them in a folder. A logo is an image that identifies businesses, government agencies, products, and other entities. In addition, you want to compress the logos into one compressed (zipped) file.

Part 1 Instructions: Finding and Saving Logo Images

1. Click the Microsoft Edge app button on the taskbar to start Microsoft Edge.

2. Type **www.google.com** in the 'Search or enter web address' box in the Microsoft Edge window and then press ENTER (Figure 3–73).

Figure 3–73

3. Locate the Google logo. Right-click the icon, click 'Save image as' on the shortcut menu, name the file Google logo, and then click the Save button (Save As dialog box) to save the logo in the Pictures folder. If you are unable to save this image, contact your instructor for an alternate image to save for this step.

4. Type **www.mcdonalds.com** in the address bar and then press ENTER. Locate the McDonald's logo and use the file name, McDonald's logo, to save the McDonald's logo in the Pictures folder.

5. Exit Microsoft Edge.

6. Make the File Explorer window the active window and navigate to the Pictures folder. The Google logo and McDonald's image appear in the Pictures folder window.

Part 2 Instructions: Displaying File Properties

1. Right-click each logo file in the Pictures folder, click Properties on the shortcut menu, answer the following questions about the logos, and then close the Properties dialog box.

   a. What type of file is the Google logo file?

   b. What type of file is the McDonald's logo file?

2. Click an open area of the Pictures folder to deselect the logo file.

Part 3 Instructions: Creating the Logos Folder in the Pictures Folder

1. Create a new folder in the Pictures folder, type **Logos** in the new folder's text box, and then press ENTER.

2. Drag each logo file to the Logos folder.

3. Refresh the image on the Logos folder.

Part 4 Instructions: Compressing the Logo Images

1. Right-click the Logos folder to display a shortcut menu.

2. Click 'Compress to ZIP file' on the shortcut menu to create a compressed (zipped) file.

3. Type **Logos Backup** as the file name and then press ENTER.

In the Labs

Design and implement a solution using creative thinking and problem-solving skills.

Lab 1: Using Search to Find Picture Files

Problem: You know that searching is an important feature of Windows. You decide to use the Search box to find images on the hard drive. You will store the files in a folder in the Pictures folder and then print the images.

Part 1 Instructions: Searching for Files in the Search Results Window

1. If necessary, start Windows and sign in to your account.

2. Display the desktop.

3. Click the File Explorer button. Navigate to the This PC window. Maximize the This PC window.

4. Double-click Windows-SSD (C:), double-click the Windows folder and then scroll to and double-click the Web folder to open it.

5. In the Search box, type **img** as the entry (Figure 3–74).

6. Copy the img30 image to the Pictures folder. If the img30 image does not appear, try another image.

Part 2 Instructions: Searching for Groups of Files

1. Navigate to the This PC window. Maximize the This PC window.

2. Double-click Windows-SSD (C:), double-click the Windows folder, and then double-click the Web folder to open it.

3. In the Search box of the Windows folder, type **img1*** as the search text.

4. How many files were found?

Continued on next page

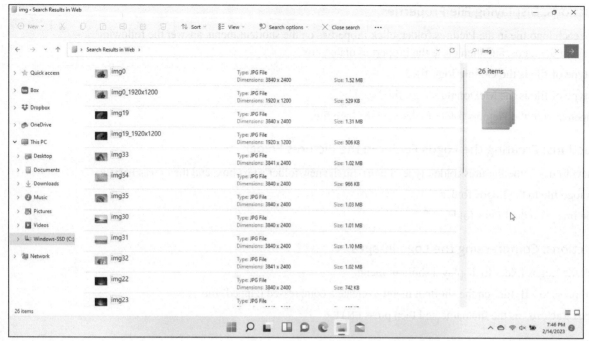

Figure 3–74

5. Click the img102 icon to select the icon. If the img102 icon does not appear, select another icon.

6. Copy the image to the Pictures folder.

Part 3 Instructions: Creating the More Backgrounds Folder in the Pictures Folder

1. If necessary, navigate to the Pictures folder. Click the New button on the toolbar, click Folder, type **More Backgrounds** in the new folder's text box, and then press ENTER.

2. Select the icons of the images you copied to the Pictures folder and then move the images to the More Backgrounds folder.

3. Right-click the More Backgrounds folder, click Properties on the shortcut menu, click the Customize tab, and then, if necessary, optimize the folder for pictures.

Part 4 Instructions: Printing the Images

1. Open the More Backgrounds folder.

2. Select the pictures.

3. Right-click the selected pictures, click 'Show more options' on the shortcut menu, click Print, and then click the Print button (Print dialog box) to print the photos.

4. Delete the More Backgrounds folder from the Pictures folder.

5. Close the Pictures folder window.

Lab 2: Backing Up Your Files

Problem: Several files exist on your computer that you would like to store in their own compressed folder and then back up to OneDrive.

Perform the following tasks:

1. Click the File Explorer button on the taskbar to open the File Explorer window.
2. Display the This PC window.
3. Display the Windows-SSD (C:) window (or the window for your primary hard drive).
4. Display the contents of the Windows folder and then display the contents of the Web folder.
5. Perform a search for all files with the file name extension, .jpg (Figure 3–75).
   (**Hint:** Search for *.jpg.)

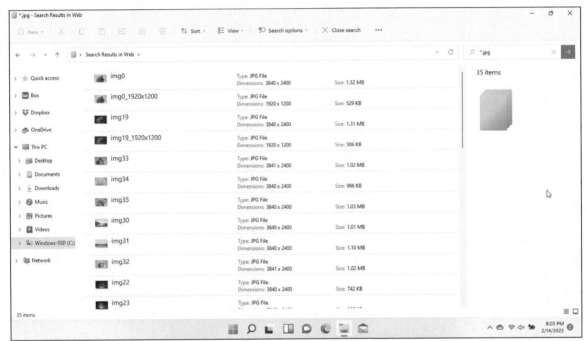

Figure 3–75

6. Copy five images of your choice to the Pictures folder. (**Hint:** If you have trouble pasting an image in the Pictures folder, try a different image.)
7. Navigate to the Pictures folder window.
8. Create a new folder named, Important Pictures - Backup, and copy the five images to it.
9. Compress the Important Pictures - Backup folder.
10. Copy the Important Pictures - Backup compressed (zipped) folder to OneDrive.
11. Delete the Important Pictures - Backup folder and the Important Pictures - Backup compressed (zipped) folder from the Pictures folder.
12. Display the contents of the OneDrive folder, and copy the compressed (zipped) Important Pictures - Backup folder to the Pictures folder.
13. Copy the Important Pictures - Backup folder from the compressed (zipped) folder to the Pictures folder.
14. Delete the Important Pictures - Backup compressed (zipped) folder from the Pictures folder.

Lab 3: Consider This: Your Turn

Researching Data Security

Problem: Stored data is one of a company's most valuable assets. If that data were to be stolen, lost, or compromised so that it could not be accessed, the company could go out of business. Therefore, companies go to great lengths to protect their data.

Part 1:   Working with classmates, research how the companies where you each work handle their backups. If you are unable to determine this information from the company where you work, contact another local company for information.

Part 2:   Find out how each company protects its data against malware, unauthorized access, and even natural disasters, such as fire and floods. Prepare a brief report that describes the companies' procedures. In your report, point out any areas where you find a company has not protected its data adequately.

Personalizing Your Work Environment

Objectives

After completing this module, you will be able to:

- Differentiate among the various types of user accounts
- Create user accounts
- Create a picture password
- Personalize the lock screen
- Customize the Start menu

- Work with multiple desktops
- Work with and customize the taskbar
- Open the Notification Center
- View and modify folder options

Introduction

One of the best ways to improve productivity while using a computer is to personalize your work environment. For example, you can change your desktop's appearance, screen resolution, screen saver, taskbar, and folder options to best suit how you work. Similarly, users often personalize their computers by adding unique touches. This includes changing their lock screen and Start menu to display the apps and colors relevant to them. By personalizing the work environment, users feel more in tune with their computers, which can put them more at ease and lead to improved productivity.

User Accounts

A **user account** is a collection of information that Windows requires about a computer user. When you are signed in to an account, the Start menu displays the user account that is signed in. Information is saved for each user account, including the user name, password, picture, and rights and permissions the user has for accessing a computer or network resources. User accounts make it possible for each user to perform tasks, such as sign in to the computer, keep information confidential and computer settings protected, customize Windows, store files in unique folders, and maintain a personal list of favorite websites.

Normally, user accounts operate in standard user mode, which allows you to use most of the capabilities of the computer. A standard user cannot install software that affects other users or change system settings that affect security. An administrator account has full control of the computer and operating system and can change user permissions, install software that affects all users, and change all system settings. When a task requires administrator access, depending on how Windows is configured, the User Account Control feature might prompt you to authorize the task.

By default, you are asked for permission only when apps attempt to make a change to the computer. Once authorized, the user has temporary administrator privileges. After the task is finished, the user returns to standard user mode. User Account Control is designed to prevent unauthorized or malicious software from being installed inadvertently, even by administrators. For standard user accounts, the user needs to know an administrator account user name and the password to authorize User Account Control. Only administrators are prompted to continue without requiring a user name and password. Table 4–1 provides a list of the different privileges for the account types.

Table 4–1: User Accounts and Privileges

User Account Type	Privileges
Administrator	Create, change, and delete user accounts
	Install programs and apps
	Set folder sharing
	Set permissions
	Access all files
	Take ownership of files
	Grant rights to other user accounts and to their own accounts
	Install or remove hardware devices
	Sign in using safe mode
Standard	Change the password and picture for their own user accounts
	Use programs that have been installed on the computer
	View permissions
	Create, change, and delete files in their libraries
	View files in shared document folders

Local Accounts

Windows supports Microsoft accounts and local accounts. A **local account** is an account that works on only one computer. A local account can be either an administrative or a standard account. A local account does not integrate automatically with the cloud, which enables features such as saving files and synchronizing your Windows settings on OneDrive.

Microsoft Accounts

When you are signed in with a Microsoft account, you can access the services provided on the web for Microsoft account holders. Apps that support Microsoft accounts will allow you to use the associated services that a local account may not be able to use, such as OneDrive. When you add a Microsoft account to your computer, as is the case with a local account, it can be an administrative or a standard account.

When using a Microsoft account, your sign-in settings can be saved on the Internet. When you sign in to Windows on another computer, your settings will be used from your Microsoft account. You can sync your account to the web, which allows you to carry your settings from computer to computer automatically. If you are signed in to Windows with a Microsoft account and you save your files on OneDrive, your files will be readily available if you sign in to another computer using the same Microsoft account. In some lab settings, you may not be able to use your Microsoft account if the lab does not allow you to sign in without a local account. Your instructor can tell you if you can sign in using your Microsoft account.

To Create a Microsoft Account

Why? You might want to have a Microsoft account so that you can save files on OneDrive and synchronize your user settings. The following steps create a Microsoft account. If you already have a Microsoft account or do not wish to create a Microsoft account, read these steps without performing them.

- Click the Search button on the taskbar, type **https://signup.live.com** in the Search box, and then press ENTER to display the Create an account webpage in the Microsoft Edge browser (Figure 4–1).

Q&A Why did a Sign In webpage appear instead of the Create an account webpage?
If you already are signed in to Windows with a Microsoft account, the Sign In webpage might be displayed. To continue creating a Microsoft account, click the links on the page to sign in with a different Microsoft account and then to create a new Microsoft account.

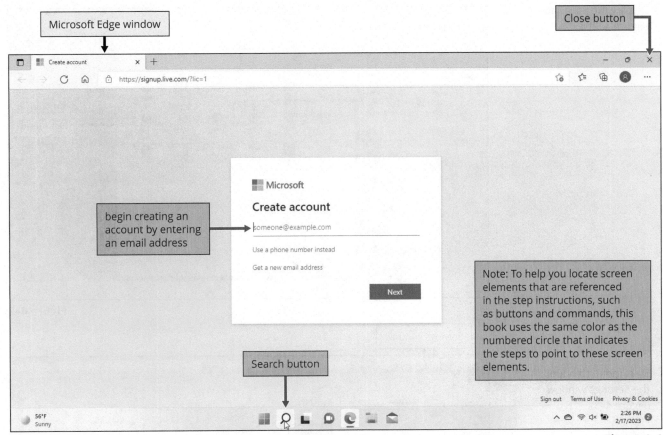

Figure 4–1

- Complete the requested information and follow the required steps to create your account.
- When the account has been created, click the Close button to close Microsoft Edge and return to the desktop.

Setting Up User Accounts

Windows users who want to allow multiple people use of their computer can add an account for each user. When adding an account, you can add either a local or Microsoft account. For the Microsoft account to be used, the computer should have an Internet connection. Once you have added the accounts, different users then can sign in to their account by selecting it on the sign-in screen. To add an account, you first must start the Settings app.

To Add a Local Account

Why? You have decided to let another person use your computer. The following steps add a local account with the user name, SC Student.

- Display the Start menu (Figure 4–2).

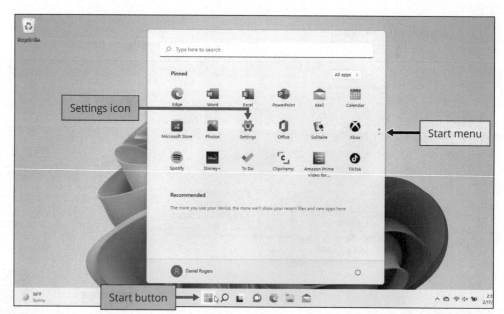

Figure 4–2

- Click Settings on the Start menu to open the Settings window (Figure 4–3).

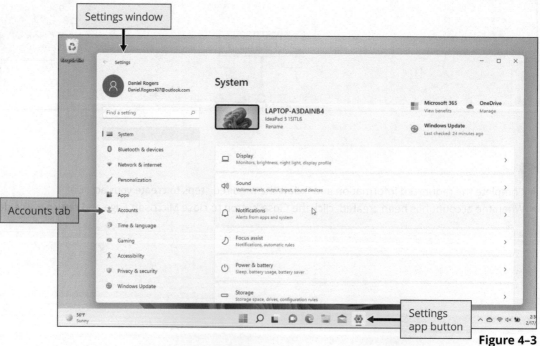

Figure 4–3

- Click the Accounts tab to view the Accounts page and related settings (Figure 4–4).

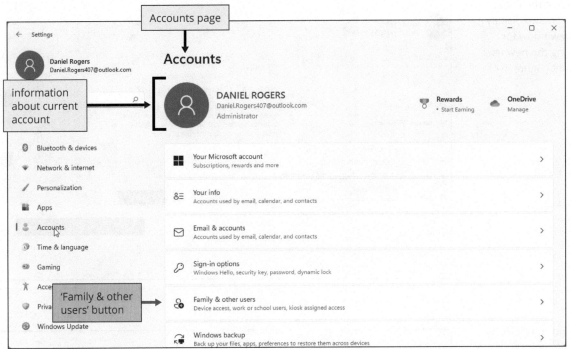

Figure 4–4

- Click the 'Family & other users' button (shown in Figure 4–4) to display the page allowing you to add accounts to Windows (Figure 4–5). If necessary, click the Yes button in the User Account Control dialog box.

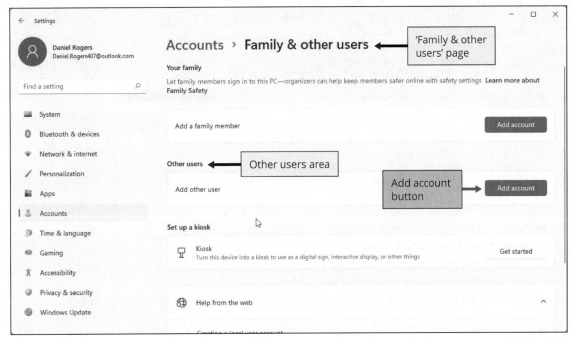

Figure 4–5

Q&A What if I do not see the 'Family & other users' option?

You might not be signed in to Windows using an Administrator account. Recall that Standard user accounts are unable to add accounts to the computer. If you are unable to sign in to the computer with an Administrator account, read these steps without performing them.

- Click the Add account button in the Other users area to display a new window for creating the new user account (Figure 4–6).

Figure 4–6

- Click the 'I don't have this person's sign-in information' link to display the create account page (Figure 4–7).

Q&A Can I also create a Microsoft account on this page?
Yes. You can create a Microsoft account at the same time you add a Microsoft account to your computer, if desired.

Figure 4–7

- Click the 'Add a user without a Microsoft account' link to display several text boxes prompting you for account information.
- Type **SC Student** in the User name text box.
- Type **Windows11** in the Enter password text box.
- Type **Windows11** in the Re-enter password text box.
- If necessary, scroll down and select three security questions and enter appropriate answers (Figure 4–8).

Q&A What password should I use when creating user accounts on my computer?
Whether you are creating a Microsoft account or a local account, you should create a secure password. Secure passwords have more than eight characters, both uppercase and lowercase letters, numbers, and special characters (such as a question mark, exclamation mark, asterisk, or ampersand). The longer your password and the more of these different types of characters, the more secure your account will become.

Q&A Why do I have to select secret questions and answers?
In the event you forget your password, answering the secret questions correctly will help you sign in to your account.

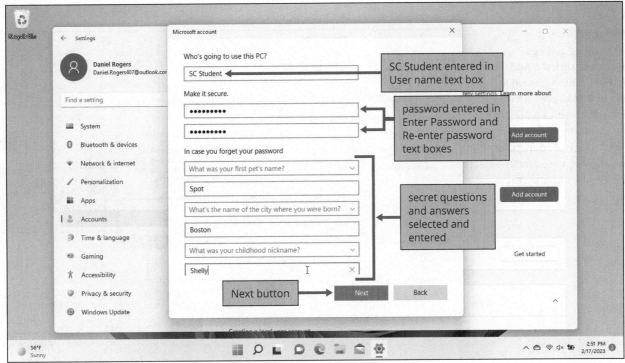

Figure 4–8

- Click the Next button to create the account. If necessary, scroll to view the SC Student user account (Figure 4–9). If necessary, click the Yes button in the User Account Control dialog box.

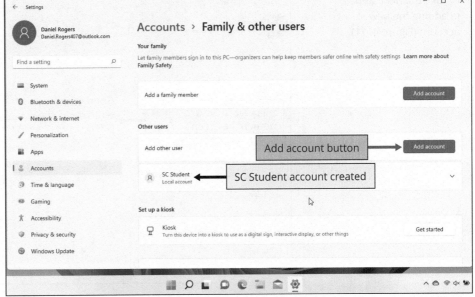

Figure 4–9

To Add a Microsoft Account

Why? You recently created a Microsoft account and would like to add it so that you easily can integrate features, such as OneDrive and Office Online, while working with your Windows account. The following steps add a Microsoft account.

1

- With the 'Family & other users' settings displayed, click the Add account button (shown in Figure 4–9) to prepare to add a Microsoft account to the computer.
- Type the email address for the Microsoft account in the 'Email or phone' text box (Figure 4–10).

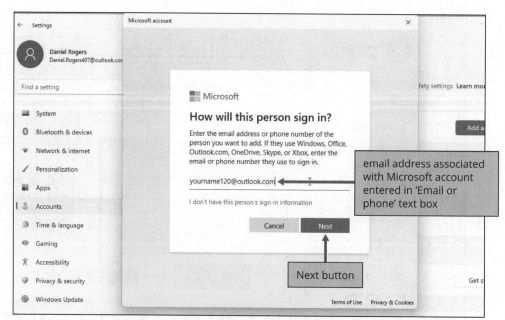

Figure 4–10

2

- Click the Next button to take the next step in adding the new account (Figure 4–11).

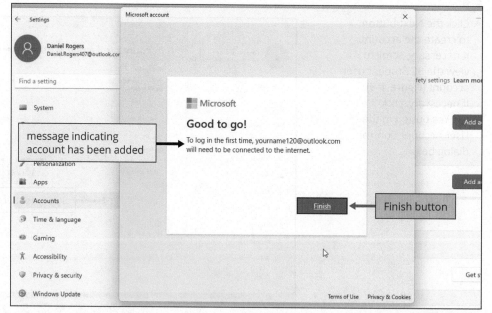

Figure 4–11

3

- Click the Finish button to add the Microsoft account to the computer (Figure 4–12).
- Click the Close button to exit the Settings app.

Q&A Why did I not have to specify a user name or password when creating the Microsoft account?
When you sign in to Windows with a Microsoft account, the email address associated with the account is the user name. The password is the same password you specified when creating the Microsoft account. If you ever change your Microsoft account password, you will need to sign in to Windows using the new password.

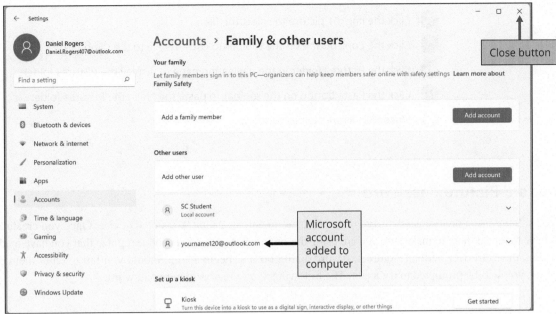

Figure 4–12

To Sign In to a Microsoft Account   After creating a Microsoft account and adding it to your computer, you can sign in to your computer using the Microsoft account. If you wanted to sign in to your computer with the newly created Microsoft account, you would perform the following steps.

1. If necessary, sign out of your existing account.
2. Click the lock screen to display the sign-in screen.
3. Click the name and email address associated with your Microsoft account.
4. Type your Microsoft account password in the text box and then press ENTER to sign in to Windows.

Picture Passwords

Instead of using a password that you have to type in, Windows allows you to use a picture password. A **picture password** involves you selecting a picture and then adding gestures to use for your password. A gesture can be a circle, a straight line, or a click. When you sign in to your account, you will use those gestures to sign in rather than a password. You always can go back and remove the picture password should you no longer want to use it. Also, you can change your picture password to use a different picture or different gestures. While a picture password can be difficult for others to guess, beware of individuals looking over your shoulder as you enter the picture password, as it may be easy for them to remember.

BTW
Picture Passwords
Picture passwords are easiest to use when you are using Windows on a computer with a touch screen, so that you can draw the gestures directly on the screen using your finger. If you are using a keyboard and mouse with your computer, it might be easier just to type a password instead of using a picture password.

To Copy a Picture

You will need a picture to use when creating a picture password. The following steps copy img101.jpg from the Web folder to the Pictures folder.

1 Click the File Explorer button to open the File Explorer window.

2 Display the contents of the Windows folder. In the Windows folder, double-click the Web folder to display its contents.

3 Type **img101.jpg** in the Search box and then press ENTER to search for the img101 picture.

Click the img101 picture to select the file.

(5) Click the Copy button on the toolbar to copy the file to the Clipboard.

(6) Click the Pictures folder in the navigation pane to display the Pictures folder.

(7) Click the Paste button on the toolbar to paste the file in the Pictures folder.

(8) Close the Pictures folder window.

To Create a Picture Password

Why? You want to use a picture password so that it is easier to enter on a touch-enabled device. Once you create the gestures, you will have to repeat them to make sure you are using the same exact gestures. If you recognize that you have made a mistake, you can click the Start over button (Picture password dialog box) to begin again. Should you fail to enter them correctly the second time, you will be prompted to try again. The following steps create a picture password.

1

- Display the Start menu.
- Click Settings to start the Settings app.
- Click the Accounts tab in the Settings window to display the account options.
- Click the Sign-in options button in the right pane to display the sign-in options for the current account (Figure 4–13).

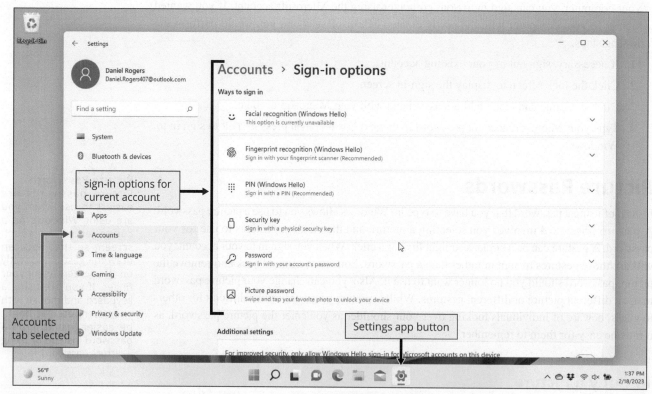

Figure 4–13

2

- Click the picture password button in the right pane to display the Add button (Figure 4–14).

Q&A The Picture password option does not appear in my list of sign-in options. What should I do?
Your computer is probably set up to use only Windows Hello to sign in with a fingerprint scan or facial recognition. Read but do not perform the steps involving a picture password.

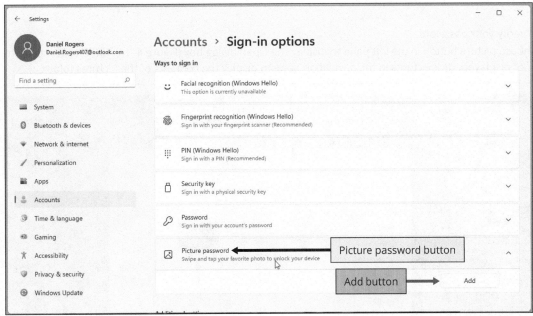

Figure 4–14

3

- Click the Add button below the Picture password heading to display the Windows Security dialog box.
- Type your current Windows password in the Password text box (Figure 4–15).

Q&A Why do I have to type my Windows password?
You have to type your Windows password as a safety precaution. If you are signed in to your Windows account and leave your computer unattended, this measure will prevent people from sitting at your computer and quickly changing your password to something else.

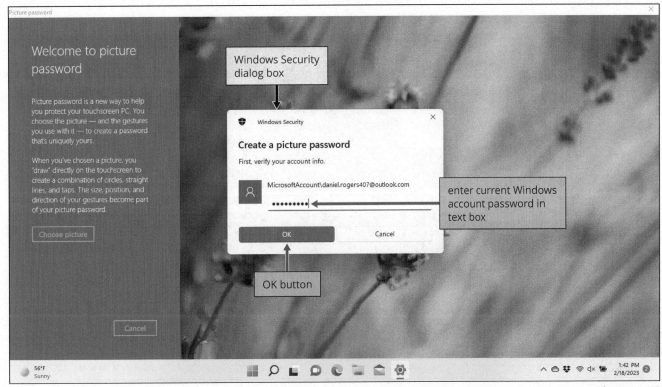

Figure 4–15

- Click OK to verify your password.
- Click the Choose picture button in the left pane to display the Open dialog box (Figure 4–16). If the contents of the Pictures folder are not displayed, click Pictures in the navigation pane to display the contents of the Pictures folder.

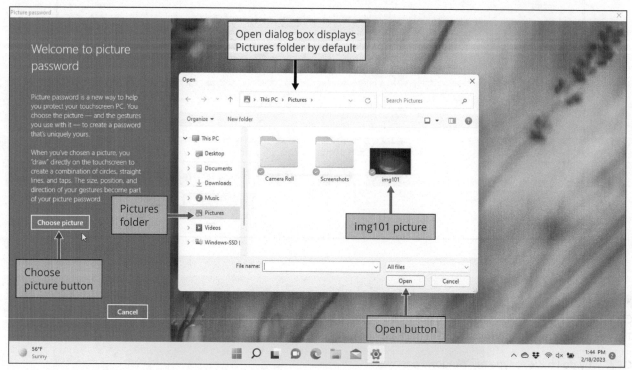

Figure 4–16

- Click the img101 picture to select it.
- Click the Open button (shown in Figure 4–16) to select the img101 image (Figure 4–17).

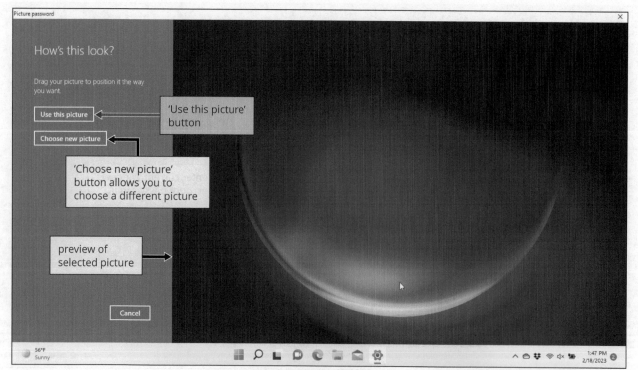

Figure 4–17

- Click the 'Use this picture' button to select this picture for use (Figure 4–18).

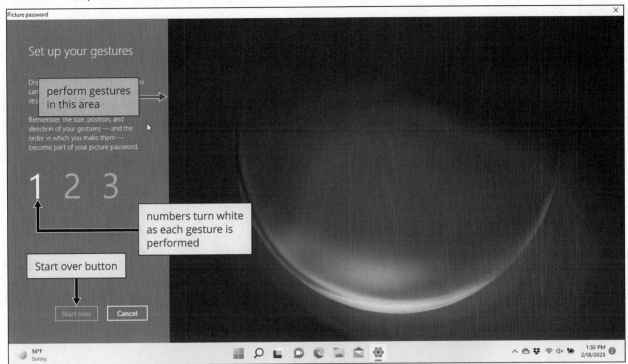

Figure 4–18

- Perform three gestures of your choice either using your mouse or finger (if you have a touch screen). Gestures might include tapping or clicking, or dragging to create a curved or straight line or a shape. If you make a mistake, click the Start over button (shown in Figure 4–18).
- Perform the three gestures again to confirm them (Figure 4–19).

Q&A What happens if I forget my picture password?
Your original password still exists, so you still have the option of signing in to Windows using that password.

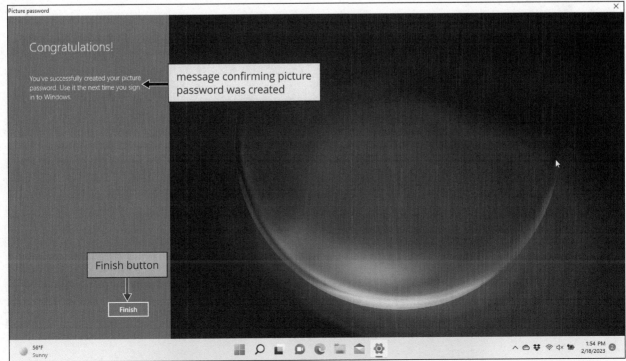

Figure 4–19

- Click the Finish button to save the picture password.
- Exit the Settings app.

Personalization

One way to personalize your Windows settings is to change the appearance of the desktop, lock screen, and Start menu. Personalization settings that you can apply to the desktop include changing the background and accent color. For the lock screen, you can change the apps that are displayed to the apps that you want or use most frequently. They will run in the background and be available whenever the lock screen is displayed. You also can change settings, such as the screen resolution and screen saver. You can change most personalization settings using the Settings app.

To Change the Desktop Background

Windows allows you to specify one of three settings for the desktop background. In this textbook, all figures showing the desktop show the default Windows background image; however, you can change the desktop background to a different picture, a solid color, or a slideshow consisting of two or more pictures that change at a set interval. **Why?** You want to change the desktop background to show something that is of interest to you. The following steps change the desktop background using a picture, solid color, and slideshow.

- Display the Start menu.
- Click Settings on the Start menu to start the Settings app and open the Settings window (Figure 4–20).

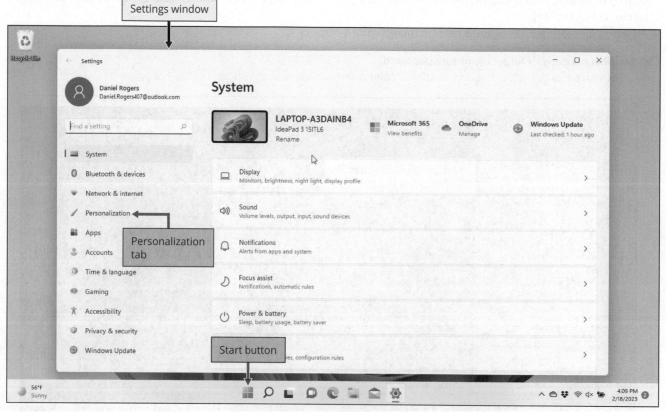

Figure 4–20

WIN 4-15

2

- Click the Personalization tab in the Settings window to display the Personalization page and its related settings (Figure 4–21).

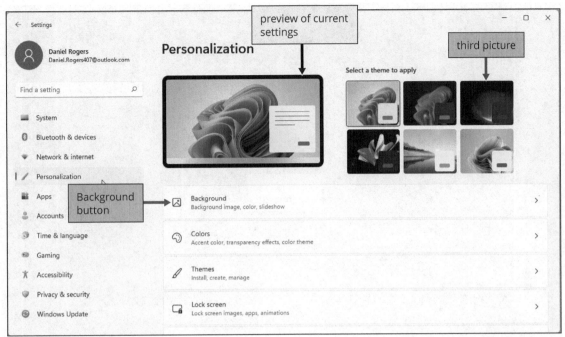

Figure 4–21

3

- Click the Background button to display the Background page.
- Click to select the third picture in the Recent Images area to change the desktop background (Figure 4–22).

Q&A Can I use a picture other than the ones shown?
Yes. If you want to use your own picture, click the Browse photos button and then navigate to and select the picture you want to use.

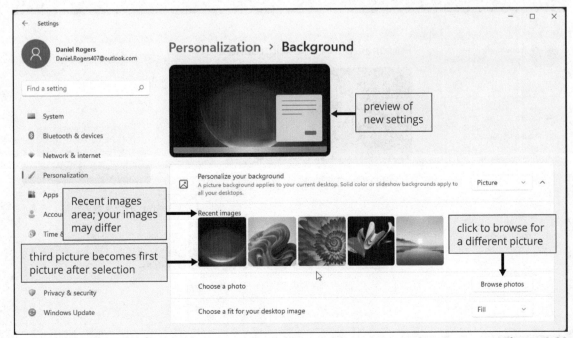

Figure 4–22

4

- Click the Show desktop button to minimize all open windows and preview the new desktop background (Figure 4–23).

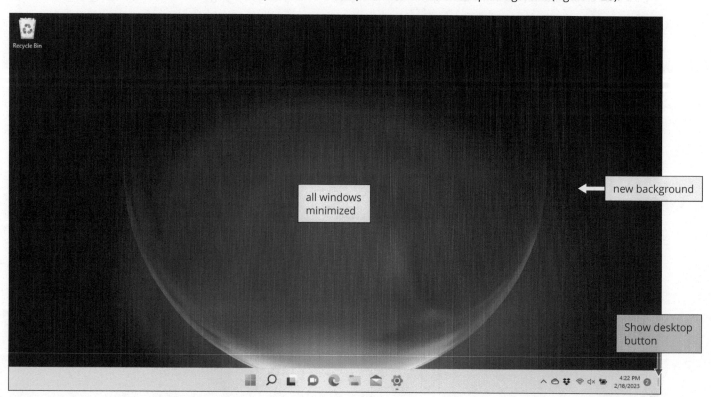

Figure 4–23

5

- Click the Settings app button on the taskbar to view the Settings window.
- Click the Picture button to display a list of background options (Figure 4–24).

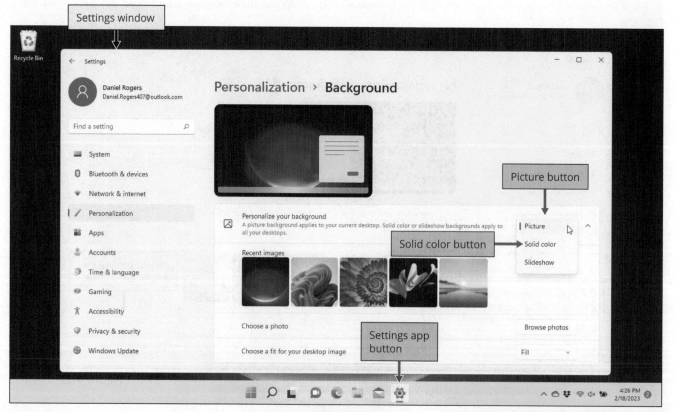

Figure 4–24

6

- Click Solid color in the Background list to display a list of available background colors.
- Click the red background color to change the desktop background to a solid color (Figure 4–25).

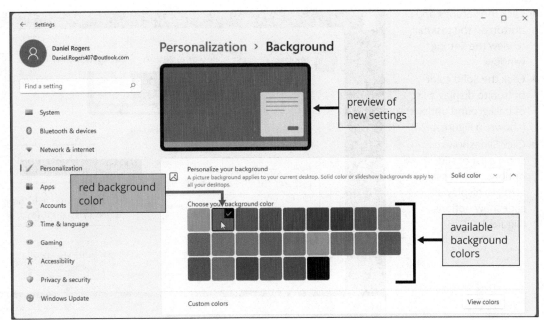

Figure 4–25

7

- Click the Show desktop button to minimize all windows so that you can preview the solid background color (Figure 4–26).

Figure 4–26

8

- Click the Settings app button on the taskbar to view the Settings window.
- Click the Solid color button to display a list of background options (shown in Figure 4–24).
- Click Slideshow to show a list of slideshow options. If necessary, scroll to display all slideshow options (Figure 4–27).

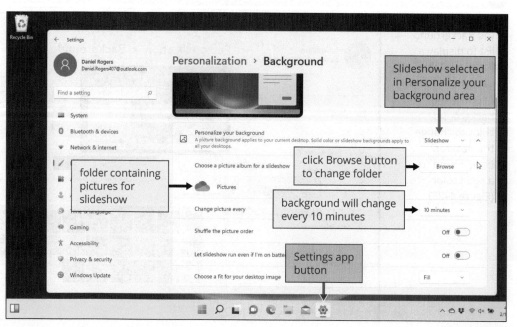

Figure 4–27

9

- Click the Slideshow button to display a list of background options.
- Click Picture to change the desktop background to a picture.
- Choose the last picture in the Recent images area to change the desktop background again.

To Change the Accent Color

The accent color you choose will specify how certain elements of the Start menu, windows, and taskbar are displayed. For example, if you choose a red accent color, accents on the Start menu, menu options, and some window elements will be red. **Why?** You want to change the accent color to your favorite color. The following steps change the accent color.

1

- Click the Personalization tab in the left pane of the Settings window to display the Personalization page.
- Click the Colors button in the right pane to display color options (Figure 4–28).

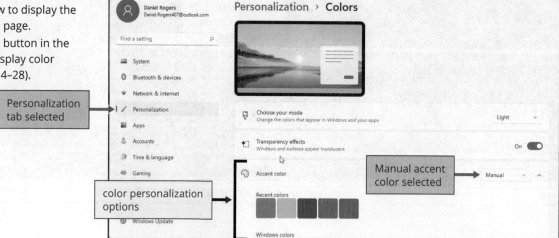

Figure 4–28

- Scroll to display the palette of available accent colors (Figure 4–29).
- Make a note of the accent color currently selected. The selected accent color is identified by a check mark located in the color sample.

Q&A Why are no accent colors being displayed?

The Automatic setting for accent color might be selected. This feature will determine an accent color that matches your desktop background and apply it automatically. To see the palette of accent colors, click the Automatic button and then click Manual.

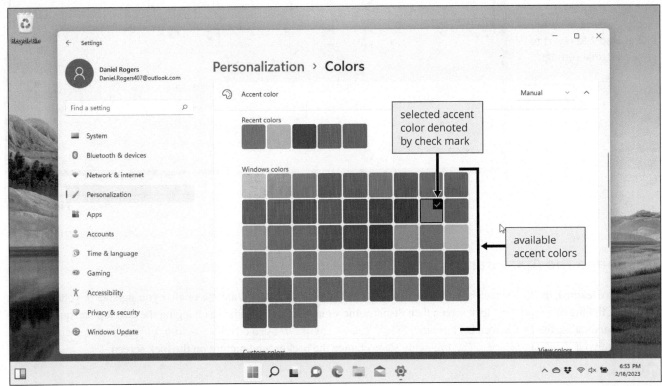

Figure 4–29

- Click the Orange bright accent color to change the accent color (Figure 4–30).

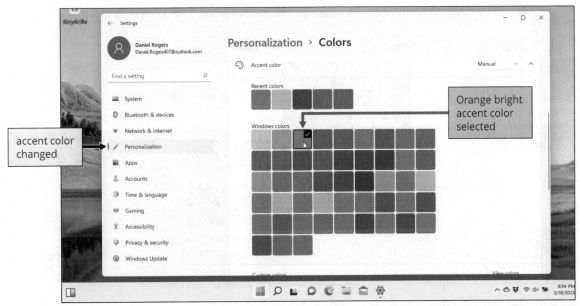

Figure 4–30

4

- Click the Start button to view how the accent color changes the appearance of the Start menu (Figure 4–31).

5

- Close the Start menu.
- Choose the accent color you made note of in Step 2 to revert to your original settings.

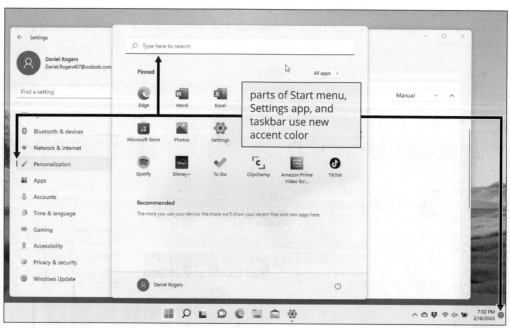

Figure 4–31

To Change the Appearance of the Lock Screen

As you have learned, the lock screen is the screen that appears when you first start Windows or after you sign out of your Windows account. Clicking or swiping the lock screen then displays the sign-in screen. Similar to changing the desktop background, you also can personalize the lock screen background. **Why?** You would like to use a different picture for your lock screen to further personalize your Windows settings. The following steps change the background picture on the lock screen.

1

- Click the Personalization tab in the left pane of the Settings window to display the Personalization page.
- Click the Lock screen button in the right pane to display options for the lock screen.
- If necessary, change the 'Personalize your lock screen' option to Picture (Figure 4–32).

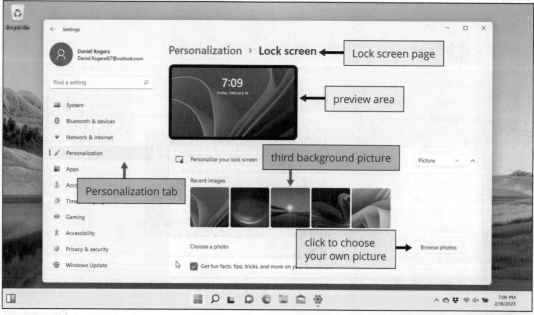

Figure 4–32

2

- Make note of the background picture currently being displayed.
- Click the third background picture to change the background on the lock screen (Figure 4–33).

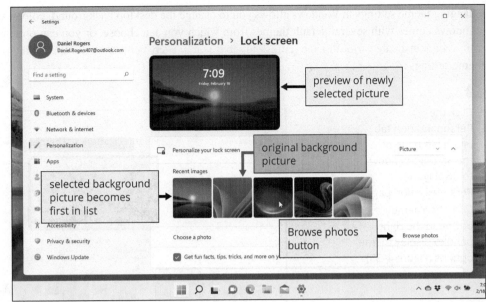

Figure 4–33

3

- Click the background picture you made note of in Step 2 to revert the lock screen background to its original setting.
- Scroll down in the right pane to view additional lock screen settings (Figure 4–34).

Q&A What other options are available for personalizing the lock screen?
Many options are available. You can use a different picture by clicking the Browse button and then navigating to and selecting the picture of your choice, you can view a slideshow of images as your lock screen background, and you can display information from selected apps on the lock screen. For example, if you have an email account configured on your computer, you can configure the lock screen to show how many new email messages are awaiting your attention.

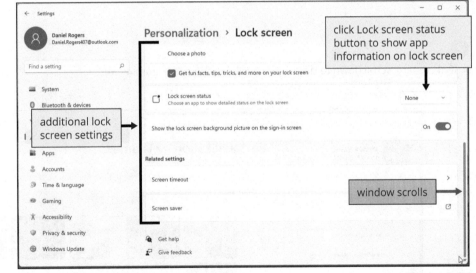

Figure 4–34

To Change Theme Settings

Changing theme settings in Windows allows you to change the desktop background, colors, and sound settings all at one time. Windows comes with several default themes from which you can choose, or you can obtain additional themes online. **Why?** You want to evaluate various theme settings to see if you like any better than the current theme. The following steps change the theme settings.

- Click the Personalization tab in the left pane of the Settings window to display the Personalization page.
- Click the Themes button in the right pane to display theme options (Figure 4–35).

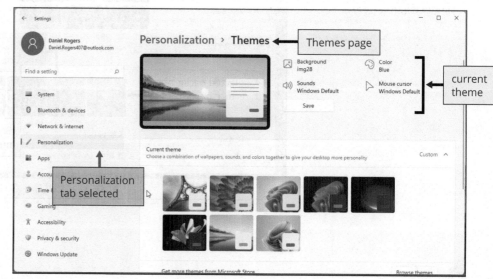

Figure 4–35

2

- If necessary, scroll down to display the available themes (Figure 4–36).

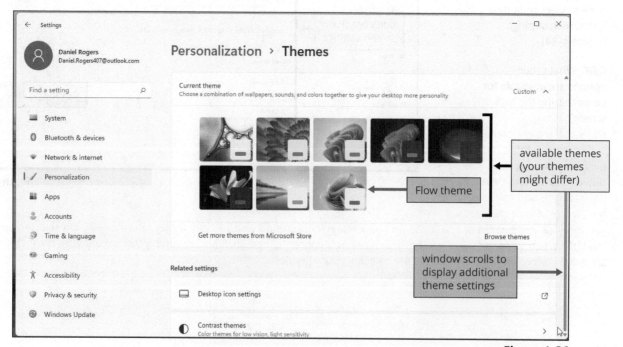

Figure 4–36

3

- Make a note of the theme that currently is selected.
- Click the Flow theme to change the theme to Flow (Figure 4–37).

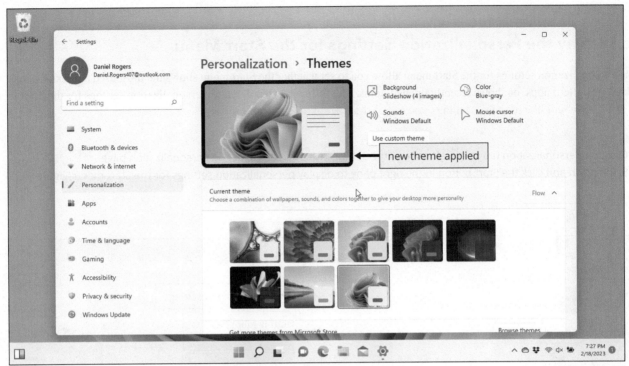

Figure 4–37

4

- Click the Show desktop button to minimize all windows and view the changes (Figure 4–38).

Q&A What changed when I selected the Flow theme?

Visible changes include a different desktop background and updated colors.

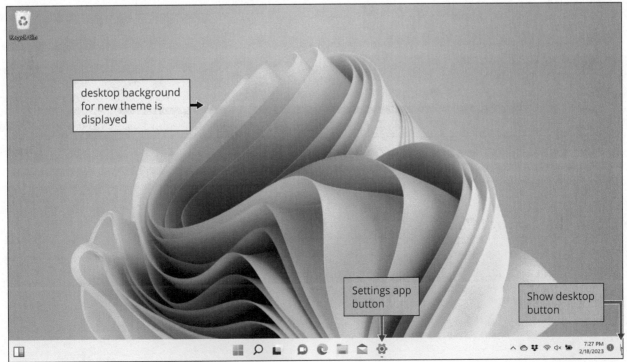

Figure 4–38

5

- Click the Settings app button on the taskbar to open the Settings window.
- Click the theme you recorded from Step 3 to restore the theme to the previous setting.

To Display the Personalization Settings for the Start Menu

The Personalization settings for the Start menu allow you to set whether the Start menu shows the most used apps, shows recently added (installed) apps, or shows recently opened items. The following step displays personalization settings for the Start menu. **Why?** You would like to see the settings you can customize for your Start menu.

- Click the Personalization tab in the left pane of the Settings window to display the Personalization page.
- Scroll down and click the Start button in the right pane to display personalization settings for the Start menu (Figure 4–39).

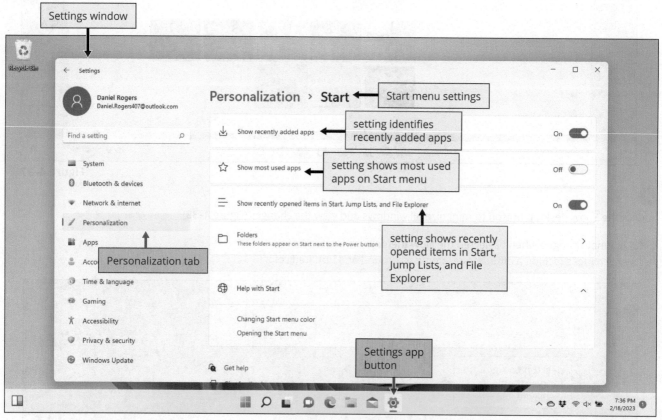

Figure 4–39

To Open the Control Panel

Why? You might need to open the Control Panel in some instances in which you would like to access and change settings you are unable to find in the Settings app. **The following steps open the Control Panel.**

1

- Click the Start button and then type **control panel** in the Search box to display the search results (Figure 4–40).

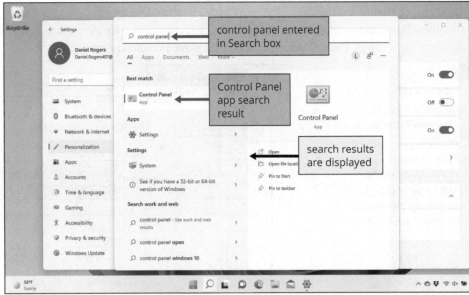

Figure 4–40

2

- Click the Control Panel app search result to open the Control Panel window (Figure 4–41).

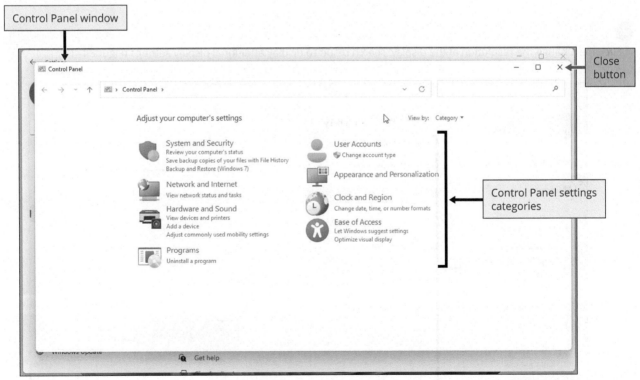

Figure 4–41

View Screen Resolution Settings

The screen resolution settings enable you to change how content appears on the screen. **Why?** You want to view the settings available that can adjust brightness, calibrate color, and change the screen resolution (which affects how much content displays on the screen at once). The following steps view the screen resolution settings.

- Click the Close button on the title bar to close the Control Panel window.
- Type **screen resolution** in the 'Find a setting' text box to display the search results (Figure 4–42).

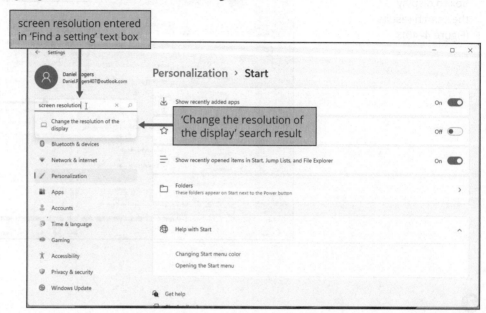

Figure 4–42

- Click the 'Change the resolution of the display' search result to display additional display settings (Figure 4–43).

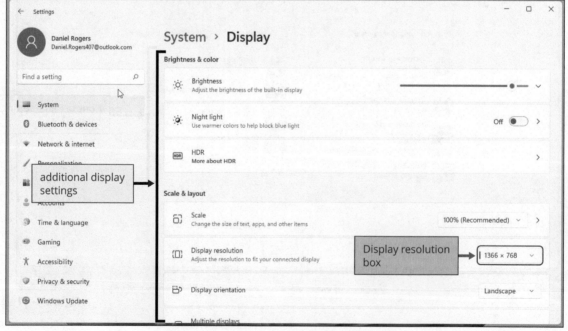

Figure 4–43

● If necessary, scroll down to
display the Display Resolution
setting and then click the
Display resolution box to
display the various resolution
options (Figure 4–44).

● Press ESC to close the
Resolution options.

Q&A What is the screen
resolution?
The screen resolution specifies
how many pixels are displayed
on the screen at one time. As you
increase the resolution, more
content will be displayed on the
screen, and all screen elements
(windows, menus, buttons, and
so on) will appear smaller.

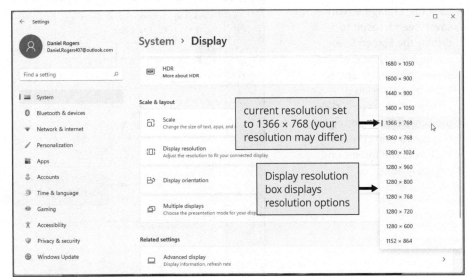

Figure 4–44

To Change the Screen Saver

Another element of a desktop theme that you can modify is the screen saver. A **screen saver** is a moving picture or pattern that
is displayed on the monitor when you have not interacted with the computer for a specified period of time. Originally, screen
savers were designed to prevent the problem of **ghosting** (where a dim version of an image would permanently be etched on the
monitor if the same image were to be displayed for a long time) by continually changing the image on the monitor. Although
ghosting is less of a problem with today's monitors, people still use screen savers. Screen savers can be animations, designs,
and other entertaining or fascinating activities that are displayed on the screen after a period of time has passed without any
computer activity. You can determine how long this interval should be. Screen savers stop executing when you press a key on
the keyboard, move the mouse, or touch the screen. Windows 11 provides a variety of screen savers from which you can choose.
The following steps change the screen saver. **Why?** Your computer currently has no screen saver configured, and you want to
select and enable one. The following steps change the screen saver.

● Type **screen saver**
in the 'Find a setting'
text box to display
the search results
(Figure 4–45).

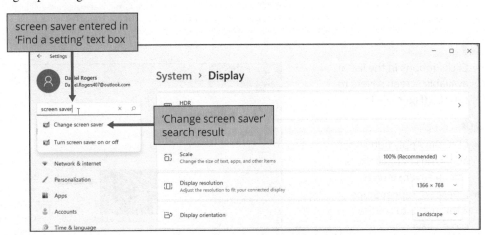

Figure 4–45

2

- Click the 'Change screen saver' search result to display the Screen Saver Settings dialog box, which shows the current screen saver and associated settings. If necessary, click the Screen Saver Settings title bar to bring the dialog box to the foreground (Figure 4–46).

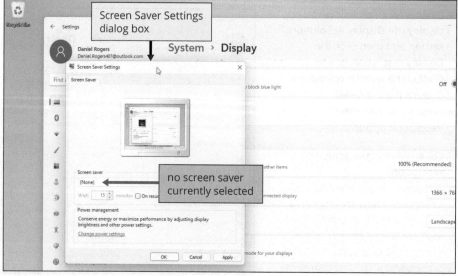

Screen Saver Settings dialog box

no screen saver currently selected

Figure 4–46

3

- Make a note of the screen saver (if any) that currently is selected.
- Click the Screen saver button to view a list of available screen savers (Figure 4–47).

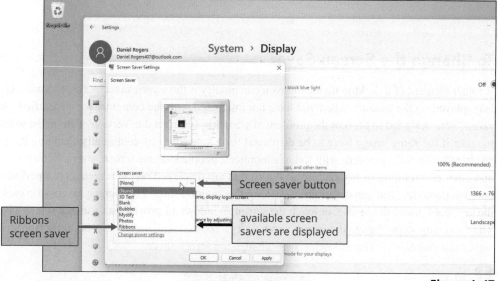

Screen saver button

available screen savers are displayed

Ribbons screen saver

Figure 4–47

4

- Click Ribbons in the list of available screen savers to select it (Figure 4–48).

5

- Click the Apply button to apply the changes to the screen saver settings.
- If desired, repeat Steps 2 through 5 to set the screen saver back to the original setting from Step 3.

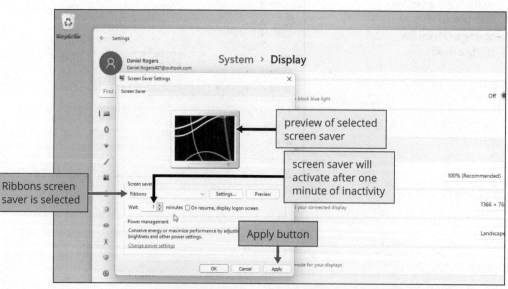

preview of selected screen saver

screen saver will activate after one minute of inactivity

Ribbons screen saver is selected

Apply button

Figure 4–48

To Display Task View and Add a Desktop

Task view allows you to see thumbnail images of all windows and apps you currently have open or running. Viewing thumbnail images of all open windows and apps makes it easy for you to switch between apps if you have multiple windows open at one time. As mentioned previously, the desktop is a workspace where your open windows and apps are displayed. **Why?** If you feel your desktop is becoming cluttered, you can add a desktop that displays some windows, while other open windows remain on your original desktop. The following steps display Task view and add a desktop.

- Click the Task View button on the taskbar to display Task view (Figure 4–49).

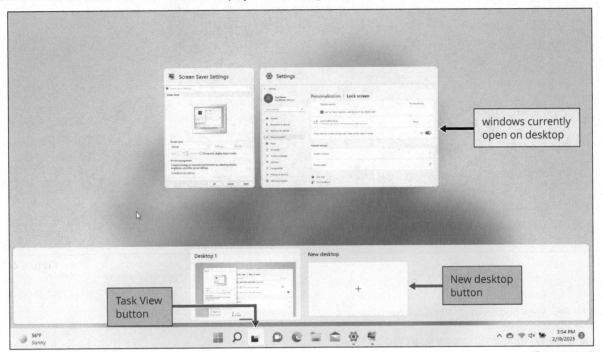

Figure 4–49

- Click the New desktop button above the taskbar to add a second desktop (Figure 4–50).

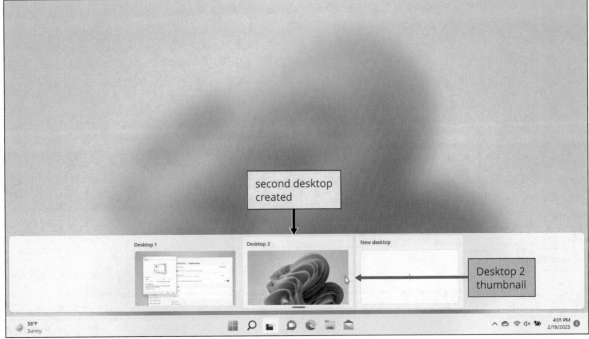

Figure 4–50

● Click the Desktop 2 thumbnail to view the second desktop (Figure 4–51).

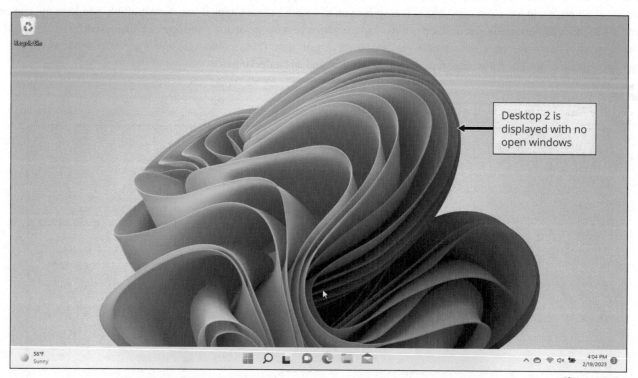

Desktop 2 is displayed with no open windows

Figure 4–51

● Click the Task View button to display Task view (Figure 4–52).

Q&A Why are no thumbnail images displayed?
You currently have no apps running or windows open on the second desktop, so no thumbnail images are displayed.

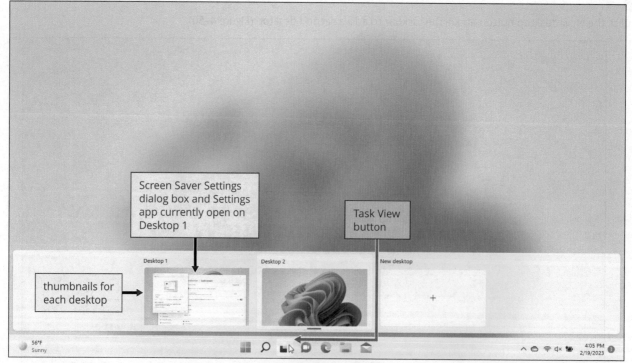

Screen Saver Settings dialog box and Settings app currently open on Desktop 1

Task View button

thumbnails for each desktop

Desktop 1   Desktop 2   New desktop

Figure 4–52

5

- Point to the Desktop 1 thumbnail until the thumbnail images of running apps and open windows are displayed (shown in Figure 4–50).
- Drag the Settings thumbnail to the Desktop 2 thumbnail to move the Settings app to Desktop 2 (Figure 4–53).

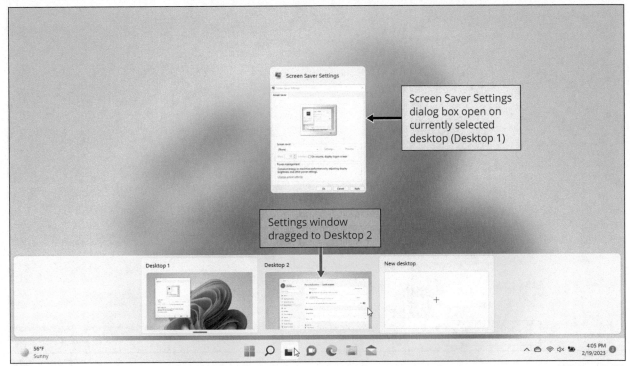

Screen Saver Settings dialog box open on currently selected desktop (Desktop 1)

Settings window dragged to Desktop 2

Figure 4–53

6

- Click the Desktop 2 thumbnail to view the Settings app on Desktop 2 (Figure 4–54).

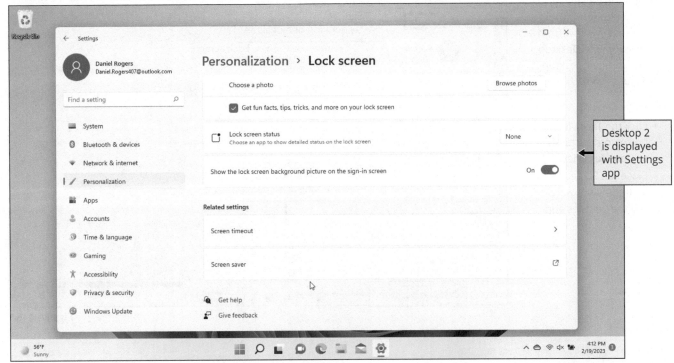

Desktop 2 is displayed with Settings app

Figure 4–54

7

- Display Task view.
- Point to the Desktop 2 thumbnail to display the Close button (Figure 4–55).

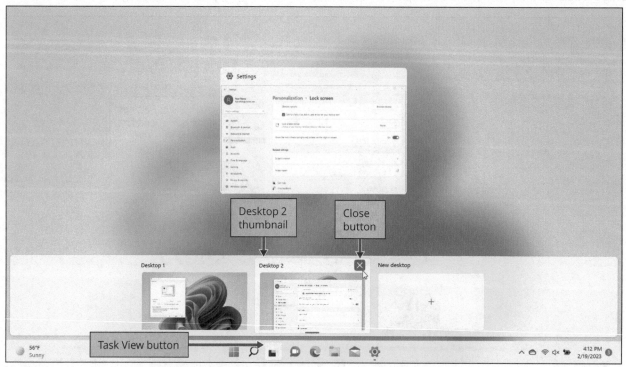

Figure 4–55

8

- Click the Close button to move the Settings window from Desktop 2 to Desktop 1 and remove Desktop 2 (Figure 4–56).

9

- Click the Task View button on the taskbar to close Task view.
- Close the Screen Saver Settings window.
- Exit the Settings app.

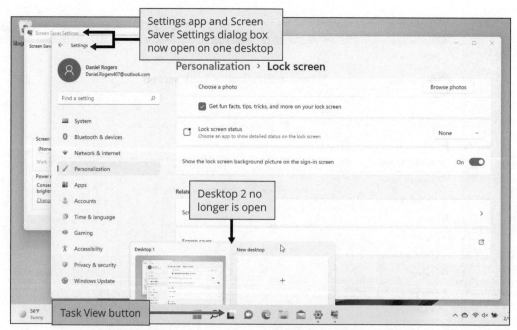

Figure 4–56

Customizing the Taskbar

Another method of modifying the desktop work environment is to customize the taskbar at the bottom of the desktop. For example, you can hide the taskbar; change the alignment of the taskbar; and manage the buttons and icons on the taskbar. The next sections illustrate how to customize the taskbar.

To Change the Taskbar Alignment

By default, the taskbar is centered at the bottom of the screen. As you start apps, Windows adds their buttons to the taskbar to preserve the center alignment. You can change the alignment of the taskbar so that the default buttons, buttons for pinned apps, and buttons for running apps appear on the left. **Why?** If you used previous versions of Windows, you may be accustomed to finding the Start button on the left side of the taskbar. The following steps change the alignment of the taskbar.

- Right-click an open area of the taskbar to display a shortcut menu
- Click Taskbar settings on the shortcut menu to open the Settings window and display the taskbar personalization settings (Figure 4–57).

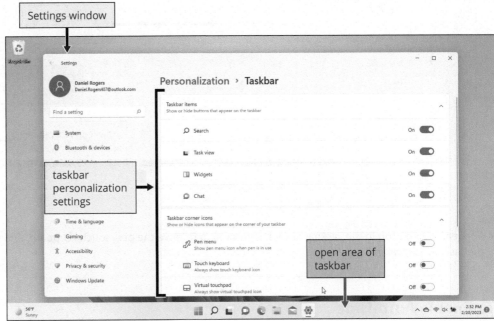

Figure 4–57

- Scroll down and then click the Taskbar behaviors button to display the settings that affect taskbar behaviors.
- Click the Taskbar alignment button and then click Left to change the taskbar alignment (Figure 4–58).

Q&A What happened to the Widgets button, which previously appeared in the left corner of the taskbar?
When the taskbar buttons are left-aligned, the Widgets button moves to the right of the Task View button.

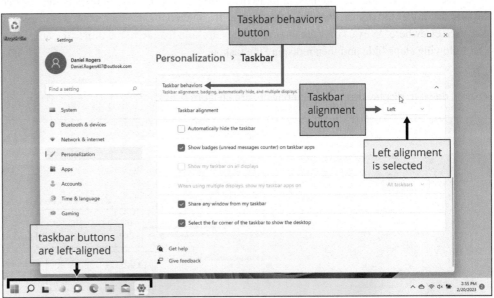

Figure 4–58

Other Ways

1. Click Start button, click Settings, click Personalization tab, click Taskbar

To Show or Hide Taskbar Corner Icons

Recall that the notification area appears in the right corner of the taskbar and displays the current date and time along with icons for other information, such as a network connection, volume control, and battery status. You can choose to display additional icons for a pen menu, touch keyboard, and virtual touchpad. **Why?** Depending on your computer hardware, you may want to access and control a digital pen, touch keyboard, or virtual touchpad. The following steps show and hide the taskbar corner icons.

- Scroll up to display the Taskbar corner icons area and then click to change each Off button to On (Figure 4–59).

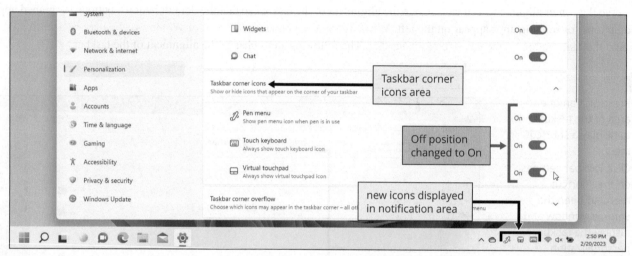

Figure 4–59

- Click each On button in the Taskbar corner icons area to remove the pen, touch keyboard, and virtual touchpad icons from the taskbar (shown in Figure 4–60).

To Enable Auto-Hide

Another way to customize the desktop is to hide the taskbar so that only its top edge is visible at the bottom of the desktop. When the taskbar is hidden, you must point to the bottom of the desktop to display the taskbar. The taskbar will remain on the desktop as long as the pointer hovers on the taskbar. If you click the taskbar when it is displayed, it remains on the desktop until you click elsewhere. **Why?** You want to enable the Auto-hide feature to maximize the amount of available space on the desktop. The following steps hide and then redisplay the taskbar.

- Scroll down to display the Taskbar behaviors area (Figure 4–60).

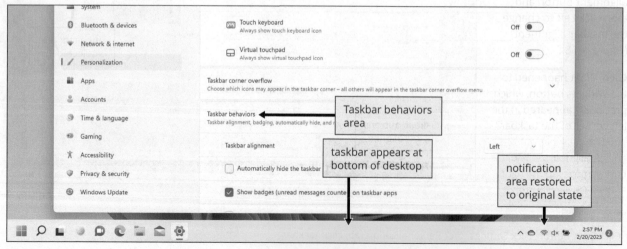

Figure 4–60

- Click the 'Automatically hide the taskbar' check box to insert a check mark and hide the taskbar (Figure 4–61).

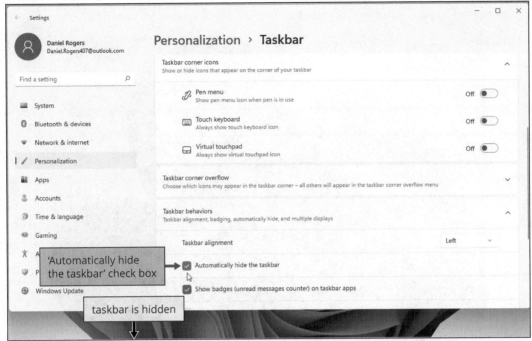

Figure 4–61

- Point to the bottom of the screen to display the taskbar (Figure 4–62).

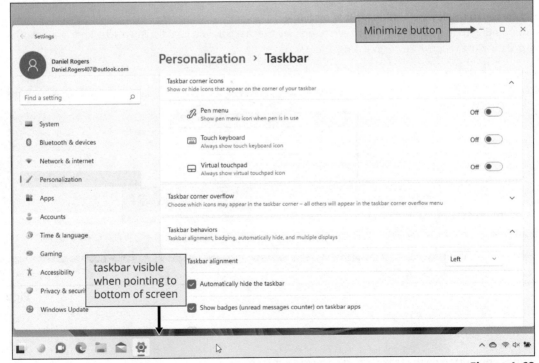

Figure 4–62

• Click the Minimize button to minimize the Settings window (Figure 4–63).

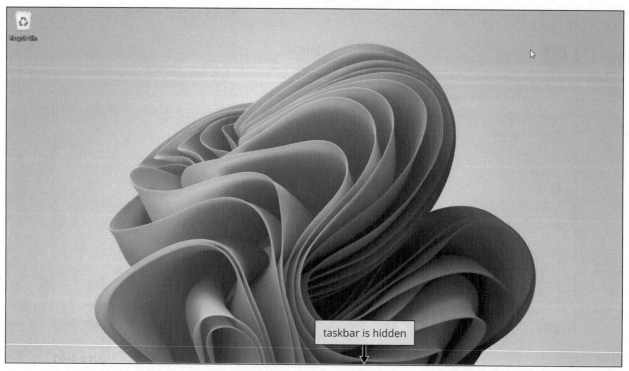

taskbar is hidden

Figure 4–63

• Point to the bottom of the screen to display the taskbar and then click the taskbar to keep it displayed (Figure 4–64).

Q&A Is another way to display the hidden taskbar available?
In addition to pointing to the bottom of the screen to display the taskbar, you can display the taskbar and the Start menu at any time by pressing the WINDOWS key or pressing CTRL+ESC.

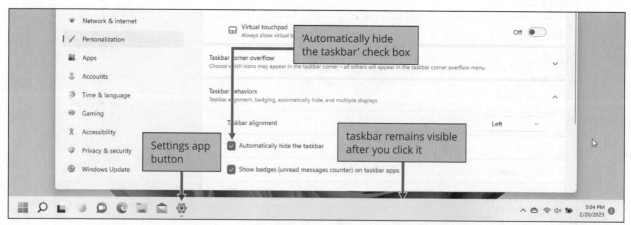

'Automatically hide the taskbar' check box

Settings app button

taskbar remains visible after you click it

Figure 4–64

• Click the Settings app button on the taskbar to display the Settings app.
• Click the 'Automatically hide the taskbar' check box to remove the check mark to turn off the Auto-hide feature.

To Show or Hide Taskbar Buttons

The Search, Task view, Widgets, and Chat buttons are displayed on the taskbar by default. You can use the Taskbar settings to show or hide these default buttons. **Why?** If you do not use the Search, Task view, Widgets, or Chat features regularly, you can hide their buttons to gain space on the taskbar. The following steps hide and show the default taskbar buttons.

- If necessary, scroll to display the Taskbar items area.
- Click to change the On button for the Chat app to Off (Figure 4–65).

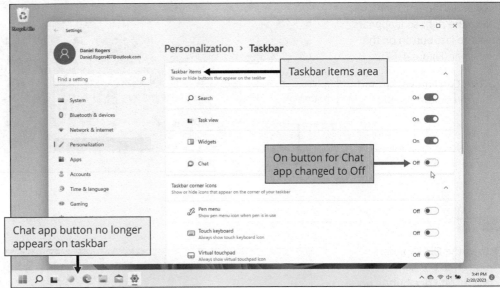

Figure 4–65

- Click the other On buttons in the Taskbar items area to change the settings to Off (Figure 4–66).

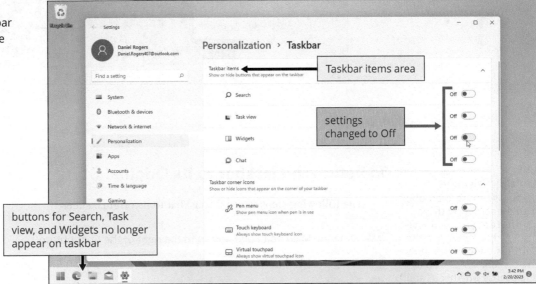

Figure 4–66

- After viewing the changes in the taskbar, click to change each Off button in the 'Taskbar items' area to On (shown in Figure 4–65).
- Exit the Settings app.

To Rearrange Taskbar Buttons

You can move the buttons on the taskbar by dragging them. **Why?** You might find it easier to access a taskbar button you use frequently if it appears in a different position. The following steps rearrange the taskbar buttons.

- Point to the Microsoft Edge button and then drag it to the right so it appears as the last button on the taskbar (Figure 4–67).

   Q&A Can I move the Start button on the taskbar? No. The Start button is always the first button on the left, even when the taskbar is centered.

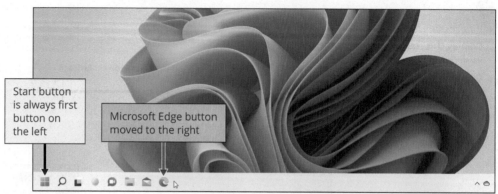

Figure 4–67

- Drag the File Explorer button to the right of the Microsoft Edge button on the taskbar (Figure 4–68).

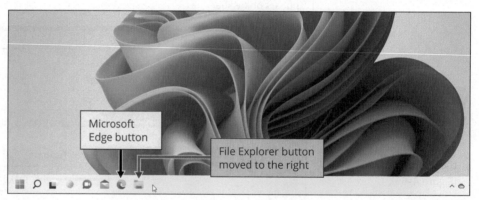

Figure 4–68

To Return the Taskbar to Its Original State

The following steps return the taskbar to its original state.

1. Drag the Microsoft Edge button to the right of the Chat button.

2. Drag the File Explorer button to the right of the Microsoft Edge button.

3. Right-click an open area of the taskbar and then click Taskbar settings on the shortcut menu to display the Taskbar settings in the Settings window.

4. Scroll down and click the Taskbar behaviors button to expand the Taskbar behaviors area.

5. Click the Taskbar alignment button and then click Center to change the alignment of the taskbar buttons.

6. Exit the Settings app.

Notification Center and Quick Settings Panel

The Notification Center is a location in Windows where you can view notifications. A **notification** is a message from either the operating system or an installed app that contains relevant information. For example, when Windows installs updates, you may receive a notification that new updates have been installed. The Notification Center also displays a scrollable monthly calendar. The Quick Settings panel consolidates settings for your computer, such as network connections and screen brightness. To display the Quick Settings panel, click a Windows icon in the notification area.

BTW
Notifications
Windows and other apps can display notifications in the Notification Center. To see more information about a notification, you can click it. You also can clear all notifications by clicking the Clear all button link in the Notification Center.

To Open the Notification Center

Why? You want to open the Notification Center to view the current notifications (if any). The following steps open the Notification Center.

- Click the date and time in the notification area on the taskbar to open the Notification Center (Figure 4–69).

Q&A Can I open the Notification Center if the Notification icon does not appear on the taskbar?
Yes. You can press WIN+N to open the Notification Center at any time.

- Click outside the Notification Center to close the Notification Center.

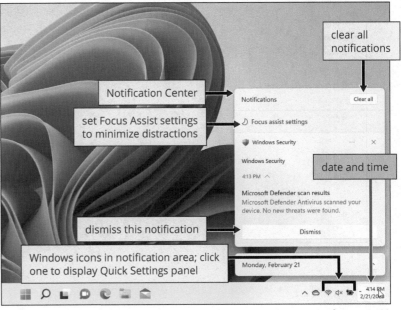

Figure 4–69

Changing Folder Options

In this module, you modified the desktop work environment by changing the desktop properties, customizing the taskbar, and viewing Start menu customization options. In addition to these changes, you also can make changes to folders, windows, and the desktop by changing folder options. Folder options allow you to specify how you open and work with icons, windows, folders, and files on the desktop.

To Display the Folder Options Dialog Box

Why? You first need to display the Folder Options dialog box so that you can view and change settings. The following step opens the This PC window and then displays the Folder Options dialog box.

- Open the File Explorer window.
- Click the See more button on the toolbar to display the See more menu (Figure 4–70).
- Click Options on the See more menu to display the Folder Options dialog box (shown in Figure 4–71).

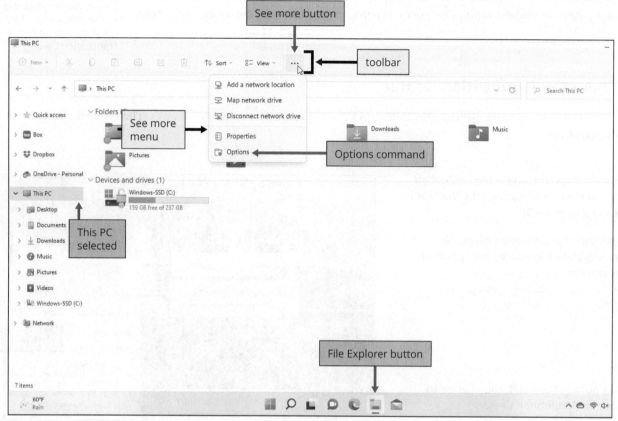

Figure 4–70

Other Ways

1. Press ALT, press RIGHT ARROW to select See more button, press DOWN ARROW to select Options command

To Select the 'Open Each Folder in Its Own Window' Option

Each time you double-click a folder icon in an open window, the new folder opens in the same window where the previously opened folder was displayed. The process of opening a folder in the same window as the previously opened folder is referred to as opening a folder in the same window, and it is the default setting in Windows 11. **Why?** Selecting the 'Open each folder in its own window' option causes each folder to open in its own window, so that you easily can view the contents of each open folder at the same time. The following step enables the 'Open each folder in its own window' option.

- Click 'Open each folder in its own window' in the Browse folders area (Folder Options dialog box) to select it (Figure 4–71).
- Click OK to apply the changes and close the Folder Options dialog box.

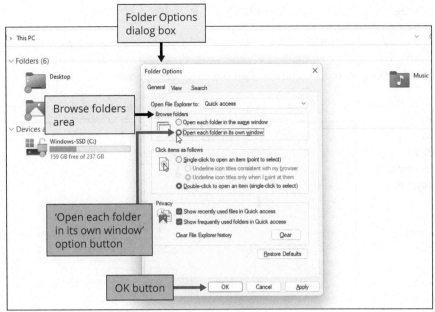

Figure 4–71

To Open a Folder in Its Own Window

Why? You want to view the result of changing the settings in the Folder Options dialog box from the previous set of steps. The following steps open the Windows-SSD (C:) folder in its own window.

1

- Double-click the Windows-SSD (C:) icon in the This PC window to display the Windows-SSD (C:) folder in its own window (Figure 4–72).

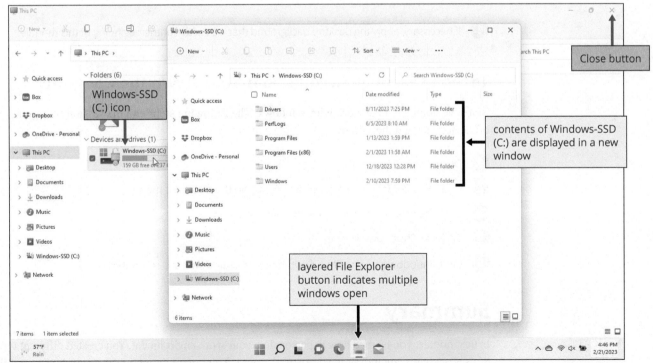

Figure 4–72

2

- Click the Close button in the Windows-SSD (C:) window to close the window.

To Restore the Folder Options to the Default Folder Options

Why? After changing one or more folder options, you can restore the default folder options you changed by manually resetting each option you changed, or you can restore all the folder options to their default options by using the Restore Defaults button. The following step restores the changed folder options to their default folder options.

- Click the See more button on the toolbar in the This PC window and then click Options on the shortcut menu to display the Folder Options dialog box.
- Click the Restore Defaults button (Folder Options dialog box) to restore the folder defaults (Figure 4–73).
- Click OK to close the Folder Options dialog box and then click the Close button to close the This PC window.

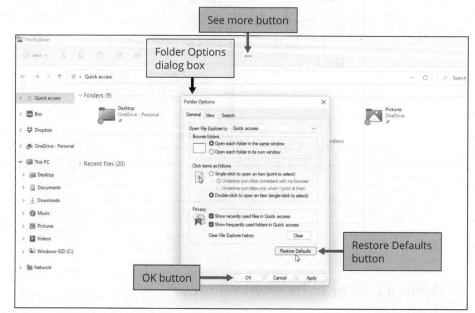

Figure 4–73

To Restore the Desktop Background

The following step restores the desktop background to the one you used at the beginning of this module.

 If necessary, apply the desktop background that was active at the beginning of this module.

To Sign Out of an Account and Shut Down the Computer

You have completed the work with Windows. The following steps end the session by signing out of the account and then shutting down the computer.

1 Display the Start menu.

2 Click the user icon and then click Sign out on the short cut menu.

3 Click the lock screen to display the sign-in screen.

4 Click the Shut down button.

5 Click Shut down on the Shut down menu to shut down the computer.

Summary

In this module, you learned how to personalize your work environment. You created different types of user accounts, including a Microsoft account. You created a picture password, changed the desktop background and accent color, and customized the lock screen. You also worked with the Task View button, managed multiple desktops, customized the taskbar, and opened the Notification Center. Finally, you viewed and adjusted folder options in the Folder Options dialog box.

Student Assignments

Apply Your Knowledge
Reinforce the skills and apply the concepts you learned in this module.

Personalizing Windows 11
Instructions: Use Personalization options in the Settings app to set the desktop background, configure Windows to automatically choose an accent color, change the lock screen background, and view additional settings.

Perform the following tasks:

1. Start the Settings app and then click the Personalization tab in the Settings window.
2. Click the Background button in the right pane (Figure 4–74) and then change the desktop background to a picture of your choosing (do not use the same picture as the one currently displayed). Describe the picture you chose.

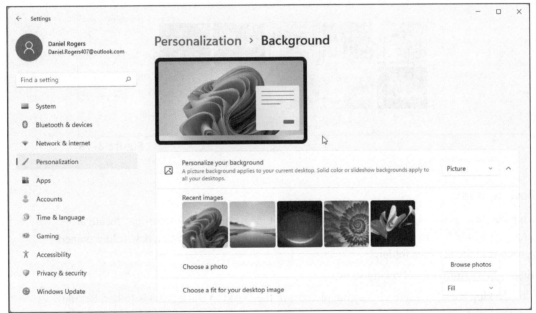

Figure 4–74

3. Click the Personalization tab in the left pane and then click the Colors button in the right pane.
4. Click the Accent color button and then click Automatic to have Windows decide the best accent color. What differences do you notice?
5. Click the Personalization tab in the left pane and then click the Lock screen button. Change the lock screen background to another picture of your choosing. Which one did you select?
6. Click the Personalization tab in the left pane, click the Themes button, and then scroll to display the available themes. What themes are available on your computer?
7. Type **change screen saver** in the 'Find a setting' box and click the 'Change screen saver' search result to display the screen saver settings. What screen savers are available on your computer?
8. Review the available screen savers. Which one do you like most? Why?
9. Change the current screen saver to Mystify and then click OK (Screen Saver Settings dialog box).
10. Close the Screen Saver Settings dialog box.
11. Exit the Settings app.

Extend Your Knowledge

Extend the skills you learned in this module and experiment with new skills. You will use the Search box to complete the assignment.

Creating Custom Themes

Instructions: Use Help if necessary to locate pictures, download them, set the desktop background, choose a screen saver, and save the settings as a new theme (Figure 4–75).

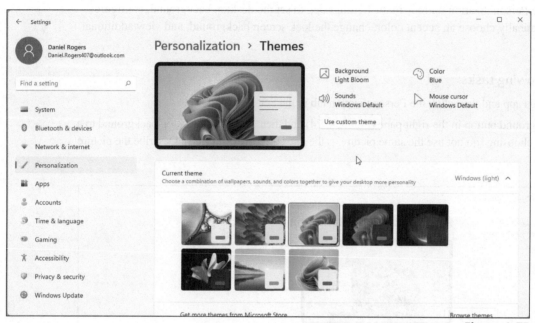

Figure 4–75

Perform the following steps:

1. Using your own pictures or pictures from the Internet that do not have copyright restrictions, locate at least five pictures you would like to use as a desktop background. Download them to a new folder named Desktop Backgrounds in the Pictures folder.

2. Using the Settings app, perform the following steps:

    a. Configure the desktop background to display the pictures in the Desktop Backgrounds folder. Set the pictures to change every 10 minutes.

    b. Configure Windows to use an accent color similar to the one in the background image. What color did you choose?

    c. Enable the setting to show the accent color on the title bars and window borders. What happened?

    d. Set the screen saver to Bubbles, and configure Windows to wait 10 minutes before starting the screen saver. Configure Windows to display the logon (sign in) screen on resume.

    e. Save the settings as a new theme and name it EYK 4-1 Theme.

3. While viewing the list of themes, click the Browse themes button to get more themes in the Store and answer the following questions:

    a. What are the names of three featured themes?

    b. Browse the available themes. Which three themes are your favorites?

    c. How can you download and use these themes?

Expand Your World

Creating and Using a Microsoft Account

Create a solution that uses cloud or web technologies by learning and investigating on your own from general guidance.

1. Click the Microsoft Edge button on the taskbar to start Microsoft Edge.

2. Navigate to the login.live.com webpage.

3. Locate and then click the link to sign up for a new Microsoft account. If you are unable to locate this link, look for a link to sign in with a different Microsoft account. Click that link and then click the link to sign up for a new Microsoft account (Figure 4–76).

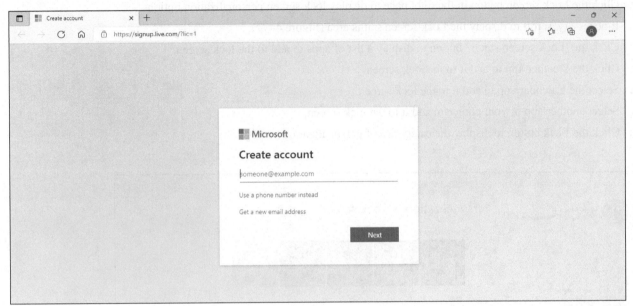

Figure 4–76

4. Complete the requested information on the Create account webpage and then click the button to create an account.

5. If necessary, create a new user account on the computer using the Microsoft account you just created.

6. Sign in to Windows with the new Microsoft account.

7. Change the desktop background to an image of your choosing.

8. Create and save a document in WordPad and then copy the file to OneDrive.

9. Sign out of the Windows account.

10. Sign in to another computer using the same Microsoft account you have just created (you may need to first add the user account to the computer), and answer the following questions:

   a. What desktop background do you see?

   b. Do you see the WordPad document that you saved on OneDrive?

   c. What happens if you delete the OneDrive document on this computer? Will it still appear on other computers?

   d. What happens to the desktop background on other computers if you change the desktop background on this computer?

In the Labs

Design and implement a solution using creative thinking and problem-solving skills.

Lab 1: Customizing Settings

Problem: You would like to customize your lock screen and add a picture password for your user account.

Perform the following steps:

1. Copy the img20 picture from the Web folder in the Windows folder to the Pictures folder. You will be using this picture as a picture password later in this exercise.
2. Start the Settings app.
3. Click the Personalization tab and then perform the following tasks:
   a. Click the Lock screen button in the right pane to display lock screen personalization options.
   b. If necessary, scroll to display the Lock screen status area (Figure 4–77).
   c. Click the 'Lock screen status' button to display a list of apps to add to the lock screen.
   d. Click the Weather app to add it to the lock screen.
   e. Select the Calendar app to add it to the lock screen.
   f. Select another app of your choice to add it to the lock screen.
   g. Click the Back button to display the categories of personalization settings.

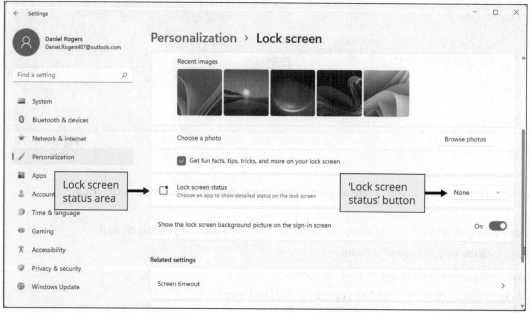

Figure 4–77

4. Click the Accounts tab in the Settings window and then perform the following tasks:
   a. Click the Sign-in options button in the right pane.
   b. Click the Picture password button and then click the Add button to create a picture password.
   c. After entering your password, click to select the img20 picture that will be used as a picture password.
   d. Use the mouse or touch gestures to add a circle, line, and a tap or click to create a picture password.

Lab 2: Customizing the Taskbar and Desktop

Problem: You want to customize the taskbar and desktop to better facilitate your working habits.

Perform the following steps.

Part 1: Customize the Taskbar

1. Right-click an open area of the taskbar to display a shortcut menu.
2. Click Taskbar settings on the shortcut menu.
3. Align the taskbar to the left side of the screen (Figure 4–78).
4. Enable the Auto-hide feature.

Figure 4–78

5. Show the taskbar corner icons for a pen menu, touch keyboard, and virtual touchpad.
6. Hide the Chat app button on the taskbar.
7. Revert all changes to their original settings.
8. Close all open windows.

Part 2: Customize the Desktop Arrangement

1. Start the Settings app, open the File Explorer window, and then start WordPad.
2. Click the Task View button on the taskbar to display Task view.
3. Add a new desktop.
4. Drag the WordPad window so that it appears on the new desktop.
5. Display the new desktop.
6. Click the Task View button on the taskbar.
7. Delete the desktop you added in Step 3. What happened to the WordPad window?

Lab 3: Consider This: Your Turn

Researching Account Types

Problem: You are working in the information technology department for a corporation. Your bosses have been wondering if they should allow users to have administrative or standard use account privileges. They want you to research this using the Internet and create a summary for them to use in making a decision.

Part 1:   Research different user account privileges. Describe the account types and then list some of the advantages and disadvantages of each. Which people would you allow to have an administrative account? Why? Which people would have a standard user account? Why? What risks are involved in giving someone an administrative account?

Part 2:   You made several decisions while performing research for this assignment. What decisions did you make? What was the rationale behind these decisions? How did you locate the required information about the different account types?

Advanced Personalization and Customization

Objectives

After completing this module, you will be able to:

- Open the Control Panel and switch views
- View system information and hardware properties
- View and configure the Windows Defender Firewall
- Defragment and optimize a hard drive
- View and adjust hardware and sound settings

- View power plan information
- Change time and region settings
- Display and adjust ease of access settings
- View privacy settings
- Display update and security settings

Introduction

Personalizing your work environment can lead to improved productivity. You can modify desktop properties by creating a new desktop theme, personalizing the taskbar, customizing folder options, and using other methods to customize Windows 11 so that you can get the most from your computer. Technology works best when it supports our lifestyles, providing the tools we need to accomplish the tasks set before us.

The Control Panel window contains categories that allow you to change the properties of an object and, thus, customize the Windows 11 environment (Figure 5–1). In addition, Control Panel provides links to other windows that contain settings, allowing you to further customize your computer. In this module, you will learn how to view and adjust system and security settings, hardware and sound settings, uninstall programs and apps, adjust time and language settings, adjust accessibility and privacy settings, and display and update security settings.

You will be able to complete some of the steps in this module only if you have an administrator account, because a user account with administrative access is capable of viewing and modifying all computer settings.

Normally, user accounts operate in standard user mode, which allows you to use most of the capabilities of the computer. A standard user cannot install software that affects other users or change system settings that affect security. An **administrator account** has full control of the computer and operating system and can change user permissions, install software that affects all users, and change system settings that affect security. When a task requires administrator access, you might be prompted to authorize the task. By default, you are asked for permission only when programs attempt to make a change to the computer. In the Control Panel window, a shield appears next to tasks requiring administrator privileges. Some of the steps in this module require administrative privileges. If you do not have administrative privileges, read the steps instead of performing them.

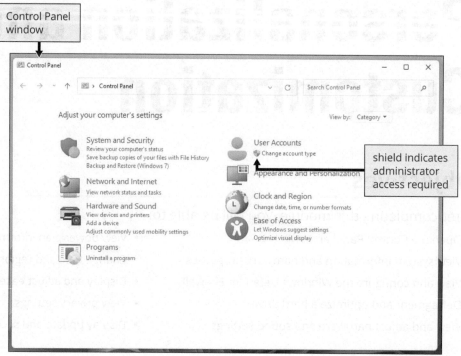

Figure 5–1

System and Security Settings

You can use the System and Security window to view security and maintenance settings, view and configure the Windows Defender Firewall, view system information, access the device manager, and defragment and optimize your hard drive. Each option provides different opportunities for you to fine-tune your computer. Be aware, however, that some of the advanced system and maintenance options require User Account Control authorization if you are not using an account with administrative privileges. User Account Control requires you to enter an administrator's user name and password before allowing the current user account temporary administrative access.

To Open the Control Panel Window

The following steps open the Control Panel window. **Why?** To access certain computer settings, you first must open the Control Panel window.

1

- Click the Search button on the taskbar and then type **control panel** in the Search box to display the search results (Figure 5–2).

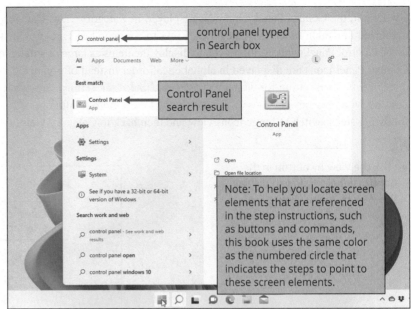

Figure 5–2

2

- Click the Control Panel search result to open the Control Panel window. If necessary, maximize the Control Panel window (Figure 5–3).

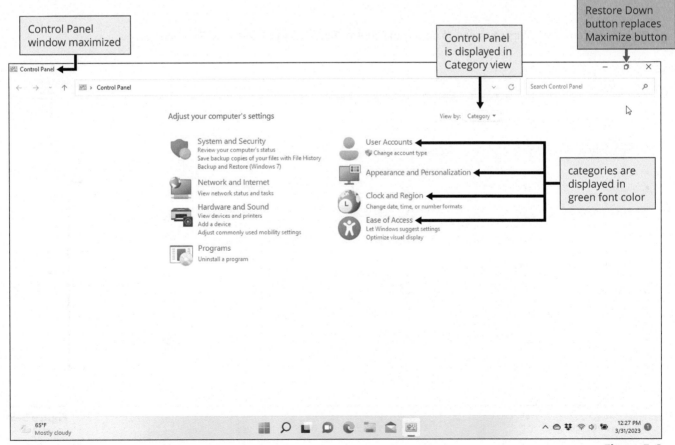

Figure 5–3

To Switch Control Panel Views

By default, the Control Panel window is displayed in Category view. Category view offers the various Control Panel options organized into eight functional categories. Links to common tasks are provided below each category name. The View by arrow in the Control Panel window allows you to display the items as large or small icons. When changed to icons, all of the individual Control Panel icons are displayed in alphabetical order instead of organized into categories. **Why?** It may be easier to locate the Control Panel setting for which you are searching if the settings are displayed alphabetically. In addition, people who are familiar with previous versions of Windows may find it more familiar to use a different view to locate a particular setting. The following steps switch to Large icons view and then back to Category view.

1

- Click the View by button in the Control Panel window to display the View by menu (Figure 5–4).

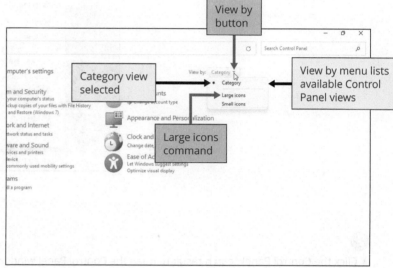

Figure 5–4

2

- Click Large icons on the View by menu to display the Control Panel in Large icons view (Figure 5–5).

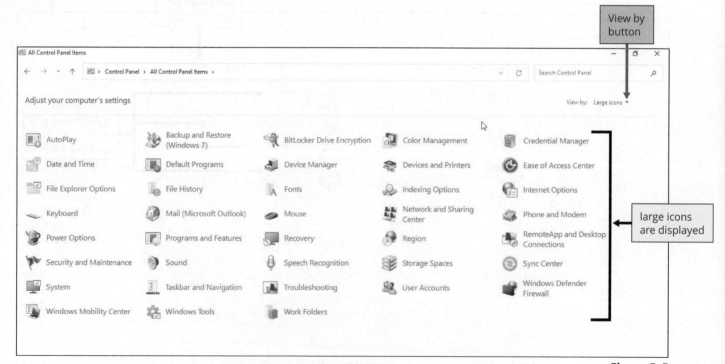

Figure 5–5

- Click the View by button in the Control Panel window to display the View by menu (shown in Figure 5–4).
- Click Category on the View by menu to return the Control Panel window to Category view (Figure 5–6).

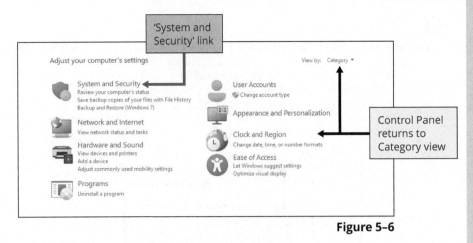

Figure 5–6

To Open the System and Security Window

The following step opens the System and Security window. **Why?** You must click the 'System and Security' link to view the system and security settings.

- Click the 'System and Security' link to open the System and Security window (Figure 5–7).

Q&A Why do my links differ from those shown in the figure?
Depending upon the configuration and the devices installed, you might see different links within the System and Security window.

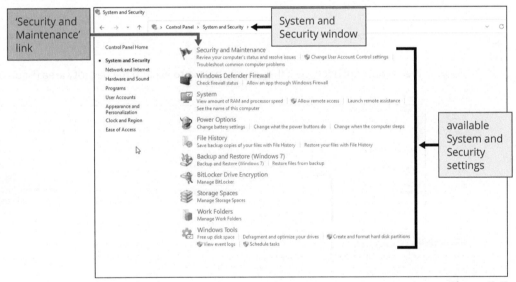

Figure 5–7

To View Security and Maintenance Settings

Why? The Security and Maintenance window allows you to view and monitor your security and maintenance settings, such as the status of your firewall or antivirus program. **The following steps display the security and maintenance settings.**

1

- Click the 'Security and Maintenance' link to view the security and maintenance settings (Figure 5–8).

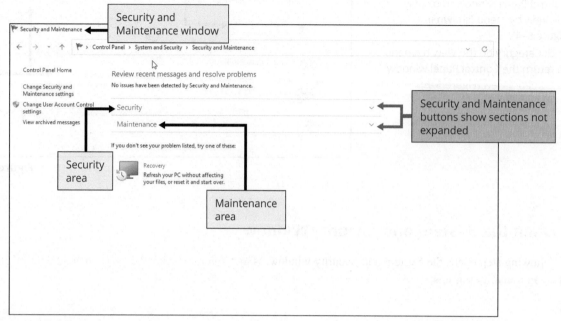

Figure 5–8

2

- If the Security area is not expanded, click the Security button to expand the Security area (Figure 5–9).

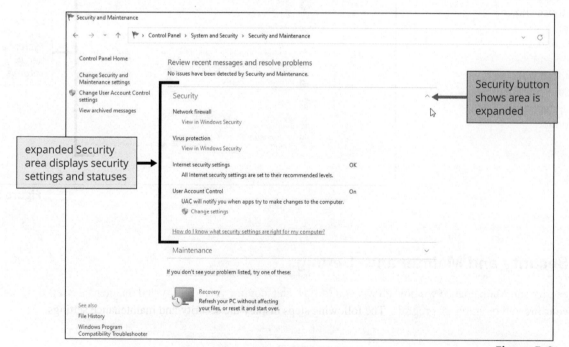

Figure 5–9

• If necessary, scroll to display the Maintenance button. Click the Maintenance button to expand the Maintenance area to view the maintenance settings (Figure 5–10).

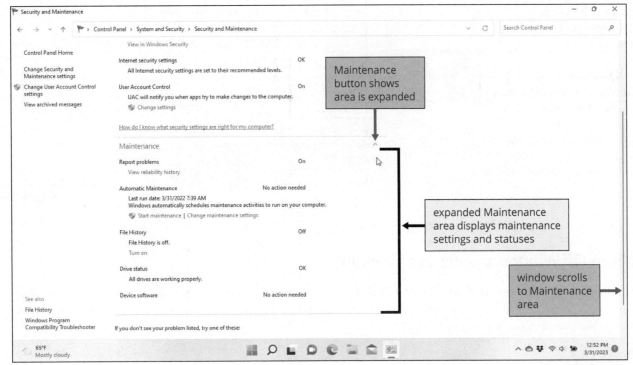

Figure 5–10

• Click the Back button to return to the System and Security window (Figure 5–11).

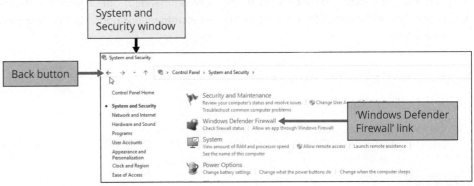

Figure 5–11

To View Windows Defender Firewall Settings

Windows Defender Firewall is a program that protects your computer from unauthorized users by monitoring and restricting information that travels between your computer and a network or the Internet. Windows Defender Firewall also helps to block malware from infecting your computer. Windows Defender Firewall automatically is turned on by default in Windows 11, and unless you have another program or app that provides a firewall, it is recommended that Windows Defender Firewall remain on. **Why?** You want to make sure that Windows Defender Firewall is protecting your computer adequately. The following step views Windows Defender Firewall settings.

1

- Click the 'Windows Defender Firewall' link (shown in Figure 5-11) to open the Windows Defender Firewall window (Figure 5-12).

Q&A Why does my Windows Defender Firewall window look different? If you have another firewall app installed on your computer, the settings in this window might differ.

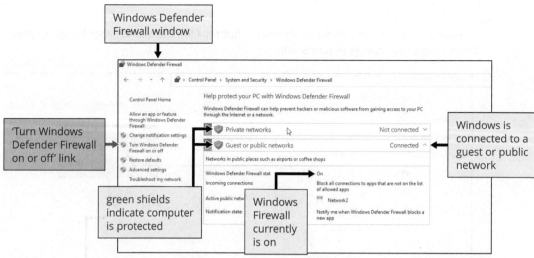

Figure 5-12

To Turn Off Windows Defender Firewall

The following steps turn off Windows Defender Firewall. **Why?** If you have another program or app that includes a firewall feature, you may need to turn off Windows Defender Firewall. It is not recommended that you connect a computer or mobile device to the Internet without an active firewall.

1

- Click the 'Turn Windows Defender Firewall on or off' link in the Windows Defender Firewall window to display the Windows Defender Firewall settings.
- Click the 'Turn off Windows Defender Firewall (not recommended)' option button in the Private network settings area.
- Click the 'Turn off Windows Defender Firewall (not recommended)' option button in the Public network settings area (Figure 5-13).

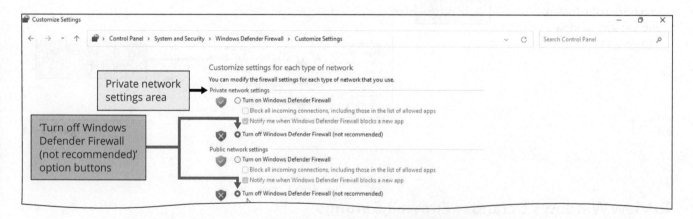

Figure 5-13

- Click OK (shown in Figure 5–13) to turn off the Windows Defender Firewall and return to the Windows Defender Firewall window (Figure 5–14).

Q&A Why does a Windows Defender Firewall notification appear?
As stated previously, it is extremely important to keep a firewall enabled. If Windows detects that no firewall is enabled, a notification will be displayed requesting that you enable Windows Defender Firewall.

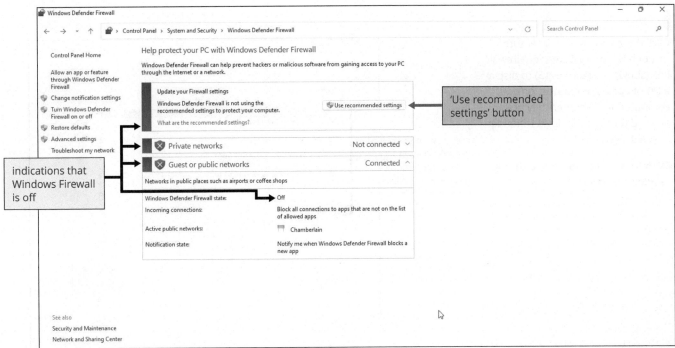

Figure 5–14

To Turn On Windows Defender Firewall

If the Windows Defender Firewall is not enabled and you want to turn it on, you can do so from the Windows Defender Firewall window. **Why?** You always should have a firewall enabled when your computer is connected to the Internet. The following step turns on Windows Defender Firewall.

- Click the 'Use recommended settings' button in the Windows Defender Firewall window (shown in Figure 5–14) to turn on Windows Defender Firewall (Figure 5–15).

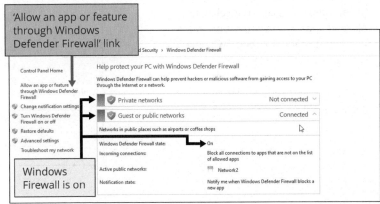

Figure 5–15

To View Allowed Apps and Features through Windows Defender Firewall

The purpose of a firewall is to block unintended communication between your computer and the Internet. Windows Defender Firewall does its best to determine what communication to allow or block, but at times, it is possible that Windows Defender Firewall is blocking communication that you want to allow. When this occurs, you can view and change the apps that Windows Defender Firewall allows to communicate using the Internet. **Why?** You have just installed a new app and want to see whether Windows Defender Firewall is allowing it to communicate using the Internet. The following steps view apps and features that are allowed to communicate through Windows Defender Firewall.

- Click the 'Allow an app or feature through Windows Defender Firewall' link (shown in Figure 5–15) to display a list of apps and features on your computer and whether they are allowed through Windows Defender Firewall (Figure 5–16).

Q&A How do I allow an app through Windows Defender Firewall?
Click the 'Allow another app' button in the Allowed apps and features list to display a dialog box where you can select the app you want to add. If the app you want to add is not listed, click the Browse button in the Add an app window to locate and select the desired app. When you have selected the app to add, click the Add button in the Add an app window. Next, scroll through the list in the Allowed apps window and select whether the app should have access through Windows Defender Firewall on private and/or public networks.

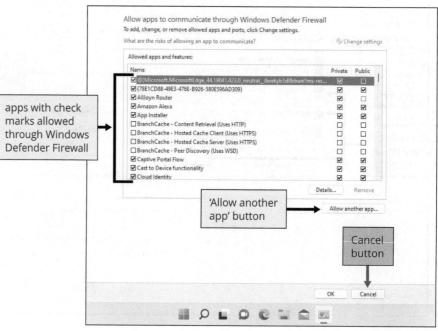

Figure 5–16

- When you have finished viewing the allowed apps, click Cancel in the Allowed apps window to return to the Windows Defender Firewall window without saving changes.
- Click the Back button to return to the System and Security window (Figure 5–17).

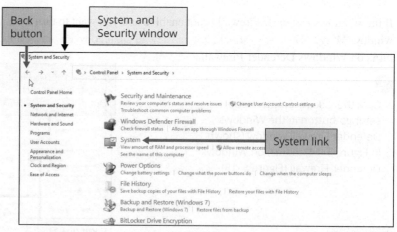

Figure 5–17

To View System Information

The System window displays summary information about your computer. You can access Device Manager, adjust remote access settings, modify system protection settings, change advanced system settings, and update Windows 11 computer or activation information using the System window. **Why?** You may need to view information about your computer so that you can determine whether it meets the system requirements for an app you want to install. The following step opens the System window.

- Click the System link (shown in Figure 5–17) to open the System window. If necessary, maximize the System window (Figure 5–18).

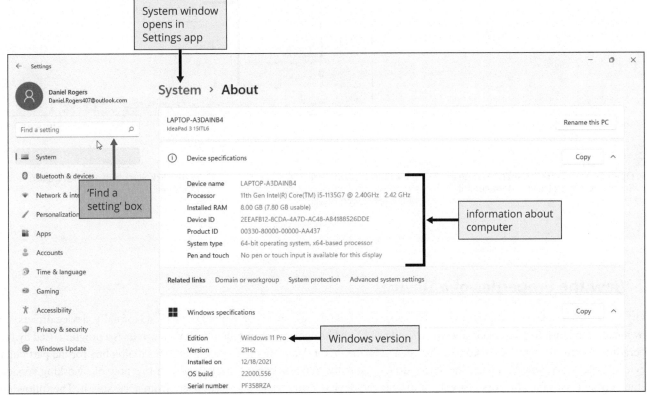

Figure 5–18

Other Ways

1. Open Control Panel window, change to Large or Small icons, click System link

2. Open This PC window, click See more button, click Properties

To Open Device Manager

Device Manager allows you to display a list of the hardware devices installed on your computer and also allows you to update device drivers, view and modify hardware settings, and troubleshoot problems. **Why?** If a device on your computer is not working, you can open Device Manager to see if the device shows up or has any problems. The following step opens the Device Manager window.

• Type **device manager** in the 'Find a setting' box (shown in Figure 5–18) and then click Device Manager in the search results to open the Device Manager window (Figure 5–19).

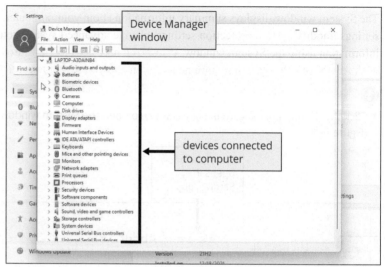

Figure 5–19

Other Ways

1. Open Control Panel, change to Large or Small icons, click Device Manager link

2. Click Start button, type **device manager** in Search box, click Device Manager search result

3. Right-click Start button, click Device Manager

To View the Properties of a Device

Why? You can use Device Manager to see the properties of the devices installed on your computer. Normally, device drivers are downloaded and installed automatically when Windows 11 and its updates are installed. A **device driver** is a program used by the operating system to control the hardware. You can view the driver details in the Device Properties dialog box for the particular device. If necessary, you can update the device driver manually. You also can roll back the driver to a previous working version if the current driver fails to work properly or disable the device if you want to prevent users from accessing it. The following steps display the properties and driver information for the keyboard.

• Click the arrow next to Keyboards to expand the list of installed keyboards (Figure 5–20).

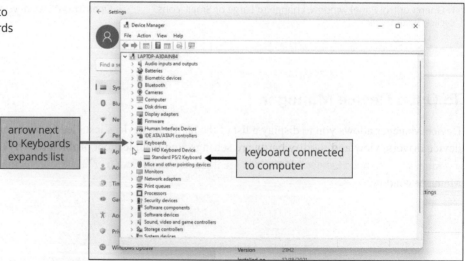

Figure 5–20

- Double-click a keyboard entry to display the Keyboard Properties dialog box (Figure 5–21).

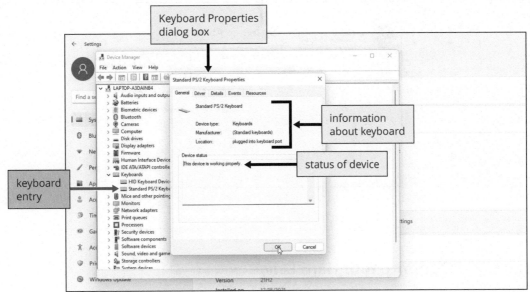

Figure 5–21

- Click the Driver tab (Keyboard Properties dialog box) to display the Driver sheet (Figure 5–22).
- After viewing the driver information, click OK to close the Keyboard Properties dialog box.

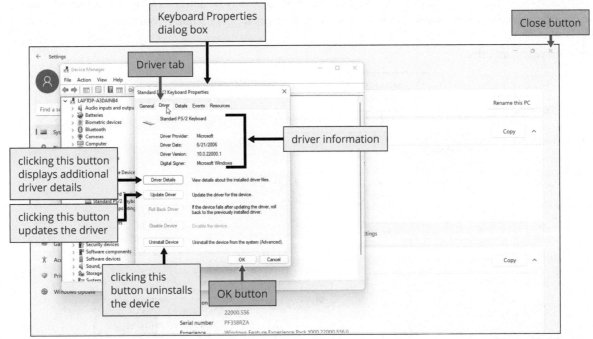

Figure 5–22

4

- Close the Device Manager window and return to the System window (Figure 5–23).

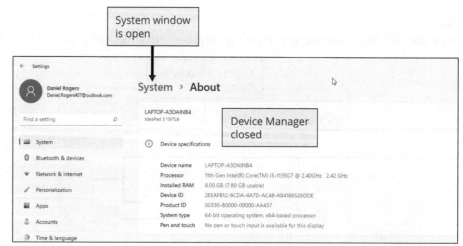

Figure 5–23

To Defragment and Optimize Your Hard Drive

Defragmenting and optimizing your hard drive will help it run more efficiently so that you can access your files more quickly. When you add files on a hard drive, Windows does not always store all the information for the file contiguously. That is, portions of the files may be stored on one location of the hard drive, while the remaining portions are stored elsewhere. As a result, it might take your computer longer to access files that are fragmented in this fashion. Defragmenting and optimizing your hard drive in Windows 11 will move files so that they all are stored contiguously, thus defragmenting your hard drive. While it is recommended you defragment and optimize the hard drive periodically, some experts argue that defragmenting a solid state drive (SSD) will shorten the life of the drive. SSDs are much faster than traditional (magnetic) hard drives, so you might not even recognize the benefits of defragmenting. Windows automatically may be defragmenting and optimizing your hard drive on a regular basis, such as every week, but you always can defragment and optimize your hard drive manually. **Why?** You want to defragment and optimize your hard drive so that you can access files more quickly. The following steps defragment and optimize your hard drive.

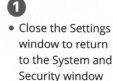

- Close the Settings window to return to the System and Security window (Figure 5–24).

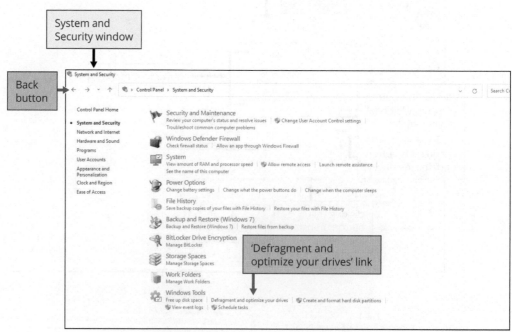

Figure 5–24

2

- Click the 'Defragment and optimize your drives' link to open the Optimize Drives window.
- If necessary, click to select the hard drive you want to optimize and defragment (Figure 5–25).

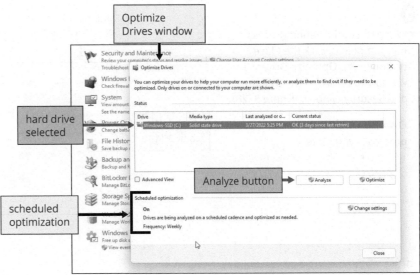

Figure 5–25

3

- Click the Analyze button to analyze the selected drive and determine whether it needs to be defragmented. Depending on the size and condition of the drive, it might take several minutes or longer to analyze. If the User Account Control dialog box is displayed, click the Yes button (Figure 5–26).

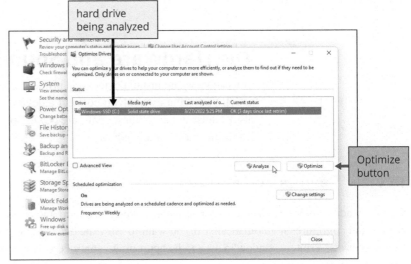

Figure 5–26

4

- Click the Optimize button (shown in Figure 5–26) to optimize and defragment the drive. This process might take several minutes or longer to complete, depending on the size and condition of the drive (Figure 5–27).

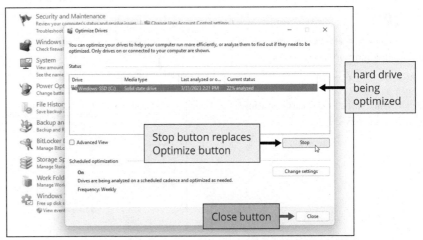

Figure 5–27

• When the optimization process has completed, click the Close button in the Optimize Drives window to return to the System and Security window (Figure 5–28).

Q&A How will I know when the process is complete?
The current status for the drive will display, OK.

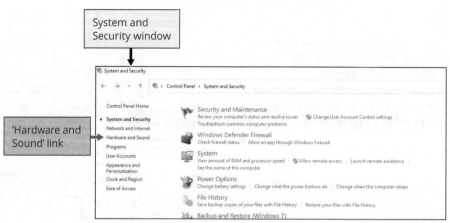

Figure 5–28

Other Ways

1. Click Start button, type **optimize** in Search box, click 'Defragment and Optimize Drives' in search results

---

The Hardware and Sound Window

You can view and install devices and printers, configure AutoPlay (**AutoPlay** refers to the default action that occurs when you connect a device, such as a USB flash drive, or insert an optical disc), adjust sound settings, configure power options, change display settings, and more, from the Hardware and Sound window.

To View Devices and Printers

When you add a device, such as a printer, scanner, camera, keyboard, mouse, or any other hardware device, Windows 11 usually installs and configures it automatically. If you want to view the devices and printers connected to your computer, you can use the Devices and Printers window to access the appropriate controls. If you connect a device or printer to your computer and it does not work, you can open the Devices and Printers window to see if Windows recognizes it. If Windows does not recognize it, you might need to install the device drivers for the device or printer. Device drivers are available either on a disc that comes with the device or printer or on the manufacturer's website. The following steps view installed devices and printers. **Why?** You have connected a device to your computer and want to see if Windows recognizes it.

• Click the 'Hardware and Sound' link (shown in Figure 5–28) in the System and Security Window to open the Hardware and Sound window (Figure 5–29).

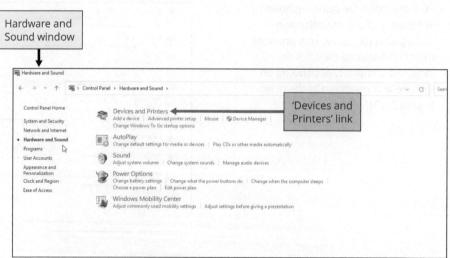

Figure 5–29

2

- Click the 'Devices and Printers' link (shown in Figure 5–29) to open the Devices and Printers window (Figure 5–30).

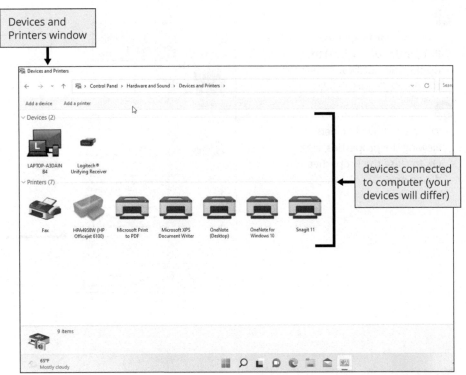

Figure 5–30

3

- Double-click a device in the Devices and Printers window to view the General sheet in the Properties dialog box for that device (Figure 5–31).

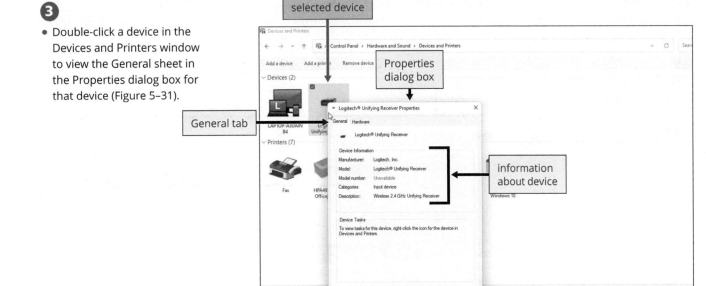

Figure 5–31

4

- Click the Hardware tab (Properties dialog box) to display the Hardware sheet for the device (Figure 5–32).

5

- When you have finished viewing the properties, click OK to close the Properties dialog box.

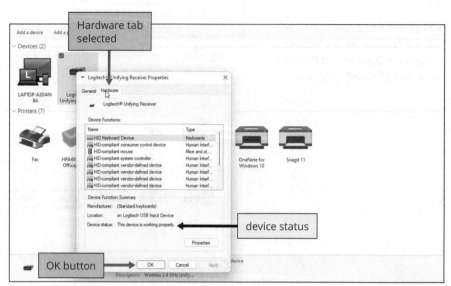

Figure 5–32

To Adjust AutoPlay Settings

Windows 11 allows you to customize the AutoPlay features for your computer. As mentioned previously, AutoPlay refers to the default action that occurs when media and devices are connected to your computer. Once set, the new action will be used the next time you insert the media or device. The following steps configure AutoPlay settings to open content on removable devices automatically when they are connected to the computer. **Why?** When you connect a removable device, you typically want to browse the files on the device. Configuring AutoPlay settings will display the removable device contents automatically so that you do not have to perform an extra step to view them.

1

- Click the Back button to display the Hardware and Sound window (Figure 5–33).

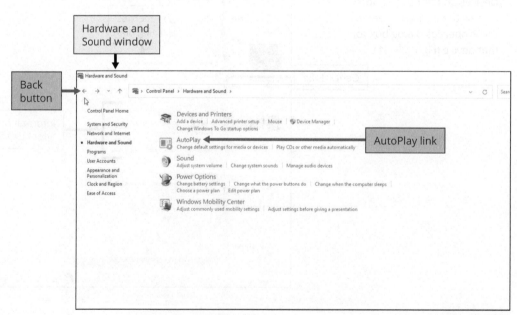

Figure 5–33

2

- Click the AutoPlay link to display the current AutoPlay settings in the AutoPlay window (Figure 5–34).

AutoPlay window

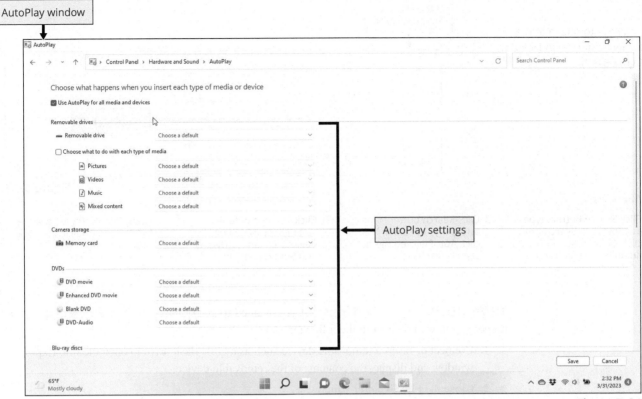

AutoPlay settings

Figure 5–34

3

- Click the Removable drive button to display a list of default options for removable devices (Figure 5–35).

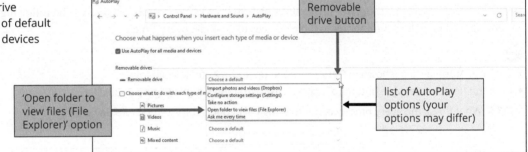

'Open folder to view files (File Explorer)' option

Removable drive button

list of AutoPlay options (your options may differ)

Figure 5–35

4

- Click 'Open folder to view files (File Explorer)' to configure Windows to open the contents of removable devices in File Explorer when they are connected to the computer (Figure 5–36).

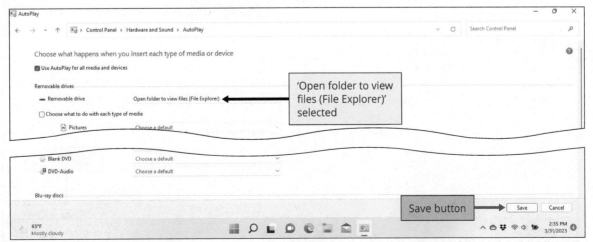

'Open folder to view files (File Explorer)' selected

Save button

Figure 5–36

5

- Click Save to return to the Hardware and Sound window (Figure 5–37).

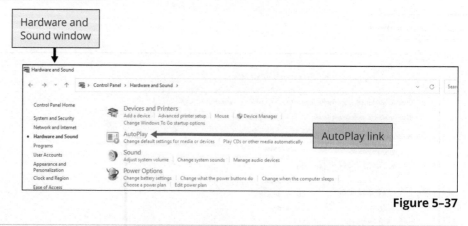

Figure 5–37

Other Ways

1. Click Search button, type **autoplay** in Search box, click 'Choose AutoPlay defaults' in search results	2. Click Search button, type **autoplay** in Search box, click AutoPlay settings in search results	3. Click 'Change default settings for media or devices' link in Hardware and Sound window	4. Open Control Panel, change to Large or Small icons, click AutoPlay link

To Verify AutoPlay Settings   If you wanted to verify that your AutoPlay settings work properly, you would perform the following steps.

1. Connect or insert a removable device such as a USB flash drive to open the File Explorer window and display the contents of the removable device.

2. Close the File Explorer window.

To Revert an AutoPlay Setting

Why? You want to change the AutoPlay settings back to how you originally had them. The following steps open the AutoPlay window and change the action for removable devices to 'Ask me every time'.

- Click the AutoPlay link (shown in Figure 5–37) to open the AutoPlay window.
- Click the Removable drive button to display a list of default actions (Figure 5–38).

Q&A What if 'Ask me every time' was not the original action set for removable devices?
Click the action that was selected before you changed the action.

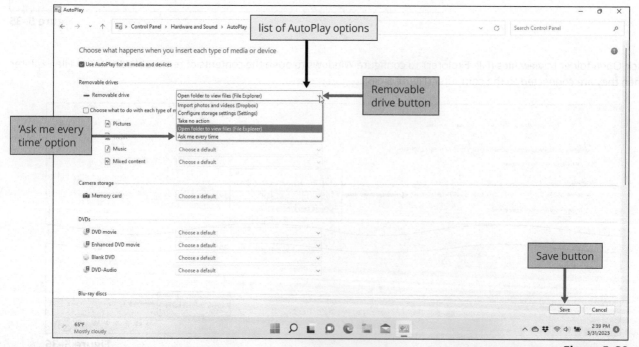

Figure 5–38

2

- Click 'Ask me every time' to configure Windows to ask you each time what you want to do when you insert or connect a removable device.
- Click the Save button in the AutoPlay window (shown in Figure 5–38) to save the AutoPlay settings and return to the Hardware and Sound window (Figure 5–39).

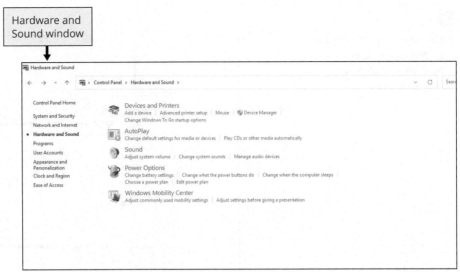

Figure 5–39

Other Ways

1. Click Search button, type **autoplay** in Search box, click 'Choose AutoPlay defaults' in search results	2. Click Search button, type **autoplay** in Search box, click AutoPlay settings in search results	3. Click 'Change default settings for media or devices' link in Hardware and Sound window	4. Open Control Panel, change to Large or Small icons, click AutoPlay link

To View Sound Settings

The sound settings in Windows 11 allow you to adjust speaker volume, change the sounds that play when certain events occur, and manage the devices on your computer that record and play sounds. The following steps view sound settings. **Why?** You would like to see the devices that are configured to play audio and see the sounds that play when certain events occur on your computer.

1

- Click the Sound link to display the Sound dialog box.
- Click the default playback device (Figure 5–40).

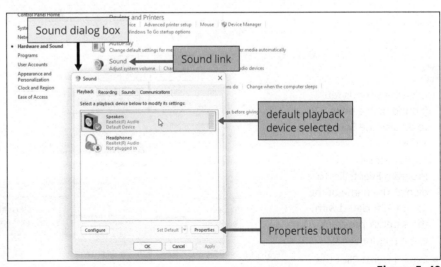

Figure 5–40

- Click the Properties button
to display the Speakers
Properties dialog box
(Figure 5–41).

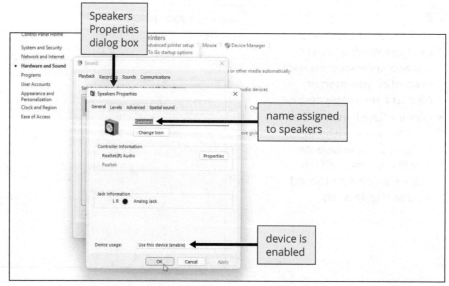

Figure 5–41

- Click the Levels tab
(Speakers Properties dialog
box) to display the Levels
sheet, which includes slid-
ers you can drag to adjust
the volume for the audio
devices on your computer
(Figure 5–42).
- Click Cancel to close
the Speakers Properties
dialog box without saving
changes.

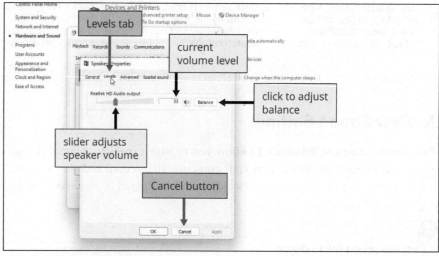

Figure 5–42

- Click the Sounds tab
(Sound dialog box)
to display the Sound
sheet.
- Click Asterisk in the
Program Events list to
display the name of the
sound associated with
the Asterisk program
event (Figure 5–43).
- **Experiment:** Click the
other program events
in the list to view their
associated sounds.

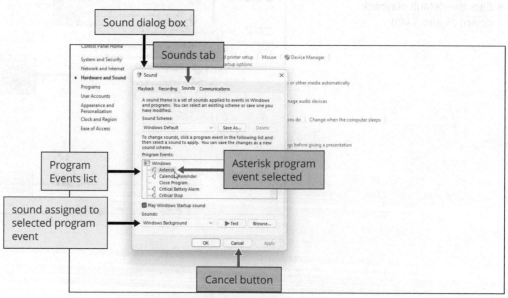

Figure 5–43

5

- Click Cancel (Sound dialog box) to close the Sound dialog box without saving changes (Figure 5–44).

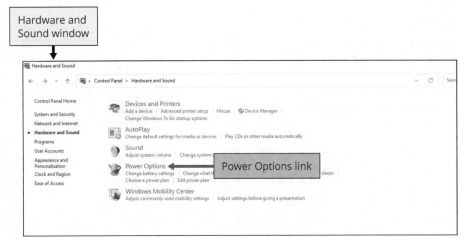

Figure 5–44

Other Ways

1. Click Search button, type **sound** in Search box, click Sound settings in search results

2. Open Control Panel, change to Large or Small icons, click Sound link

To View Power Plan Information

You can adjust power options in Windows 11 to help conserve energy when your computer is not being used. When you customize a power plan, you can determine how the computer should conserve energy when it is plugged in or running on a battery (if you are using a mobile device, such as a laptop or tablet). One way you can conserve energy is by configuring Windows to turn off the computer's display after a set period of time. Another way you can conserve energy is by putting the computer to sleep (a low-powered state) after a specified period of time. The following steps view power plan information. **Why?** You think it is important to conserve energy and want to make sure your computer is configured to use minimal energy when it is not in use.

1

- Click the Power Options link in the Hardware and Sound window to open the Power Options window (Figure 5–45).

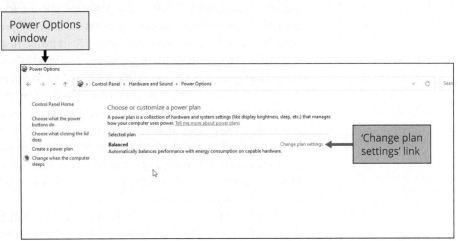

Figure 5–45

2

- Click the 'Change plan settings' link next to the Balanced power plan to view the settings for the Balanced power plan in the Edit Plan Settings window (Figure 5–46).

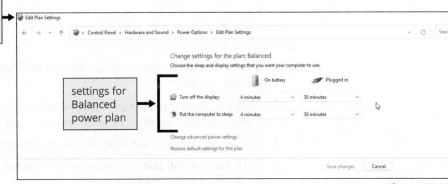

Figure 5–46

- Click the 'Turn off the display' button in the On battery list (if necessary) to view a list of options for when the computer should turn off the display (Figure 5–47).

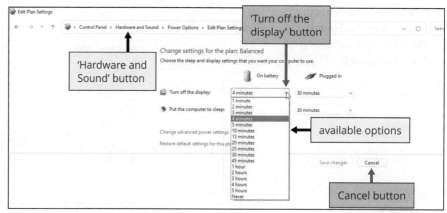

Figure 5–47

- Click outside the list to close it.
- Click Cancel to return to the Power Options window without saving changes.

Programs and Apps

The Programs window in the Control Panel brings together all of the tools you need when working with the various programs and apps on your computer. From the Programs window, you can uninstall programs and apps, as well as turn a variety of Windows features on and off, view installed updates, run programs made for previous versions of Windows, and view and change default programs.

Some programs and apps include uninstall options as a part of their installation. For example, some programs and apps, when installed, add a folder to the Start menu, which includes an uninstall command that you can use to run the uninstall program. Other programs and apps do not offer an uninstall option or a folder on the Start menu. Instead, a command is available during the installation process to uninstall the software. You also can uninstall many programs and apps by right-clicking the program or app name on the Start menu and then clicking the Uninstall command on the shortcut menu. Other programs and apps must be removed by deleting the files that compose the program or app. Although you can remove programs and apps by dragging the program's or app's folder to the Recycle Bin, it is recommended that you uninstall the program or app using the Programs and Features window. This ensures that the program or app is completely removed from the system without leaving any extraneous files to potentially interfere with the normal processes of the computer. Most of the programs and apps you install can be uninstalled from the Programs and Features window, as well.

When installing or uninstalling programs, you will be required to provide the proper User Account Control authorization. If you are not using an account with administrator privileges or do not have the user name and password of an administrator account, you will be unable to install or uninstall a program or app.

To Uninstall a Program or App   If you wanted to uninstall a program or app, you would perform the following steps.

1. Click the Programs link in the left pane of the System and Security window to open the Programs window.
2. Click the 'Programs and Features' link to display the Programs and Features window, which contains a list of all installed programs and features.
3. If necessary, scroll to and then click the desired program or app to uninstall.
4. Click the Uninstall button to uninstall the selected program or app. If necessary, follow the remaining on-screen instructions.

To View Programs Associated with File Types

When you double-click a file to open it, Windows starts the default program or app associated with the type of file you double-clicked. For example, if you double-click a file that has a .docx file name extension, Windows might open that file using Microsoft Word. If you double-click a file with a .pdf file name extension, Windows might open that file using Adobe Acrobat. The following steps view programs associated with file types. **Why?** If you have multiple programs and apps on your computer that are capable of opening the same type of file, you can see which program or app is designated as the default program for that file type. If necessary, you can change the default program associated with that file type.

1

- Click the 'Hardware and Sound' button on the address bar (shown in Figure 5–47) to return to the Hardware and Sound window.
- Click the Programs link in the left pane to open the Programs window (Figure 5–48).

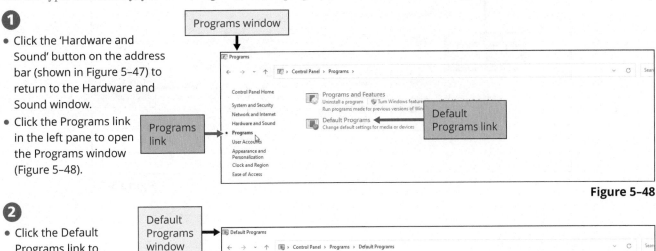

Figure 5–48

2

- Click the Default Programs link to open the Default Programs window (Figure 5–49).

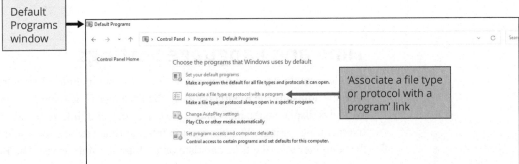

Figure 5–49

3

- Click the 'Associate a file type or protocol with a program' link to display a list of file types and their current default programs in the Settings window (Figure 5–50).

Q&A How can I change a default program?
Click the default app you wish to change and then select the desired app to open the respective file type.

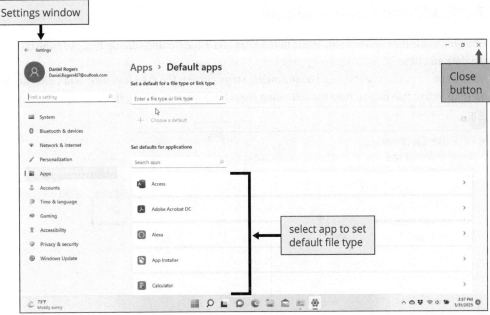

Figure 5–50

4
- Click the Close button in the Settings window to return to the Default Programs window.
- Click the Control Panel button on the address bar to return to the Control Panel (Figure 5–51).

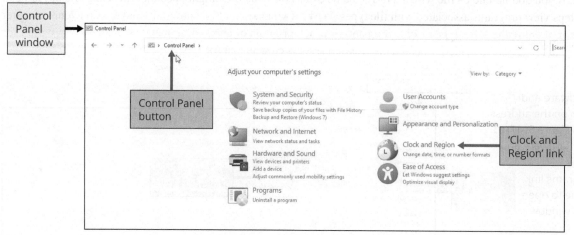

Control Panel window

Control Panel button

'Clock and Region' link

Figure 5–51

Time and Language Settings

The Clock and Region window in the Control Panel includes the controls for setting the date and time and adjusting the Region options. The Date and Time dialog box is where you can change the Windows display language; change the date, time, and time zone; add additional clocks; and alter Internet time settings. You can use the Internet time settings to synchronize the time and date on the computer with the time and date on an Internet time server. The Region dialog box is where you can change and customize date formats.

To Change the Date and Time

Changes to the date and time are made in the Date and Time Settings dialog box. Administrative privileges are required to change the date and time. **Why?** You do not think the time on your computer is accurate, so you want to change it so that it displays the same time as your smartphone. The following steps change the date and time and then cancel the changes. If you do not have administrative privileges, read the following steps without performing them.

1
- Click the 'Clock and Region' link in the Control Panel window (shown in Figure 5–51) to open the Clock and Region window (Figure 5–52).

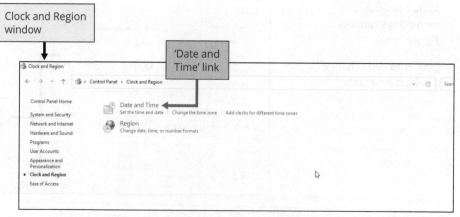

Clock and Region window

'Date and Time' link

Figure 5–52

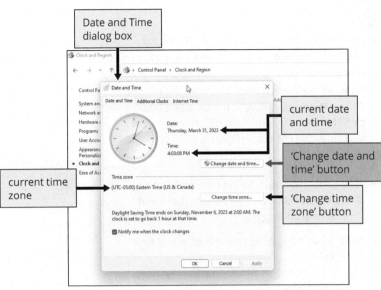

- Click the 'Date and Time' link to display the Date and Time dialog box (Figure 5–53).

Q&A Do I need to manually adjust the clock for daylight savings time?
No. Windows automatically changes the time for daylight savings time.

Should I change the time or the time zone if I travel?
If you travel to a different time zone, you can use the 'Change time zone' button (Date and Time dialog box) to update the day and time on your computer so that the clock displays the correct time, or you can configure an additional clock to display the time and date of your destination.

Figure 5–53

- Click the 'Change date and time' button (Date and Time dialog box) to display the Date and Time Settings dialog box (Figure 5–54).

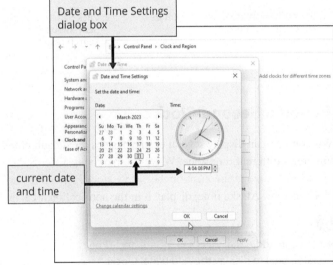

Figure 5–54

- Click the right month arrow until the month changes to November. If November already is the current month, you do not need to click the right arrow.
- Click the number 7 in the monthly calendar to select November 7 (Figure 5–55).

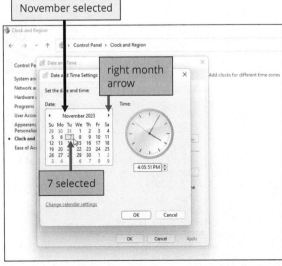

Figure 5–55

5

- Double-click the hour value in the Time text box and then type **1** as the new value to change the hour.
- Type **45** as the new value to change the minute.
- If the AM entry displays in the time text box, click the AM entry and then click the up arrow to display the PM entry (Figure 5–56).

6

- Click Cancel to return to the Date and Time dialog box without saving changes (Date and Time Settings dialog box).

Q&A What if I want to save the date and time changes?

If you want to save the date and time changes, you should click OK instead of Cancel.

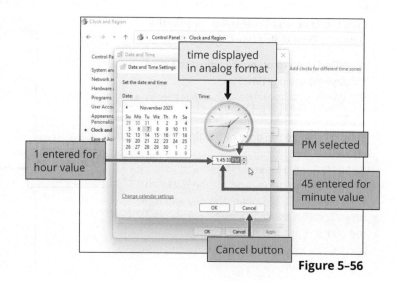

Figure 5–56

Other Ways

1. In notification area, right-click time, click 'Adjust date/time'
2. Click Search button, type **date** in Search box, click 'Date & time settings' search result
3. Open Control Panel, change to Large or Small icons, click 'Date and Time' link

To Add a Second Clock

Windows 11 can display several clocks besides the default clock in the notification area. Each clock that you add can show the time for a different time zone. **Why?** International students, business travelers, and tourists might find it useful to have a clock to show the time in the location they are visiting, as well as the time in their home location. The following steps add a second clock to show Alaska time, display it in the notification area, and then delete it.

1

- Click the Additional Clocks tab (Date and Time dialog box) to display the Additional Clocks sheet (Figure 5–57).

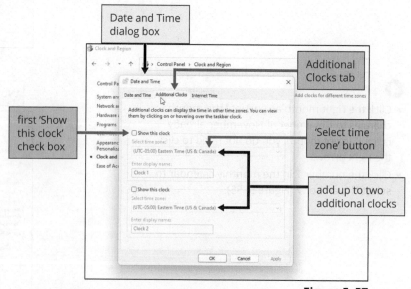

Figure 5–57

- Click the first 'Show this clock' check box to select it.
- Click the 'Select time zone' button (shown in Figure 5–57) to display a list of time zones.
- If necessary, scroll until you see Alaska in the list (Figure 5–58).

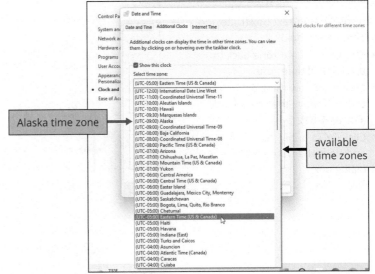

Figure 5–58

- Click the Alaska list item to select it. If your time zone already is set for Alaska, select another time zone.
- Type **Alaska** in the 'Enter display name' text box to name the clock (Figure 5–59).

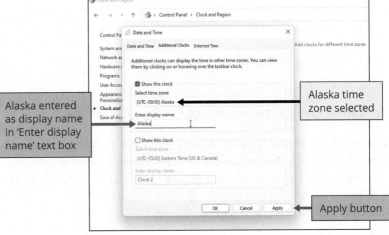

Figure 5–59

4

- Click the Apply button to apply the changes.
- Point to the clock on the taskbar to display the additional clock (Figure 5–60).

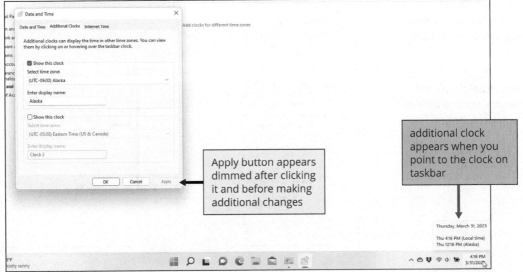

Figure 5–60

5

- Type **Clock 1** in the 'Enter display name' text box (Date and Time dialog box).
- Change the time zone back to the original time zone.
- Click the 'Show this clock' check box to remove the check mark (Figure 5–61).
- Click OK to apply the changes and close the Date and Time dialog box.

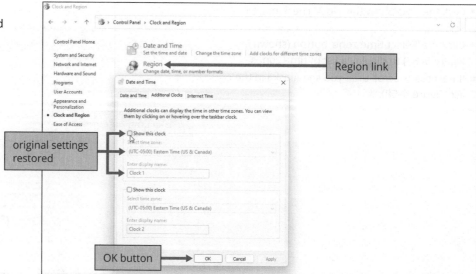

Figure 5–61

Other Ways

1. In notification area, right-click time, click 'Adjust date and time' on shortcut menu, click Additional clocks

2. Click Search button, type **date** in Search box, click 'Change the date and time' search result, click Additional clocks

3. Open Control Panel window, change to Large or Small icons, click 'Date and Time' link, click Additional Clocks tab (Date & Time dialog box)

To View the Date Formats

Windows 11 is designed to work in many regions of the world and in many different languages. Countries often have different conventions for displaying dates and time. For example, many countries in Europe use the 24-hour clock when displaying time. You can use the Region dialog box to view the formats that Windows 11 uses to display dates. **Why?** If you are planning to visit other countries, you can change the date formats so that they will match the formats used by the countries you visit. The following step displays the Region dialog box.

1

- Click the Region link in the Clock and Region window (shown in Figure 5–61) to display the Region dialog box (Figure 5–62).
- After viewing the date formats, click Cancel to close the dialog box.
- **Experiment:** Try changing the current format selection and review the various date formats used by other countries.

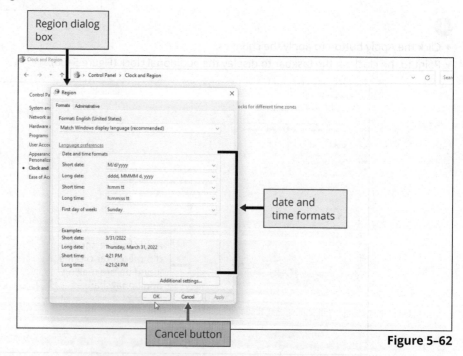

Figure 5–62

Other Ways

1. Click Search button, type **region** in Search box, click Region settings search result

2. Open Control Panel, change to Large or Small icons, click Region link

Ease of Access Settings

Windows 11 provides specialized customization tools, which are known as **accessibility features**, for people with specific mobility, hearing, or vision impairments. All of the accessibility features can be found in the Ease of Access Center. People who have restricted movement and cannot move the mouse have the option of using Mouse Keys that allow them to use the numeric keypad to move the pointer, click, double-click, and drag. People who are Deaf or hard-of-hearing can enable Sound Sentry, which generates visual warnings when the computer makes a sound and can turn on captions when a program speaks or makes sounds, if captions are available. People who are blind or have difficulty seeing the screen can select a High Contrast theme. High Contrast themes rely on a black or white background and bold colors to create a greater contrast between objects on the screen, which improves an individual's ability to read the text. Windows 11 also offers Narrator, which translates text to speech, and Magnifier, which creates a separate window to display a magnified part of the screen.

These are just a few of the accessibility features that are available in Windows 11. From the Ease of Access Center, you also can access a questionnaire that allows Windows to determine the right accessibility features for you. If you are unsure of where to begin, start with the questionnaire. The following section demonstrates some of the accessibility features.

To Display the Ease of Access Center

Why? The Ease of Access Center provides access to Windows 11 accessibility settings. **The following steps display the Ease of Access Center.**

1

- Click the Control Panel button in the address bar to open the Control Panel window (Figure 5–63).

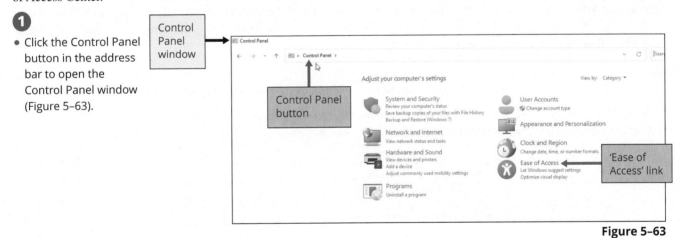

Figure 5–63

2

- Click the 'Ease of Access' link in the Control Panel window to open the Ease of Access window (Figure 5–64).

Figure 5–64

- Click the 'Ease of Access Center' link in the Ease of Access window to open the Ease of Access Center window (Figure 5-65).

Q&A What do I hear when I open the Ease of Access Center window?

To help those who are visually impaired when they first open the Ease of Access Center window, Windows 11 reads aloud the content on the screen.

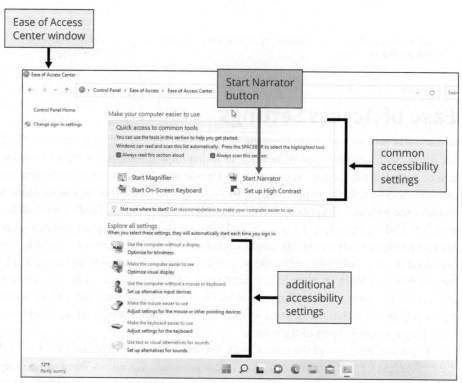

Figure 5-65

To Enable and Configure Narrator

Narrator is an accessibility feature in Windows 11 that reads aloud the content that displays on the screen. While Narrator is reading aloud the screen content, a blue outline surrounds the portion of the screen that currently is being read. **Why?** If you are visually impaired and need help knowing what currently is being displayed on the screen, Narrator can read the content to you. The following steps enable and configure Narrator.

- Click the Start Narrator button in the Ease of Access Center window to start Narrator (Figure 5-66).

Q&A The Narrator dialog box appeared when I clicked the Start Narrator button. What should I do?

Read the information in the Narrator dialog box and then click OK.

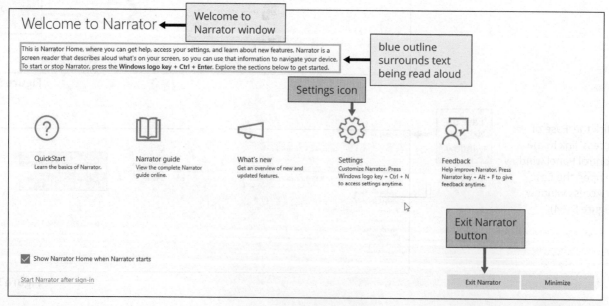

Figure 5-66

- Click the Settings icon to open the Narrator Settings window (Figure 5–67).

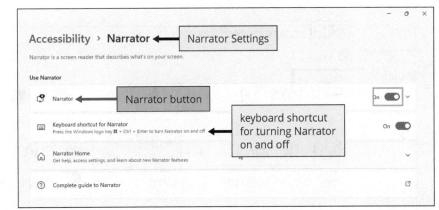

Figure 5–67

- Click the Narrator button in the Narrator Settings window to view the settings for starting Narrator (Figure 5–68).

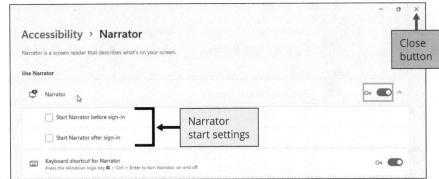

Figure 5–68

- Click the Close button to return to the Welcome to Narrator window (shown in Figure 5–66).
- Click the Exit Narrator button (shown in Figure 5–66) to exit Narrator.

To Enable and Configure Magnifier

Magnifier increases the size of all objects on the screen so that visually impaired individuals can see the content on the screen more easily. When Magnifier is enabled, the entire contents of the desktop cannot fit on the screen at one time; it is necessary to scroll horizontally and vertically to see areas of the desktop that are not displayed currently. **Why?** Magnifier helps individuals who require larger objects on the screen. The following steps enable and configure Magnifier.

- Click the Start Magnifier button in the Ease of Access Center window to start the Magnifier and increase the size of everything on the screen (Figure 5–69).

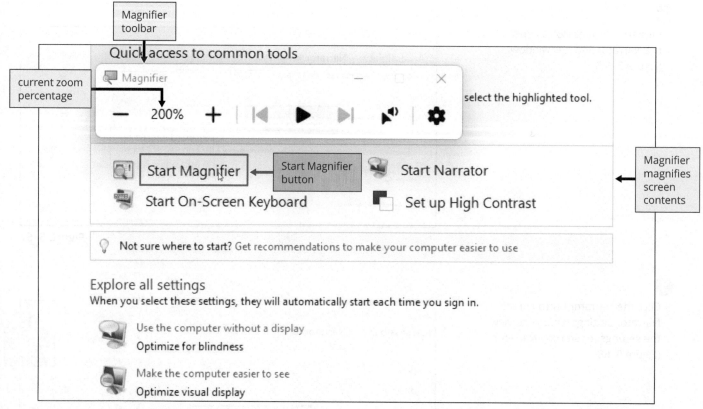

Figure 5–69

2

• Move the pointer around the screen to see different portions of the screen (Figure 5–70).

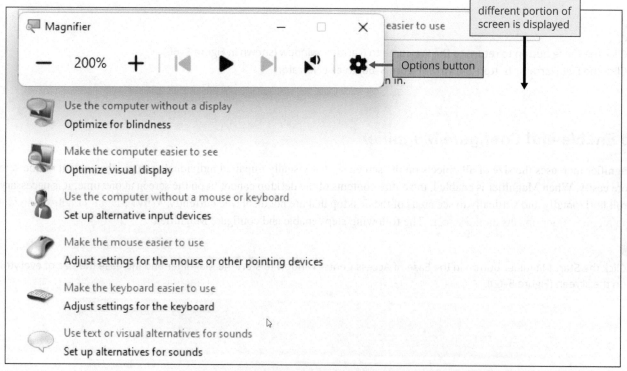

Figure 5–70

● Click the Options button on the Magnifier toolbar to display the Magnifier options in the Settings app (Figure 5–71).

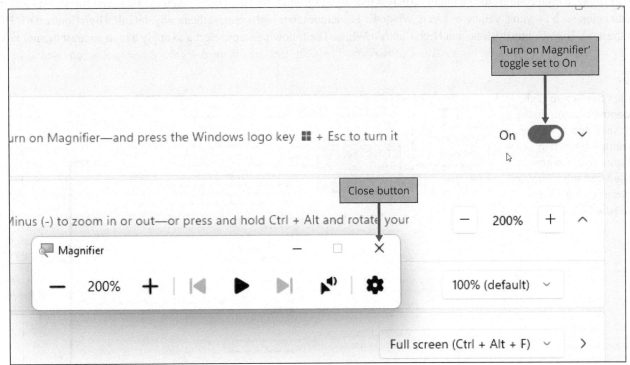

Figure 5–71

● Click the Close button on the Magnifier toolbar to close Magnifier (Figure 5–72).

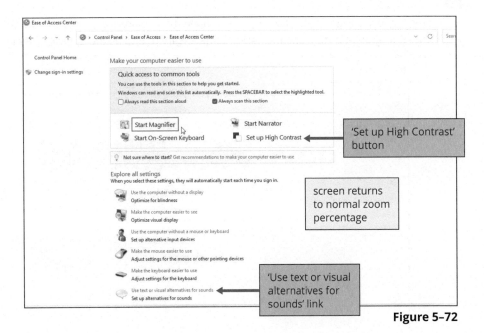

Figure 5–72

To Select and Apply a High Contrast Theme

High contrast themes help individuals who are visually impaired by providing greater contrast between objects on the screen. For example, a high contrast theme might display window backgrounds in a dark color, such as black, and foreground text in a bright color, such as white, yellow, or green. Windows 11 includes four high contrast themes by default: High Contrast #1, High Contrast #2, High Contrast Black, and High Contrast White. The following steps select and apply a high contrast theme. **Why?** Using a high contrast theme makes it easier to differentiate between elements in the foreground and background on the screen.

- Click the 'Set up High Contrast' button in the Ease of Access Center window (shown in Figure 5–72) to open the Make the computer easier to see window (Figure 5–73).

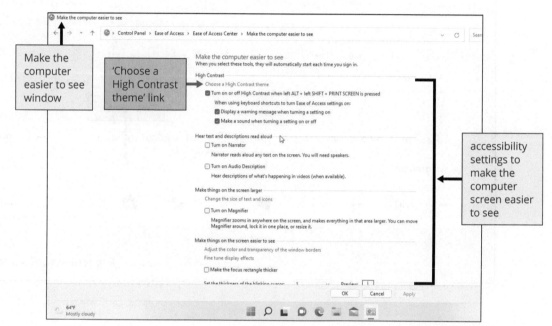

Figure 5–73

- Click the 'Choose a High Contrast theme' link to open the Personalization page in the Settings window.
- Click the Background button and then scroll as necessary to display the Contrast themes button (Figure 5–74).

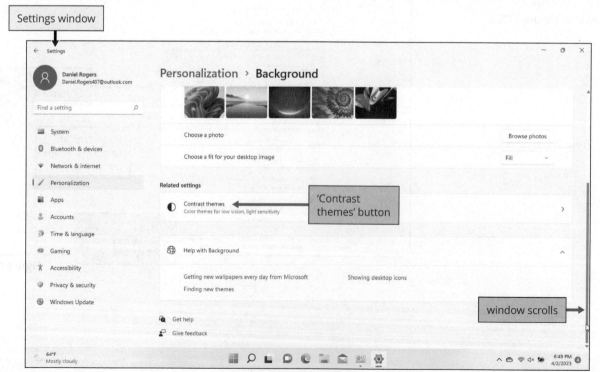

Figure 5–74

3

- Click the Contrast themes button to display the high contrast options in the Settings app.
- Click the None button and then click Aquatic to select a high contrast theme (Figure 5–75).

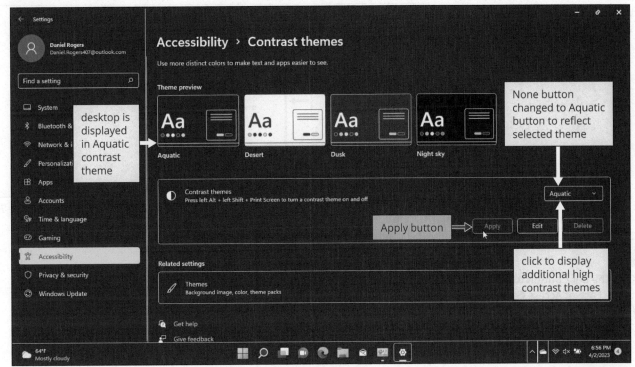

Figure 5–75

4

- Click the Aquatic button and then click None to deselect a high contrast theme.
- Click the Apply button to disable high contrast.
- Click the Close button to close the Settings app window.
- Click the 'Ease of Access Center' button on the address bar to return to the Ease of Access Center.

Other Ways

1. Press LEFT ALT+LEFT SHIFT+PRINT SCREEN, click Yes

To View Text or Visual Alternatives for Sound

Computer users who have difficulty hearing can enable text or visual alternatives for sounds. For example, when a sound otherwise would play, you can enable visual warnings, such as flashing the active caption bar, flashing the active window, or flashing the desktop. You also can enable text captions for spoken dialog. **Why?** Visual alternatives for sounds make it easier for those with hearing impairments to know when a sound plays on their computer. The following steps display the settings for text or visual alternatives for sounds.

- Click the 'Use text or visual alternatives for sounds' link (shown in Figure 5–72) to open the Use text or visual alternatives for sounds window (Figure 5–76).

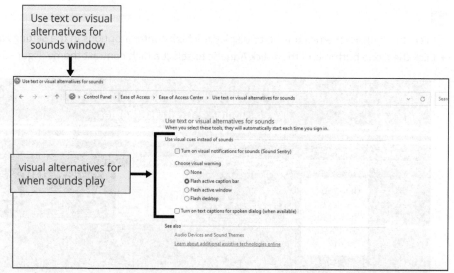

Figure 5–76

- Click the Back button to return to the Ease of Access Center (Figure 5–77).

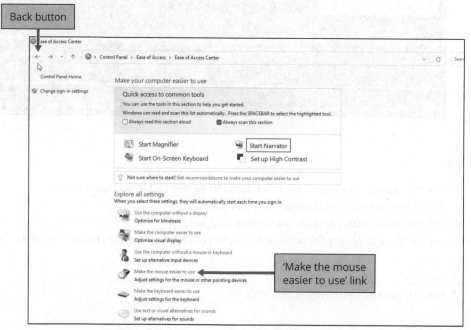

Figure 5–77

To Display Mouse Accessibility Settings

Mouse accessibility settings in the Ease of Access Center allow you to change the appearance of pointers, turn on Mouse Keys (which enables you to move the pointer using keys on the keyboard), and make it easier to manage windows. The following steps display mouse accessibility settings. **Why?** You want to know what mouse accessibility settings are available in case any can help you work more efficiently.

1

- Click the 'Make the mouse easier to use' link (shown in Figure 5–77) in the Ease of Access Center to display the mouse accessibility settings (Figure 5–78).

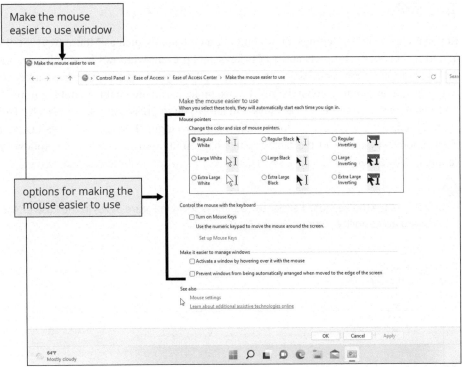

Figure 5–78

2

- Click the Back button to return to the Ease of Access Center (Figure 5–79).

Figure 5–79

To Display Keyboard Accessibility Settings

Keyboard accessibility settings allow you to turn on features such as Mouse Keys, Sticky Keys, Toggle Keys, and Filter Keys; underline keyboard shortcuts and access keys; and prevent windows from being arranged automatically if you drag them to the edge of the screen. The **Sticky Keys** feature allows you to press and release a key on the keyboard, and Windows will act as if you still are holding down the key. For example, if you are unable to hold multiple keys simultaneously and want to press ALT+F4 to exit a program, Sticky Keys will allow you to press and release the ALT key and then press and release F4 to exit the program. Filter Keys plays a tone when you press a toggle key, such as CAPS LOCK, NUM LOCK, or SCROLL LOCK. Filter Keys ignores keystrokes of the same key that happen in rapid succession. The following steps display keyboard accessibility settings. **Why?** You would like to see whether keyboard accessibility settings will help you as you work.

- Click the 'Make the keyboard easier to use' link (shown in Figure 5-79) in the Ease of Access Center window to display the keyboard accessibility settings (Figure 5-80).

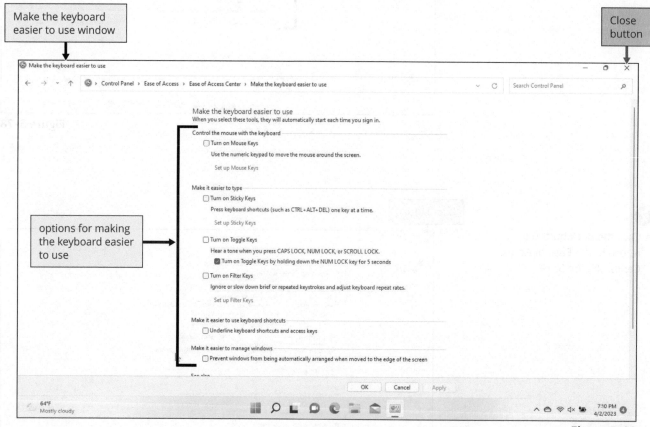

Figure 5-80

- Click the Close button to close the window.

Privacy Settings

Windows 11 has a myriad of privacy settings that allow you to control how much information you share, as well as which peripheral devices apps can access on your computer or mobile device. Windows can share information with Microsoft and third-party apps to provide you with a customized experience when using your computer or mobile device. For example, the Weather app can detect your location automatically and display the current weather in your area. Apps may be able to access the camera on your computer or mobile device so that you can take and share pictures and video, or host a video call with someone on the other side of the country. Some individuals are concerned with their privacy and want to limit the amount of information shared without their knowledge. In addition, they might want to control which apps have access to particular peripheral devices on their computer or mobile device. Table 5–1 shows various privacy categories in Windows 11.

Table 5–1 Windows 11 Privacy Settings

Category	Description
Windows permissions	
General	Contains general privacy settings, including whether to allow Microsoft to collect information across apps for advertising purposes, to track app launches, and to show suggested content in the Settings app, and whether websites can access your language list
Speech	Settings control the Microsoft online speech recognition feature to use your voice with apps
Inking & typing personalization	Settings control whether to use your typing history and handwriting patterns to create a personal dictionary
Diagnostics & feedback	Settings control whether (or how frequently) Windows asks for feedback or shares device data with Microsoft
Activity history	Settings control whether to store your activity history, including websites you visit
App permissions	
Location	Settings control whether Windows can detect your location, keep a history of your locations, and which apps can access your location
Camera	Settings control which apps can use your camera
Microphone	Settings control which apps can use your microphone
Account info	Settings control which apps can use your account information, such as your name, picture, and other account information
Contacts	Settings control which apps can access and use your contacts
Calendar	Settings control which apps can access and use your calendar
Messaging	Settings control which apps can read or send messages, such as text messages and MMS messages
Radios	Settings control which apps can use radios, such as Bluetooth
Other devices	Settings control whether apps can share information and synchronize with other devices, such as smartphones

To Display Privacy Settings

Why? You want to view your Windows privacy settings to see what Windows is storing and sending, as well as what features various apps are able to access. The following steps display privacy settings.

- Display the Start menu.
- Click Settings on the Start menu to start the Settings app and open the Settings window (Figure 5–81).

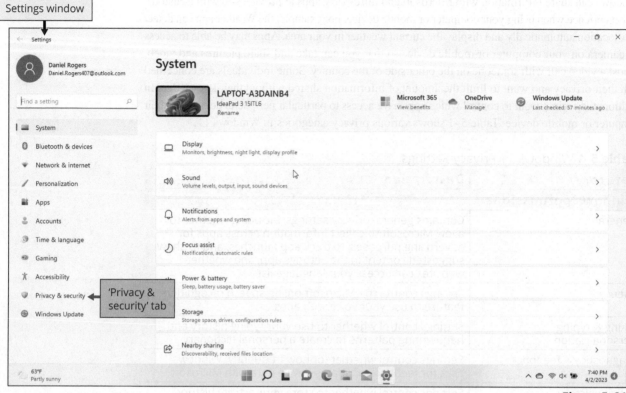

Figure 5–81

- Click the 'Privacy & security' tab to display the privacy settings (Figure 5–82).
- **Experiment:** Click the various categories to see the privacy settings for each category.

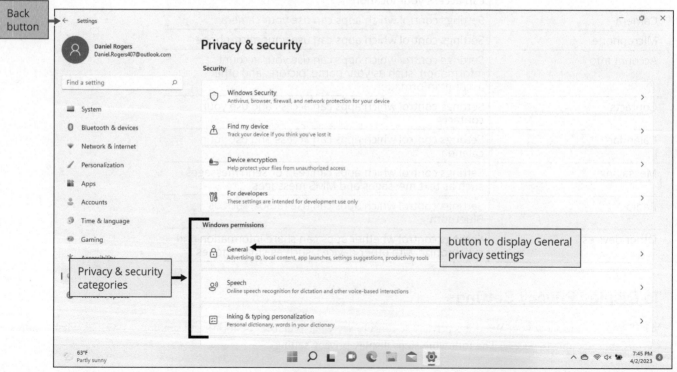

Figure 5–82

Update and Security Settings

Update and security settings in Windows 11 allow you to perform functions such as checking for and installing updates to the Windows operating system, configuring how Windows Security finds and removes malware from your computer, configuring backups for your data using File History, and recovering your computer if it is not running well.

To Display Windows Update Settings and Check for Updates

Why? Microsoft releases Windows updates periodically to enhance performance and add features. You would like to make sure you have all the latest updates installed. **The following steps display Windows Update settings and check for updates.**

- Click the Back button (shown in Figure 5–82) to return to the list of categories in the Settings app (Figure 5–83).

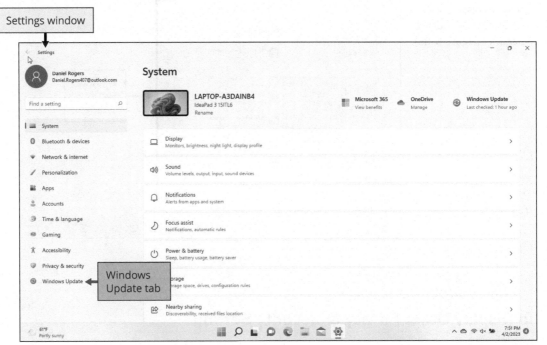

Figure 5–83

- Click the Windows Update tab in the Settings window to display the Windows Update settings in the Settings app (Figure 5–84).

Figure 5–84

To Display Windows Security Settings

Why? You want to make sure Windows Security is enabled and actively protecting your computer. **The following step displays Windows Security settings.**

1

- Click the 'Privacy & security' tab in the Settings window and then click the Windows Security button in the right pane to display the settings for Windows Security (Figure 5–85).

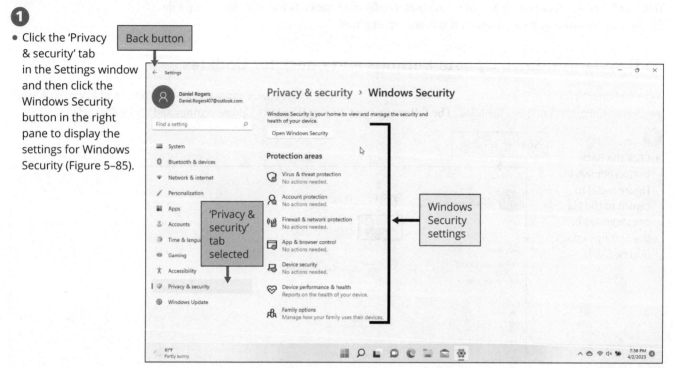

Figure 5–85

To Display Other Privacy & Security Settings

Why? You want to view the other privacy and security settings available in Windows 11. **The following steps display other privacy and security settings.**

1

- Click the Back button (shown in Figure 5–85) and then click the 'Find my device' button to display the Find my device settings (Figure 5–86).

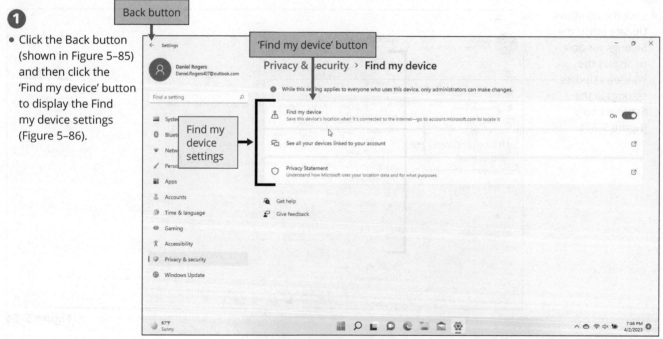

Figure 5–86

- Click the Back button (shown in Figure 5–85) and then click the Device encryption button to display the Device encryption settings (Figure 5–87).

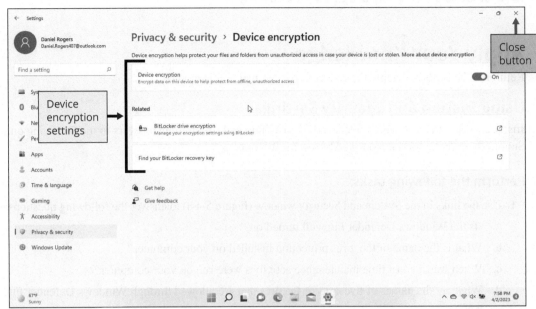

Figure 5–87

- Click the Close button to exit the Settings app.

To Sign Out of Your Account and Shut Down the Computer

After completing your work with Windows, you should follow these steps to end your session by signing out of your account and then shutting down the computer.

1. Display the Start menu.

2. Click the user icon and then click Sign out.

3. Click the lock screen to display the sign-in screen.

4. Click the Shut down button.

5. Click the Shut down on the Shut down menu to shut down the computer.

Summary

In this module, you learned how to customize Windows 11 using various links in the Control Panel window. You customized the keyboard, mouse, and date and time. You viewed devices and printers and viewed the properties of the hardware devices attached to the computer. Using the Ease of Access Center, you explored settings for mobility impaired and visually impaired users. You also viewed privacy settings, viewed and adjusted Windows Defender Firewall settings, viewed power plan information, and updated security settings.

Student Assignments

Apply Your Knowledge

Reinforce the skills and apply the concepts you learned in this module.

Using System and Security Settings

Instructions: Increase your understanding of Windows 11 by finding answers to the following questions. Submit them in the format requested by your instructor.

Perform the following tasks:

1. Use the links in the System and Security window (Figure 5–88) to answer the following questions:
   a. Is the Windows Defender Firewall turned on?
   b. What is the name of the virus protection installed on your computer?
   c. When was the last time maintenance activities were run on your computer?
   d. What are the names of five apps or features that are allowed through Windows Defender Firewall?
   e. What type of processor does your computer have?
   f. How much memory (RAM) is installed on your computer?
   g. What is your computer name?
   h. What is the current power plan selected for your computer?
   i. With the currently selected power plan, how long is it before Windows turns off the display?
   j. With the currently selected power plan, how long is it before Windows puts the computer to sleep?

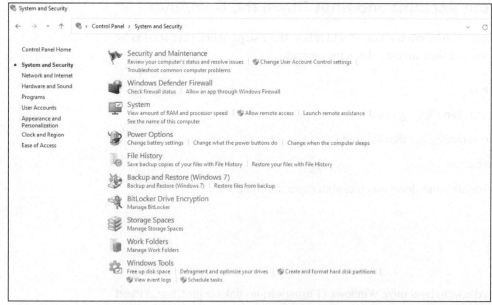

Figure 5–88

2. Use the links in the Hardware and Sound window to answer the following questions:
   a. What are the names of five devices that currently are connected to your computer?
   b. What type of keyboard is connected to your computer?
   c. Are there any devices displaying in the Devices and Printers window that you did not expect to appear?
   d. What is the AutoPlay setting for memory cards? If one is not selected, which one would you choose? Why?

e. What sound does Windows play for a calendar reminder?

f. What sound does Windows play for a new mail notification?

3. Use the Programs and Features window to answer the following questions:

a. What are the names of five programs or apps installed on your computer?

b. If you begin to run out of space on your hard drive, what are two apps you would uninstall? Why?

Extend Your Knowledge

Extend the skills you learned in this module and experiment with new skills. You might need to use Help to complete the assignment.

Troubleshooting Hardware Problems

Instructions: Use the troubleshooting features in Windows 11 to find answers to questions regarding hardware. Display the Control Panel using Small icons view and then click the Troubleshooting link. Use the links in the Troubleshooting window (Figure 5–89) to answer the following questions and then submit your answers in the format requested by your instructor.

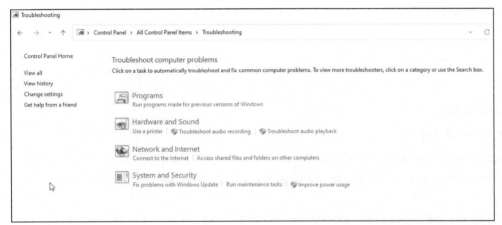

Figure 5–89

Perform the following tasks:

1. What are the steps required to run a program or app that was made for a previous version of Windows? Explain what happens during the troubleshooting process.

2. What steps are required to configure devices that are not working correctly? Explain what happens during the troubleshooting process.

3. What steps should you take if you are having problems recording audio? Explain what happens during the troubleshooting process.

4. What steps are required if you need assistance accessing shared files and folders on other computers? Explain what happens during the troubleshooting process.

5. What steps should you take if you are having problems with Windows Update? Explain what happens during the troubleshooting process.

6. If you continue having problems with Windows after using the troubleshooting features, how can you use Remote Assistance?

7. What is the Steps Recorder? Explain how it might help someone troubleshoot a problem you are experiencing.

Expand Your World

Create a solution that uses cloud or web technologies by learning and investigating on your own from general guidance.

Researching Third Party Apps

Instructions: As you have learned in this module, Windows Defender Firewall (Figure 5–90) helps control whether apps installed on your computer can communicate using the Internet. Other apps are available that can provide the same or similar functionality. You will research various apps and answer questions about your findings.

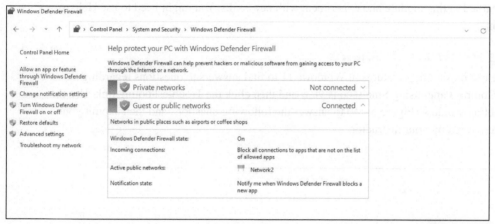

Figure 5–90

Perform the following tasks:

Part 1: Researching Firewall Apps

1. What are the names of at least three other firewall apps that are compatible with Windows 11?

2. Do the three other firewall apps have any features that the Windows Defender Firewall does not? If so, what are they?

3. Does Windows Defender Firewall have any features that the other firewall apps do not? If so, what are they?

4. Of the four firewall apps you have reviewed (Windows Defender Firewall and the three other apps), which one do you prefer? Why?

Part 2: Researching Antivirus Apps

Windows Security scans for and removes viruses and other malware from your computer. Research other apps that can scan for and remove viruses and other malware and then answer the following questions:

1. What are the names of at least two other antivirus apps that are compatible with Windows 11?

2. Do the three other antivirus apps have features that the Windows Security does not? If so, what are they?

3. Does Windows Security have any features that the other antivirus apps do not? If so, what are they?

4. Of the three antivirus apps you have reviewed (Windows Security and the two other apps), which one do you prefer? Why?

5. Are the apps you researched free or do they charge a fee? Is an annual subscription fee required that you must pay to receive the latest updates?

Part 3: Researching Accessibility Apps

Windows 11 provides many accessibility features designed to help individuals with various impairments. In addition to the features Windows provides, other companies develop software that can offer additional accessibility features designed to make Windows and its apps more accessible. Research other apps compatible with Windows 11 that provide accessibility features and answer the following questions:

1. What are the names of two apps providing accessibility features?

2. What types of accessibility features do these apps provide?

3. How much do these apps cost?

4. Why might someone use a third-party app instead of the features built into Windows 11?

In the Labs

Design and implement a solution using creative thinking and problem-solving skills.

Lab 1: Developing a Control Panel Guide

Problem: Although most people like to use the Category view when working with Control Panel, your boss favors the Small icons view (Figure 5–91). Your boss asks you to create a Control Panel guide so that other employees can familiarize themselves with the Small icons view and the Control Panel icons. Using WordPad, create a guide with a title and description of the following icons in the Control Panel window: Date and Time, File Explorer Options, Programs and Features, and Windows Defender Firewall.

Perform the following tasks:

1. Open the Control Panel window and change to Small icons view (Figure 5–91).

2. Run WordPad and maximize the Document - WordPad window.

3. Type **The Control Panel Window (Small Icons View)** as the title.

4. Type a brief statement about how Small icons view is different from Category view.

5. Type **Date and Time** and then type a brief description of the date and time settings.

6. Type **File Explorer Options** and then type a brief description of the available options for File Explorer.

7. Type **Programs and Features** and then type a brief description of what tasks you can accomplish in the Programs and Features window.

8. Type **Windows Defender Firewall** and then type a brief description of the various Windows Defender Firewall settings.

9. Save the completed document using the file name, Control Panel Guide.

10. Print the completed document.

11. Exit WordPad and then close the Control Panel window.

12. Submit the Control Panel Guide in a format requested by your instructor.

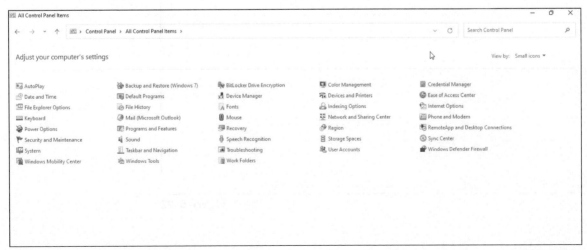

Figure 5–91

Lab 2: Customizing the Computer Using the Ease of Access Center

Problem: You are volunteering at a local community center for older adults, and you have noticed that a number of the members have difficulty reading the text on the screen and using the keyboard to type text. You decide to change the settings to help them access the computer more easily. You will make the screen easier to read and make it easier to type in WordPad. After seeing how these changes helped some of the seniors to use the computer, you decide to explore additional accessibility options.

Perform the following steps:

1. Open the Ease of Access Center window (Figure 5–92).
2. Click the Start Magnifier button to start the Magnifier and display the Magnifier toolbar.
3. Click the Views button on the Magnifier toolbar. What types of views are listed?
4. Click the Options button on the Magnifier toolbar. What options are available to set?
5. Exit Magnifier.
6. Click the 'Start On-Screen Keyboard' link in the Ease of Access Center. The on-screen keyboard allows you to type text in a document window using the mouse.
7. If necessary, drag the on-screen keyboard window to position the window at the bottom of the desktop.
8. Start WordPad. Resize and position the WordPad window at the top of the desktop.
9. Using the pointer and on-screen keyboard, type the following sentence: **The on-screen keyboard helps individuals type if they are unable to use a traditional keyboard.**   and then click ENTER on the on-screen keyboard two times. (**Hint:** To type using the on-screen keyboard, click the key on the on-screen keyboard corresponding to the character you want to type. Click SHIFT on the on-screen keyboard to capitalize text. Click the SPACEBAR on the on-screen keyboard to insert a blank space.)
10. Use the on-screen keyboard to type your first and last name and then click ENTER.
11. Print the document.
12. Close the On-Screen Keyboard window and then exit WordPad without saving your changes.

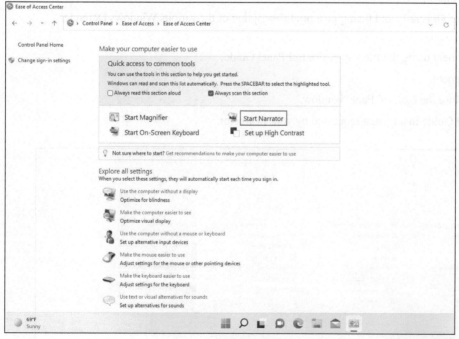

Figure 5–92

13. Make a note of the current desktop background, color options, and other display settings.

14. Return to the Ease of Access Center and click the 'Get recommendations to make your computer easier to use' link. As you answer the questions in the accessibility questionnaire, select the appropriate options as if you had a vision and hearing impairment.

15. After you complete the questionnaire, turn on the suggested options.

16. Display the Start menu.

    a. What color is the background color on the Start menu?

    b. Did the size of the commands on the Start menu change? If so, how?

    c. Is each icon on the Start menu fully visible?

17. Open and maximize the Control Panel window.

    a. Are the icons in the Control Panel window easy to see?

18. Close the Control Panel window.

19. Restore the computer to the original settings you noted in Step 13.

20. Turn off the options you turned on in the Ease of Access Center.

21. Submit the printed WordPad document and the answers to the questions to your instructor.

Lab 3: Consider This: Your Turn

Verifying Privacy Settings

Problem: You have just purchased a new computer that comes with Windows 11. You are very concerned about privacy and want to make sure your personal information is not shared without your knowledge. In addition, you want to strictly limit the features on your computer that installed apps can access.

Part 1: Review the privacy settings on your computer and prepare a list of privacy settings you would configure to guarantee the type of privacy you desire. In addition, prepare a list of other privacy concerns you might have while using your computer.

Part 2: You made several decisions while researching for this assignment. What decisions did you make? What was the rationale behind these decisions? How did you locate the required information about which privacy settings to configure?

Advanced Searching Techniques

Objectives

After completing this module, you will be able to:

- Understand advanced searching techniques
- Find a file by using Boolean operators
- Search for a file by specifying properties
- View and modify the index

- Search for media files using specialized properties
- Save a search and find a file using a saved search
- Refine searches using the Search box
- Configure Search box settings

Introduction

In addition to the search techniques you learned in previous modules, other methods for searching are available in Windows 11. Searching for files and folders can be an everyday activity. If you want to work with your budget, you need your budget files. If you want to edit some photos, you need to locate your photos. If you want to send an important document to a colleague, you need to know where the document is located.

Windows 11 provides a variety of methods for searching. The easiest method is to use the Search box in the folder where the files you are searching for should be located. You performed this basic type of search in earlier modules. Another way is to use file list headings to organize your files so that you can find items faster. You can use file list headings to organize the contents of folders by filtering or sorting items, after which you can search to find what you want. If you are unable to find your files in one folder, you can use the customize option to change the search location without having to completely re-create the search. Finally, you can search using the Search button on the taskbar to locate your programs and files. The Search button offers efficient searching without first having to open a folder.

In this module, you will learn how to use these search tools and how indexing decreases search times. You will search for files on the local hard drive by specifying the date, file type, or word or phrase that appears in the file. You also will learn techniques for searching for files using properties (Figure 6–1).

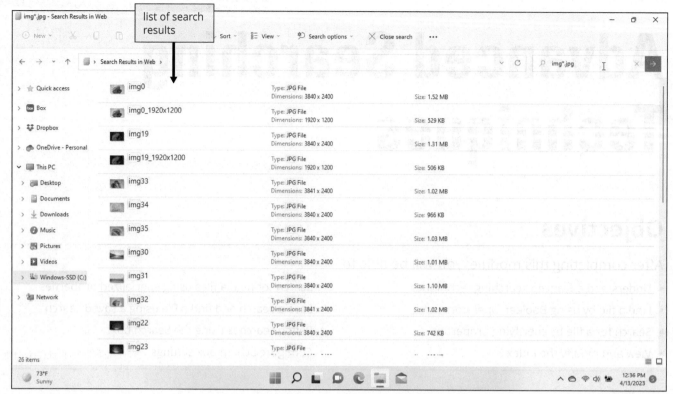

Figure 6–1a

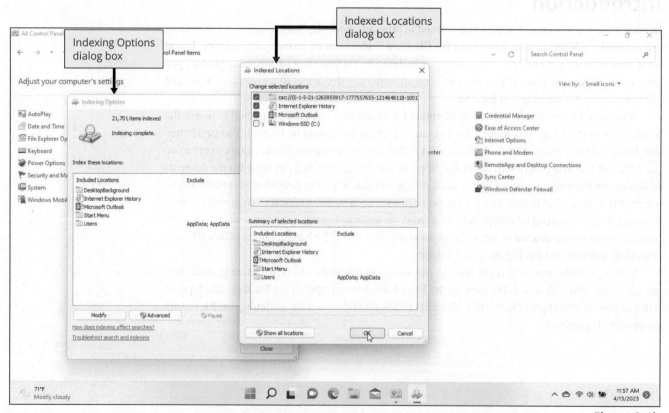

Figure 6–1b

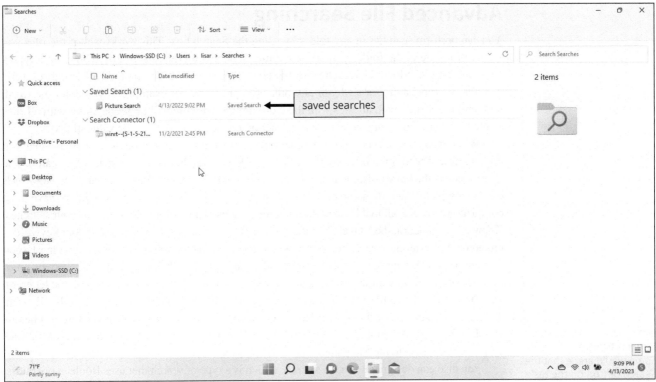

Figure 6–1c

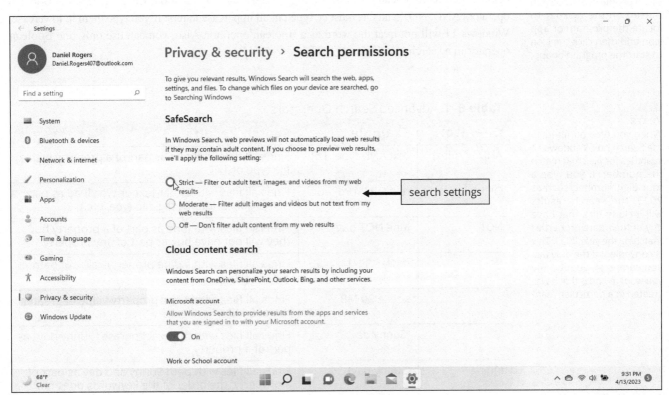

Figure 6–1d

Advanced File Searching

You can perform searches in any folder by using the Search box. This works well if the files you want to find are in the folder you are searching. When using the Search box, you simply type a keyword, and Windows 11 searches for matches. Search results can include all or part of a file name, a file type, a tag for a file, or any other file property. For example, if you enter the word, text, into the Search box, all files with the word, text, in the title will be found along with all files of the type text, with a tag value of text, or any other file property with the value of text.

When designing a search, it can be helpful to consider what you know as well as what you do not know. Try to think of keywords or parts of keywords that you can use in your search. The more specific the keywords, the more likely that you will locate the files you want. The keywords can be any part of the file name or located in tags or properties. Keywords also do not have to be complete words. Recall that in an earlier module, you used an * (asterisk) as part of your searches. Known as a wildcard, the * takes the place of one or more characters when part of your keyword is unknown. For example, searching for *rd would result in matches for all words that end in rd, such as word, board, and herd, whereas *.bmp would match all files that have a file name extension of .bmp. If you know that a file you want to find begins with the letter, h, and ends with the letter, m, you can use the wildcard to create the search keyword, h*m. Perhaps you know that the file is an MP3, but you know only that the name has the word, hey, as part of it. You are unsure if it begins with hey, has hey in the middle, or ends with hey. You would use *hey*.mp3 to find all MP3 files with the word, hey, in the file name.

You also can design a **Boolean search**, which is a type of search that uses Boolean operators. A **Boolean operator** is used to expand or narrow a search. Table 6–1 lists the Boolean operators with examples and explanations. If you know that a photo you want to find was taken on vacation and you added the tag, our vacation, to your photos, as well as saved them as JPEG files, you could structure your search as follows: *.jpg AND tag: our vacation. Be aware that the Boolean operators AND, NOT, and OR must be typed in all uppercase letters. If you type them in lowercase, Windows 11 will not treat the word as a Boolean operator. Also, you can use only one Boolean operator in a search at a time.

Table 6–1: Advanced Search Operators

Operator	Example	Search Results
AND '+' (plus)	text AND type: TXT	Finds all files with text as part of a property with a file type of TXT
OR '–' (hyphen)	text OR WordPad	Finds all files with either text or WordPad as part of a property (name, tag, file type, etc.)
NOT	June NOT bug	Finds all files with June as part of a property but they will not have bug as part of any property
<	date: < 11/11/2023	Finds all files with a date property value of before 11/11/2023
>	size: > 20 MB	Finds all files with a size property value of greater than 20 MB
" "	"Sunny day"	Finds all files with the exact phrase "Sunny day" as part of a property
( )	(Sunny day)	Finds all files with both Sunny and day as part of a property; the order of the keywords does not matter

To Search Using Boolean Operators

Why? You want to locate files meeting two criteria. The following steps use the Boolean operator, AND, to find all files that have the keywords, blue and jpg.

- Open the This PC window.
- If necessary, maximize the This PC window.
- Display the contents of the hard drive.
- Display the contents of the Windows folder (Figure 6–2).

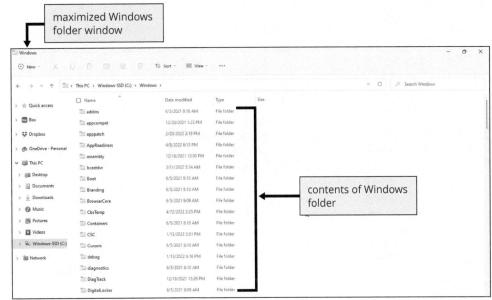

Figure 6–2

- Display the contents of the Microsoft.NET folder.
- Type ***blue* AND jpg** in the Search box to specify what you want to find, and wait for the search to finish and the search results to appear (Figure 6–3).

Q&A Windows did not start searching as I typed. What should I do?
Press ENTER after typing the search text to start the search.

Why do my results differ from the figure?
Depending upon your computer's contents, you might have different files appear or none at all.

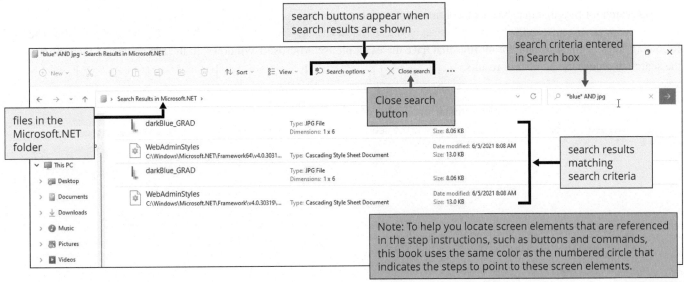

Figure 6–3

- After viewing the results, click the Close search button on the toolbar to end the search.
- Display the contents of the Windows folder.
- Click an open area of the window (Figure 6–4).

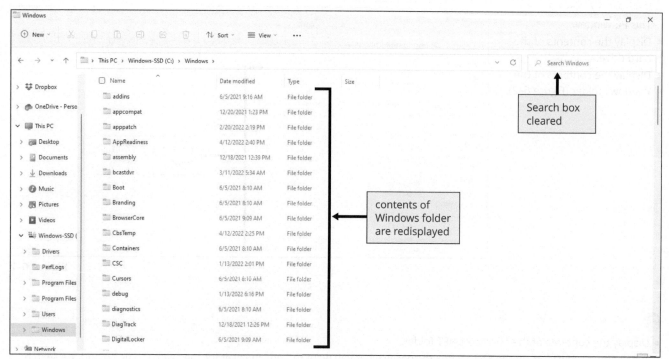

Figure 6–4

To Search for an Exact Phrase

You can search for files that match an exact phrase as part of its properties using double quotation marks. **Why?** You know two words that appear together in the file name, so searching for an exact phrase will help limit the number of search results. The following steps begin searching for all files that have the exact phrase, Microsoft Windows, in the file name and then modify the search to reduce the number of results.

- Display the contents of the SystemApps folder.
- Type **"Microsoft Windows"** in the Search box as the search criteria and to begin searching for results (Figure 6–5).

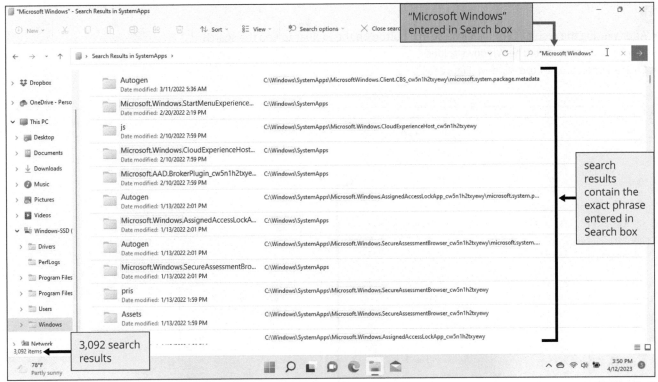

Figure 6–5

- Type **NOT assets** in the Search box following "Microsoft Windows" to narrow your search and reduce the number of search results and then press ENTER (Figure 6–6).

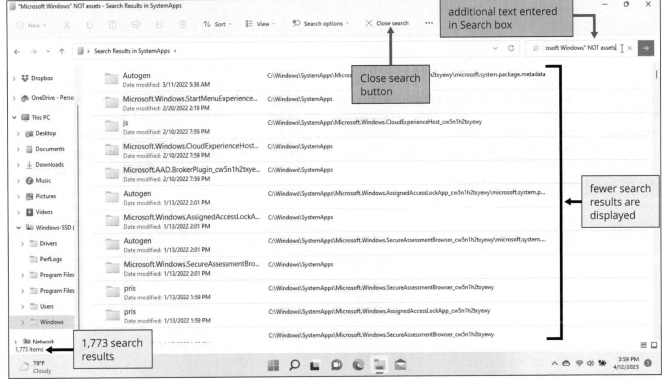

Figure 6–6

- After viewing the results, click the Close search button on the toolbar to end the search.
- Display the contents of the Windows folder.
- Click an open area of the window (Figure 6–7).

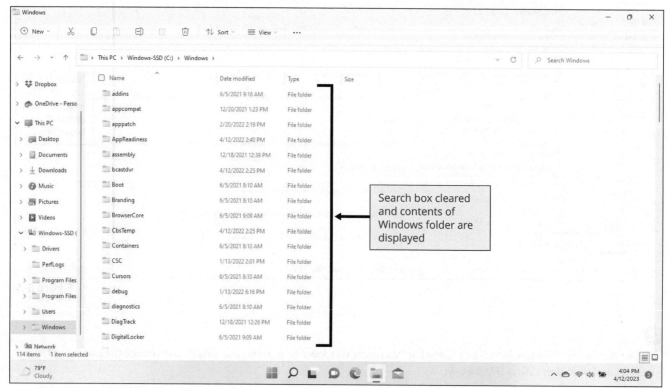

Figure 6–7

To Structure a Complex Search Combining a File Property and a Range

All files have properties. When searching a folder, you can be more specific by adding a property, such as file name, type, tag, or author, to the search text. For example, when you search using the search text, type: text, the search will find text files only. Any property can be used in this fashion. You need to type the colon (:) after the property name for the search to execute properly. You can create complex searches by combining searches for specific property values with Boolean operators. Why? You want to search for files with properties falling within a range of values. The following step searches for all files that range in size between 1 and 5 megabytes (MB).

- Display the contents of the Speech folder.
- Type **size:>1MB AND <5MB** in the Search box to specify that you want to see all files that are between 1 and 5 MB in size (Figure 6–8).

Q&A Can I specify size in kilobytes (KB) or gigabytes (GB)?
Yes. When working with the Search box to search using file size as the criteria, you can specify kilobytes (KB), megabytes (MB), or gigabytes (GB).

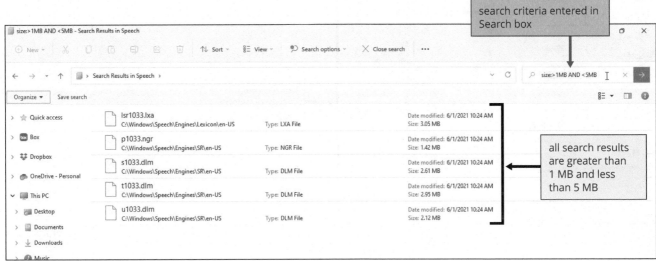

Figure 6–8

To Filter Files Using File List Headings

When using the file list headings, you can sort or filter files according to their headings. **Sorting** files arranges them in increasing or decreasing order, depending upon the file list heading you select. You also can filter files by choosing a date or date range or by choosing a timeframe specified by Windows, such as today, yesterday, or last week. Both options for filtering are based on the existing titles of the files and folders and are available by clicking the file list headings arrow. For example, filtering by the name heading includes options for organizing the files and folders by alphabetical groups (such as A–H), whereas filtering by the type heading includes a list of the file types found in the current folder. These options are most helpful when searching for files about which you already have some information. To sort and filter using file list headings, the contents must be displayed in Details view.

An increasing number of programs are using XML (Extensible Markup Language) files. The following steps filter the Windows folder to display only XML files. **Why?** You want to see the XML files in the Windows folder on your computer.

- Click the Close search button on the toolbar.
- Display the contents of the Windows folder.
- Click the View button on the toolbar to display the View menu.
- Click Details on the View menu to display the window contents in Details view (Figure 6–9).

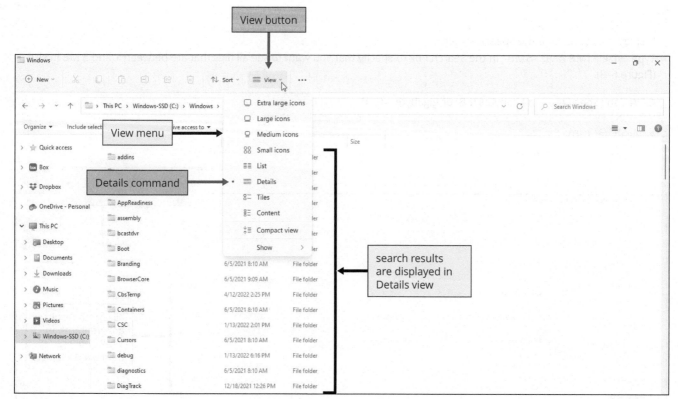

Figure 6–9

2

- Point to the Type heading to display the Type arrow.
- Click the Type arrow to display the list of filter options for file types (Figure 6–10).

Q&A Can I change which file list headings are displayed in the window?
Yes. By right-clicking a list heading, you can select which file list headings are displayed. You can add or remove file list headings based on your needs. You also can add or remove file list headings and associated columns by right-clicking a column heading and clicking the columns you want to add or remove.

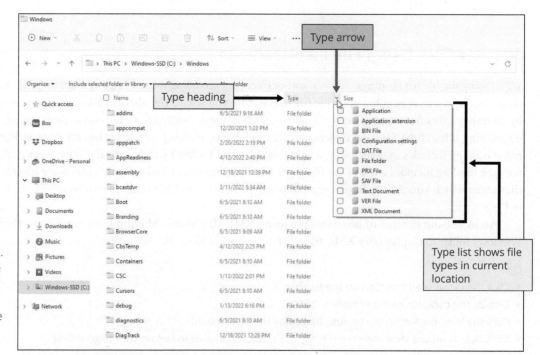

Figure 6–10

- If necessary, scroll to display the XML Document check box in the Type list.
- Click the XML Document check box to filter the Windows folder for XML files only (Figure 6–11).

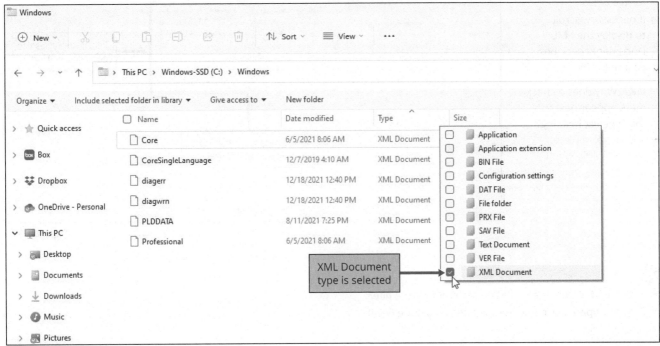

Figure 6–11

❹
- Click any open space in the folder window to close the list of filter options (Figure 6–12).

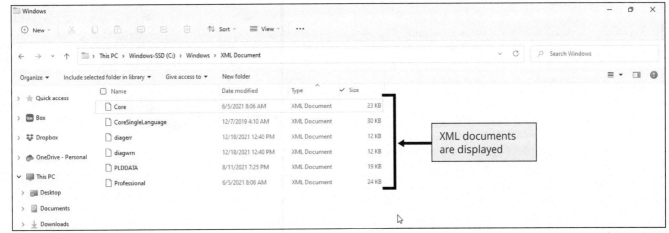

Figure 6–12

5

- After viewing the results, click the Type check mark to display the list of filter options for file types.
- If necessary, scroll to display the XML Document check box (Figure 6–13).

Q&A Why does a check mark appear next to the Type list heading? The check mark indicates that the window is displaying only certain (and not all) file types.

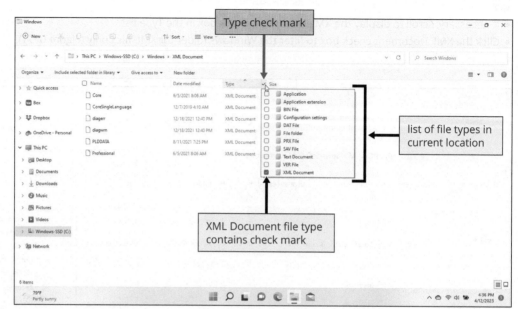

Figure 6–13

6

- Click the XML Document check box to remove the filter.
- Click any open space to close the filter list (Figure 6–14).

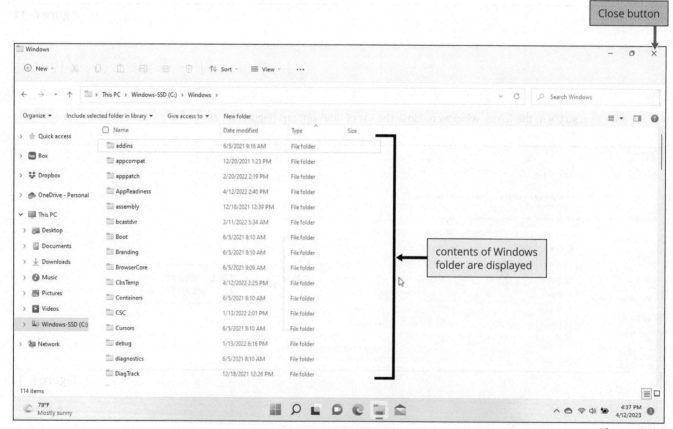

Figure 6–14

7
- Close the Windows folder window (Figure 6–15).

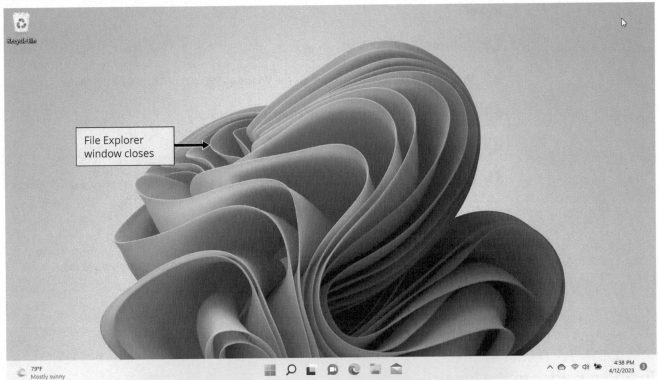

File Explorer
window closes

Figure 6–15

Other Ways

1. Click Search box, type **fileextension:xml**

Understanding Indexing

Windows 11 uses indexing to increase the speed at which it searches selected folders and files. By default, Windows 11 indexes each user's personal folders, which contain the Documents, Pictures, Music, and Videos folders. Program and system files, such as the C:\Windows folder, are not included as indexed locations. Excluding these folders keeps the index small. In addition, to keep the index at a manageable size, Windows 11 prevents you from indexing network locations, unless specifically designated.

As you have seen while searching the C:\Windows folder, a folder does not have to be indexed to be searchable. If you want to improve performance when searching, however, you might want to add additional folders to the index. It is important to note that the Search folder window relies on the index by default.

To Create a Folder and Files for Indexing

First, you will create a new folder and some files that you will then add to the index. The following steps create a folder named SCFiles and create both a text file and a WordPad file within the new folder.

1 Open the This PC window.

2 Open the hard drive folder, such as the Windows-SSD (C:) or Local Disk (C:) folder.

3 Create a folder and then type **SCFiles** as the name.

4 Open the SCFiles folder.

5 Create a text file named Homework containing the following lines: **1) Must read 15 pages from my Chemistry book**   and   **2) Write summary about Save the Planet's social media campaign.**

6 Create a WordPad file named ToDo containing the following two lines: **1) Respond to email messages**   and   **2) Update social media with the Koala exhibit photos.**

7 Close the File Explorer window.

To Add a Folder to the Index

Why? Adding a folder to the index will allow Windows to search for files in that folder more quickly. You can add any folders to the index, but remember that the index will not perform well if it grows too large. It is recommended that you add only those locations that contain personal files, and never add program or system files. If your computer uses an SSD instead of a hard disk, creating an index might not increase performance very much. SSDs are very fast and can locate search results in indexed and nonindexed locations very quickly. The following steps add the SCFiles folder to the Search Index by using the Indexing Options dialog box.

- Open the Control Panel window.
- Change the view to Small icons (Figure 6–16).

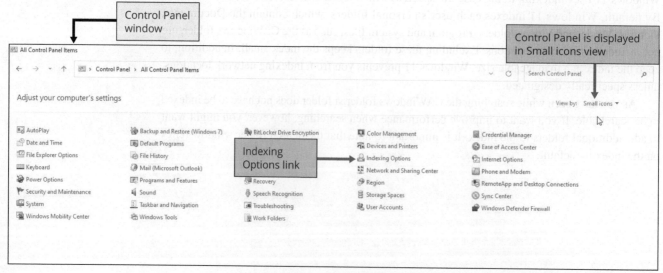

Figure 6–16

2

- Click the Indexing Options link to display the Indexing Options dialog box (Figure 6–17).

Q&A Why is my list of indexed locations different?
Your index might have been modified by the administrator. Also, the number of files you have installed in various indexed locations might be different.

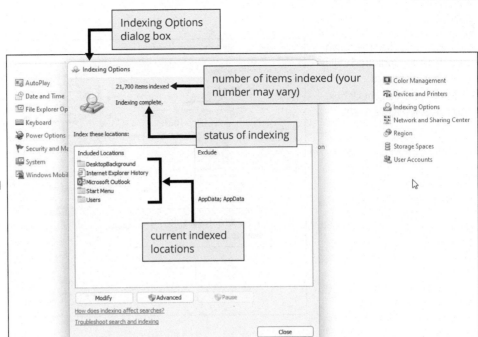

Figure 6–17

3

- Click the Modify button (Indexing Options dialog box) to display the Indexed Locations dialog box (Figure 6–18).

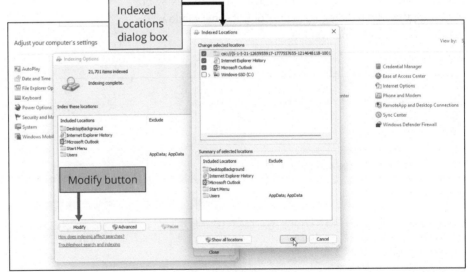

Figure 6–18

4

- Click the Windows-SSD (C:) arrow to display the list of folders (Figure 6–19).

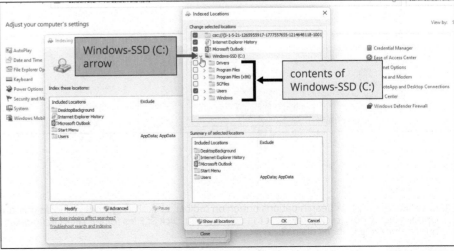

Figure 6–19

- If necessary, click the down scroll arrow until the SCFiles folder is displayed.
- Click the SCFiles check box to select it (Figure 6–20).

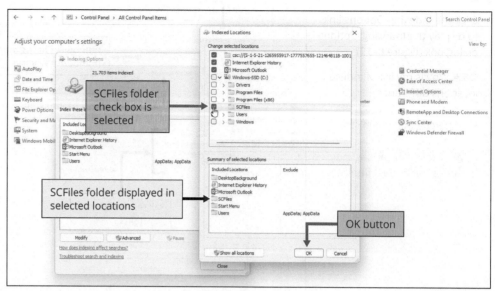

Figure 6–20

6

- Click OK (Indexed Locations dialog box) to add the SCFiles folder to the Search Index (Figure 6–21).
- Click the Close button to close the Indexing Options dialog box.
- Change the view to Category in the Control Panel window.
- Close the Control Panel window.

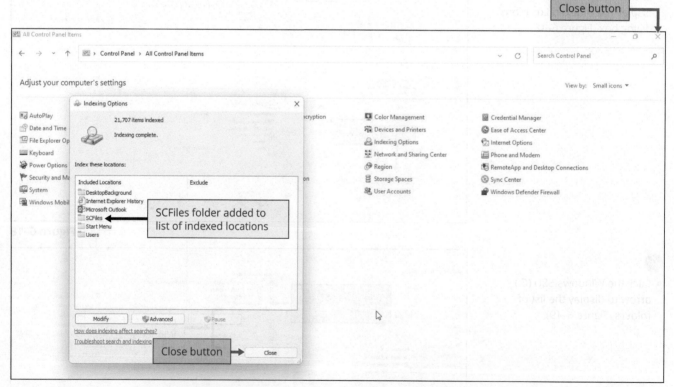

Figure 6–21

Other Ways

1. Click Search box, click Search options button on toolbar, click 'Change indexed locations' on menu, click Modify button (Indexing Options dialog box), click arrow next to Local Disk (C:), click SCFiles folder, click OK (Indexed Locations dialog box), click Close button (Indexing Options dialog box)

To Search for a File Using a Word or Phrase in the File

When searching an indexed location, you can search for a file using a word or phrase that appears within the file. **Why?** You might not remember the name of the file containing the contents for which you are searching, but you might remember some of the text within the file. The following steps find all files containing the words, Chemistry and social media, and the phrase, Respond to email messages.

- Open the This PC window.
- Display the contents of the hard drive folder, such as the Windows-SSD (C:) or Local Disk (C:) folder.
- Open the SCFiles folder.
- If necessary, maximize the SCFiles folder window.
- Type **Chemistry** in the Search box to search for all files containing the word, Chemistry (Figure 6–22).

Q&A Why was the search result not displayed?
When you add a folder to the indexed locations, it might take a while for Windows to index all the file contents. If Windows has not finished indexing the contents of the files in the SCFiles folder, the Homework file might not appear in the search results.

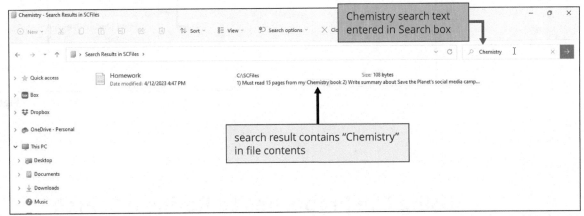

Figure 6–22

- After viewing the results, clear the Search box.
- Type **Respond to email messages** in the Search box to search for all files containing the phrase, Respond to email messages (Figure 6–23).

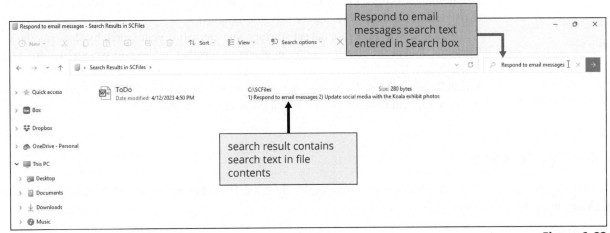

Figure 6–23

- After viewing the results, clear the Search box.
- Type **social media** in the Search box to search for all files containing the words, social media (Figure 6–24).

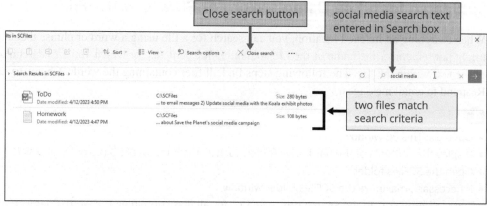

Figure 6–24

- After viewing the results, click the Close search button on the toolbar to clear the search results (Figure 6–25).

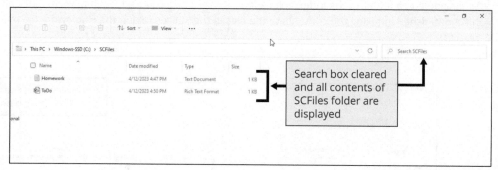

Figure 6–25

Using File Properties to Refine a Search

As discussed earlier in this module, you can search for files using any of the file properties, such as the file's name, author, size, and type. Media files, however, often have additional specialized properties that are searchable. These specialized properties often are assigned values by the file's creators. For example, if you want to find all the photos taken using your Nikon camera, you can enter, camera maker: Nikon, in the Search box to find these pictures. You also can search for a file based on when you last worked with the file or search for files containing specific text. Additionally, if you have edited the properties of a file or folder and added tags, you then will be able to find those files and folders using the tags you assigned.

If your search results are not satisfactory, you can refine your search by changing the search keywords, looking in other locations, or changing whether hidden and system files are included in the search. If no files were found, a message (No items match your search) will appear in the Search Results window. In this case, you might want to double-check the search criteria you entered or select different parameters with which to continue your search.

To Add a Tag to a File

Why? To search for files using tags, you must first add the tags to the files. The following steps add the tag, landscape, to the desert picture in the Pictures folder.

- Display the contents of the hard drive folder, such as the Windows-SSD (C:) or Local Disk (C:) folder.
- Display the contents of the Windows folder and then display the contents of the Web folder.
- Type **img*.jpg** in the Search box to display all files with img in the file name and jpg as the file type (Figure 6–26).

Q&A What if no search results are returned?

Type ***.jpg** in the Search box to display other images, and choose one to use for the following steps.

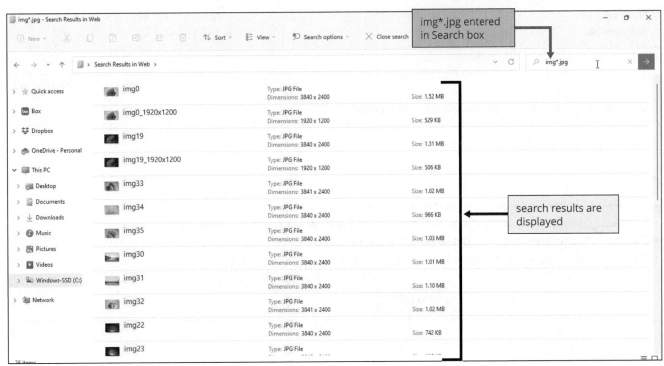

Figure 6–26

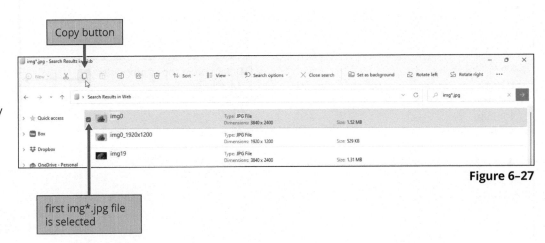

Figure 6–27

- Click the first img file to select it.
- Click the Copy button on the toolbar to copy the selected image (Figure 6–27).

3

- Display the SCFiles folder window.
- Click the Paste button on the toolbar to paste a copy of the img*.jpg file in the SCFiles folder.
- If necessary, click the img*.jpg file to select it (Figure 6–28).

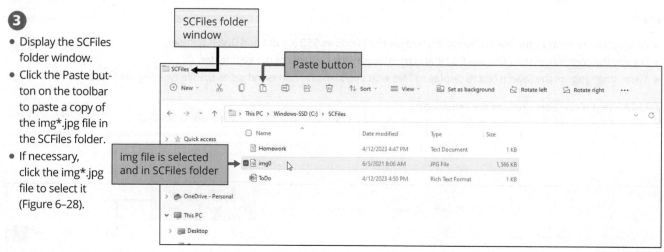

Figure 6–28

Q&A Why did I have to copy the file to a different location?

Windows does not allow you to edit the properties for certain files in the Windows folder. By copying the file to a different location, you then can modify its properties.

4

- Click the View button on the toolbar to display the View menu.
- If necessary, point to Show on the View menu and then click Details pane to open the Details pane.
- Click the Add comments label in the Details pane to display a text box.
- Type **desktop background** in the text box to assign the comment to the picture (Figure 6–29).

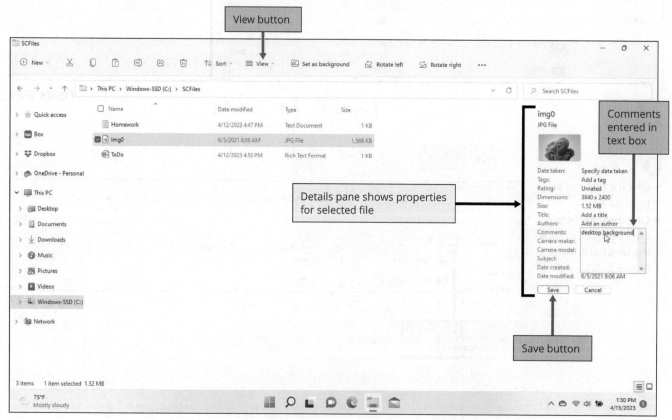

Figure 6–29

● Click the Save button in the Details pane to save the change (Figure 6–30).

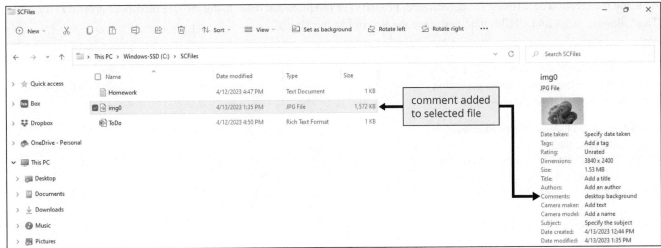

Figure 6–30

To Search Using the Comments Property

Why? If you have added tags to your files, you can search for files by using the tags property in your search. The following steps find all files in the SCFiles folder with the words, desktop background, in the Comments property.

● Type **comments: desktop background** in the Search box to enter the search criteria (Figure 6–31).

Figure 6–31

● After viewing the results, click the Close search button on the toolbar to clear the Search box (Figure 6–32).

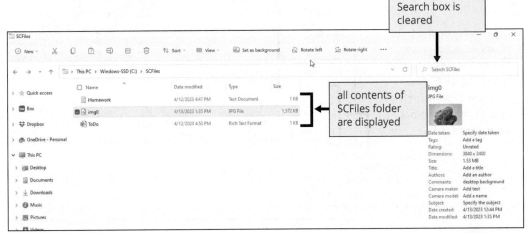

Figure 6–32

To Search Using the Date Property

When searching for a file, Windows 11 allows you to search using date properties. **Why?** This can be helpful if you are searching for a file you modified recently, but you do not remember the name of the file or where it is stored. You can select to find files by using the creation date (using the datecreated: property) or modification date (using the datemodified: property) for a file. The following steps find all files modified since the first of last month.

 1

- Type **datemodified:** in the Search box to list the files in the SCFiles folder according to modification date (Figure 6–33).

  Q&A How can I see all the properties available for a file?
  Click to select the file for which you want to view properties, click the See more button on the toolbar, click Properties on the See more menu to display the Properties dialog box, click the Details tab to display the Details sheet, and then scroll to display all properties. When you have finished, click OK (Properties dialog box) to close the dialog box.

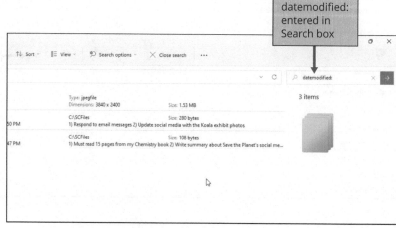

Figure 6–33

 2

- Click the Search options button on the toolbar to display a list of search options.
- Point to Date modified to display a list of date options (Figure 6–34).

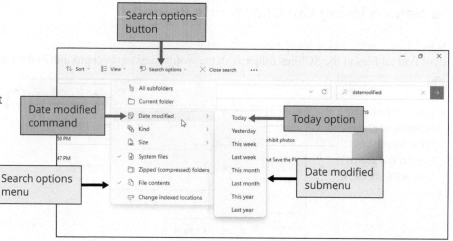

Figure 6–34

 3

- Click Today on the Date modified submenu to search for files modified today (Figure 6–35).
- Click the Close search button on the toolbar to clear the search.

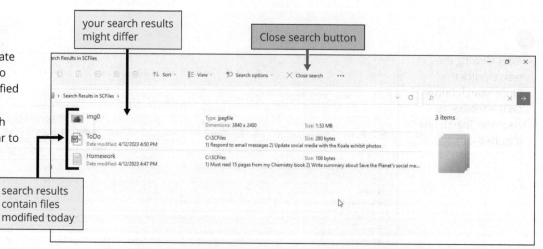

Figure 6–35

To Search for a File by Kind

Windows 11 allows you to search for specific kinds of files, such as documents, games, movies, and pictures. **Why?** You store many pictures on your computer and want to display all the pictures. The following steps search for pictures on your hard drive and display them as search results.

- Click the Windows-SSD (C:) button on the address bar to display the contents of the hard drive.
- Display the contents of the Windows folder and then display the contents of the Web folder.
- Type **kind:** in the Search box to display the contents of the Web folder and its subfolders.
- Click the Search options button on the toolbar and then point to the Kind command to display a list of the different kinds of files (Figure 6–36).

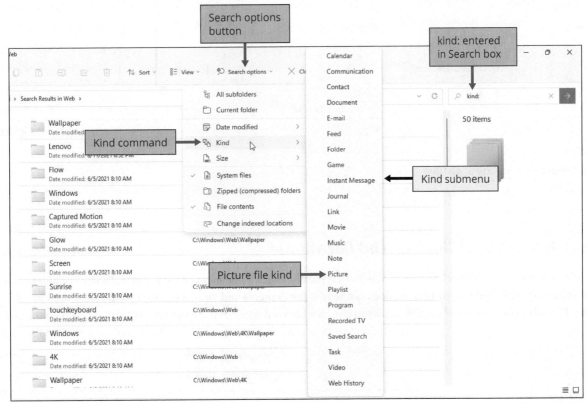

Figure 6–36

- Click Picture on the Kind submenu to display a list of pictures stored in the Web folder and its subfolders.
- Scroll to display the search results (Figure 6–37).

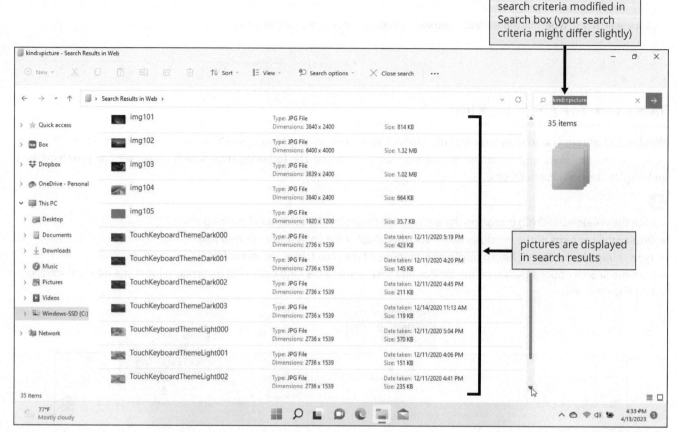

search criteria modified in Search box (your search criteria might differ slightly)

pictures are displayed in search results

Figure 6–37

Other Ways

1. Click Search box, type **kind: picture**

To Search Additional Nonindexed Locations

As mentioned previously, the search feature in Windows typically searches the indexed locations and some nonindexed locations (such as system files). Windows, by default, does not search file contents and zipped (compressed) files stored in nonindexed locations. The following steps configure Windows to search additional nonindexed locations. **Why?** If you are looking for a file that could be stored anywhere on your hard drive and you want Windows to perform a full search of nonindexed locations, you will need to configure Windows to perform this action.

● Click the Search options button on the toolbar to display the Search options menu (Figure 6–38).

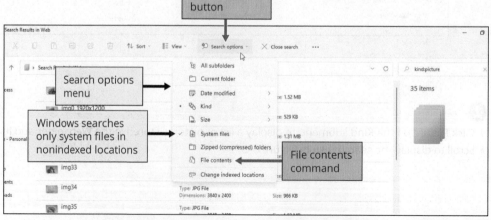

Search options button

Search options menu

Windows searches only system files in nonindexed locations

File contents command

Figure 6–38

2

- Click File contents on the Search options menu to configure Windows to search the file contents in nonindexed locations.
- Click the Search options button on the toolbar to display a list of search options (Figure 6–39).
- Click 'Zipped (compressed) folders' on the Search options menu to configure Windows to search zipped (compressed) folders stored in nonindexed locations.

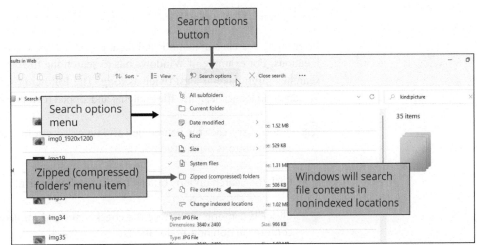

Figure 6–39

3

- Close the search results.
- Display the contents of the Windows folder.
- Type **screen** in the Search box to perform a search using the text, screen, in the additional nonindexed locations (Figure 6–40). The search might take a long time to complete, depending on the number of files in the Windows folder. If you do not want to wait for all search results to appear, skip ahead to Step 4.

Q&A Why does the search take so long to complete?
Windows is searching every file, as well as the contents of each file, which can take several minutes or longer to complete.

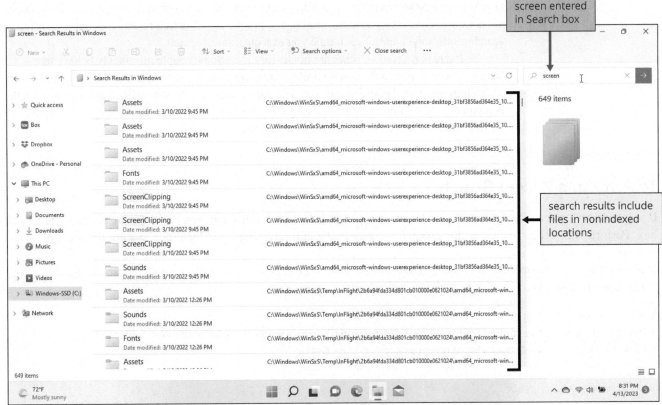

Figure 6–40

4

- After viewing the search results, close the search.

To Reset the Nonindexed Location Search Settings

Performing searches in nonindexed locations is not always as efficient as searching only indexed locations. For example, if Windows has to search the file contents in every nonindexed location, searches might take at least twice as long. The following steps reset the search settings so that Windows no longer searches file contents and zipped (compressed) folders in nonindexed locations.

1 If necessary, click the Search box and type **computer** as the search text to display the search buttons on the toolbar.

2 Click the Search options button on the toolbar to display a list of search options.

3 Click File contents to remove the check mark and configure Windows not to search file contents in nonindexed locations.

4 Click the Search options button on the toolbar to display a list of search options.

5 Click 'Zipped (compressed) folders' on the Search options menu to remove its check mark and configure Windows not to search compressed folders in nonindexed locations.

Working with Saved Searches

Every user has a Searches folder that is created by Windows when their user account is created. The Searches folder is the default location for all saved searches. Any searches that you have saved will appear in your Searches folder. It is important to note that a **saved search** is a set of instructions about how to conduct a particular search, and not the actual search results themselves. Different search results might appear each time you execute a saved search.

Be aware that saved searches are not history lists. Some people mistakenly believe that some searches, such as a recently modified file search, are history lists, like those found when working with a browser. They believe that if they delete the search results, they will clear the history on the computer, which is not the case. Deleting search results deletes the files from your computer, so be very careful when choosing to delete search results.

To Perform a Recent Search

If you have performed a search recently and want to perform the same search again, you can do so by clicking the Search box. Performing a recent search in this manner will search the currently displayed locations and not the location of the original search. **Why?** You want to perform another search for all pictures in the Web folder because you closed the previous search results before having a chance to review them completely. The following steps use the Search box to perform a recent search.

- If necessary, display the contents of the Windows folder and then display the contents of the Web folder.
- Click the Search box to display a list of recent searches (Figure 6–41).

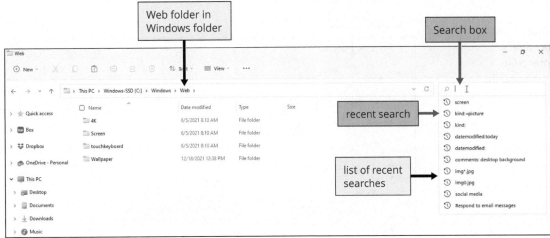

Figure 6–41

2

- Click 'kind: = picture' in the Recent searches list to perform a search for pictures (Figure 6–42).

Q&A What if I perform this same search when the SCFiles folder is displayed?
Because recent searches only search the currently displayed location, performing the search would display only the pictures stored in the SCFiles folder.

Figure 6–42

To Save a Search

After defining search criteria, you can save a search. By using a saved search, you can perform the same search repeatedly without having to re-create the search each time. The next time you execute a saved search, the search results might differ from the results you received when the search was first performed. **Why?** You anticipate performing searches for pictures on a regular basis. The following steps save the current search as Picture Search.

- Right-click the file icon in the right pane to display a shortcut menu (Figure 6–43).
- Click Save search on the shortcut menu to display the Save As dialog box.

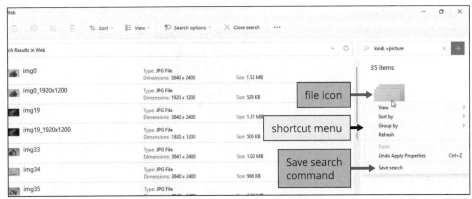

Figure 6–43

- Type **Picture Search** in the File name box to enter a file name for the search (Figure 6–44).

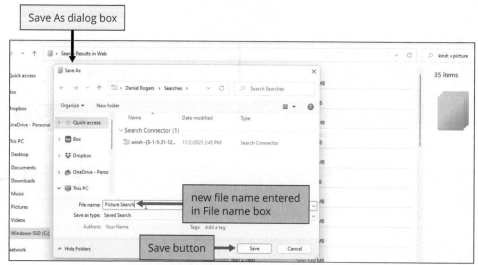

Figure 6–44

- Click the Save button (Save As dialog box) to save the search (Figure 6–45).
- Close the Picture Search window.

Figure 6–45

Q&A Why can I not just continue performing this search from the Recent searches list?
The searches that appear in the Recent searches list do not stay there permanently and can be cleared at any time. If you want to ensure that you can perform the same search again in the future without having to reenter the search criteria, you should save the search.

To Open the Searches Folder

Why? To access saved searches you have created, you first must open the Searches folder. The Searches folder is located in your user folder, which is created when you create your user account. The following steps open the Searches folder.

- Click the Search button on the taskbar and then type **searches** in the Search box to display a list of search results (Figure 6–46).

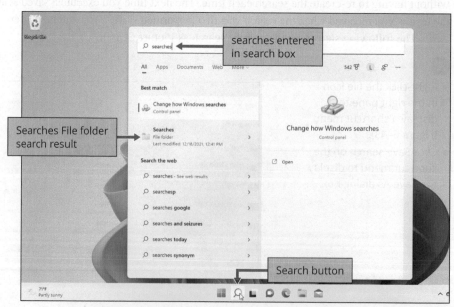

Figure 6–46

● Click the Searches File folder search result to open the Searches folder window (Figure 6–47).

Searches folder window

Picture Search saved search

Figure 6–47

Other Ways

1. Open This PC window, display contents of hard drive, open Users folder, open folder corresponding to your user account, open Searches folder

To Create a Search from a Saved Search

You can use an existing saved search as a starting point for more searches. For example, if you want to search for pictures containing the text, img, in the file name, you can open the saved Picture Search and enter additional search criteria. **Why?** The Picture Search search results were too extensive, and you want to further limit the search results. The following steps search for results using the keyword, img, in the saved Picture Search and then save the search using the name, Picture Search - img.

● Double-click the Picture Search saved search in the Searches folder window (shown in Figure 6–47).
● Scroll to display the search results (Figure 6–48).

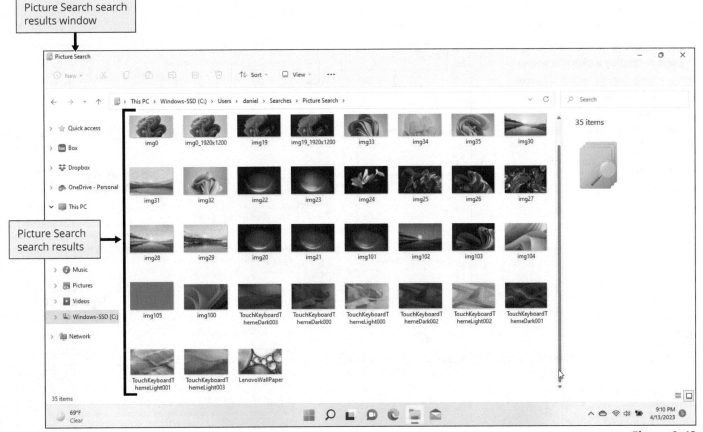

Picture Search search results window

Picture Search search results

Figure 6–48

- Type **img** in the Search box to enter the additional search criteria (Figure 6–49).

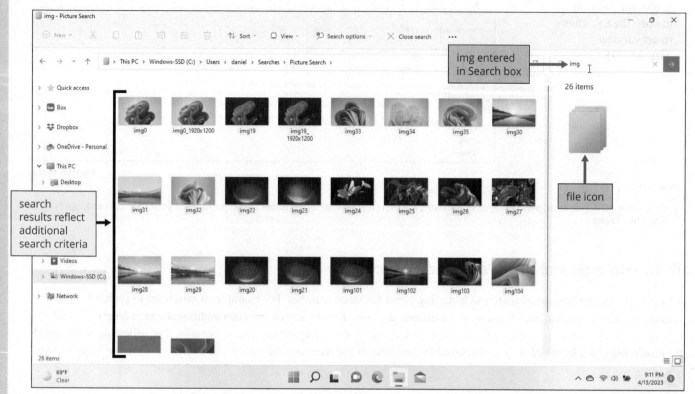

Figure 6–49

- Right-click the file icon in the right pane to display a shortcut menu.
- Click Save search on the shortcut menu to display the Save As dialog box.
- Type **Picture Search - img** in the File name box to enter a file name for the search (Figure 6–50).

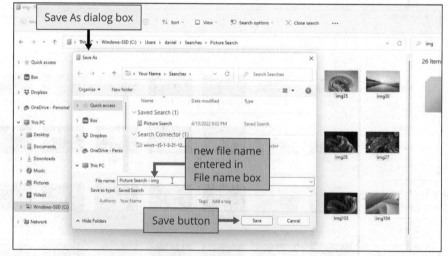

Figure 6–50

- Click the Save button (Save As dialog box) to save the search and display the search results (Figure 6–51).

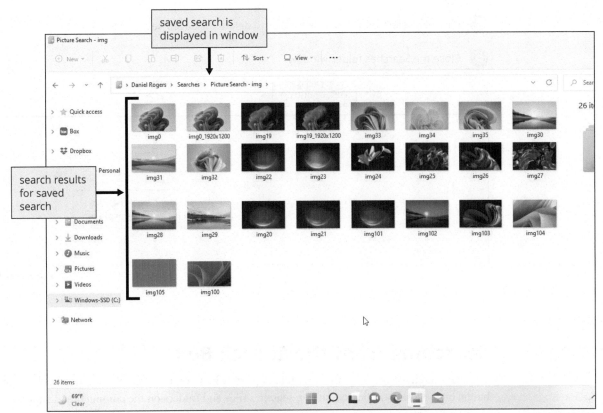

Figure 6–51

5
- Click the Searches button on the address bar to display a list of saved searches (Figure 6–52).

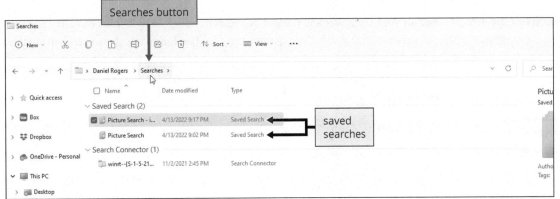

Figure 6–52

To Delete a Saved Search

You can delete any saved search in your Searches folder. Before deleting a saved search, you should be sure that you no longer need it. The following steps delete the saved searches you created in the previous steps.

1 Click the Picture Search saved search to select it.

2 Click the Delete button on the toolbar to delete the Picture Search saved search.

3 Click the Picture Search - img saved search to select it.

④ Click the Delete button on the toolbar to delete the saved search (Figure 6–53).

⑤ Close the Searches folder window.

Figure 6–53

Searching from the Search Box

You can search using the Search box that appears when you click the Start button or the Search button on the taskbar. The Search box searches files and folders on the computer and additionally searches the Internet to find webpages that match your search criteria. The Search box also provides a way to configure web searches so that only the most appropriate results are displayed.

To Search Using the Search Box

The Search box, by default, searches your computer and the web for search results. **Why?** You would like to use the Search box to search the computer, apps, settings, and the web for your search criteria. **The following steps search using the Search box.**

①
• Click the Search button on the taskbar to display search information (Figure 6–54).

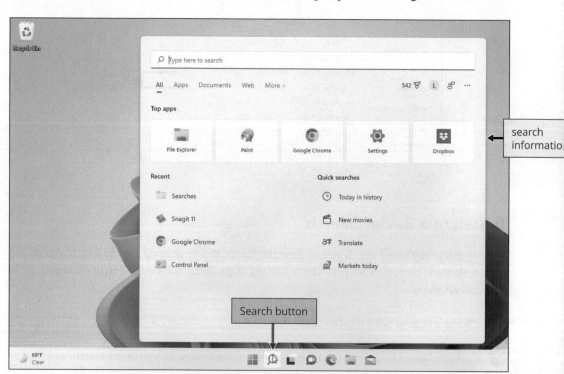

Figure 6–54

2

- Type **pictures** in the Search box to display search results related to pictures (Figure 6–55).

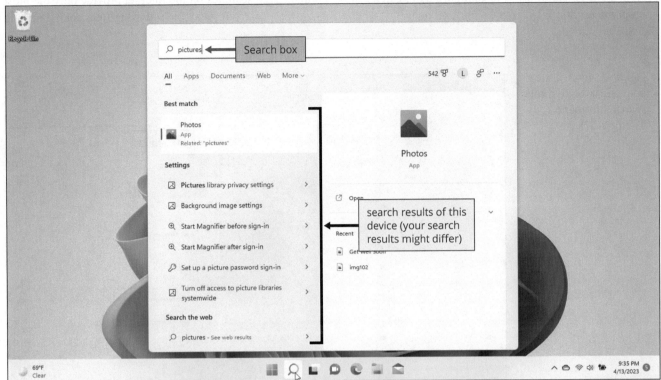

Figure 6–55

3

- Click the More button to display additional locations to search (Figure 6–56).

4

- Click an empty area on the desktop to close the search results.

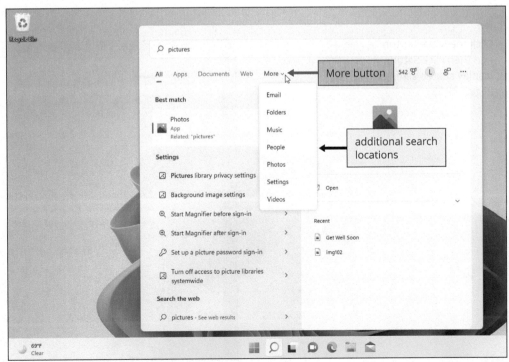

Figure 6–56

To Configure Bing SafeSearch Settings

The Internet contains a wealth of information, and some information might not be appropriate for all audiences. For this reason, Windows allows you to configure SafeSearch settings to make sure searches on the Internet provide only the most appropriate results. **Why?** You do not want to include adult content in your search results. The following steps configure Bing SafeSearch settings.

● Click the Search button on the taskbar to display search information (Figure 6–57).

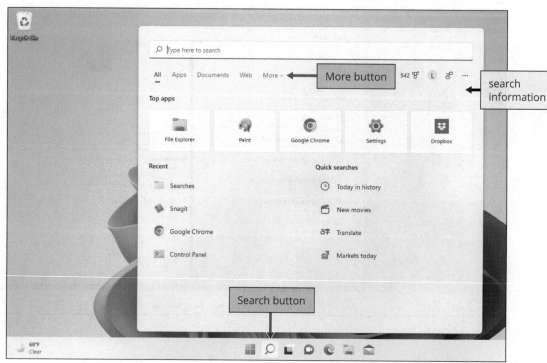

Figure 6–57

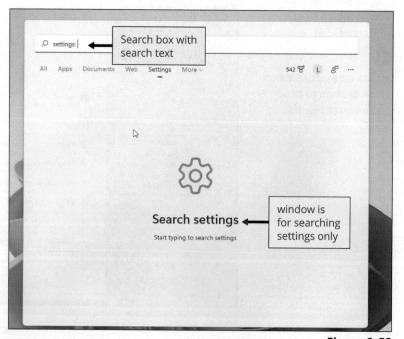

● Click the More button and then click Settings to display search settings (Figure 6–58).

Figure 6–58

- Type **SafeSearch settings** in the Search box and then press ENTER to open the Search permissions window in the Settings app.
- Click the Strict option button in the SafeSearch area to configure Windows to filter out adult text, images, and videos from the search results (Figure 6–59).

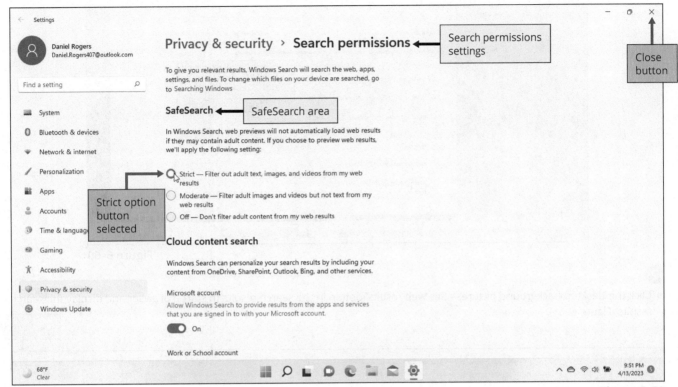

Figure 6–59

- Click the Close button to close the Settings window.

To Search the Web Using the Search Box

In addition to the Search box allowing you to exclude information on the web from the search results, you also can choose to display search results only from the web. **Why?** You have searched your computer for desktop backgrounds you would like to use but could not find any that are suitable. You now want to see the desktop backgrounds available on the web. The following steps search the web using the Search box.

- Click the Search button on the taskbar and then type **desktop background pictures** in the Search box to display the search results (Figure 6–60).

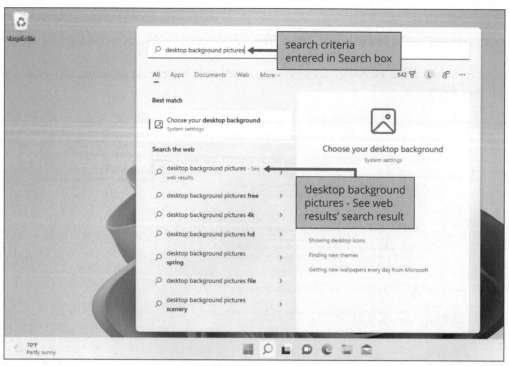

Figure 6–60

2

- Click the 'desktop background pictures - See web results' option in the search results to start a browser and display the search results (Figure 6–61).

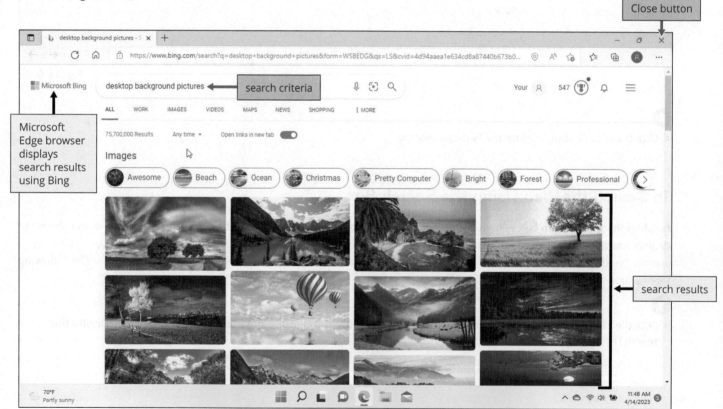

Figure 6–61

 3

- Click the Close button to exit Microsoft Edge.

To Use the Search Box to Search for Other Information

In addition to using the Search box to search for files, settings, apps, and results on the web, you also can use the Search box to perform actions such as conversions and mathematical calculations or to display weather and time information and sports scores. **Why?** You would like to use the Search box to search for additional information, such as conversion information, weather and time information, and to perform mathematical calculations. The following steps use the Search box to perform conversions, display weather information, display time information, and perform a mathematical calculation.

- Click the search button on the taskbar to display search information.
- Type **How many cups are in a gallon?** in the Search box to display the search results (Figure 6–62).

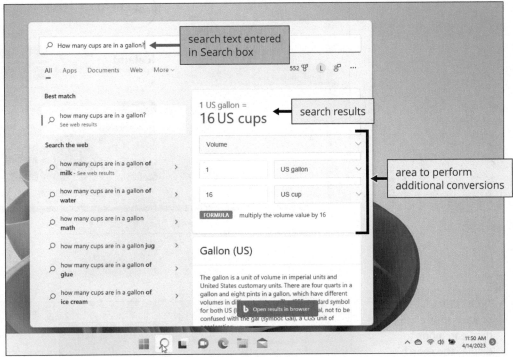

Figure 6–62

- Type **What is the weather forecast for nyc tomorrow?** in the Search box to display the search results (Figure 6–63).

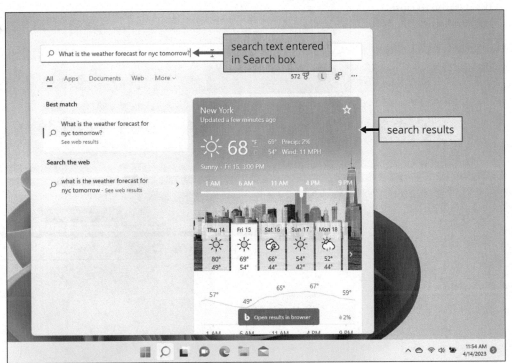

Figure 6–63

3

- Type **What is the current time in Iceland?** in the Search box to display the search results (Figure 6–64).

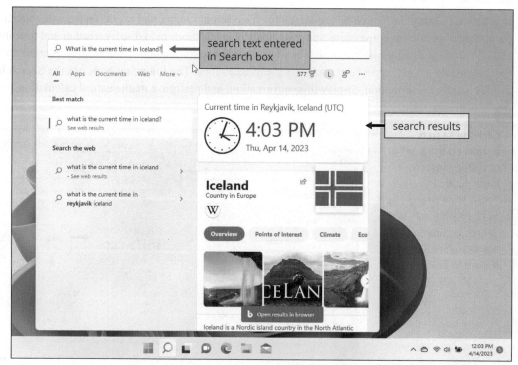

Figure 6–64

4

- Type **Calculate the square root of 25** in the Search box to display the search results (Figure 6–65).
- Click an empty area on the desktop to close the Search box.

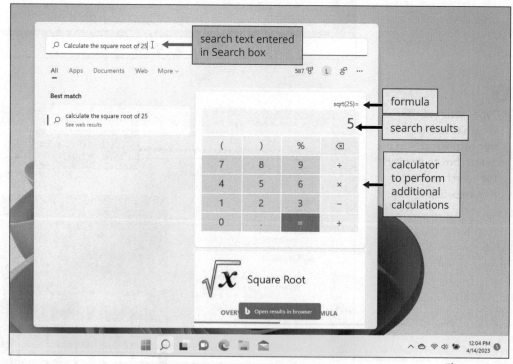

Figure 6–65

To Show the Cortana Icon on the Taskbar

Windows 11 displays the Search button on the taskbar by default, but you also have the option of pinning the Cortana icon to the taskbar. **Why?** It would be convenient to give voice commands to Cortana using an icon on the taskbar. The following steps show the Cortana icon on the taskbar.

- Click the Search button on the taskbar to display search options.
- Type **Cortana** in the Search box to display the search results (Figure 6–66).

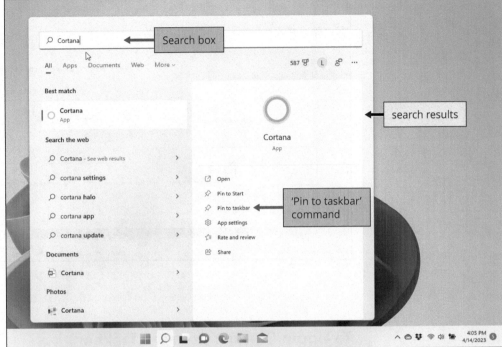

Figure 6–66

- Click 'Pin to taskbar' in the search results to show the Cortana icon on the taskbar (Figure 6–67).

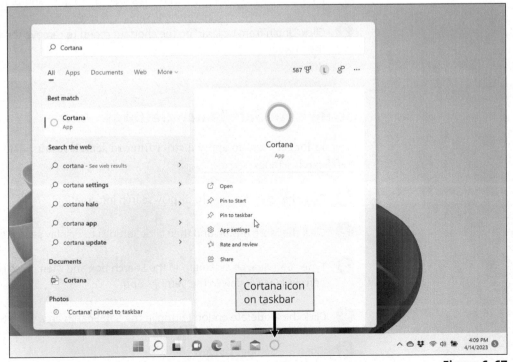

Figure 6–67

3

- Click the Cortana icon on the taskbar to start the Cortana app (Figure 6–68).
- Click the Close button to exit Cortana.

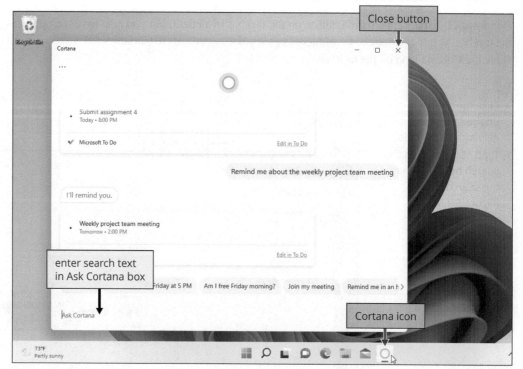

Figure 6–68

To Unpin Cortana from the Taskbar

The following steps unpin Cortana from the taskbar.

1 Right-click the Cortana icon on the taskbar to display a shortcut menu.

2 Click 'Unpin from taskbar' on the shortcut menu to remove the Cortana icon from the taskbar.

To Restore SafeSearch Settings

You no longer want to apply a strict filter to search results. The following steps restore the SafeSearch settings.

1 Click the Search button to display search information.

2 Click the More button and then click Settings to display search settings.

3 Type **SafeSearch settings** in the Search box and then press ENTER to open the Search permissions window in the Settings app.

4 Click the Moderate option button in the SafeSearch area to restore the SafeSearch settings.

5 Close the Settings window.

To Remove a Folder from the Index

Why? When you no longer need a folder to be indexed, you should remove it from the index. This means that if you search the folder at a later time, the search might be slower, depending upon the size of the folder. The following steps remove the SCFiles folder from the Search Index.

 1

- Open the Control Panel window.
- Change the view to Small icons (Figure 6–69).

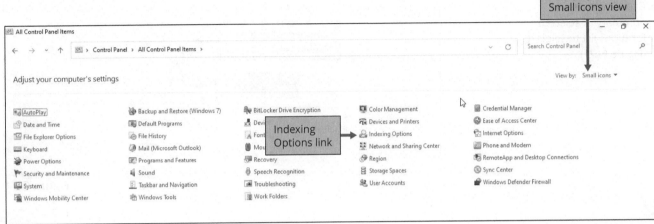

Figure 6–69

 2

- Click the Indexing Options link to display the Indexing Options dialog box.
- Click the Modify button (Indexing Options dialog box) to display the Indexed Locations dialog box (Figure 6–70).

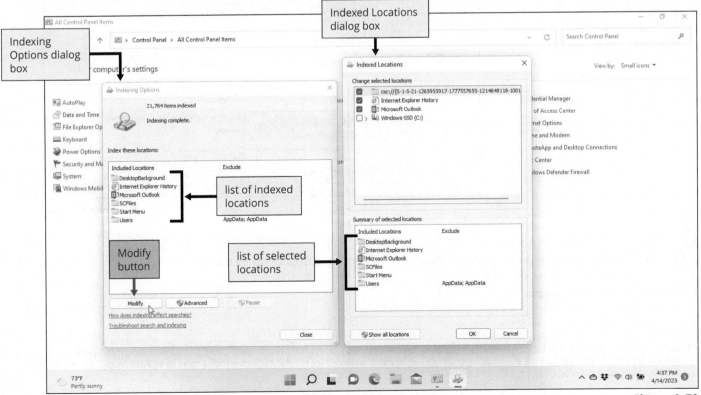

Figure 6–70

- Click the Windows-SSD (C:) arrow to display the list of folders on Windows-SSD (C:).
- If necessary, click the SCFiles folder check box to place a check mark.
- Click SCFiles in the Summary of selected locations list to select it (Figure 6–71).

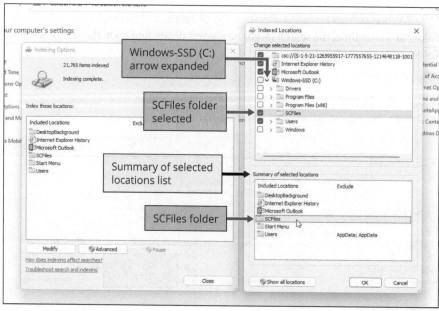

Figure 6–71

- Click the SCFiles folder check box in the Change selected locations list to remove the check mark (Figure 6–72).
- Click OK (Indexed Locations dialog box) to remove the SCFiles folder from the Search Index and to close the Indexed Locations dialog box.

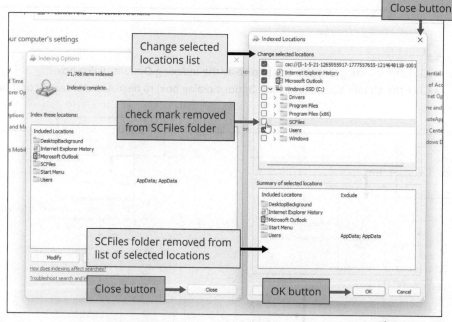

Figure 6–72

- Click the Close button (Indexing Options dialog box) to close the Indexing Options dialog box.
- Change the Control Panel view to Category.
- Close the Control Panel window.

Other Ways

1. In File Explorer, click Search box, type search text, click Search options button on toolbar, click 'Change indexed locations', click Modify button (Indexing Options dialog box), click SCFiles in list of indexed locations, click check box next to SCFiles folder, click OK (Indexed Locations dialog box), click Close button (Indexing Options dialog box)

To Delete the SCFiles Folder

Now that you have removed the SCFiles folder from the index, you can delete it. The following steps delete the SCFiles folder and the files it contains.

1 Open the This PC window.

2 Display the contents of your hard drive, such as Windows-SSD (C:) or Local Disk (C:).

3 Delete the SCFiles folder.

4 Close the This PC window.

5 Empty the Recycle Bin.

To Sign Out of Your Account and Shut Down the Computer

After completing your work with Windows, you should end your session by signing out of your account and then turning off the computer. The following steps sign out of your account and shut down the computer.

1 Display the Start menu.

2 Click the user account icon and then click Sign out.

3 Click the lock screen to display the sign-in screen.

4 Click the Shut down button.

5 Click Shut down on the Shut down menu to shut down the computer.

Summary

In this module, you learned how to use advanced search techniques. Using the Search box, you learned how to search a folder using keywords, Boolean operators, and property data. You filtered files using the file list headings. You added a location to the index and learned the differences between using indexed and nonindexed locations when searching. You learned how each file type has different properties and that you can search using those properties. Using the advanced Search options of the Search box, you found files based on additional properties. You also configured the Search box to exclude search results from the web. You also configured SafeSearch settings and displayed the Cortana icon on the taskbar.

Student Assignments

Apply Your Knowledge

Reinforce the skills and apply the concepts you learned in this module.

Exploring Different Search Techniques

Instructions: Open the This PC window and navigate to the Windows folder. Maximize the window if necessary and then search for images as instructed below.

Perform the following tasks:

1. Open the This PC window and navigate to the Web folder in the Windows folder. If necessary, maximize the window.

2. Search for pictures with the file name, img3 (Figure 6–73).

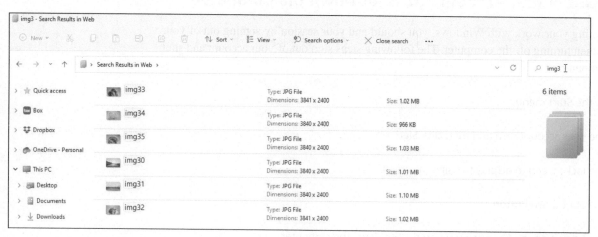

Figure 6–73

3. Select each search result and copy it to the Pictures folder.

4. Return to the Web folder and search for pictures containing the word, light, in the file name.

5. Select each search result and copy it to the Pictures folder.

6. In the Windows folder, search for all files with names that contain the word, chimes, or the word, town, using the Boolean OR operator.

7. Select each picture search result and copy it to the Pictures folder, skipping any duplicates.

8. Search for all files with names that contain the keyword, grad, but not the keyword, darkblue.

9. Select each picture search result and copy it to the Pictures folder, skipping any duplicates.

10. Search for pictures in the .jpg file format with file names that contain the keyword, wmp.

11. Select each search result and copy it to the Pictures folder.

12. Search for pictures that begin with the letters, pe, and have a Tiny file size (0 – 16 KB).

13. Select one search result and copy it to the Pictures folder.

14. Record the list of the files that you have copied to the Pictures folder in this exercise and then submit the list to your instructor.

15. Open the Pictures folder.

16. Select all the files you copied to the folder in this exercise.

17. Right-click one of the picture icons to display a shortcut menu and then click Delete on the shortcut menu.

18. Close the Pictures folder.

Extend Your Knowledge

Extend the skills you learned in this module and experiment with new skills. You might need to use Help to complete the assignment.

Using the Search Box to Search for Information

Instructions: Use the Search box to find information on the Internet and on your computer.

Perform the following steps:

1. Design a search statement for each of the following topics, click the Search button on the taskbar, and then type the statement into the Search box. Expand each search to the Internet; find and print an appropriate webpage for each statement. Create a WordPad document, and record your search text for each example given.

   a. You want to find journals that are available through the UCF libraries (Figure 6–74).

   b. You want to see current temperature readings for major cities in the United States.

   c. You need information to write a report about the senators that represent your state in the U.S. Senate.

   d. You want to shop for the best prices for a new computer. You already have prices for Dell and Lenovo computers, so you do not want to include those in your search results.

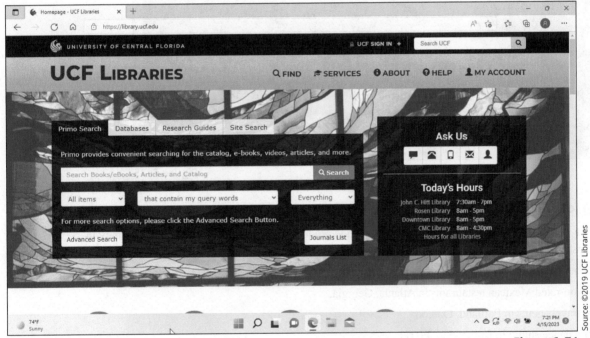

Source: ©2019 UCF Libraries

Figure 6–74

2. Design a set of search keywords for each of the following topics, type the keywords you come up with in the Search box on the taskbar to test them (expand if necessary), and then write a summary of your results in a WordPad document.

   a. You want to find files you have that contain information about creating an Excel spreadsheet.

   b. You know that you have saved webpages about buying a new motorhome.

   c. You have applied for admission to Kansas State University and have received email messages from the admissions department.

3. Submit your answers and printouts to your instructor.

Expand Your World

Searching the Web

Create a solution that uses cloud or web technologies by learning and investigating on your own from general guidance.

Instructions: If necessary, connect to the Internet. Start Microsoft Edge and then perform the following searches using search techniques introduced in this module. Type **bing.com** in the address bar and then press enter to display the Bing search engine (Figure 6–75). Determine the best search criteria to use and then click the link for your preferred search result. Print the webpage for the search result you choose for each item and submit it to your instructor.

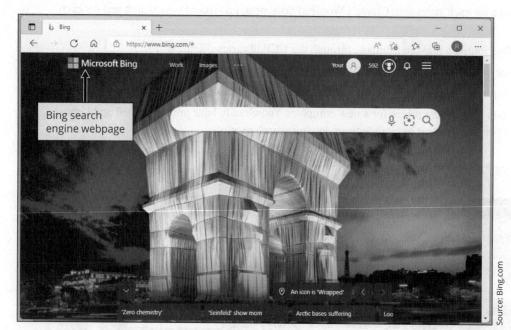

Figure 6–75

Source: Bing.com

Perform the following tasks:

1. Search for a webpage containing information about an undergraduate psychology degree from a university in New Hampshire.

2. Search for a professional photographer in your hometown.

3. Search for top-rated Mexican restaurants in Atlanta, Georgia.

4. Search for travel agents in Portland, Oregon.

5. Search for a dance studio in Hollywood, Florida.

6. Search for a company in Phoenix, Arizona, that builds custom cabinets.

7. Search for a secondhand children's clothing and/or toy store in California.

8. Exit Microsoft Edge.

In the Labs

Design and implement a solution using creative thinking and problem-solving skills.

Lab 1: Using Windows 11 to Search for Files and Folders

Problem: In addition to using the Search box to search for files when all you know is their file names, you also can search for files using various file properties (Figure 6–76). Perform searches for files using the following guidelines. Create a WordPad document and type the answers to the questions that follow.

Figure 6–76

1. Search for files and folders in your Windows folder that were modified today. How many files or folders were found?

2. Search for files and folders in your Windows folder that were modified since your last birthday. How many files or folders were found?

3. Modify the advanced search options to search compressed files, system files, and file contents in nonindexed locations. Search for files and folders in your Windows folder that were modified in the last month. How many files or folders were found? Restore the advanced search options so that compressed files and file contents in nonindexed locations are not searched.

4. Search your Windows folder for .jpg files.

5. List the first five .jpg files found during the search.

6. Scroll to make the first icon visible and then double-click the first icon. Which image is displayed? In which app is the image displayed?

7. Scroll to make the last icon visible and then double-click the last icon. Which image is displayed?

8. Search your Windows folder for music files in the .wav file format using the keyword, WAV.

   a. How many files or folders were found?

   b. Double-click one of the files that was found. What do you hear?

9. Search your Windows folder for video files.

   a. How many files or folders were found?

   b. Double-click one of the videos. What is displayed?

10. Search your Windows folder for all text documents containing the keyword, homework. How many files or folders were found?

11. Search your Windows folder for files with the .gif extension. (**Hint:** Type ***.gif** in the Search box.)

    a. How many files were found?

    b. What happens when you double-click one of these files?

12. Close the Search Results window.

Lab 2: Searching for Files Based on Content

Problem: You want to test the way Windows 11 can find files based on content. You plan to create four files using WordPad and then practice your search techniques to list files based on content.

1. Create a folder in the Documents folder titled, Lab 2.

2. Create the four documents shown in Figure 6–77 using WordPad and save them in the Lab 2 folder.

3. Search for your classes using the keyword, class. How many results appear?

4. Search for homework assignments using the keyword, lab 2. How many results appear?

5. Search for your work task list using the keyword, work. How many results appear?

6. Submit your answers to your instructor.

7. Delete the folder and files that you added to the Documents folder.

Continued on next page

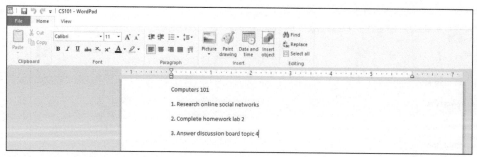

Figure 6–77a

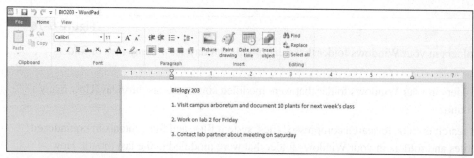

Figure 6–77b

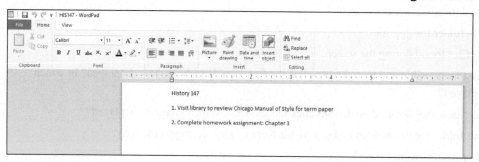

Figure 6–77c

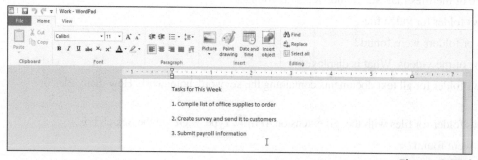

Figure 6–77d

Lab 3: Consider This: Your Turn

Understanding Wildcards

Problem: Wildcard characters often are used in a file name to locate a group of files while searching. For example, to locate all files with the file name, Physics, regardless of the file extension, an entry (Physics.*) containing the asterisk wildcard character would be used. Your supervisor has asked you to create a guide to using wildcards so that other employees in your organization can perform more effective searches.

Part 1:   Using the Internet, computer publications, or any other resources, develop a guide to using wildcards. Summarize what a wildcard character is, what the valid wildcard characters are, and provide several examples to explain their use.

Part 2:   You made several decisions while searching for this assignment. What decisions did you make? What was the rationale behind these decisions? How did you determine what to include in this guide?

Microsoft Edge

Objectives

After completing this module, you will be able to:

- Personalize the home page
- Use tabbed browsing
- Display webpages by address
- Open an InPrivate window
- Search using the Search box
- Change search providers
- Find information on a webpage
- Use Cortana to search the web

- Use the Immersive Reader
- Save an article to a collection
- Add a website to favorites
- Open a saved webpage
- Display the favorites bar
- Search for information with the sidebar
- Display the Edge bar

What Is Microsoft Edge?

Microsoft Edge is the default browser with the release of Windows 11. For most users, the browser is a common tool for locating and accessing information every day. In the previous modules, you already have explored basic features of Edge as a browser, using it to access different websites.

Microsoft designed Edge to be more than a basic browser, placing a focus on creating a tool ready for the newest web development practices, including **predictive browsing**, a feature that predicts which links you will visit next and preloads them into memory, and the **semantic web**, which is a web of linked data that supports the creation of data stores on the web. Although Edge provides many features consistent with other browsers, such as favorites, tabbed browsing, and InPrivate windows, several features make Edge unique. Edge also is a **Universal Windows app**, meaning that one application runs on computers, smartphones, tablets, and other mobile devices running Windows 11.

One way in which Edge is different from other browsers is through its integration of Windows 11 and Bing, Microsoft's search engine. You already have experienced the integration of Windows 11 and Edge by opening webpages in Edge directly from Windows search results. Bing is integrated in the browser through the address bar and contextual help options. In addition to providing access to webpages, Edge can be used to provide useful details about information on a webpage, such as definitions, conversions, and related content, or it can respond to queries typed directly in Edge's address bar.

Other unique features of Edge are the Edge bar, a pane that serves as a mini browser, and the sidebar, a vertical toolbar you can use to visit websites and access Edge tools without leaving the current webpage tab. If your browser does not display a sidebar, read the related steps without performing them. Alternatively, you may be able to access the same features from the sidebar using another menu in Edge.

An additional feature of Edge makes it different from other browsers: the Immersive Reader. The **Immersive Reader** is a distraction-free view of articles on the web that hides extra webpage content, such as navigation and advertisements, to allow focus on the article content. It also provides grammar and read-aloud tools.

In this module, you will learn how to use Microsoft Edge for more efficient and effective browsing of the web. You will save content for later access. You will configure settings to personalize Edge. You also will use the Immersive Reader to make webpages more accessible (Figure 7–1).

additional security with InPrivate browsing windows

Figure 7–1a

fewer distractions in Immersive Reader

sidebar

Figure 7–1b

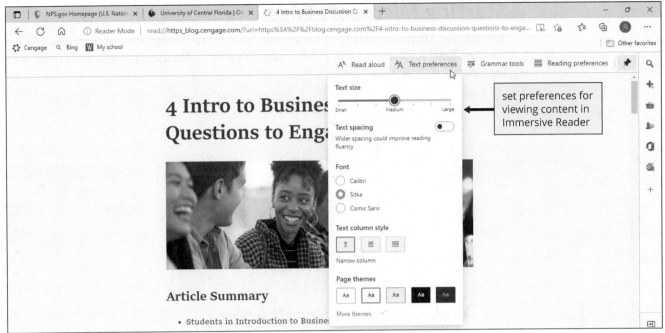

Figure 7–1c

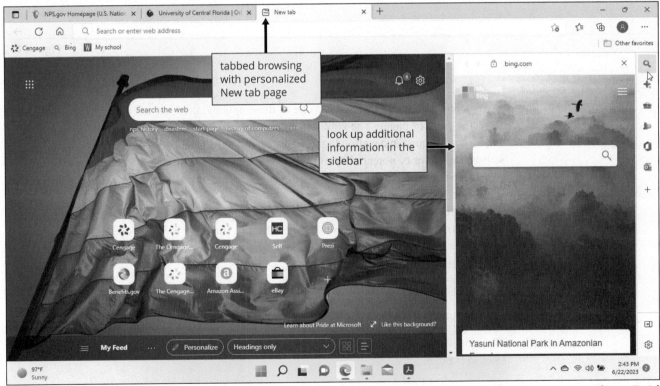

Figure 7–1d

Starting Microsoft Edge

You can start Microsoft Edge from the app button on the taskbar or from the Start menu. When you start Edge for the first time, you can take a tour of its features or start searching the web immediately (Figure 7–2).

Figure 7–2

Future sessions in Edge open to one of three options: the New tab page, previous pages, or a specific page or pages. The **New tab** page provides a Search box and a row of website tiles that allows for quick navigation to the websites you most frequently visit or suggestions for new websites and apps of potential interest. The New tab page also displays news content from MSN (short for Microsoft Network), a Microsoft web portal that provides access to online news, weather, sports, and more.

Using the previous pages option will restore a browsing session to the most recent set of tabs that were open when Edge last was exited. The specific page or pages option provides choices of MSN or Bing and provides the capability to specify any page or pages to be displayed when Edge is started.

To Start Microsoft Edge

First, you will start Microsoft Edge to display the configured home page. The following step starts Microsoft Edge.

1 Click the Microsoft Edge button on the taskbar to start Microsoft Edge (Figure 7–3).

Q&A Why does my home page look different?

If you are using Microsoft Edge at school or work, or you are using a computer where Microsoft Edge might have previously been customized, your home page may look different.

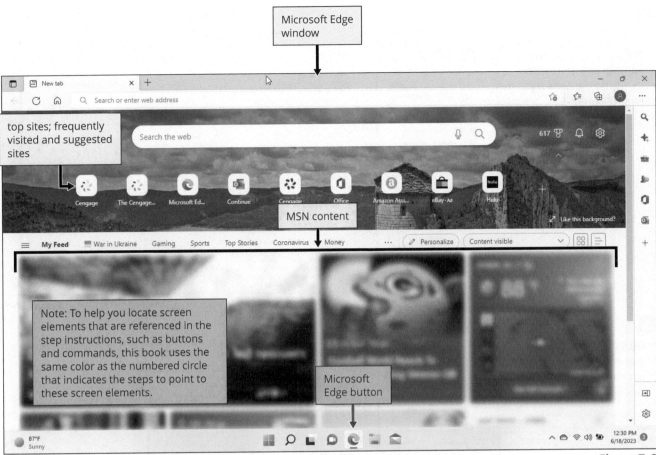

Figure 7–3

To Personalize the Home Page

Why? You want to display the National Park Service's website each time you start Microsoft Edge. Many times, people visit the same websites at the start of a new browsing session to catch up on the latest news or information. The following steps will set the National Park Service's website to display when Edge first is started.

1

- Click the 'Settings and more' button in the address bar to display the Settings and more menu (Figure 7–4).

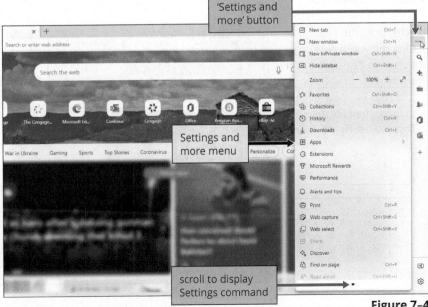

Figure 7–4

2

- If necessary, scroll down and click Settings on the Settings and more menu to display the Settings page (Figure 7–5).

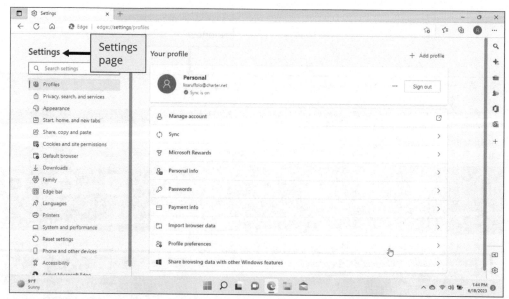

Figure 7–5

3

- Click the 'Start, home, and new tabs' tab in the left pane to display start settings (Figure 7–6).

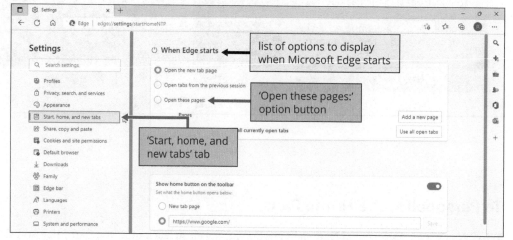

Figure 7–6

4

- Click the 'Open these pages:' option button to activate its options.
- Click the 'Add a new page' button to display the Add a new page dialog box and select a specific page to load when Microsoft Edge starts (Figure 7–7).

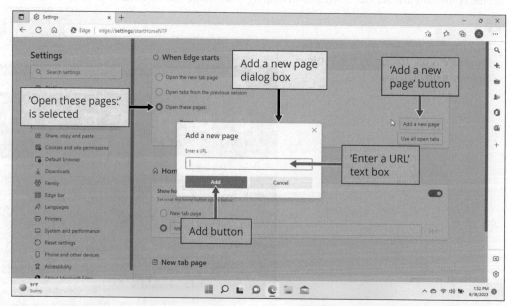

Figure 7–7

5

- Type **https://www.nps.gov** in the 'Enter a URL' text box (shown in Figure 7–7).
- Click the Add button (shown in Figure 7–7) to specify the National Park Service website as the home page.
- Click the 'Add a new page' button to add another page to open when Microsoft Edge starts.
- Type **https://www.ucf.edu** in the 'Enter a URL' text box, and then click the Add button (Figure 7–8).
- Exit Microsoft Edge.

Q&A Can a page be removed from the list?
Yes. Click the More actions button to the right of the page you want to remove and then click Delete on the More actions menu.

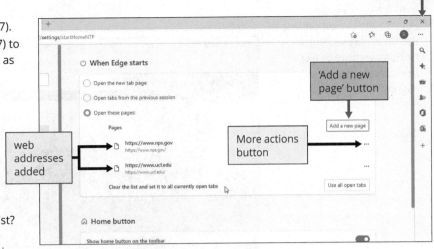

Figure 7–8

Browsing the Web

Microsoft Edge supports browsing the web in traditional ways, either through hyperlinks on displayed webpages, access to websites located by Cortana searches, direct access by web address, or through integrated search features.

When you click a link on a webpage, the new webpage is displayed, replacing the old webpage in the window. **Tabs** represent additional webpages that are open in the browser and display them across the top of the browser window. By using tabs, you can keep multiple webpages open at the same time. You can switch between the tabs without having to redisplay webpages repeatedly in the same browser window.

When the New tab page is displayed in the current browser tab, the web address for the desired webpage or a search phrase can be entered in the Search box to display the webpage or search results in the current tab. To replace a currently displayed webpage with another in the same tab, you can type the new webpage address or a search phrase directly in the address bar text box.

To Switch between Tabs

Why? You may need to access content in a different tab without closing the current tab. The following steps start Microsoft Edge again and then switch to the tab containing the University of Central Florida's website.

1

- Start Microsoft Edge.
- Point to the tab containing the University of Central Florida's website to display the tab's thumbnail (Figure 7–9).

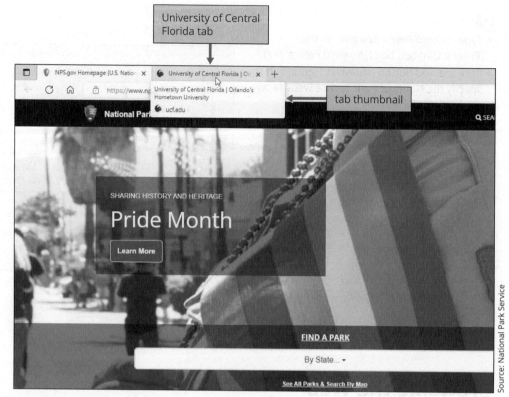

University of Central Florida tab

tab thumbnail

Figure 7–9

Source: National Park Service

2

- Click the tab to display the University of Central Florida's webpage (Figure 7–10).

active tab

University of Central Florida webpage

Figure 7–10

Source: University of Central Florida

Other Ways

1. Press CTRL+TAB to cycle clockwise through open tabs in browser

To Change New Tab Settings

When opening new tabs in Microsoft Edge, the default option is to display the new tab page with top websites and suggested content similar to what is provided on the New tab page; however, you can choose to display only some content or only headings when opening a new tab. **Why?** You are opening a new tab to display a specific website and do not want all the suggested content to be displayed. The following steps change the new tab settings to display only headings without suggested content.

1

• Click the New tab button to add a new tab displaying top sites and suggested content (Figure 7-11).

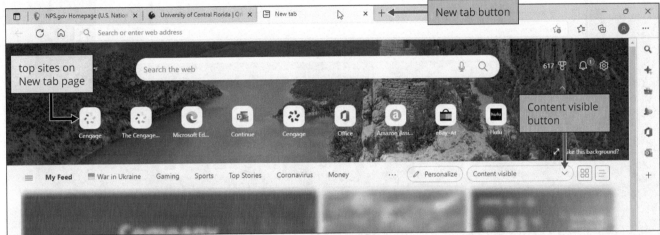

Figure 7-11

2

• Click the Content visible button to display a list of content options.
• Click Headings only to display top sites and only headings for suggested content (Figure 7-12).

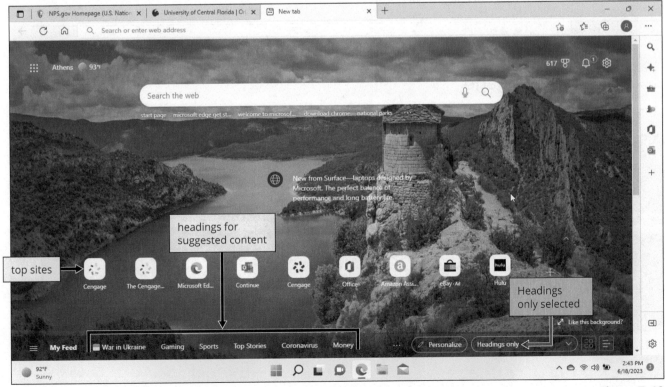

Figure 7-12

• Type **www.cengage.com** in the address bar (Figure 7–13).

text entered in address bar

site suggestions

Figure 7–13

• Press ENTER to view the Cengage webpage (Figure 7–14).

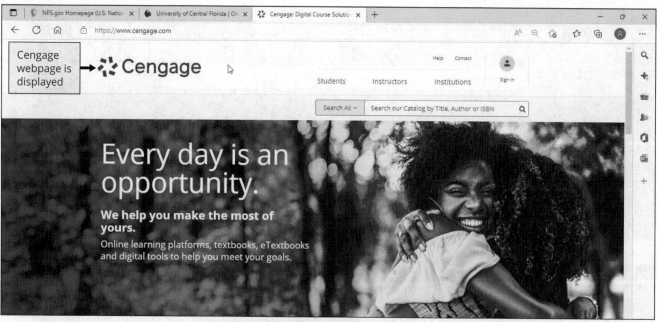

Cengage webpage is displayed

Figure 7–14

Other Ways

1. Press CTRL+T

To Display a Webpage by Address

Why? You want to find information about data sets. The following steps display the data.gov webpage.

• Type **www.data.gov** in the address bar (Figure 7–15).

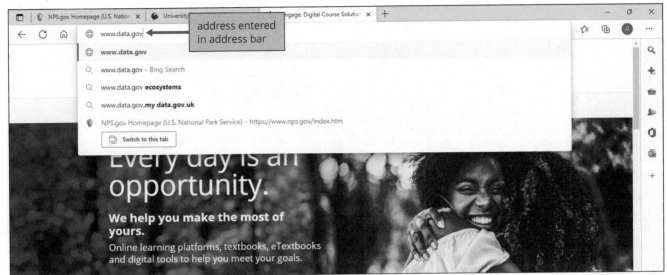

Figure 7–15

• Press ENTER to display the Data.gov webpage in the current tab (Figure 7–16).

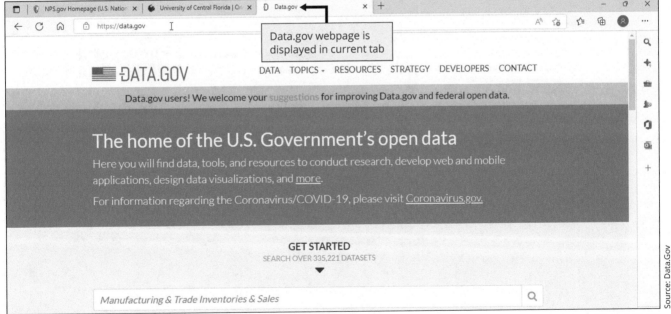

Source: Data.Gov

Figure 7–16

To Open a Link in a New Tab

The following steps open the contents of a link in a new tab. **Why?** You can open links from the webpage you are viewing in new tabs for later viewing.

1

- Scroll to the bottom of the Data.gov webpage (Figure 7–17).

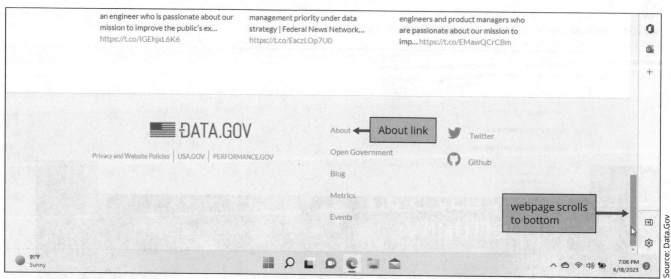

Figure 7–17

Source: Data.Gov

2

- Right-click the About link to display the shortcut menu (Figure 7–18).

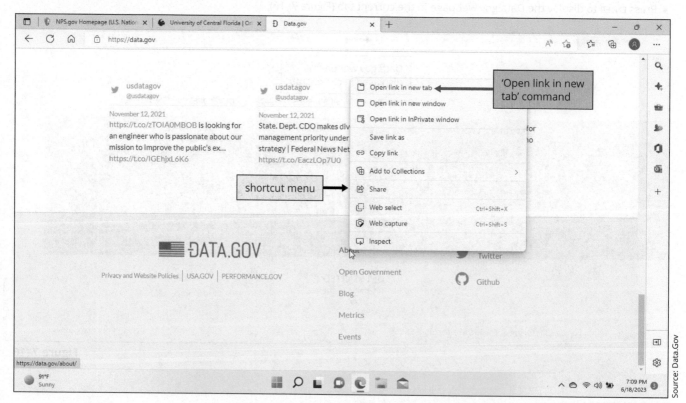

Figure 7–18

Source: Data.Gov

- Click 'Open link in new tab' on the shortcut menu to display the webpage in a new tab (Figure 7–19).

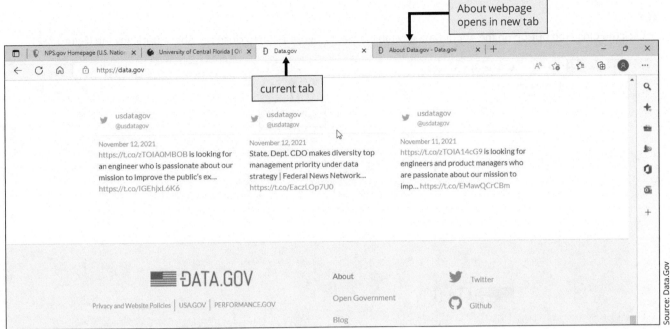

About webpage opens in new tab

current tab

Figure 7–19

Source: Data.Gov

- Click the new tab to switch to the new tab (Figure 7–20).

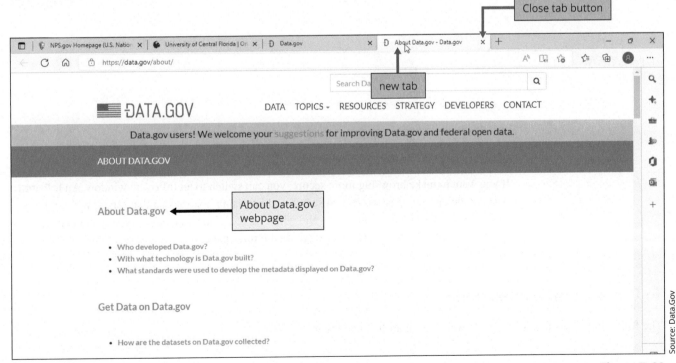

Close tab button

new tab

About Data.gov webpage

Figure 7–20

Source: Data.Gov

To Close a Tab

When you are finished using a tab and no longer need it displayed, it can be closed. **Why?** Too many tabs can make it difficult to keep track of your browsing. The following step closes the About Data.gov tab.

- Click the Close tab button on the About Data.gov tab (shown in Figure 7–20) to close the About Data.gov tab (Figure 7–21).

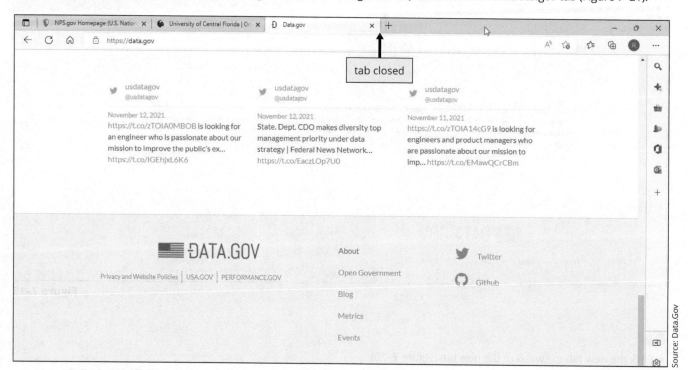

Figure 7–21

Source: Data.Gov

Other Ways

1. Press CTRL+W

Using an InPrivate Window

If you want to make browsing more secure, you can switch to an InPrivate window. An **InPrivate window** deletes any passwords and search and browsing histories so that others will not be able to see them after you are done using the window. You also can clear browsing data and change other settings for Microsoft Edge through the Settings page.

To Open an InPrivate Window

The following steps display the Bing webpage in an InPrivate window. **Why?** You want to keep your search history on this computer private.

1

- Click the 'Settings and more' button in the address bar to display the Settings and more menu (Figure 7–22).

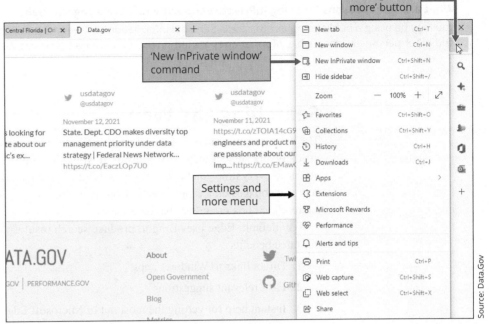

'Settings and more' button

'New InPrivate window' command

Settings and more menu

Source: Data.Gov

Figure 7–22

2

- Click 'New InPrivate window' on the Settings and more menu to open a new InPrivate window (Figure 7–23).

InPrivate browsing window

Figure 7–23

3

- Type **www.bing.com** in the address bar in the InPrivate window and then press ENTER to display the Bing webpage (Figure 7–24).
- Click the Close button to close the InPrivate window.

Close button

www.bing.com entered in address bar

Bing displayed in InPrivate browsing tab

Figure 7–24

Searching the Web

The wealth of information available on the World Wide Web provides a variety of resources on virtually any subject matter. As a result, it would be impossible to know exactly which website you need every time you browse the web. With Microsoft Edge's built-in search, you quickly can access webpages on a topic directly from your browser window using the 'Search or enter web address' text box or address bar text box.

By default, Edge uses Bing to produce search results. According to Microsoft, using Bing has three benefits:

1. Direct links to Windows apps
2. Fast, relevant suggestions
3. Instant help for getting the most out of Microsoft Edge and Windows

If you want to change search providers, you simply need to know the search engine's website and, through OpenSearch technology, Edge will produce results from your favorite search engine instead.

To Search Using the Search Box

Why? You need to find information about a search topic. The following steps search for information about Windows 11.

1

• Click the New tab button to open a new tab (Figure 7–25).

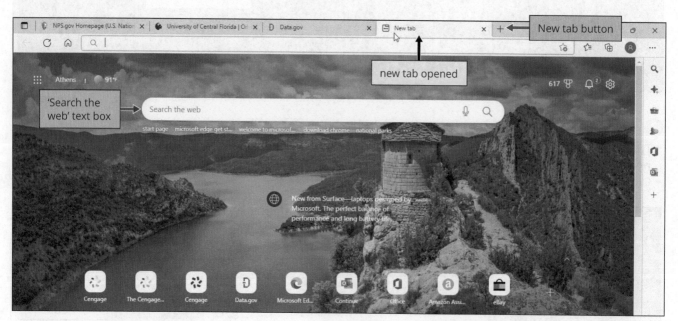

Figure 7–25

2

• Type **Windows 11** in the 'Search the web' text box and then press ENTER to begin the search (Figure 7–26).

Q&A Why are my search results different?

Search results are based on the most current information available on the web.

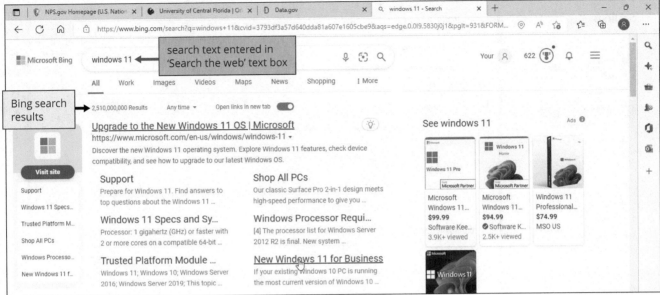

Figure 7–26

To Change Search Providers

The following steps set Google as the default search engine for Microsoft Edge. **Why?** You want to compare the results produced by a different search provider.

1

• Type **www.google.com** in the address bar text box and then press ENTER to display the Google search engine (Figure 7–27).

Source: Google

Figure 7–27

2

- Click the Settings button on the sidebar to display the Settings page (Figure 7–28). If your browser does not display a sidebar, click the 'Settings and more' button and then click Settings on the Settings and more menu.

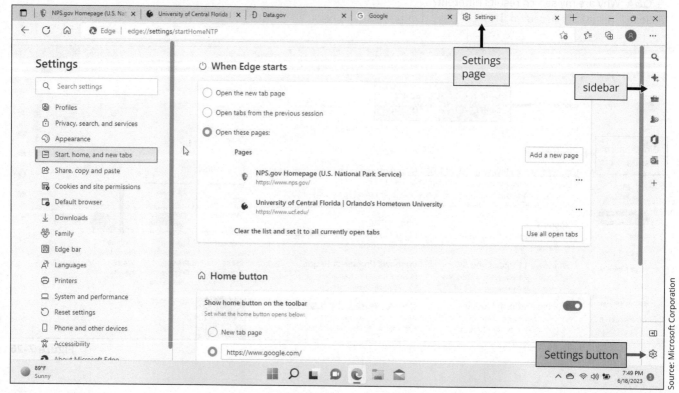

Figure 7–28

3

- Click the 'Privacy, search, and services' tab in the left pane to display the Privacy, search, and services settings and then scroll to display the Services settings (Figure 7–29).

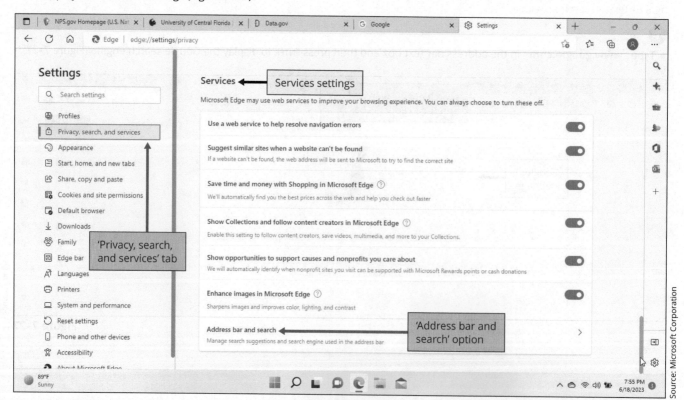

Figure 7–29

4

- Click the 'Address bar and search' option to display the Address bar and search settings.
- Click the 'Bing (Recommended, default)' button to display a list of search engines (Figure 7–30).

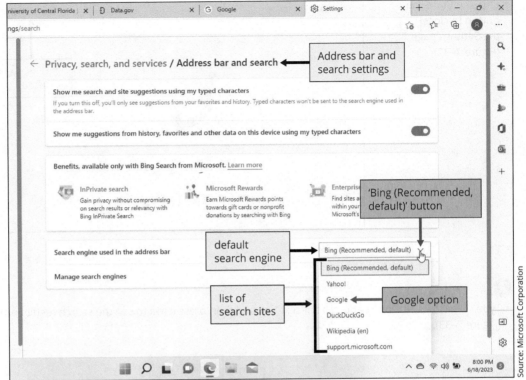

Figure 7–30

Source: Microsoft Corporation

5

- Click the Google option to specify the default search engine (Figure 7–31).

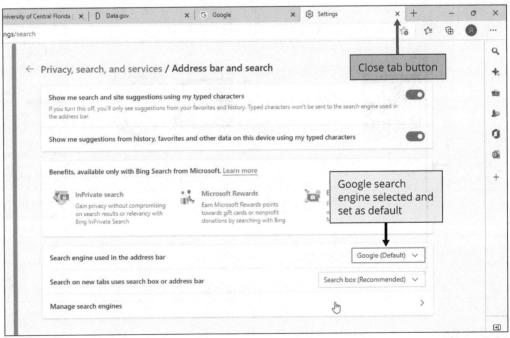

Figure 7–31

- Click the Close tab button to close the Settings page (Figure 7–32).

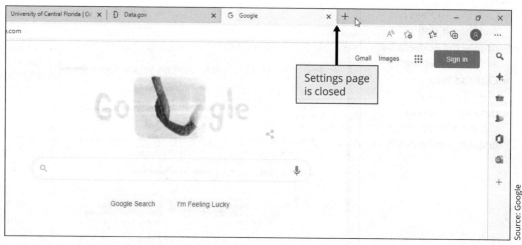

Settings page is closed

Source: Google

Figure 7–32

- Type **Windows 11** in the address bar text box and then press ENTER to see the search results produced by Google (Figure 7–33).

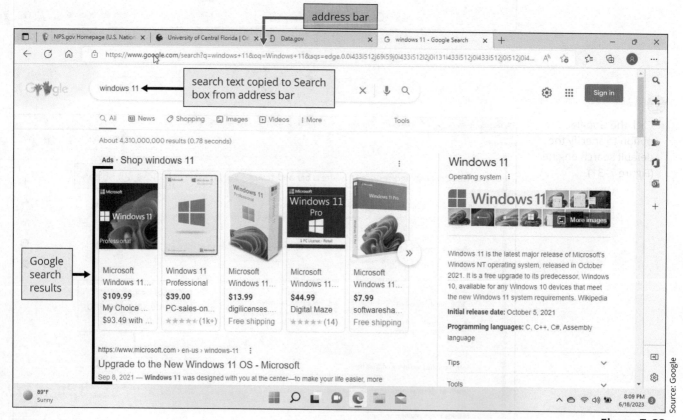

address bar

search text copied to Search box from address bar

Google search results

Source: Google

Figure 7–33

To Find Information on a Webpage

Microsoft Edge also provides ways for you to search for information within a webpage. **Why?** A page may contain a great deal of information, and you need to find just one part of the page or keyword(s) on the page. The following steps search for the text, Microsoft, on the Google search results page.

- Click the 'Settings and more' button in the address bar to display the Settings and more menu (Figure 7–34).

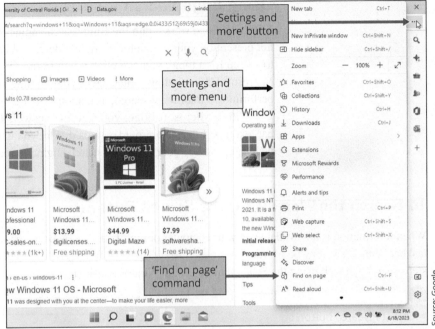

Figure 7–34

2

- Click 'Find on page' on the Settings and more menu to display the Find on page toolbar.
- Type **Microsoft** in the 'Find on page' text box to enter the search text (Figure 7–35).

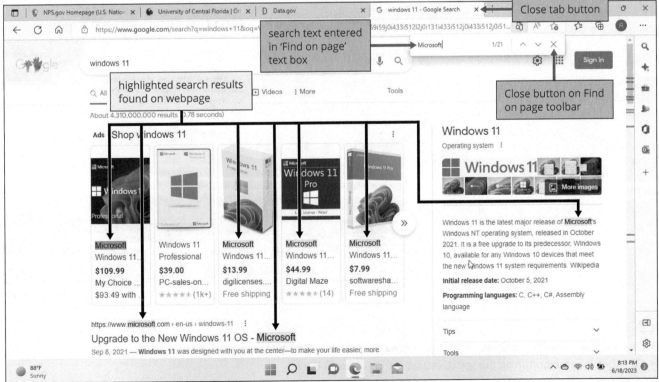

Figure 7–35

- Click the Close button on the Find on page toolbar.
- Close the search results tab.

Using Edge Search Tools

Microsoft Edge works with the Bing search engine in Windows 11 to search the web for content not present on your computer or mobile device. When you use the Search button on the taskbar to search for a topic, you can click a link in the search results to display the result directly in a Microsoft Edge window, which saves you the time associated with starting the browser and then performing a traditional search, as demonstrated previously.

Within Microsoft Edge, you can find answers to questions entered directly in the address bar text box. Edge also provides tools that let you look up the definition of a word, find text on a webpage, and use your preferred search engine to search for information about highlighted text.

To Search the Web Using the Search Button

When information is not available on your computer or mobile device, you can perform a web search quickly from the Windows taskbar. **Why?** You may be working on a paper using Microsoft Word and need information on a specific subject. The following steps search the web using the Search button on the Windows taskbar.

- Click the Search button on the Windows taskbar.
- Type **history of computers** in the Search box to display search results (Figure 7–36).

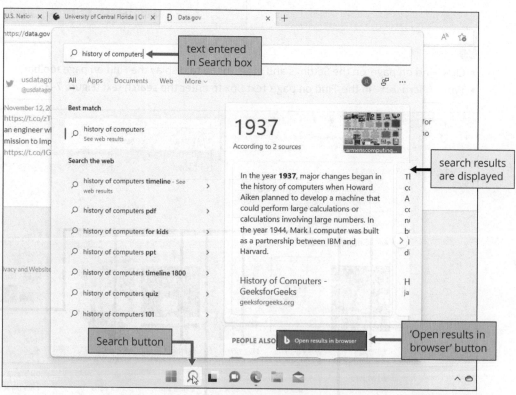

Figure 7–36

- Click the 'Open results in browser' button to display the search results in Microsoft Edge (Figure 7–37).
- Click the Close tab button on the search results tab in Microsoft Edge.

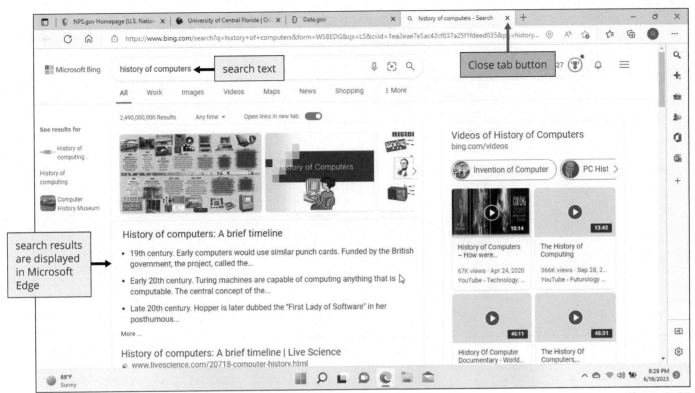

Figure 7–37

To Use Bing Search from the Sidebar

If you have changed the default search engine to Google or another search engine other than Bing, you can still start Bing from the sidebar. If you wanted to use Bing search from the sidebar, you would perform the following steps.

1. If the sidebar is not displayed, click the 'Settings and more' button in the address bar to display the Settings and more menu.

2. Click Show sidebar to display the sidebar.

3. Click the Search button on the sidebar to open a bing.com Search pane and Search text box.

To Get Instant Answers in Edge

Edge can access the answers to many questions and provide instant answers. **Why?** Some questions can be answered without needing search results. To save time, Edge can provide the answers quickly in the address bar. The following step asks a question in the address bar in Microsoft Edge and find an instant answer.

- Type **What is the square root of 64?** in the address bar and then press ENTER.
- Edge displays the results (Figure 7–38).

Q&A Why does the answer not appear until I have typed the whole question?
Edge waits until enough information is provided to answer the question before responding.

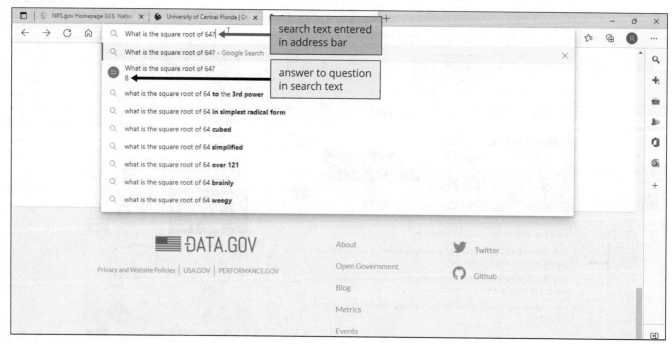

Figure 7–38

To Look Up Webpage Content

You can look up information within Edge to find content related to highlighted information on a webpage, including definitions and related webpages. **Why?** When reviewing information on a webpage, you may need additional details. You can find related information without having to open a new tab or window in the browser. The following steps look up a definition on a webpage.

- Type **www.healthcare.gov /self-employed** in the address bar text box and then press ENTER to display the webpage (Figure 7–39).

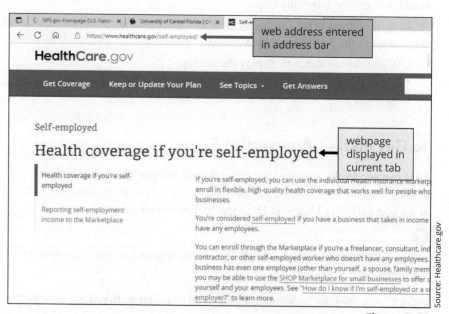

Figure 7–39

2

- Select the words, self-employed, somewhere on the page.
- Right-click the selected text to display a shortcut menu (Figure 7–40).

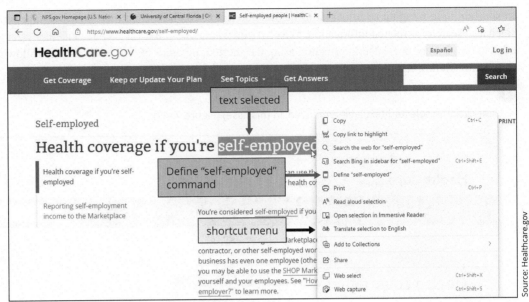

Figure 7–40

Source: Healthcare.gov

3

- Click Define "self-employed" on the shortcut menu to display a definition of the term (Figure 7–41).

Q&A Why do my results look different?

Search results will be based on the information currently available to Edge through the Bing search engine.

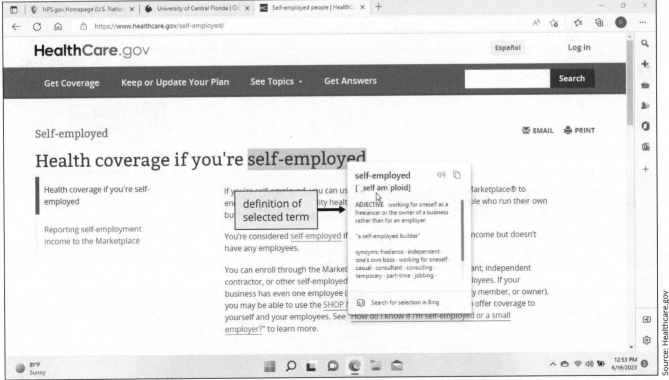

Figure 7–41

Source: Healthcare.gov

Consider This

Why would you use the Edge tools rather than performing a Bing search?

Conducting a Bing search requires opening a new tab or otherwise leaving the current webpage to find the related information. Edge tools display related information in the same tab.

To Obtain Additional Information from Bing

In addition to looking up additional information about text you have identified on a webpage, you also can use Bing in the sidebar to search for related information. **Why?** If you want to search for content found on a webpage, it is faster to locate the content and search for related information using the shortcut menu in Microsoft Edge. The following steps use Bing to search for additional information about the selected text.

1

- Right-click the selected text (self-employed, in this case) (Figure 7–42).

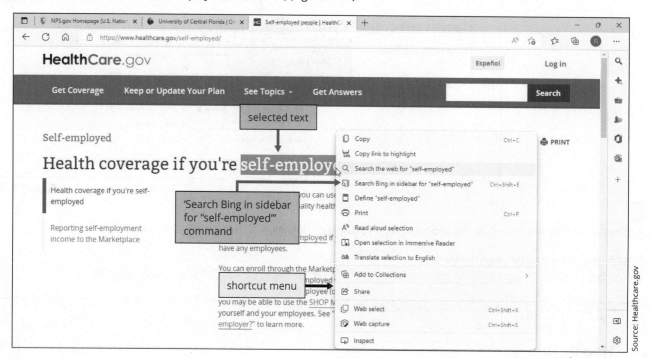

Source: Healthcare.gov

Figure 7–42

2

- Click 'Search Bing in sidebar for "self-employed"' to view the search results (Figure 7–43).

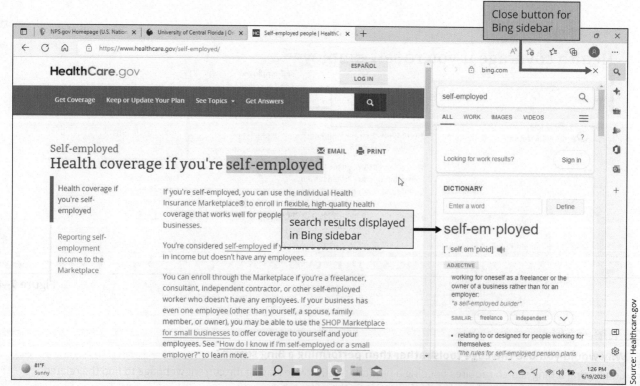

Source: Healthcare.gov

Figure 7–43

- Close the Bing sidebar containing the search results.

Reading Now or Later

Much of the content consumed by users on the World Wide Web is in the form of articles. Blogs have become popular business and personal tools for sharing information on the Internet. A **blog** is an informational website consisting of time-stamped articles (posts) in a diary or journal format, usually listed in reverse chronological order. As a result of their growing popularity, many of the links provided by search engines, such as Bing, direct visitors to blog articles with answers to their questions.

Microsoft Edge provides tools for assisting with distraction-free reading of those articles when they are displayed in the Immersive Reader. The reading list tool in Edge allows for saving of articles, making them available for later reading.

Using the Immersive Reader

The Immersive Reader view is designed to remove extra content from the screen while reading articles online. Navigation and advertisement features of the webpage are hidden from view as the article is displayed in a simplified interface. The Immersive Reader provides tools for setting text and reading preferences that can reduce eyestrain while reading articles online and a Read Aloud feature that reads webpage text audibly.

To Use the Immersive Reader

Why? When you need to read content without distractions, the Immersive Reader removes additional content, such as navigation and advertisement elements, from the screen so that you can focus on the article content on the webpage. The following steps display an article on the Cengage Learning website in the Immersive Reader.

- Type **blog.cengage.com** in the address bar text box and then press ENTER to display the Cengage Learning webpage.
- Locate a link to a blog post (Figure 7–44).

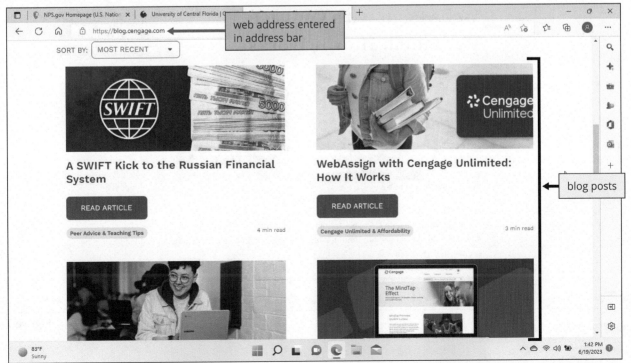

Figure 7–44

2

- Click the link for a blog post of interest to display the article in Normal view (Figure 7–45).

Figure 7–45

3

- Click the 'Enter Immersive Reader' button in the address bar to display the article in the Immersive Reader (Figure 7–46).

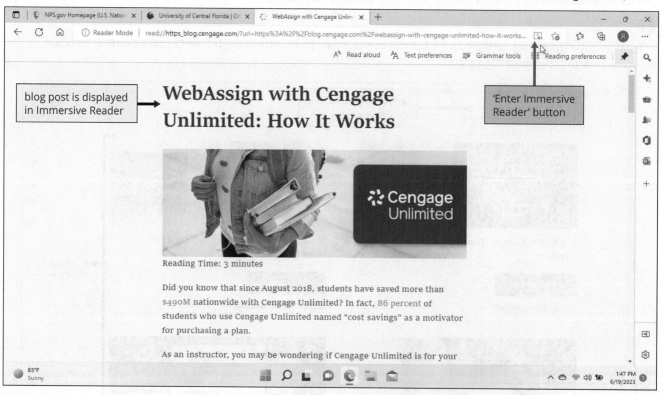

Figure 7–46

Other Ways

1. Press F9

To Customize the Immersive Reader

Why? Changing the color scheme or font size in the Immersive Reader can reduce eyestrain. The following steps apply a Dark grey page theme and increase the Immersive Reader font size.

- If necessary, click an area of the webpage to display the Immersive Reader toolbar (Figure 7–47).

Figure 7–47

2
- Click the Text preferences button on the Immersive Reader toolbar to display the Text preferences menu (Figure 7–48).

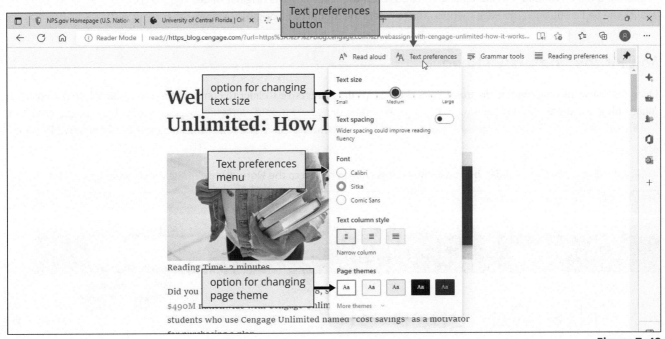

Figure 7–48

3

- Drag the slider button in the Text size area to one mark to the right of Medium to increase the font size.
- Click the Dark grey button in the Page themes area to change the theme to Dark grey (Figure 7–49).

Figure 7–49

4

- Click Medium on the slider in the Text size area to revert the text size to its original value.
- Click the Sepia button in the Page themes area to revert the theme to its original setting.

To Exit the Immersive Reader

Once you have finished reading an article, you should exit the Immersive Reader to continue browsing the original website or other online locations. **Why?** The Immersive Reader eliminates navigational elements from the current webpage; therefore, exiting the Immersive Reader is necessary to continue browsing the website. The following step exits the Immersive Reader.

1

- Click the 'Exit Immersive Reader' button in the address bar to return to the Normal view of the article webpage (Figure 7–50).

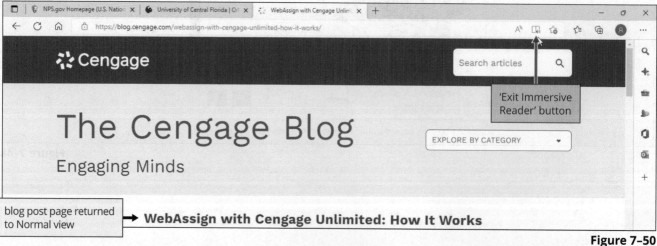

Figure 7–50

Saving an Article to a Collection

A **collection** is a place to save webpages, links, or images for later access. Similar to favorites, this feature is accessible through the Edge toolbar is available on all Windows 11 devices associated with your Microsoft account.

To Add an Article to a Collection

The following step adds an article to a Collection. **Why?** Maintaining a Collection saves articles for later reading or review, making them easily accessible when reading time is available.

- If necessary, navigate to a blog post on the Cengage Learning website at blog.cengage.com.
- Right-click the webpage to display a shortcut menu.
- Click 'Add page to Collections' on the shortcut menu to display an option for starting a new collection.
- Click 'Start new collection' to add the webpage to a new collection.
- Click the Collections button in the address bar to open the Collections pane (Figure 7–51).
- Close the Collections pane.

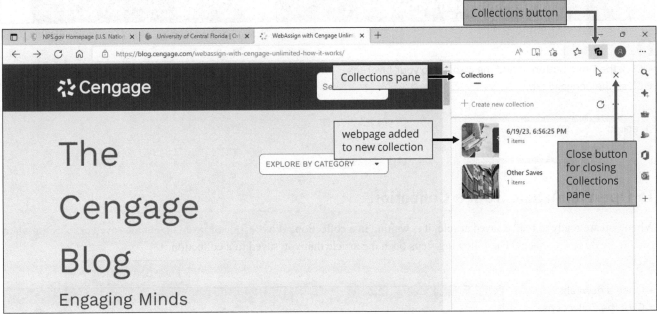

Figure 7–51

Saving a Website to Favorites

In Microsoft Edge, **favorites** is a place to store permanent links to your favorite or frequently visited webpages. Accessible through the Edge toolbar and available on all Windows 11 devices using your Microsoft account, the name and address of the webpage are stored for easy access.

To Add a Website to Favorites

The following steps add the Cengage webpage to favorites. **Why?** You can add a website to your favorites for easy access in the future.

1

- In the address bar text box, type **www.cengage.com** and then press ENTER to display the Cengage website.
- Click the 'Add this page to favorites' button in the address bar to display the Favorite added dialog box.
- In the Name text box, type **Cengage** (Figure 7–52).

Figure 7–52

2

- Click the Done button to add the website to your favorites.
- Close the Cengage tab.

Other Ways
1. CTRL+D

To Open an Article from a Collection

When you are ready to read a saved article, it is waiting in a collection. **Why?** Collections maintain the saved articles for when you are ready to read them. The following steps open the article that you saved to a collection.

1

- Open a new tab.
- Click the Collections button to open the Collections pane (Figure 7–53).

Figure 7–53

2

- Point to the collection you saved to display additional controls (Figure 7–54).

Q&A How can I use the additional controls in the Collections pane? Click the plus sign to add the current page to the collection. Click the three dots button to display a menu with options for renaming or deleting the collection.

saved collection

add the current page to the collection

display a menu with option for renaming or deleting the collection

Figure 7–54

3

- Click the name of the collection to display its contents in the Collections pane.
- Click the article you saved earlier to open the article in a new tab (Figure 7–55).
- Close the new article tab.
- Close the Collections pane.

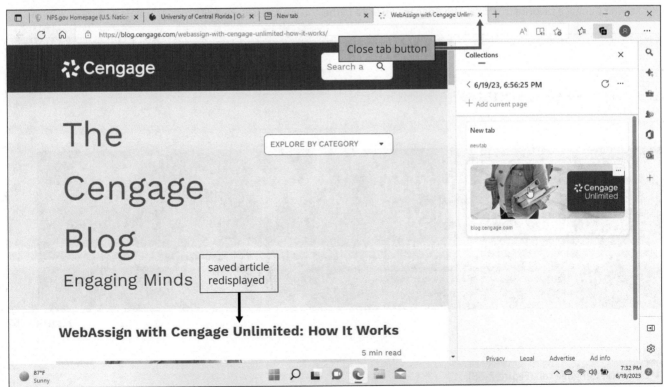

Close tab button

saved article redisplayed

Figure 7–55

To Display a Website from Favorites

The following steps redisplay the Cengage website from favorites. **Why?** Instead of retyping the web address or searching for a website, items in favorites can be accessed quickly.

1

- Click the Favorites button in the address bar to open the Favorites pane (Figure 7–56).

Figure 7–56

2

- Click the Cengage favorite to display the Cengage website in the current tab (Figure 7–57).

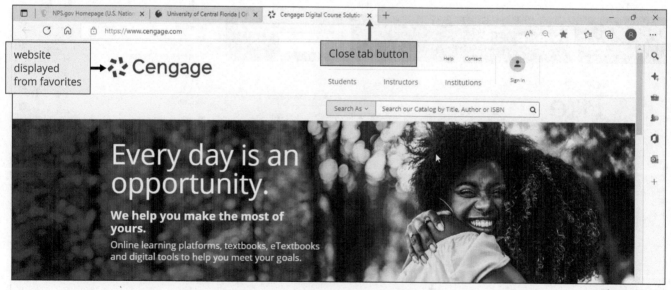

Figure 7–57

3

- Close the Cengage tab (Figure 7–58).

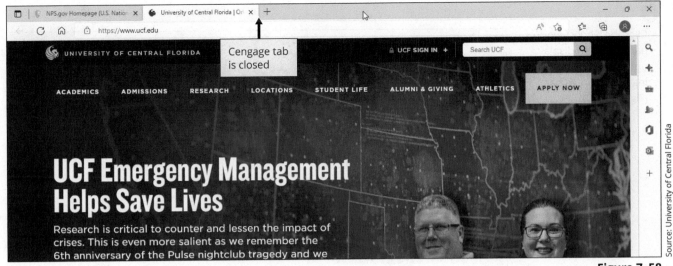

Figure 7-58

To Display the Favorites Bar

The **favorites bar** appears below the address bar in Microsoft Edge and provides easy access to favorites added to it. **Why?** By adding favorites to the favorites bar, you do not need to access the favorite through the Favorites pane. The following steps display the favorites bar in Microsoft Edge.

1

- Click the Settings button in the sidebar to display the Settings page. If your browser does not display a sidebar, click the 'Settings and more' button, and then click Settings on the Settings and more menu.
- If necessary, click the Appearance tab and then scroll down to display the Customize toolbar section (Figure 7–59).

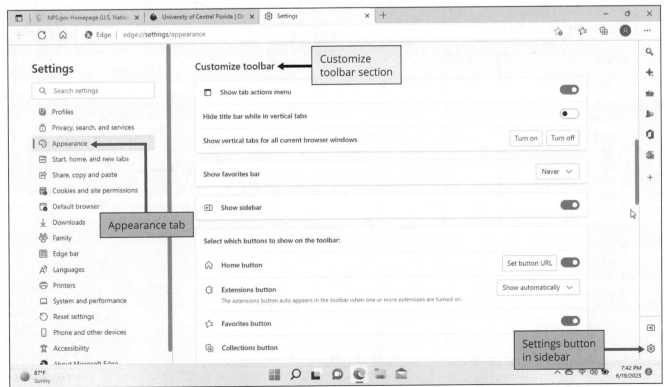

Figure 7–59

- Click the 'Show favorites bar' button to display options for displaying the favorites bar (Figure 7–60).

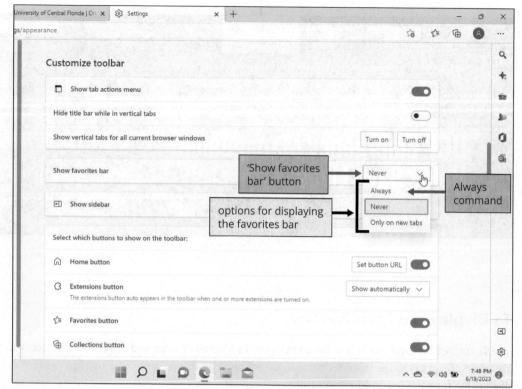

Figure 7–60

- If necessary, click Always on the menu to display the favorites bar below the address bar (Figure 7–61).

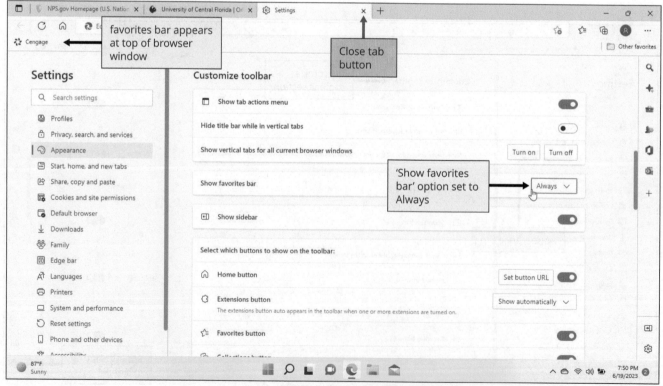

Figure 7–61

● Click the Close tab button to close the Settings page (Figure 7–62).

Figure 7–62

Other Ways

1. CTRL+SHIFT+B

To Add a Favorite to the Favorites Bar

If you wanted to add a favorite to the favorites bar so that it is easy to access, you would perform these steps.

1. Navigate to the desired website.
2. Click the 'Add this page to favorites' button on the address bar.
3. Type the desired name for the favorite in the Name text box.
4. Click the Folder arrow and select Favorites Bar.
5. Click the Done button.

Consider This

How many favorites should you add to the favorites bar?

While the actual number will vary based on individual needs and preferences, you should keep the number of favorites on the favorites bar to a minimum and reserve this storage location for the websites you access most frequently.

To Sync Favorites and Collections

Using the same Microsoft account on multiple devices running Windows 11 allows you to take advantage of the sync feature in Microsoft Edge. This feature synchronizes, or syncs, your favorites and collections across all devices associated with your account. If you wanted to enable sync features from Microsoft Edge, you would follow these steps.

1. Turn on syncing on your Windows device.
    a. Click the Start button on the taskbar to display the Start menu.
    b. Click Settings to start the Settings app.
    c. Click the Accounts icon in the Settings window to display account settings.

    d. Click Your info in the right pane of the Settings window.

    e. Make sure a Microsoft account is set up in the Account settings section and that you do not need to verify your identity.

2. Turn on syncing in Microsoft Edge on your computer.

    a. Start Microsoft Edge.

    b. Click the Settings button in the sidebar to display the Settings page.

    c. Click Profiles in the left pane of the Settings page.

    d. Click Sync in the right pane.

    e. If necessary, click the toggle buttons on the Sync section to set them to the On position.

Using and Customizing the Sidebar

You have already used the sidebar to access settings and search for selected text in Bing. The sidebar also lets you initiate a new Bing search, discover information related to the current webpage, and use tools such as a calculator and unit converter. The sidebar also provides quick access to games and Microsoft Office apps, including Outlook.

Searching for Information with the Sidebar

When you click a button on the sidebar, a pane opens on the right side of the Edge window where you can search for information without leaving the current webpage. Clicking the Search button opens the Bing search pane, which is a compact version of the Bing search engine that includes a Search text box and trending content.

To Use the Bing Search Pane

The following steps open the Bing Search pane and search for information related to an open webpage. **Why?** The Bing search pane lets you research information online without losing the context of the main webpage.

- Display the NPS webpage in the browser (Figure 7–63).

Source: National Park Service

Figure 7–63

2

- Click the Search button in the sidebar to open the Bing Search pane (Figure 7–64).

Q&A What if my browser does not display a sidebar?

Type **bing.com** in the address bar and then press ENTER to display the Bing search page.

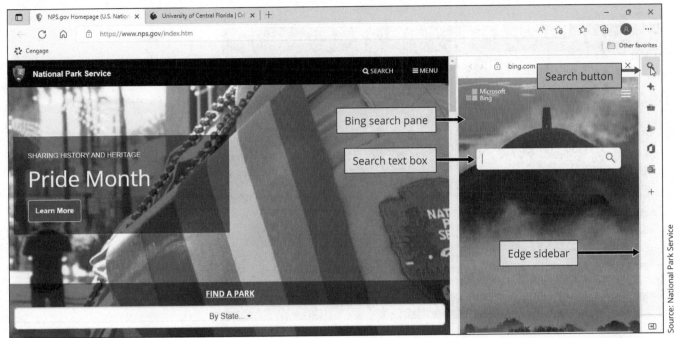

Figure 7–64

3

- Type **history of nps** in the Search text box and then press ENTER to display the results (Figure 7–65).

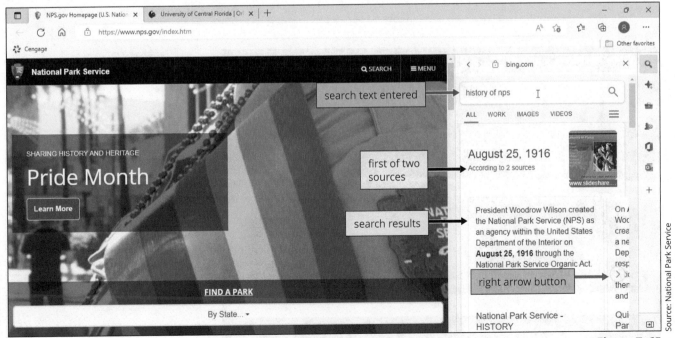

Figure 7–65

4

- Click the right arrow button to display the second source of information.
- Scroll down to display the PEOPLE ALSO ASK section of the Bing search pane (Figure 7–66).

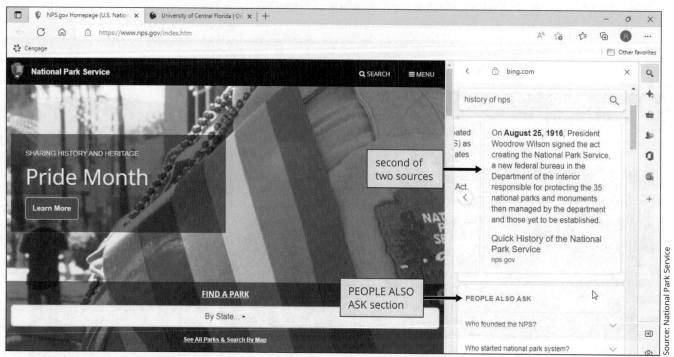

Figure 7–66

5

- Click the first link in the PEOPLE ALSO ASK section to display a brief explanation (Figure 7–67).
- Close the Bing search pane.

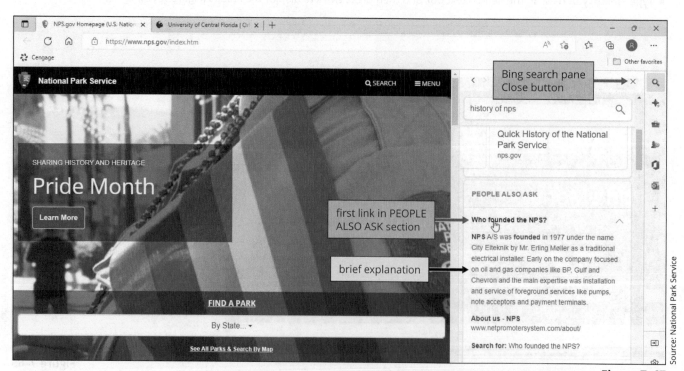

Figure 7–67

To Discover Information

Why? Bing may be able to provide useful information related to the current webpage. The following step opens the Discover pane.

1

- Display the University of Central Florida webpage.
- Click the Discover button in the sidebar to open the Discover pane with information related to the current webpage (Figure 7–68).

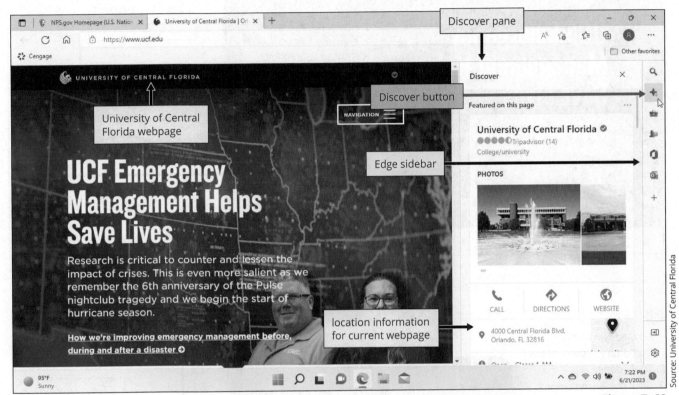

Figure 7–68

To Use the Sidebar Tools

Besides finding facts by entering questions in the address bar, you can use the sidebar tools to perform calculations, convert units, translate text, and more. **Why?** You may want to find facts without entering a specific question. The following steps use the sidebar tools.

1

- Click the Tools button on the sidebar to display the sidebar tools.
- Scroll down to the 'Unit converter' section of the Tools pane.
- Click the Length button to display the units to convert and then click Temperature to display the Celsius to Fahrenheit temperature conversion (Figure 7–69).

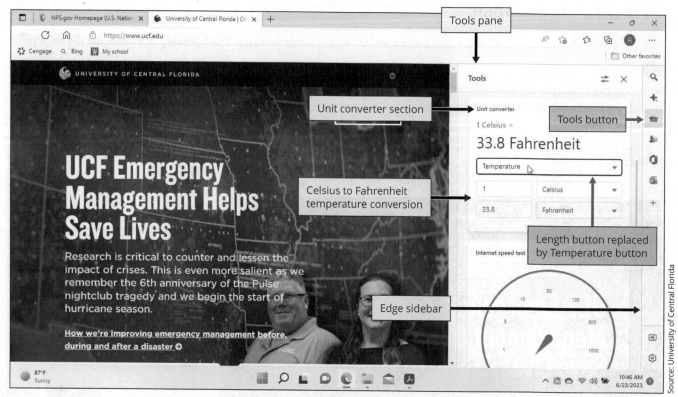

Figure 7–69

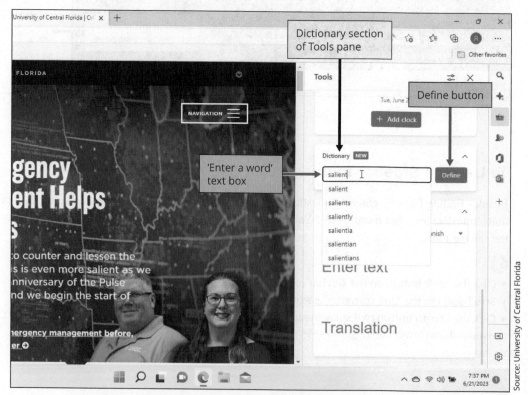

2

- Scroll down to the Dictionary section of the Tools pane.
- Click the 'Enter a word' text box and type **salient** to enter a word to define (Figure 7–70)

Figure 7–70

3

- Click the Define button to display the definition (Figure 7–71).
- Click the Back button to return to the main Tools pane.

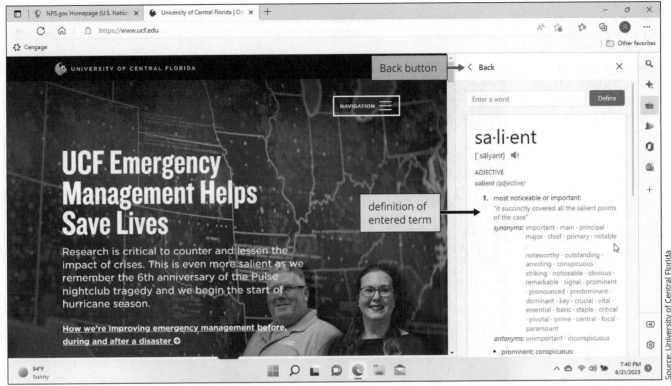

Figure 7–71

To Enable and Disable Sidebar Tools

Why? You may prefer using some sidebar panes and not others. **The following steps enable and disable a sidebar pane.**

1

• Click the Customize sidebar button in the sidebar to open the Customize sidebar pane (Figure 7–72).

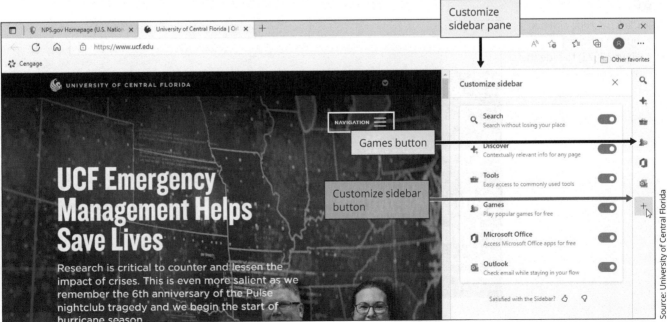

Figure 7–72

• Click the Games toggle to disable the Games pane (Figure 7–73).
• Click the Games toggle to open the Games pane.

Figure 7–73

To Hide and Show the Sidebar

The sidebar is displayed by default to the right of the Edge window, but you can hide it if necessary. **Why?** If the sidebar proves distracting, you can hide it. The following steps hide and show the sidebar.

• Click the Hide sidebar button (shown in Figure 7–73) to hide the sidebar (Figure 7–74).

Figure 7–74

- Click the 'Settings and more' button on the address bar to display the Settings and more menu (Figure 7–75).
- Click Show sidebar to display the sidebar.

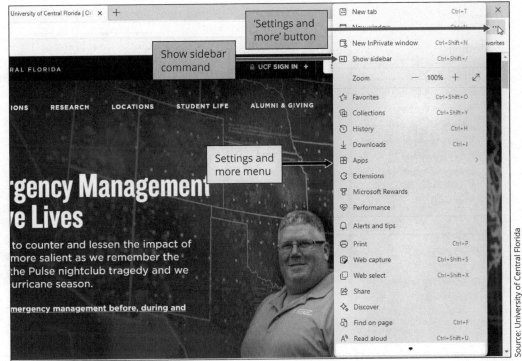

Figure 7–75

Customizing Edge

You have already customized some parts of Edge, including the New tab page. You can also customize the appearance of Edge by changing its theme, which is a set of coordinated colors for window elements. Instead of displaying webpage tabs horizontally across the top of the Edge window, you can display them vertically in a pane on the left. In addition to the sidebar, you can display the Edge bar, which is a pane that can display a personalized news feed or other content, depending on your preferences.

To Change the Appearance of Edge

The following steps apply a new theme to Edge. **Why?** You may want to add visual interest to the Edge window.

- Click the Settings button on the sidebar to display the Settings page and display settings for customizing the appearance of Edge (Figure 7–76).

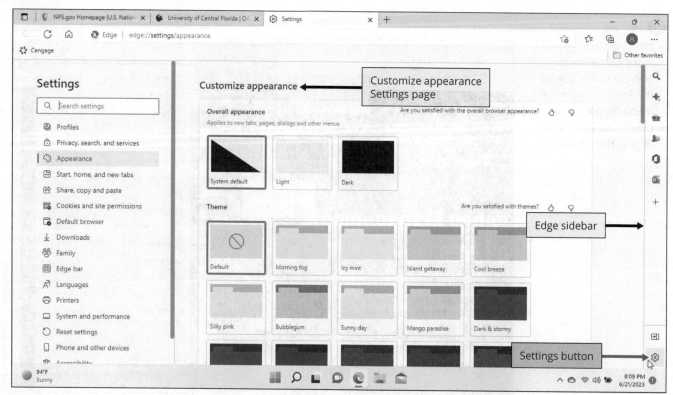

Figure 7–76

2

- In the Theme area, click the Cool breeze theme to apply the theme to the Edge window (Figure 7–77).

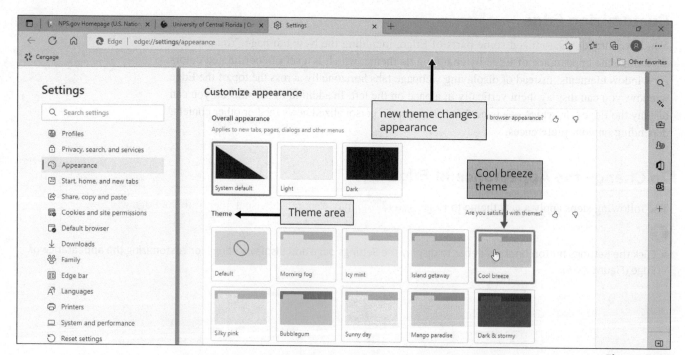

Figure 7–77

To Display Vertical Tabs

Besides changing the appearance of the Edge window, you can change how you interact with it by displaying vertical tabs. **Why?** Displaying the tabs in a vertical list makes them easier to find, select, and organize. The following steps display tabs vertically in the Edge window.

- Click the 'Tab actions menu' button on the title bar to display the Tab actions menu (Figure 7–78).

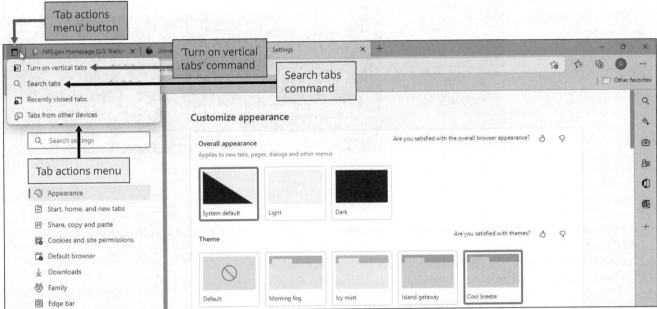

Figure 7–78

2

- Click 'Turn on vertical tabs' to display the open tabs vertically in a pane on the left side of the Edge window (Figure 7–79).

Q&A How do I use the Search tabs command?
Click Search tabs on the Tab actions menu to display a list of open and recently closed tabs. Click a tab in the list to reopen it.

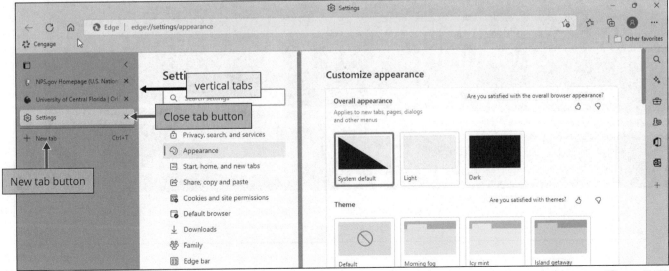

Figure 7–79

3

- Click the Close tab button to close the Settings tab.
- Click the New tab button to open a new tab.
- Open the Cengage tab from the favorites bar to display the webpage on the new tab (Figure 7–80).

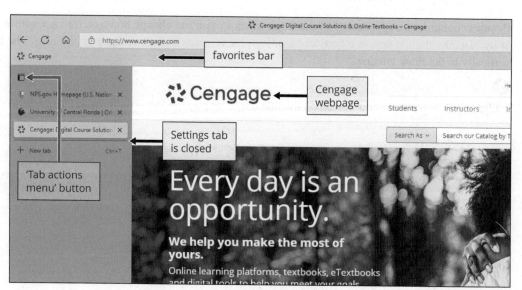

Figure 7–80

4

- Click the 'Tab actions menu' button in the left pane and then click 'Turn off vertical tabs' to restore the original horizontal tabs (Figure 7–81).
- Click the Settings button in the sidebar to display the Settings page.
- Click Default in the Theme section to restore the default theme.

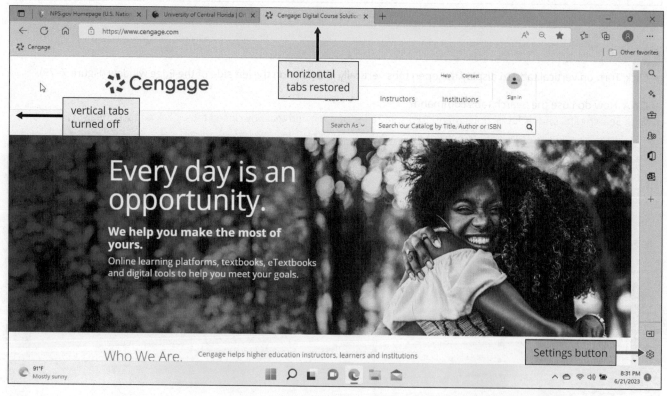

Figure 7–81

To Display the Edge Bar

In addition to the sidebar, you can display the Edge bar in the Edge window. **Why?** The Edge bar displays personalized content, such as weather and news, to keep you up to date. The following step displays and closes the Edge bar.

- Click Edge bar in the left pane of the Settings window to display the Edge settings.
- Click 'Open Edge bar' to display the Edge bar (Figure 7–82).
- Close the Edge bar.
- Close the Settings page.

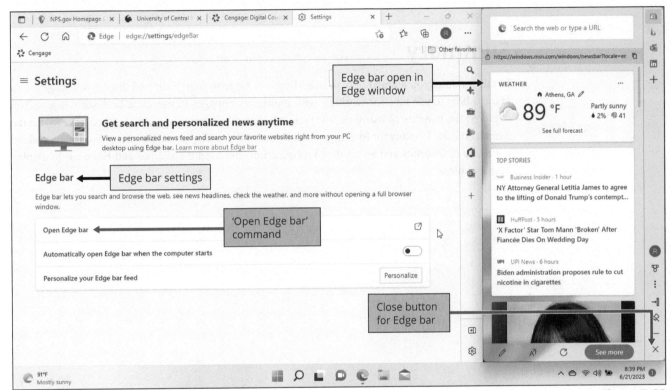

Figure 7–82

Sharing Web Content

One of the greatest benefits of the web is the ability to share content with friends, coworkers, family, or anyone else in the world. Supported by the Share pane in Windows 11, Edge can use any communication or social networking app installed on your computer or mobile device to share webpages and web notes with others.

Sharing features are available in all views of Edge discussed in this module. You can share webpages directly during normal browsing.

To Share a Webpage

A webpage can be shared quickly from the toolbar in Microsoft Edge using any app installed on your computer for communicating with others, including OneNote, Mail, Skype, and all of your favorite social networking apps. If you wanted to share a webpage, you would perform the following steps.

1. Navigate to the webpage you want to share.
2. Click the 'Settings and more' button on the address bar to display the Settings and more menu.
3. Click Share on the Settings and more menu to open the Share pane.
4. Click the app you want to use to share the webpage.

Summary

In this module, you learned how to use Microsoft Edge to search for and display webpages. You learned how to use tabs for working with multiple webpages in the same browser window. You explored the benefits of using an InPrivate window while browsing. You learned how to use the Search box and Cortana for locating new information. You displayed the Immersive Reader, added a website to favorites and an article to a collection, and used the sidebar and Edge bar to display online content.

Student Assignments

Apply Your Knowledge

Reinforce the skills and apply the concepts you learned in this module.

Using the Immersive Reader

Instructions: You want to locate information on government programs. Use Microsoft Edge to perform the following tasks.

Perform the following tasks:

1. Start Microsoft Edge.
2. Type   **US government programs**   in the address bar text box and then press ENTER to search for websites (Figure 7–83).

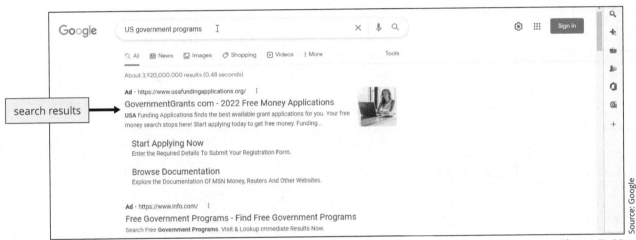

Figure 7–83

3. In the search results list, locate a link for the Benefits.gov website.
4. On the website, find the popular benefits in your state.
5. Note how many programs are available in your state.
6. Navigate the website as necessary and then click the link for a news story.
7. Review the news story.
8. Switch to the Immersive Reader for the selected news story.
9. Complete the following tasks in the Immersive Reader:
    a. Change the text size and page theme.
    b. Select a word in the news story and then open Bing in the sidebar for the selected word.
    c. Select the same word in the news story and then display its definition.
10. Press PRINT SCREEN to capture screen content.
11. Open a new document in WordPad.
12. Click the Paste button (Clipboard group | Home tab) to paste the screen clipping into the document.
13. Save the document and submit it in the format required by your instructor.

Extend Your Knowledge

Extend the skills you learned in this module and experiment with new skills. You might need to use Help to complete the assignment.

Understanding Privacy and Services in Edge

Instructions: Use the Learn more link in the advanced settings of Edge to find information about privacy and services in the Edge browser.

Perform the following steps:

1. Start Microsoft Edge.

2. Open the Settings page by completing the following steps:

   a. Click the 'Settings and more' button in the address bar to display the Settings and more menu.

   b. Click Settings on the Settings and more menu to display the Settings page.

   c. Click the 'Privacy, search, and services' tab on the Settings page.

   d. In the Privacy area, click the Learn more link to display the Microsoft Edge, browsing data, and privacy webpage in the browser (Figure 7–84).

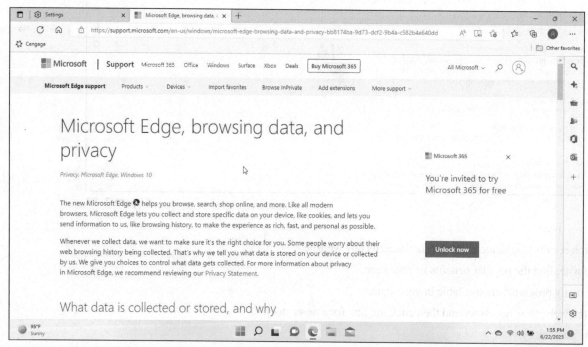

Figure 7–84

3. Open a new document in WordPad and answer the following questions:

   a. What are cookies, and how can they be cleared in Microsoft Edge?

   b. What settings control the sending of browsing history information to Microsoft?

   c. How do you prevent Edge from remembering information entered in forms?

4. Submit your answers in the format required by your instructor.

Expand Your World

Create a solution that uses cloud or web technologies by learning and investigating on your own from general guidance.

Comparing Browsers

Instructions: Now that you are familiar with the features of Microsoft Edge, you will conduct a comparison of several common browsers and summarize the features of each. Create a new document in WordPad to gather your results into a brief report.

Perform the following tasks:

1. Search for the names of three other browsers that can be run on Windows 11.
2. For each identified browser, through either personal installation and review or cited resources, do the following:
   a. List the features that the browser has in common with Edge.
   b. List additional features, if any, in the identified browser that are not present in Edge.
   c. List additional features, if any, in Edge that are not present in the identified browser.
3. Submit the WordPad document in the format requested by your instructor.

In the Labs

Design and implement a solution using creative thinking and problem-solving skills.

Lab 1: Browsing the Web

Problem: You have been working hard in all of your classes to keep up with the course requirements this semester. You have begun working on the final project for your English class, and the instructor has required a graphic presentation. Although you are familiar with Microsoft PowerPoint for creating the presentation, you want to know what other options exist. You have searched the web and found four alternatives that may be useful in completing your project.

1. Start Microsoft Edge.
2. Type **www.visme.com**   in the address bar text box and then press ENTER.
3. Write a brief description of Visme and how it is different from a PowerPoint presentation.
4. Type **www.prezi.com**   in the address bar text box and then press ENTER (Figure 7–85).

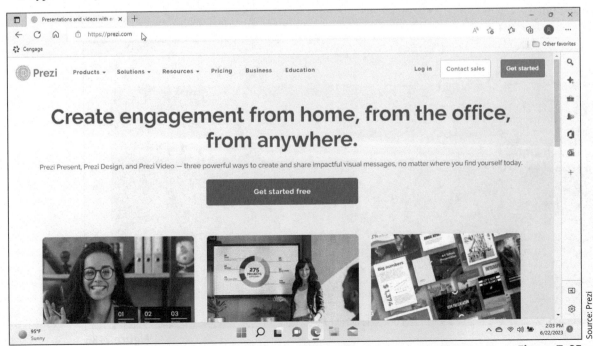

Figure 7–85

Continued on next page

5. Write a brief description about Prezi and how it is different from a PowerPoint presentation.

6. Type **www.emaze.com** in the address bar text box and then press ENTER.

7. Write a brief description about Emaze and how it is different from a PowerPoint presentation.

8. Type **www.powtoon.com** in the address bar text box and then press ENTER.

9. Write a brief description about Powtoon and how it is different from a PowerPoint presentation.

10. Submit your findings in a format required by your instructor.

Lab 2: Populating the Favorites Bar

Problem: In this module, you learned how to display the favorites bar in Microsoft Edge. You will now add several websites to the favorites bar.

Perform the following tasks:

1. Start Microsoft Edge.

2. Click the Favorites button in the address bar.

3. Click the More options button in the Favorites pane to display the More options menu.

4. If necessary, click 'Show favorites bar' on the More options menu and then click Always to display the favorites bar below the address bar.

5. Type **www.bing.com** in the address bar text box and then press enter to display the Bing.com webpage.

6. Click the 'Add this page to favorites' button in the address bar.

7. If necessary, click the Folder button and then click Favorites bar in the list.

8. Click the Done button in the Favorite added box.

9. Type the web address for your school in the address bar.

10. Click the 'Add this page to favorites' button in the address bar.

11. Type **My School** in the Name text box.

12. Save the webpage in the favorites bar.

13. Click the Done button.

14. Click the Bing button on the Favorites Bar (Figure 7–86).

15. Click the My School button on the favorites bar.

16. Exit Microsoft Edge.

Figure 7–86

Lab 3: Consider This: Your Turn

Conducting Scholarly Research

Problem: You have been assigned a research paper on the history of the Internet. To locate scholarly articles, you will use Google Scholar to find information. You have decided to keep track of your thoughts for each article. After reading the articles, you will save and submit your notes to your instructor.

Part 1: Navigate to the Google Scholar website (scholar.google.com). Use the search text, history of the Internet, to find relevant information. In the Google search results, locate an article to read and then use the Immersive Reader to review the article and summarize it in a WordPad document.

Part 2: You used several tools to complete this assignment. What differences did you notice when using Google Scholar rather than the Google search engine? How did you determine which article was the best to use for your research? How does using the Immersive Reader compare to not using it?

Mastering Digital Media

Objectives

After completing this module, you will be able to:

- Use the Photos app
- Organize photos using albums
- Edit album properties
- Enhance pictures with editing tools
- Listen to music on a computer or mobile device in the Media Player

- Work with playlists
- Browse music in the Microsoft Store
- Play video on a computer or mobile device using the Movies & TV app
- Adjust video playback options using controls
- Modify closed captioning settings

Introduction

Digital media includes pictures, audio, and video and is stored in picture files, audio files, and video files. The Photos, Media Player, and Movies & TV apps, shown in Figure 8–1, are included with Windows 11 to allow you to view and organize your digital media collections.

The **Photos app** allows you to view the photos on your computer. The **collection** is a complete set of image files displayed in reverse chronological order based on the date the photo was taken. Photos are further organized into albums and folders. **Albums** organize images into related sets of photos automatically or based on user preferences. **Folders** represent one or more physical storage locations for photos stored locally on the computer, OneDrive, or external devices. The Photos app lets you view, print, burn, send via email, and open the photos in the collection.

Media Player is used to organize and play your music collection. Audio files added to the Media Player app are categorized automatically by album, artist, and song. Music files can be organized further into custom playlists.

The **Movies & TV app** is the Windows 11 app for viewing, renting, and buying movies and television shows. A wide range of video file types is supported for videos stored on the local computer.

image in Photos app

Figure 8–1a

music collection in
Media Player

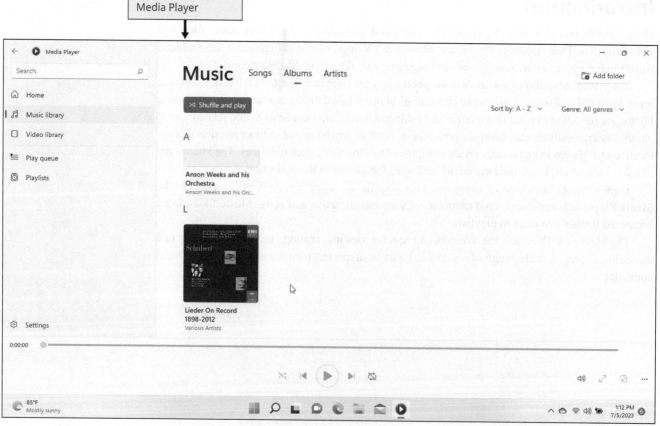

Figure 8–1b

video collections in
the Movies & TV app

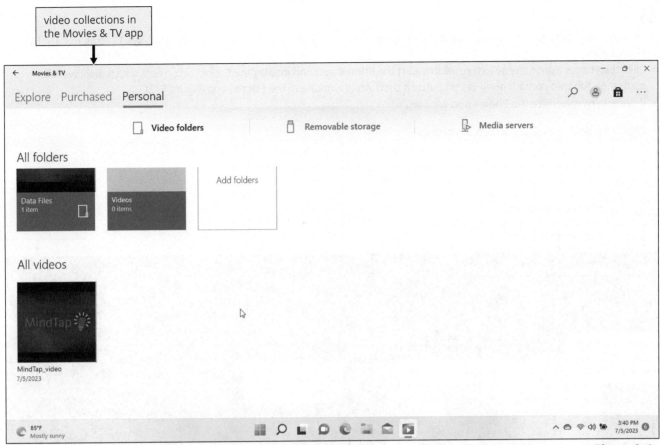

Figure 8–1c

Managing Photos

The Photos app provides tools for viewing or editing photos and videos stored on your computer
or OneDrive. Photos can be viewed as an entire collection, in custom albums, as a slide show, or
in their original storage locations.

The Photos app provides a wide range of editing tools that can be used to resize, crop, rotate,
recolor, enhance, or fix photos. After making the desired enhancements, the sharing features available throughout the app make it easy to save files on OneDrive or share individual photos or albums
through email, messaging, or social media.

The Collection

The collection represents images saved in the Pictures folder, on OneDrive, or in additional folders
specified in the Photos app settings. Organized automatically to display the newest images first,
the collection also provides navigational tools for locating your photos quickly, regardless of when
they were taken.

To Start the Photos App

The following step starts the Photos app from the Search box. **Why?** You would like to use the Photos app to view photos on
your computer.

- Click the Search button on the taskbar and then type **photos** in the Search box to instruct Windows 11 to search for the Photos app.
- Click the Photos app in the search results to start the Photos app and display the Collection screen, which displays tabs across the top that contain options and buttons used while working in the Photos app (Figure 8–2).
- If necessary, maximize the Photos app window.

Q&A Why does my collection contain photos?
The Photos app automatically detects pictures and videos located in the Pictures folder or on OneDrive and then displays those images in the collection.

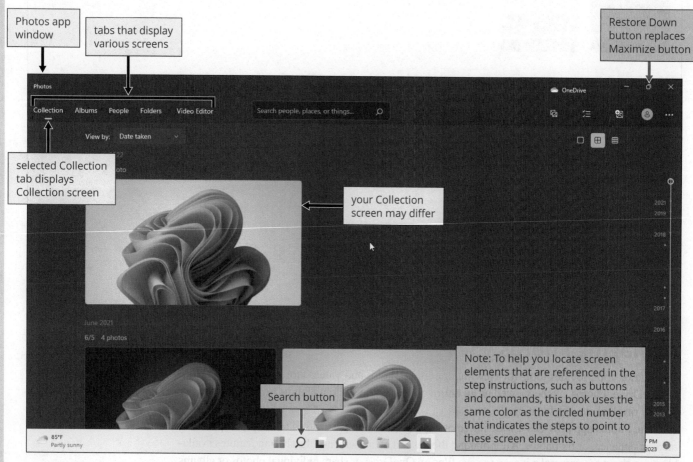

Photos app window

tabs that display various screens

Restore Down button replaces Maximize button

selected Collection tab displays Collection screen

your Collection screen may differ

Search button

Note: To help you locate screen elements that are referenced in the step instructions, such as buttons and commands, this book uses the same color as the circled number that indicates the steps to point to these screen elements.

Figure 8–2

Other Ways

1. Click Start button on taskbar, click Photos tile

Working with Folders

Although the Pictures folder provides a central location for storing and accessing photos and other images on your computer, image files may be stored in a variety of locations on your computer. Adding image folders to the collection in the Photos app gives you access to all of your images in a single place, regardless of where they are stored.

Consider This

What are some reasons for storing photos in a variety of locations?

Photos are used for different purposes. Some photos are used for business or marketing. Others are used for personal enjoyment. Some are edited for print, and others for web or electronic purposes. Keeping multiple versions of the same file in the same location can be challenging. By organizing your photos in folders or locations relative to their intended use, subject area, or other classification, you can avoid confusion from duplicate or similar file names and types.

To Add a Folder to the Collection

You have some images saved in another location that are not displayed automatically in the collection. **Why?** You want to include images from another storage location in the Photos app for viewing and management but do not want to move the images to the default locations searched by the Photos app. The following steps add the contents of the W11_M8_Images folder from the Data Files to the collection.

- Click the See more button to display the See more menu (Figure 8–3).
- Click Settings on the See more menu to display the Settings screen.

Figure 8–3

- Click the 'Add a folder' button to display the Select Folder dialog box.
- Navigate to the location of the W11_M8_Images folder in the Data Files (Figure 8–4).

Q&A Why are no pictures displayed in the W11_M8_Images folder? The Select Folder dialog box displays only folder names, not individual files within the folders.

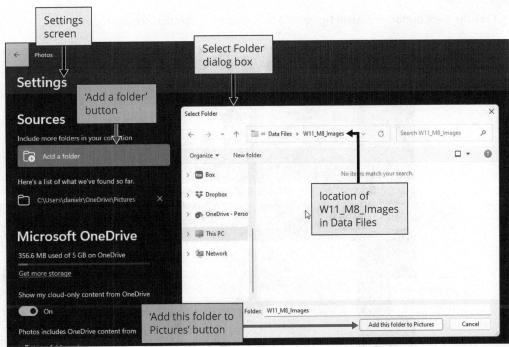

Figure 8–4

- Click the 'Add this folder to Pictures' button (Select Folder dialog box) so that the folder appears in the Sources area (Figure 8–5).

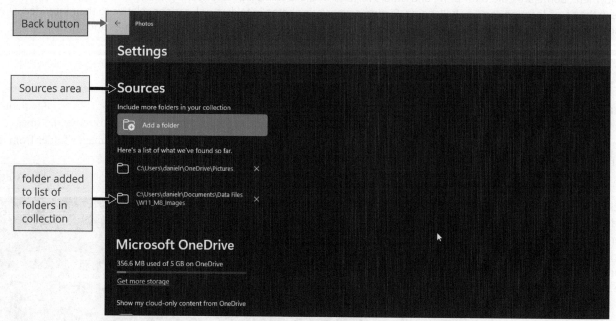

Figure 8–5

To View the Collection

Why? Once you have added the source location to the Photo app sources, you are able to view the additional images in the collection. The following steps display the collection and verify the inclusion of images found in the new source location.

- Click the Back button (shown in Figure 8–5) to display the Collection screen (Figure 8–6).

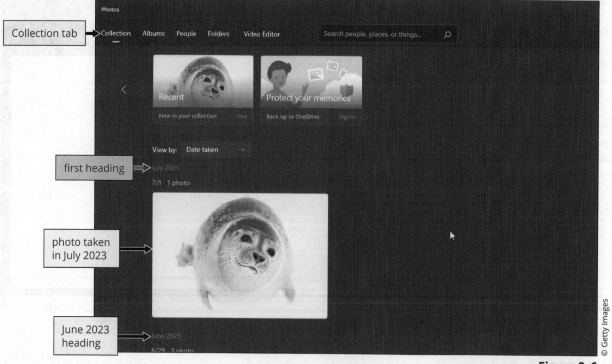

© Getty Images

Figure 8–6

2

- Click the first heading shown in the collection to display a list of months included in the collection (Figure 8–7).

Q&A How are the groups in the collection determined?
Photos in the collection are grouped by date taken (in reverse chronological order — newest to oldest).

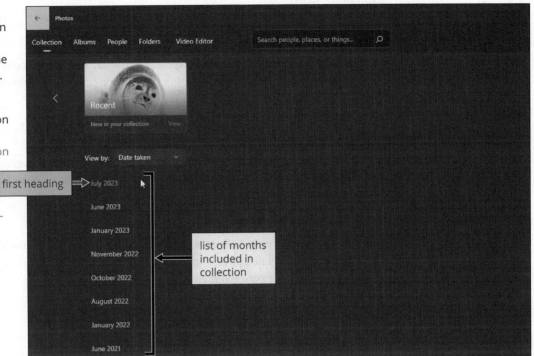

Figure 8–7

3

- Click the June 2023 heading. If necessary, scroll to locate the link.
- Verify that the tiger.jpg file from the Data Files is shown in the collection (Figure 8–8).

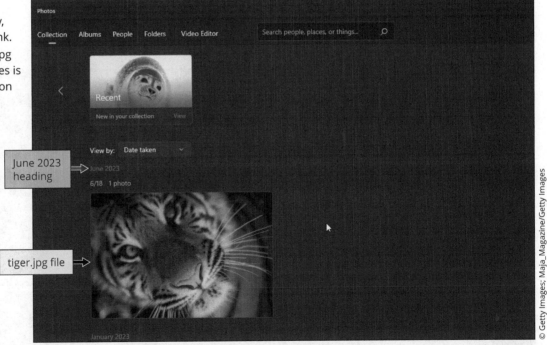

Figure 8–8

To Import Photos from a Device

Many pictures are taken with digital devices that store the photos on the device or a memory card external to your Windows 11 computer. When photos are taken with a digital camera or mobile device, it may be necessary to import the photos into the Photos app for viewing and editing. If you wanted to import photos from an external device, you would perform the following steps.

1. Connect your device to your Windows 11 computer using an available USB connection.

2. Start the Photos app and display the Collection screen.

3. Click the Import button on the toolbar to display the Import menu and then click 'From a connected device' to start searching the device for items to import.

4. Select or clear items as desired for import.

5. If desired, click the Import settings link to change the import settings, including the location of the imported photos.

6. Click the Import selected button in the Select the items you want to import dialog box to display the Start importing? dialog box and initiate the import process.

Working with Albums

The Photos app will create **albums**, or groups of related photos, automatically when it identifies a large number of related photos in your collection. Additional albums can be created to group photos based on your personal preferences.

To Create an Album

The photos you added to the collection included several photos of animals and several other landscape photographs. You have decided that it would be a good idea to create albums for each group of images. **Why?** You want to be able to quickly locate similar images regardless of when they were taken. The following steps create two albums in the Photos app.

- Click the Albums tab to display the Albums screen (Figure 8–9).

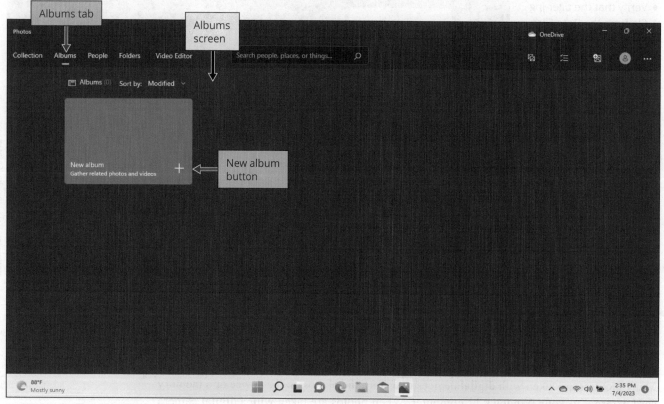

Figure 8–9

2

- Click the New album button on the Albums screen to display the Create new album screen for the first album.
- Click to select the seal image from 7/1 below the July 2023 heading (Figure 8–10).

Figure 8–10

3

- Scroll to view the kitten image from 5/26 below the May 2023 heading.
- Click to select the kitten image (Figure 8–11).

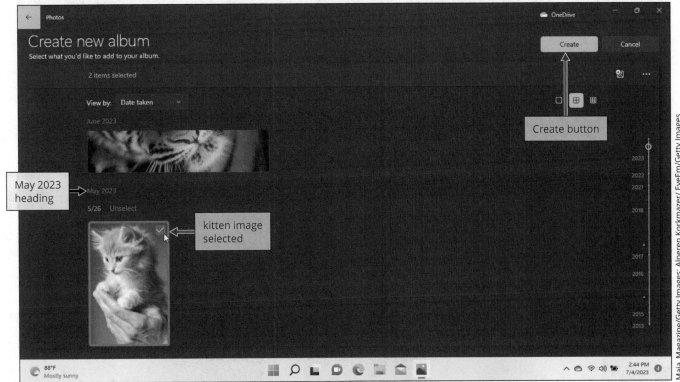

Figure 8–11

4

- Scroll to view and select the puppy image from 1/24 below the January 2023 heading.
- Scroll to view and select the tiger image from 6/18 below the June 2023 heading.
- Click the Create button on the toolbar to add the four images to the new album.

• Select the title text if necessary and then type   **Animals**   to replace the default title text on the album and then click the Done button (Figure 8–12).

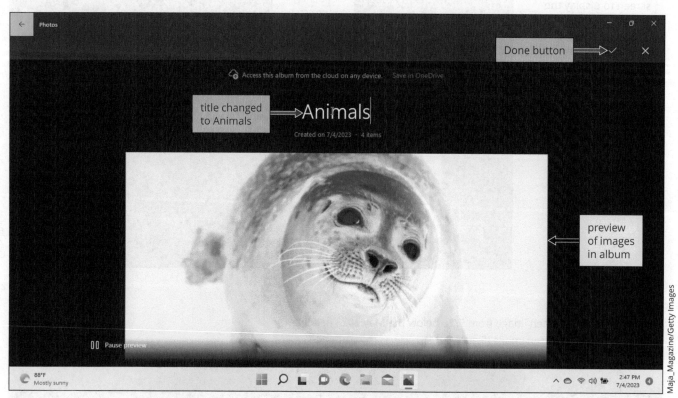

Figure 8–12

• Scroll down to view the four images in the album (Figure 8–13).

Figure 8–13

7

- If necessary, scroll to the top of the album to display the Watch button.
- Click the Watch button to display a video containing the album's photos, as well as options for customizing the video (Figure 8-14).

Figure 8-14

8

- Click the Close button to close the video preview.
- Click the Back button on the title bar to return to the Albums screen (Figure 8-15).

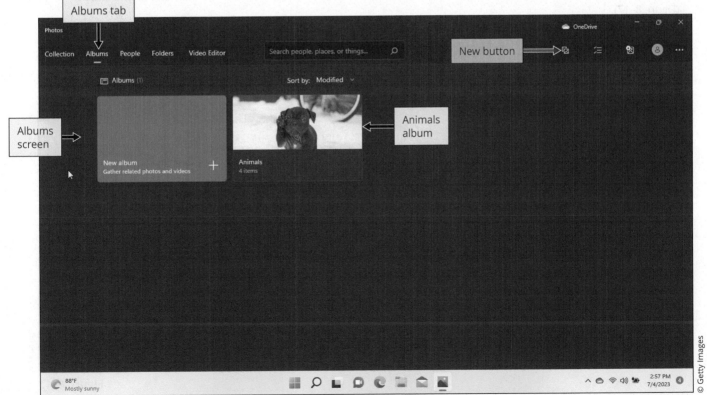

Figure 8-15

9

- Click the New album button on the Albums screen to display the Create new album screen for the second album.
- Scroll as necessary and click to select the London morning image from 11/23 below the November 2022 heading, the sunset boat image from 6/29 below the June 2022 heading, and the river sunrise image from 5/25 below the May 2022 heading (Figure 8–16).
- Click the Create button on the toolbar to add the three images to the new album.

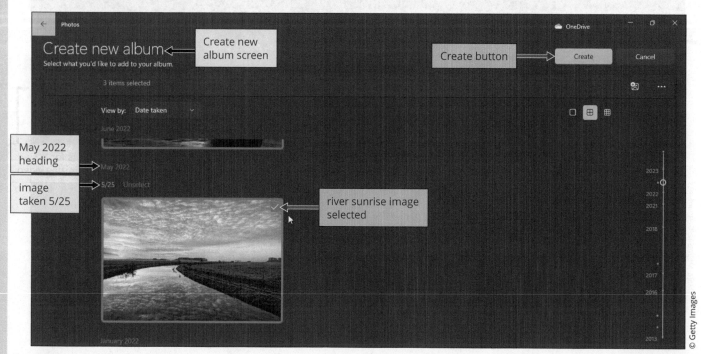

Figure 8–16

10

- Select the title text if necessary, type **Landscapes** and then press ENTER to replace the default title text on the album (Figure 8–17).

Figure 8–17

11

- Scroll down to view the three images in the album (Figure 8–18).

Back button

three images
in album

Figure 8–18

12

Albums screen

- Click the Back button on the title bar to return to the Albums screen (Figure 8–19).

Q&A Can an image be added to multiple albums?
Yes. Just as traditional photo albums can contain copies of the same image, your digital images can be included in multiple albums.

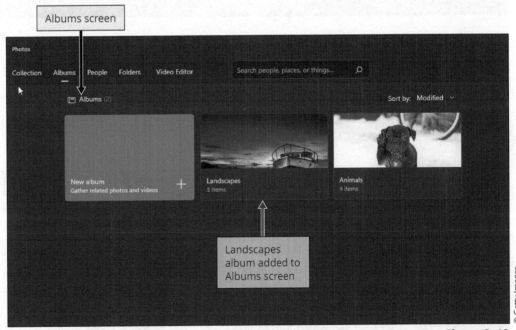

Landscapes album added to Albums screen

Figure 8–19

To Edit an Album Title and Cover

Why? You want to represent the album with a specific image and appropriate title. The following steps change the title and cover image on the Landscapes album.

- Click the Landscapes album tile to open the album.
- Replace the existing title text with the title, Sunlit Landscapes.
- Right-click the video preview to display a shortcut menu (Figure 8–20).

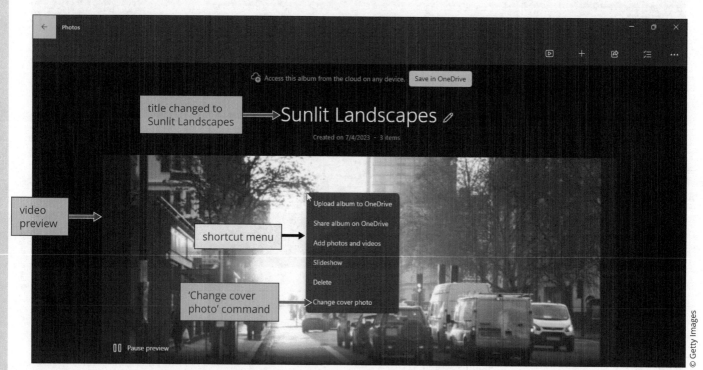

Figure 8–20

- Click 'Change cover photo' to display the Choose a cover photo screen.
- Click to select the river sunrise image (Figure 8–21).

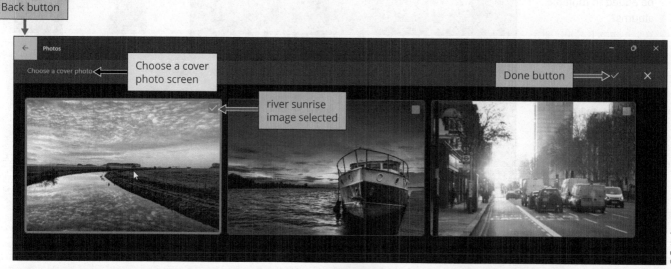

Figure 8–21

3

- Click the Done button on the toolbar to update the cover photo and return to the album editing screen.
- Click the Back button on the toolbar to return to the Albums screen (Figure 8–22).

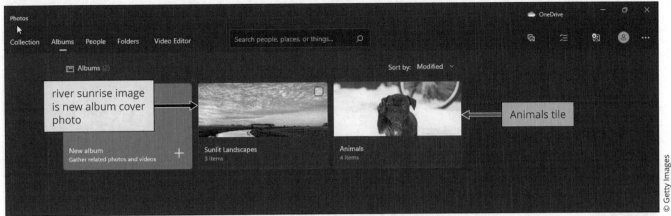

Figure 8–22

To Edit Album Contents

While reviewing your Animals album, you realize that the kitten picture seems out of place with the other images in the album and decide that it should be removed from the album. **Why?** As images in your collection change, you may want to update the contents of your albums by adding or removing photos. The following steps remove the kitten image from the Animals album.

1

- Click the Animals tile to open the album.
- Scroll down to view the photos in the album and then right-click the kitten image to display a shortcut menu (Figure 8–23).

Figure 8–23

2

- Click 'Remove from album' on the shortcut menu to display the Remove this file? dialog box (Figure 8–24).

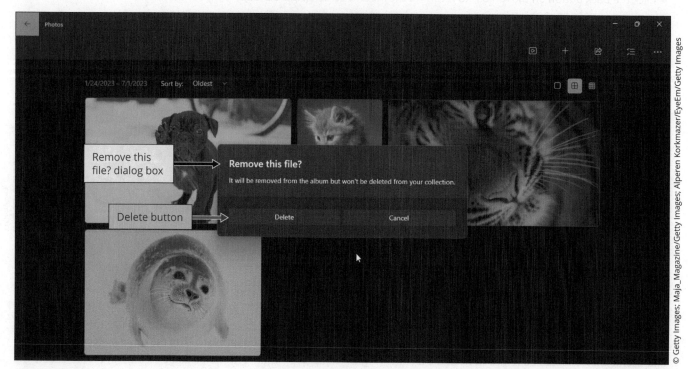

Remove this file? dialog box

Delete button

Remove this file?

It will be removed from the album but won't be deleted from your collection.

Delete   Cancel

Figure 8–24

3

- Click the Delete button in the Remove this file? dialog box to remove the kitten image from the album (Figure 8–25).

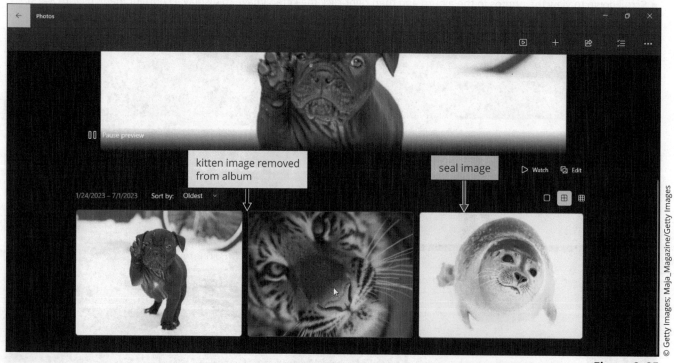

kitten image removed from album

seal image

Figure 8–25

Q&A Does removing an image from an album delete the photo from the collection?

No. Removing an image from an album has no impact on the file or the full collection of images in the Photos app.

Photo Editing

The Photos app provides tools for editing photos. These tools fall into the four categories outlined
in Table 8–1, including: Crop, Adjustment, Filter, and Mark-up.

Table 8–1: Editing Options in the Photos App

Category	Options
Crop	Trim, rotate, and flip an image
Adjustment	Change light and color settings
Filter	Apply automatic enhancements or filter effects
Mark-up	Draw and write on an image

To Enhance a Picture

While reviewing the Animals album, you notice that the blue colors in the seal image are not as defined as you expected and
decide to use the image enhancement options in the Photos app to improve the image coloring. **Why?** You may want to explore
the photo editing options in the Photos app to crop, resize, or improve the image. The following steps display the seal image
and use the enhance option to improve the coloring.

- Click the seal image (shown in Figure 8–25) to display it as a full screen image (Figure 8–26).

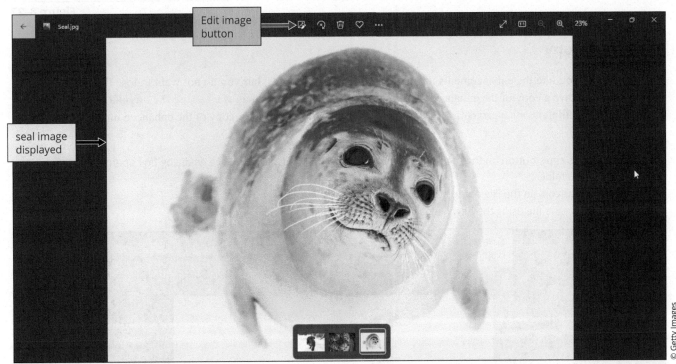

© Getty Images

Figure 8–26

- Click Edit image on the toolbar to display the editing tools.
- Click Filter on the toolbar and then click the Auto Enhance button to automatically enhance the colors and lighting effects in
  the image (Figure 8–27).

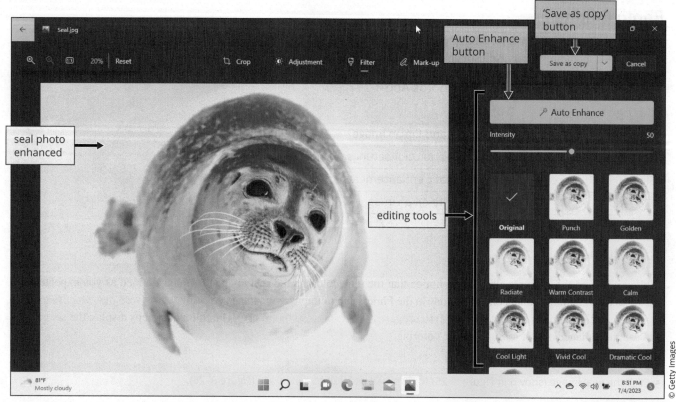

Figure 8–27

© Getty Images

To Save a Copy

You decide that you like the enhancements made by the photo editing tools, but you do not want to lose the original image, so you decide to save a copy of the enhanced image as a new file. **Why?** You may want to use the original image for another purpose or make different enhancements at a later time. The following steps save a copy of the enhanced image as a new file.

1

- Click the 'Save as copy' button on the toolbar (shown in Figure 8–27) to display the Save As dialog box open to the W11_M8_Images folder.
- Type **Seal enhanced** in the File name box (Figure 8–28).
- Click Save to save the file using the new file name, Seal enhanced.jpg.

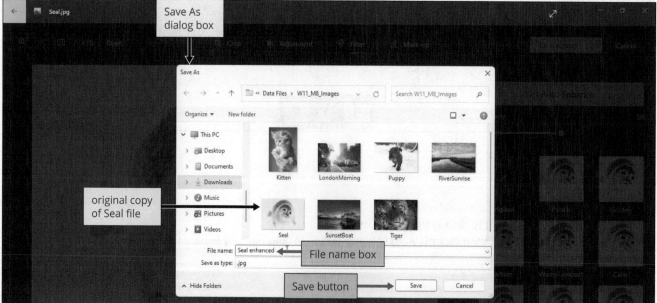

Figure 8–28

© Getty Images

Q&A Can I save the enhanced version and overwrite the original file?
Yes. Click the 'Save as copy' arrow on the toolbar and then click Save.

2
- Click the Back button on the title bar two times to return to the Albums screen.
- Click the Collection tab on the menu to display the Collection screen.
- If necessary, scroll to display the 7/1 date below the July 2023 heading to see the two versions of the seal image (Figure 8–29).

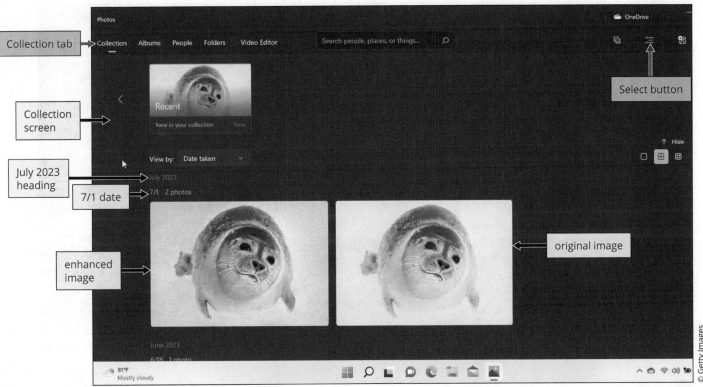

Figure 8–29

Q&A Why was the image in the Animals album not updated based on the enhancements?
Because you saved the enhancements as a copy, the new image file would need to be added to the album and the original image removed to replace the photo within the album.

Why was the enhanced copy listed below the July 2023 heading when I created it today?
The collection organizes files based on the date the photo was taken, not when the file was last modified.

Other Ways

1. Press CTRL+S

To Share Photos

Images can be shared quickly from the toolbar in the Photos app using any app installed on your computer or mobile device for communicating with others, including Mail, OneNote, and all of your favorite social networking apps. If you wanted to share an image from your collection, you would perform the following steps.

1. Locate the image you want to share in the collection in the Photos app.
2. Click the image you want to share to select it.
3. Click the See more button on the toolbar to display the See more menu and then click Share.
4. Click the app you want to use to share the image.

To Delete Photos

The following step removes the original seal image from your collection. **Why?** You may decide that multiple versions of the same image are difficult to manage and it is easier to keep only the enhanced version.

- Click the Select button on the toolbar (shown in Figure 8–29) to enable selection of images in the collection.
- Click to select the unenhanced version of the seal image (Figure 8–30).

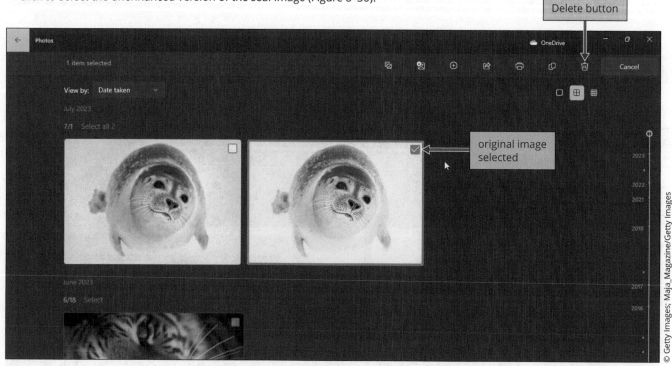

Delete button

original image
selected

Figure 8–30

- Click the Delete button on the toolbar to delete the image from the collection (Figure 8–31).
- Exit the Photos app by clicking the Close button on the title bar.

Q&A Is the file removed from the Data Files folder or just the collection?
The file is deleted from both the collection and the original storage location.

What if I accidentally delete the wrong file?
Depending on the original location of the file, it may be possible to restore the deleted file from the computer's Recycle Bin.

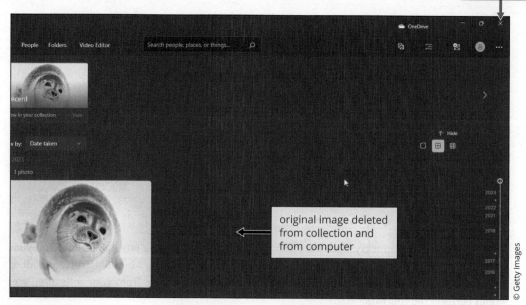

Close button

original image deleted
from collection and
from computer

Figure 8–31

Listening to Music with Media Player

Media Player is the Windows 11 app for organizing and playing your audio files. Automatically organized by albums, artists, and songs, Media Player makes it easy to find your music quickly. The built-in search feature of Media Player makes it possible to locate songs that you cannot quite remember by name.

The Media Player app supports the creation of playlists across albums and artists and will even import your existing iTunes playlists. Upload your mp3 files to OneDrive to access your Media Player library on other computers and devices.

To Start the Media Player App

Why? You want to manage audio files that you have stored on your computer. The following step starts the Media Player app from the Search box.

- Click the Search button on the taskbar and then type **media** in the Search box to search for the Media Player app.
- Click the Media Player app in the search results to start the app.
- If necessary, maximize the Media Player window (Figure 8–32).

Figure 8–32

Other Ways
1. Click Start button on Windows taskbar, click Media Player icon

To Choose a Custom Music Folder

Similar to other digital media files, music files may be stored in locations other than the Music folder. Being able to access those locations with the Media Player app is essential. The following steps add the W11_M8_Music folder from your Data Files to the Media Player app as a custom music folder. **Why?** You may want to add a custom location to your Media Player app to access music from different storage locations.

• Click the Settings button in the left pane to display the Settings screen (Figure 8–33).

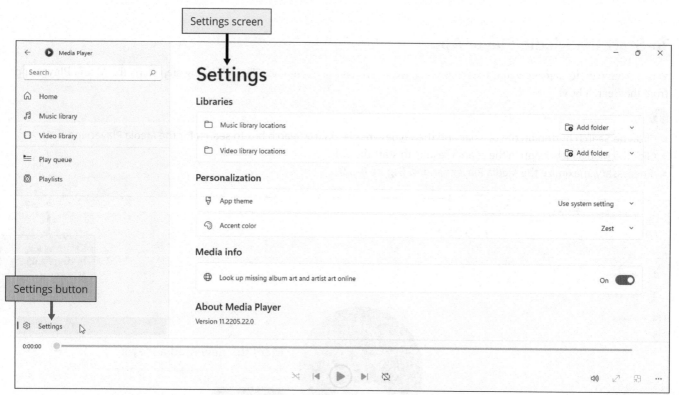

Figure 8–33

• Click the Add folder button for the Music library locations to display the Select Folder dialog box (Figure 8–34).

Figure 8–34

3

- Navigate to the location of the W11_M8_Music folder in the Data Files (Figure 8–35).

Q&A Why are no music files displayed in the W11_M8_Music folder?
The Select Folder dialog box displays only folder names, not individual files within the folders.

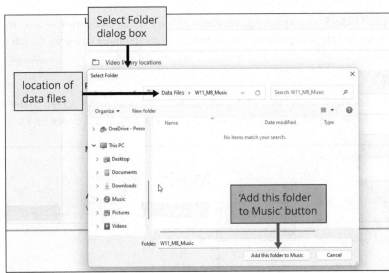

Figure 8–35

4

- Click the 'Add this folder to Music' button to add the folder to the Media Player app Music Library locations (Figure 8–36).

Q&A What file formats are supported by the Media Player app?
The Media Player app supports the following file extensions: .mp3, .flac, .aac, .m4a, .wav, .wma, .3gp, and .3g2.

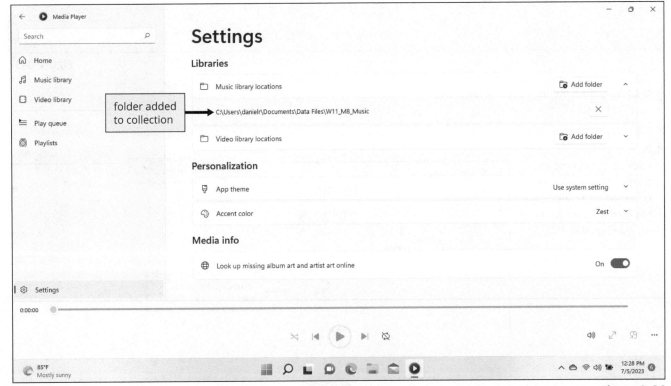

Figure 8–36

To Browse Music by Album, Artist, or Song

The Media Player app organizes audio files into three categories — albums, artists, and songs — accessible from the menu. The following steps explore the music library using the three category search options. **Why?** You may want to listen to music in a variety of ways, either by a specific artist, one of your favorite albums, or a particular song.

- Click Music library in the left pane to view a list of all music added to the music library.
- If necessary, click the Songs tab to display all songs found by Media Player (Figure 8–37).

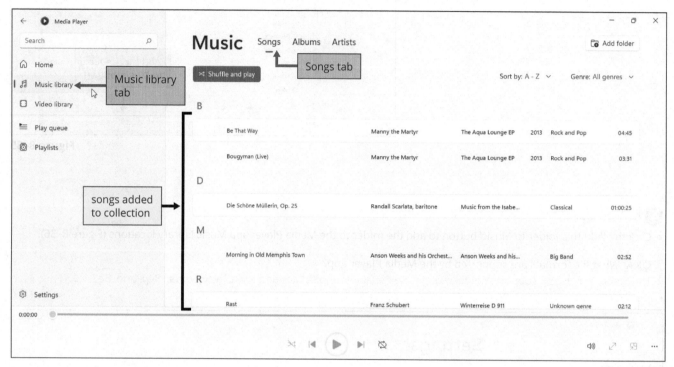

Figure 8–37

Q&A Why does my song list look different?
Your song list will include any songs saved in your Music folder or other locations where Media Player is monitoring.

- Click the Artists tab to display all artists associated with the songs in the Media Player Music library (Figure 8–38).

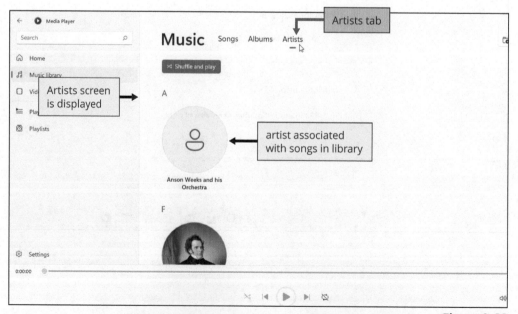

Figure 8–38

● Click the Albums tab to display all albums associated with the songs in the Media Player Music library (Figure 8–39).

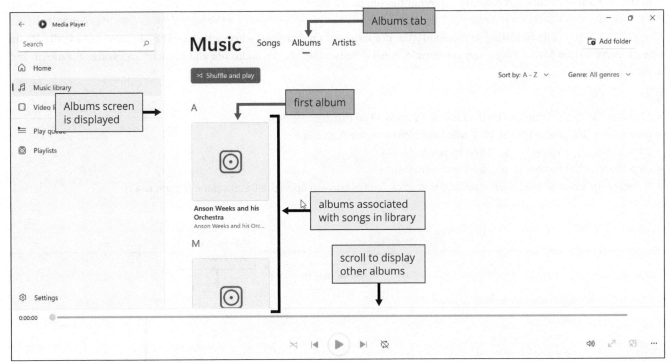

Figure 8–39

● Click the first album to display its contents (Figure 8–40).
● Click Music library in the left pane to return to the album list.

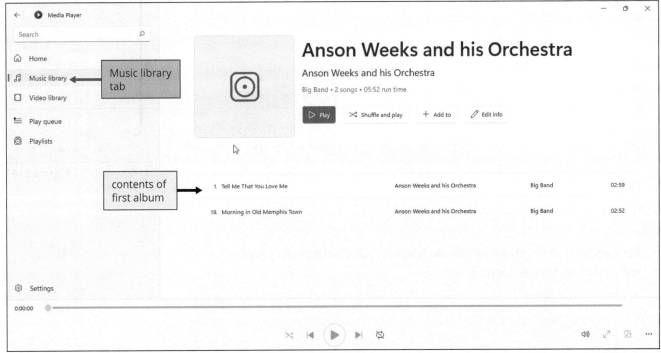

Figure 8–40

To Add Information to Music File Properties

Editing the file properties to include one or more additional details about the source of the audio can enable Media Player to find the remaining details and properly represent the file in the library. **Why?** When you add additional properties for music files, it is easier to search for the music on your computer. When possible, having an accurate representation of the file in the library is preferred. The following steps modify the properties of the Schubert - Prometheus - D 674 file to include the album title property so that Media Player can get the additional details related to the audio file and properly categorize the album and artist for the song.

- Click the File Explorer button on the taskbar to open a File Explorer window.
- Navigate to the location of the W11_M8_Music folder in the Data Files.
- Click 'Schubert - Prometheus - D 674' to select the file.
- Click View on the toolbar to display the View menu.
- If necessary, point to the Show command then click Details pane to open the Details pane (Figure 8–41).

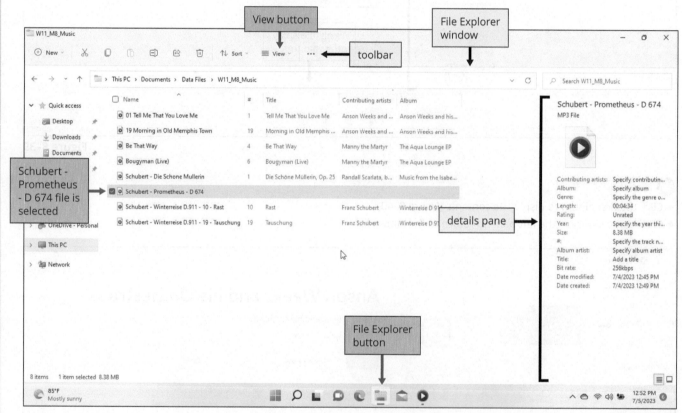

Figure 8–41

- Click the Specify album placeholder for the Album property in the Details pane.
- Type **Lieder on Record** (Figure 8–42).

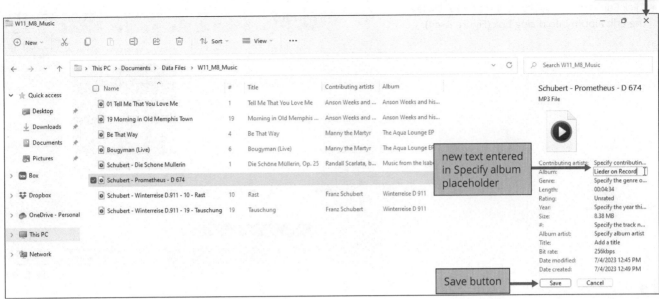

Figure 8–42

3

- Click the Save button in the Details pane to save the album name in the file properties.
- Close the File Explorer window to return to the Media Player app on the Albums screen.

To Find Album Information

Now that the Schubert - Prometheus - D 674 file has an album association, Media Player is able to locate the remaining details about the artist. The following steps update the album information with the artist details. **Why?** You may want to locate songs by artist instead of album and need the artist details to do so.

1

- Scroll down and then right-click the 'Lieder on Record' album tile to display the shortcut menu (Figure 8–43).

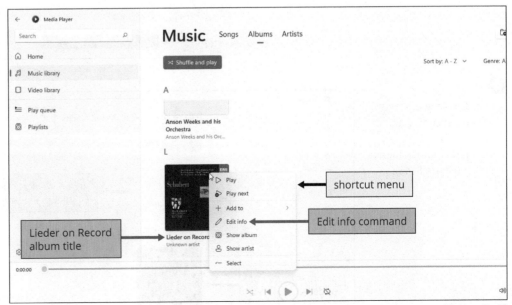

Figure 8–43

2

- Click Edit info on the shortcut menu to display the Edit album info dialog box (Figure 8–44).

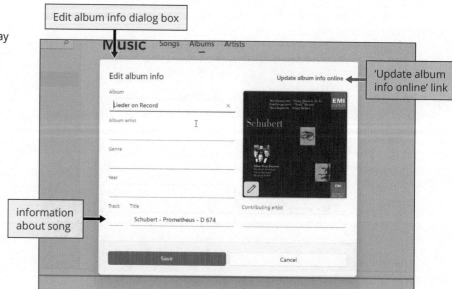

Edit album info dialog box

'Update album info online' link

information about song

Figure 8–44

3

- Click the 'Update album info online' link (Edit album info dialog box) to display a list of albums that match the associated album information.
- Click the Lieder On Record 1898-2012 album to select it (Figure 8–45).

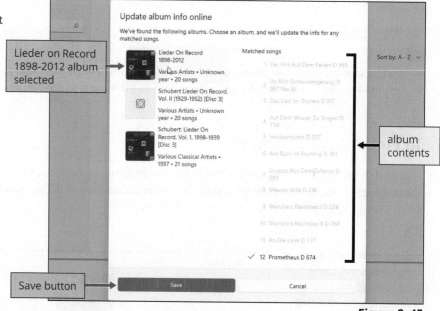

Lieder on Record 1898-2012 album selected

album contents

Save button

Figure 8–45

4

- Click the Save button to finish associating album information with the selected album in Media Player (Figure 8–46).

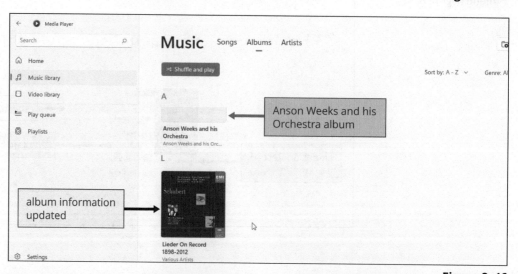

Anson Weeks and his Orchestra album

album information updated

Figure 8–46

To Play an Album

Albums make it convenient to play songs from the same source as a set. **Why?** You may want to listen to all of the songs from a specific digital collection. The following step plays the songs in the library associated with the album titled Anson Weeks and his Orchestra.

- Click the Anson Weeks and his Orchestra album to open the album and view its contents.
- Click the Play button to begin playing the first song in the album (Figure 8–47). If you want to stop the music from playing before it has finished, click the Pause button that replaced the Play button in the media controls.

   Q&A What if I want to play just one of the songs in an album?
   Instead of clicking the Play button for the album, click the song you want to play and then click the Play button.

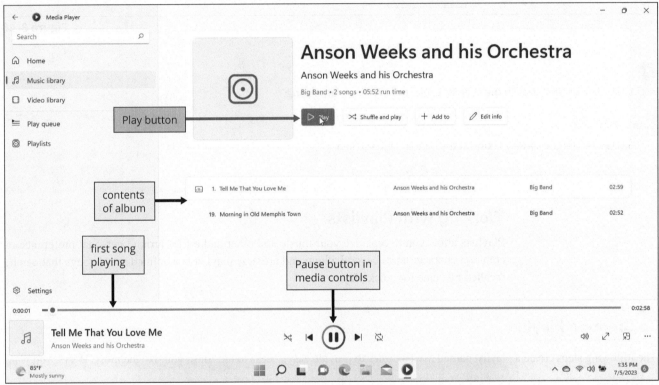

Figure 8–47

Other Ways
1. Right-click album cover on Albums screen, click Play on shortcut menu   2. Point to album cover, click Play button at bottom of screen

To Search for Music

The following steps will use the search feature of the Media Player app to locate the song Be That Way by Manny the Martyr. **Why?** You may remember part of a song title but not know what album it is on or who the artist is and need to find the song quickly.

- Click the Search text box on the menu.
- Type **that way** and press ENTER to display the search results (Figure 8–48).

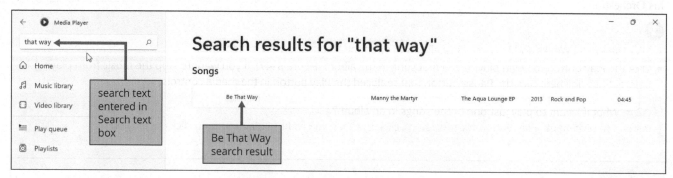

Figure 8–48

- Double-click Be That Way in the search results to play the located song.

Other Ways

1. Click located song, click Play button at the bottom of the screen

Working with Playlists

Playlists allow you to organize your music and other audio files around personal preference or common characteristics beyond album and artist. A playlist is a defined set of songs that can be recalled by name for quick play.

To Create a Playlist

The following steps create a playlist named My Favorites to provide easy access to the songs you like the most. **Why?** You want to be able to listen to your favorite songs quickly and easily in Media Player.

- Click Playlists in the left pane to display the Playlists screen.
- Click the 'Create a new playlist' button on the Playlists screen to start the process of creating a playlist.
- Type **My Favorites** in the text box (Figure 8–49).

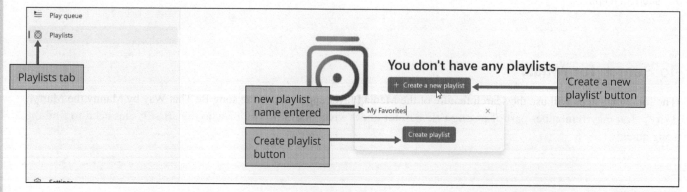

Figure 8–49

- Click the Create playlist button to add the playlist to the Playlists screen (Figure 8–50).

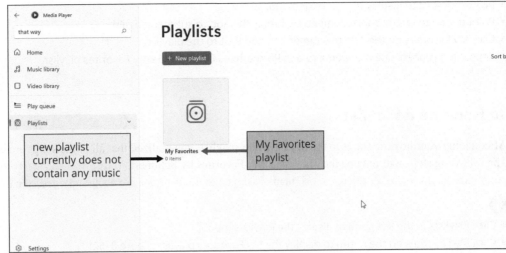

Figure 8–50

To Add Songs to a Playlist

Once a playlist is created, you need to add songs to the list. **Why?** You want to have songs from a variety of albums play without needing to monitor your computer and change albums or songs manually. **The following steps add three songs to the My Favorites playlist.**

①

- Click Music library in the left pane to display the music library.
- Click the Songs tab to display a list of songs in your music library.
- Right-click Tauschung to display the shortcut menu.
- Point to Add to on the shortcut menu to display the Add to submenu, which lists available playlists (Figure 8–51).
- Click My Favorites on the Add to submenu to add Tauschung to the My Favorites playlist.

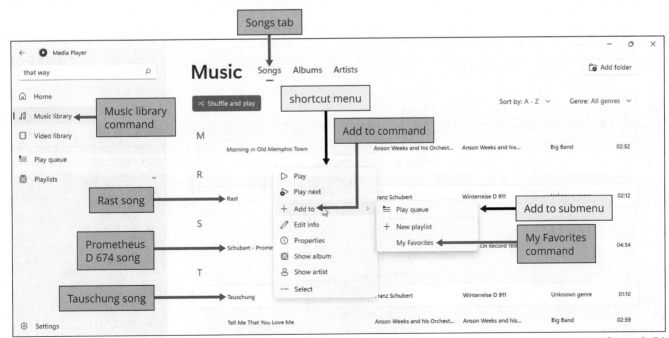

Figure 8–51

- Right-click Rast to display the shortcut menu.
- Point to Add to on the shortcut menu to display the Add to submenu again.
- Click My Favorites on the Add to submenu to add Rast to the playlist.
- Repeat the process one more time to add Prometheus D 674 to the My Favorites playlist.

To Rename a Playlist

After adding your favorite songs to the My Favorites playlist, you realized that all of the songs are composed by Franz Schubert. The following steps will rename the playlist as My Favorites by Schubert. **Why?** You add songs to a playlist based on personal preference, and sometimes the name originally assigned to the list does not accurately describe its contents.

- Click Playlists in the left pane to display the Playlists menu.
- Click My Favorites on the menu to display the My Favorites playlist (Figure 8–52).

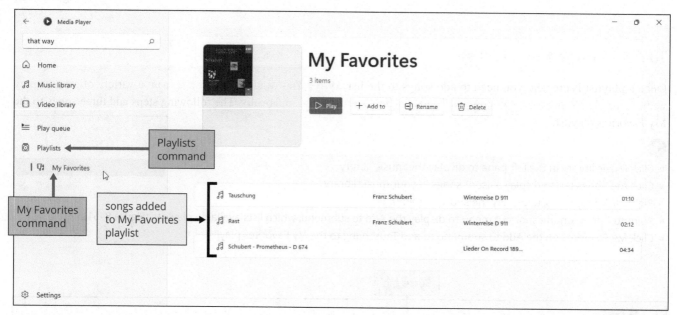

Figure 8–52

- Click the Rename button to display a dialog box to rename the playlist.
- Replace the contents of the name text box with the text, My Favorites by Schubert (Figure 8–53).

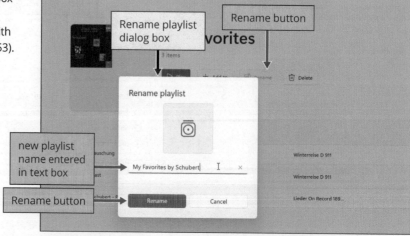

Figure 8–53

3

- Click the Rename button in the Rename playlist dialog box to update the name on the menu and playlist screen (Figure 8–54).

Q&A Media Player displayed the Music screen after I clicked the Rename button. What should I do?
Click the 'My Favorites by Schubert' playlist in the left pane to display the songs in the playlist.

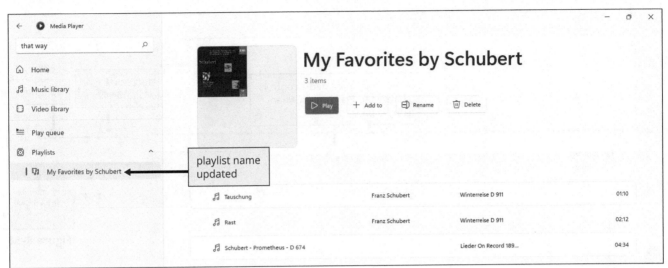

Figure 8–54

To Play the Songs in a Playlist

When you play the songs in a playlist, you can control the music playback by adjusting the volume, for example, or reducing the Media Player app to a mini player. **Why?** You may want to change the volume level or play a song in the mini player as you perform other computer tasks. The following steps play a song in the My Favorites by Schubert playlist.

1

- Click the Play button on the Playlist screen to play the first song in the playlist and display the media controls (Figure 8–55).

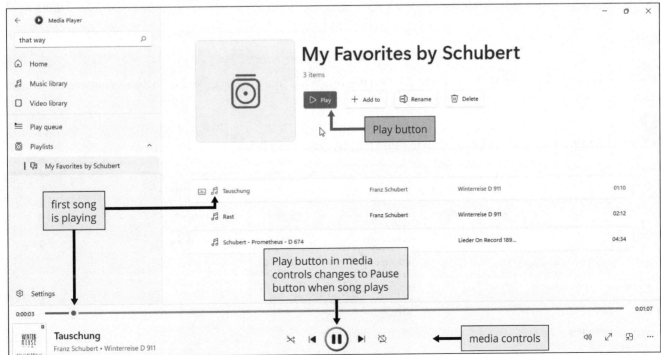

Figure 8–55

- Click the Pause button in the media controls to pause the playback.
- Click the Volume button in the media controls to display a volume slider (Figure 8–56).

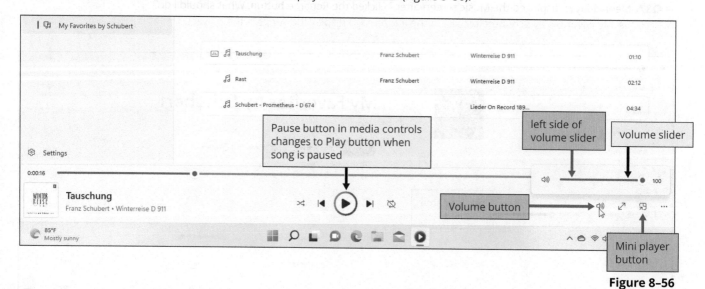

Pause button in media controls changes to Play button when song is paused

left side of volume slider

volume slider

Volume button

Mini player button

Figure 8–56

- Click the left side of the volume slider to reduce the volume.
- Click the Play button in the media controls to play the song again.
- Click the Mini player button in the media controls to reduce the Media Player window to a mini player (Figure 8–57).

- Click the 'Exit mini player' button on the mini player to return to the full-screen Media Player.

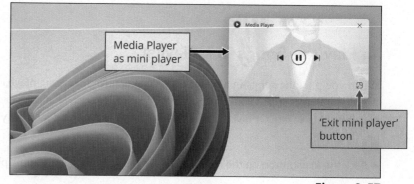

Media Player as mini player

'Exit mini player' button

Figure 8–57

To Delete a Playlist

The following steps delete the My Favorites by Schubert playlist. **Why?** You may have playlists that no longer interest you and need to be removed.

1

- Click the Pause button in the media controls to pause the playback (Figure 8–58).

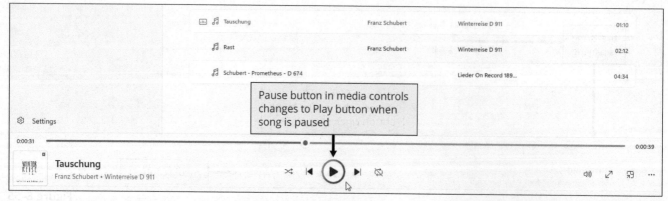

Pause button in media controls changes to Play button when song is paused

Figure 8–58

• Click the Delete button to display the Delete playlist permanently? dialog box (Figure 8–59).

Figure 8–59

• Click Delete (Delete playlist permanently? dialog box) to delete the playlist from Media Player (Figure 8–60).

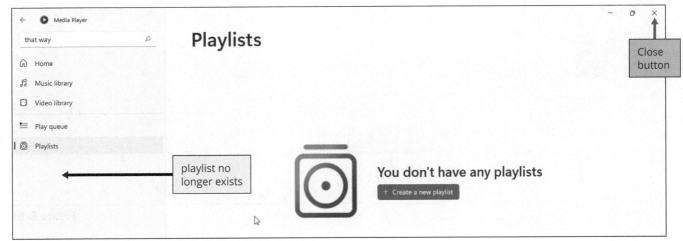

Figure 8–60

• Click the Close button to exit the Media Player app.

Enjoying Video Content in Windows 11

Windows 11 provides access to the latest HD movies and television shows through the Movies & TV app. Integrated with the Microsoft Store, the Movies & TV app provides options for rental or purchase of your favorite movies and shows.

The app provides access to detailed descriptions and customer and critic ratings to make finding something to watch quick and easy. Closed captioning is available for most movies and television shows accessed through the Microsoft Store.

Supporting most of the common video file formats, the Movies & TV app is able to import and manage your personal video collection as well. Playback options include the ability to view in full screen mode or to cast the video to an external device.

To Start the Movies & TV App

Why? You want to manage video files that you have stored on your computer. The following step starts the Movies & TV app from the Search box.

- Click the Search button on the taskbar and then type   **movies**   in the Search box to search for the Movies & TV app.
- Click the Movies & TV app in the search results to start the Movies & TV app.
- If necessary, click the Personal tab and maximize the Movies & TV window (Figure 8–61).

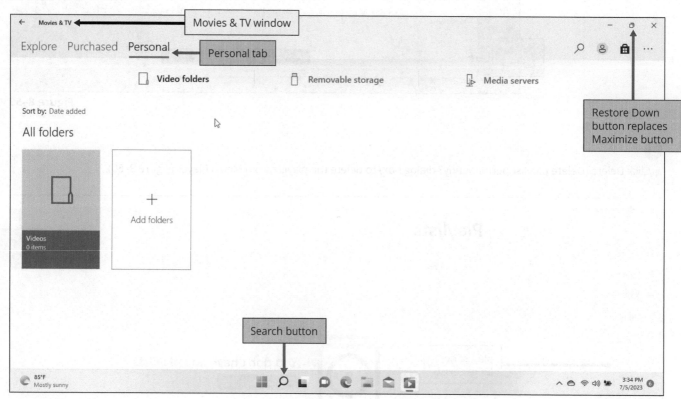

Figure 8–61

Other Ways

1. Click Start button on taskbar, click 'Movies & TV' tile

To Choose a Custom Video Folder

The following steps add the contents of the Data Files folder to the video collection. **Why?** You want to include video from another storage location and do not want to move the videos to the default locations searched by the Movies & TV app.

- Click the Add folders tile to display the Build your collection from your local video files dialog box (Figure 8–62).

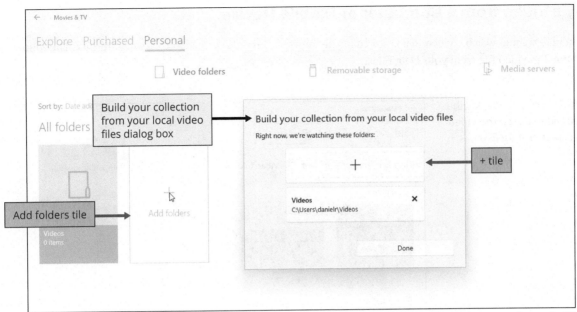

Figure 8–62

2

- Click the + tile to display the Select Folder dialog box.
- Navigate to the location of the Data Files (Figure 8–63).

Q&A Why are no videos displayed in the Data Files folder?
The Select Folder dialog box displays only folder names, not individual files within the folders.

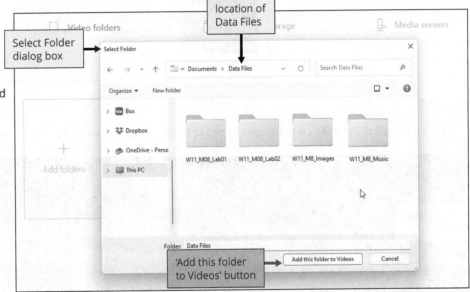

Figure 8–63

3

- Click the 'Add this folder to Videos' button (Select Folder dialog box) to add the folder to the Movies & TV app watch list (Figure 8–64).
- Click the Done button to close the Build your collection from your local video files dialog box.

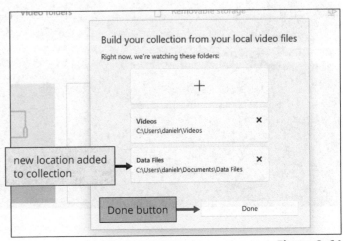

Figure 8–64

To Play a Video from a Computer or Mobile Device

Why? You may want to watch a video that is stored locally on your computer in a supported video format. **The following steps play the MindTap video file from your Data Files.**

- If necessary, scroll to display the MindTap_video tile on the Video folders screen (Figure 8–65).

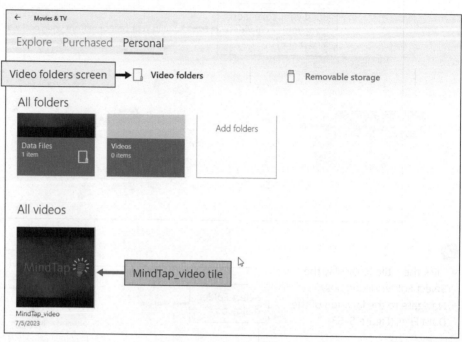

Figure 8–65

②

- Click the MindTap_video tile on the Videos screen to begin playing the video file (Figure 8–66).

Figure 8–66

Q&A What file formats are supported by the Movies & TV app?
The Movies & TV app supports the following file extensions: .m4v, .mp4, .mov, .asf, .avi, .wmv, .m2ts, .3g2, .3gp2, and .3gpp.

Playback Controls

While viewing a video in the Movies & TV app, playback controls are available, such as cast to device, aspect ratio, play/pause, volume, full screen, and toggle repeat.

The **cast to device** feature of the app supports the sharing of content with other networked devices capable of receiving the content. The **aspect ratio** toggles between standard and widescreen formatting during playback. The Play button is replaced by a Pause button while the video content is playing. The Pause button is replaced by a Play button when the video content is paused. The volume control provides a slider tool to adjust from volume levels of 0 to 100. The **full screen** feature expands the video player to fit the size of the display device and hides the title bar, taskbar, and other interface components. The **toggle repeat** feature allows for continuous play of the video content by automatically restarting the video each time it ends.

To Adjust Volume

Why? You may need to increase or decrease the volume while watching the video. The following step sets the volume for the video to a level of 50.

- If necessary, move the pointer down in the video playback screen to display the playback controls.
- Click the Volume button to display the Volume slider.
- Adjust the Volume slider to a value of 50 (Figure 8–67).

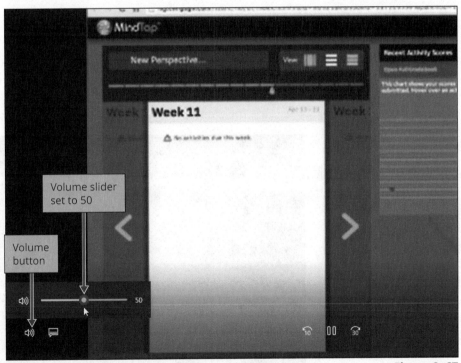

Volume slider set to 50

Volume button

Figure 8–67

To Play in Mini View

Playing a video in mini view allows you to view the video in a small window on the screen. **Why?** You want to work in other apps on your computer while the video continues to play. The following steps play the video in mini view.

- Point to the 'Play in mini view' button (Figure 8–68).

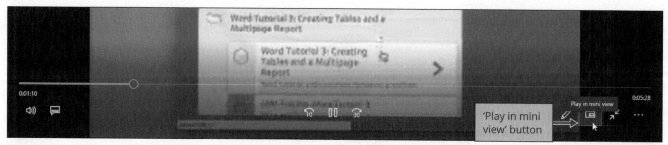

'Play in mini view' button

Figure 8–68

- Click the 'Play in mini view' button to display the video in mini view (Figure 8–69).

- Click the 'Leave mini view' button to return to playing the video in full screen.

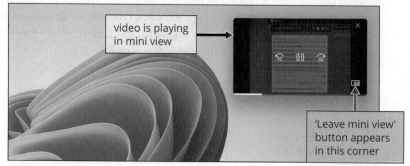

video is playing in mini view

'Leave mini view' button appears in this corner

Figure 8–69

To Change Repeat Option

The repeat option controls whether the video restarts after reaching the end of playback. **Why?** You may want to display a video presentation on a computer during an event and allow the video to continuously play without user interaction. **The following step enables the repeat option on the current video.**

- Click the 'Show more options menu' button to display the Show more options menu (Figure 8–70).
- Click Repeat on the Show more options menu to toggle the repeat on.

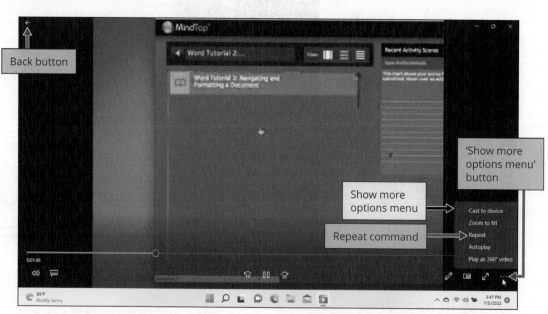

Back button

'Show more options menu' button

Show more options menu

Repeat command

Figure 8–70

Other Ways

1. CTRL+T

To Quit Video Playback

Once the video has ended, you want to return to the videos list. **Why?** You may want to watch another video or are finished with the Movies & TV app. The following step quits the video playback.

- If necessary, move the mouse down in the video playback screen to display the playback controls. Click the Back button (shown in Figure 8–70) to return to the Videos screen (Figure 8–71).

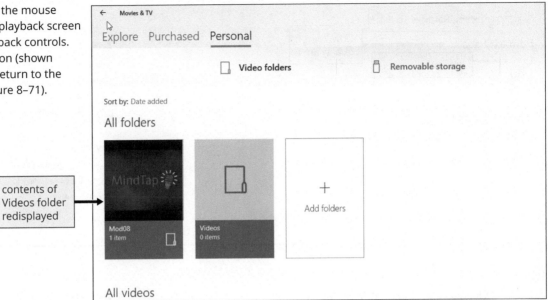

contents of Videos folder redisplayed

Figure 8–71

Movies and Television Content from the Microsoft Store

The Microsoft Store provides access to movies and TV shows as soon as the day after they air. Streaming video allows for instant delivery of purchased or rented content to Windows devices and on the web.

To Set Download Quality

The movies and television content provided through the Store includes both HD and standard-definition (SD) quality video. The actual display quality depends on the capability of the computer's equipment, screen resolution, and cables. **Why?** If your hardware does not support HD video or your network connection is too slow to support the streaming of HD video, you may want to use SD video quality or choose to be prompted prior to download. The following steps set the download quality to HD.

- Click the More options button to display the More options menu and then click Settings to display the Settings screen (Figure 8–72).

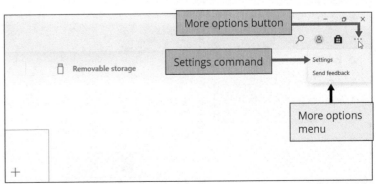

Figure 8–72

2

- Click to select the HD option button in the Download quality area (Figure 8–73).

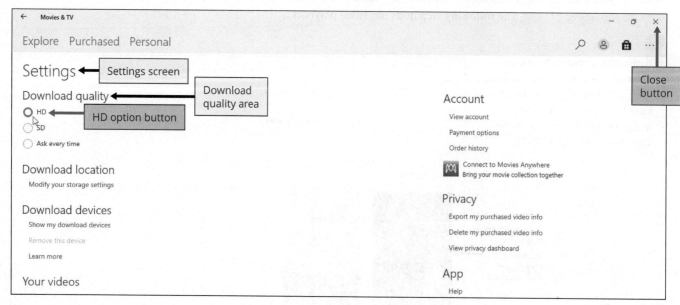

Figure 8–73

3

- Click the Close button to exit the Movies & TV app.

To Adjust Closed Captioning Settings

Closed captioning settings are managed through the Accessibility settings in Windows 11. **Why?** You may want to view closed captions on a video when playback with sound is not available. **The following steps modify the closed captions settings.**

1

- Click Settings on the Start menu to start the Settings app. If necessary, maximize the Settings app window (Figure 8–74).

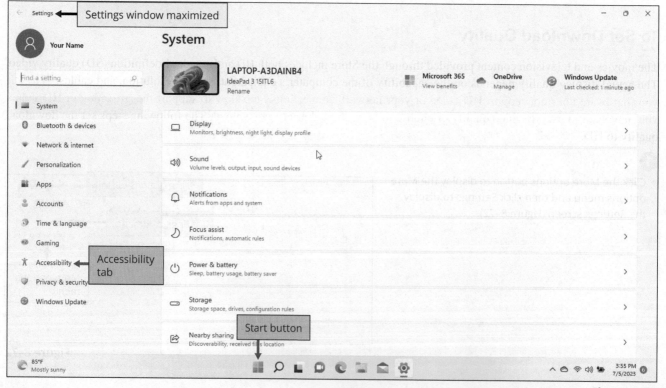

Figure 8–74

2
- Click the Accessibility tab in the Settings window to display the Accessibility settings.
- If necessary, scroll to display Captions below the Hearing heading in the right pane.
- Click Captions in the right pane to display the current captioning settings.
- Click the Caption style button and then click Large text in the list (Figure 8–75).

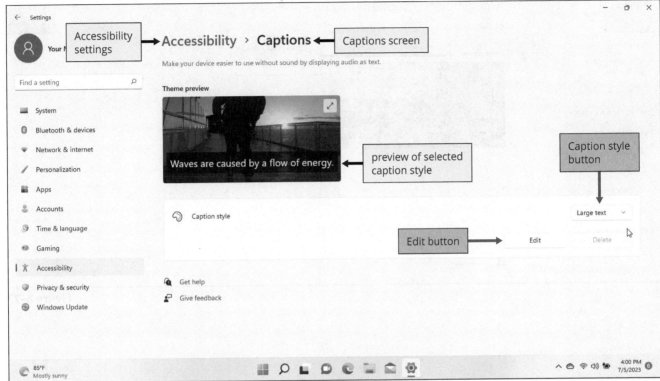

Figure 8–75

3
- Click the Edit button to display the Caption style screen.
- Click the Background tab in the Name your caption style area.
- Click the Opacity button and then click 100% in the list (Figure 8–76).

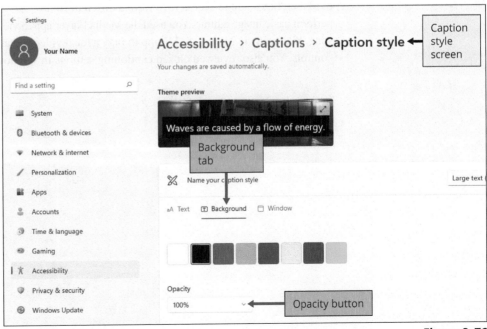

Figure 8–76

- Click the Back button and view the effects of the updated caption settings in the Theme preview area (Figure 8–77).
- Click the Close button to exit the Settings app.

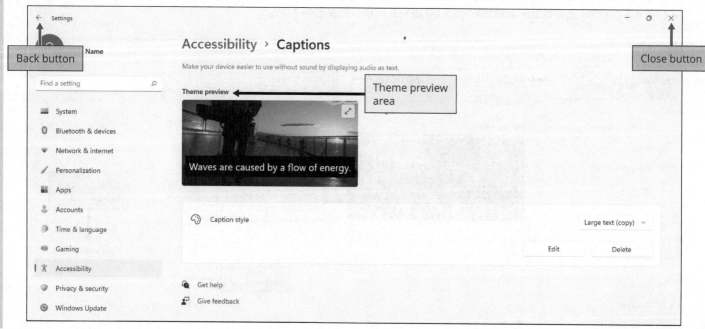

Figure 8–77

Summary

In this module, you learned how to use the Photos, Media Player, and the Movies & TV apps. You used the Photos app to access files from a different folder, to organize photos into albums, and to perform basic image editing. You used the Media Player app to view music files by artist, album, and song. You used the Movies & TV app to play a local video file and explored the various playback controls. You also reviewed closed captioning settings in Windows 11.

Student Assignments

Apply Your Knowledge

Reinforce the skills and apply the concepts you learned in this module.

Creating a Photo Album

Instructions: You want to create a photo album of images for an upcoming project. Use Microsoft Edge and the Photos app to accomplish this.

Perform the following tasks:

1. Start Microsoft Edge.
2. Type **www.skitterphoto.com** in the address bar text box and then press ENTER to display the Skitterphoto webpage (Figure 8–78).

Source: Skitterphoto.com

Figure 8–78

3. Click 'Browse free photos' at the top of the window and review the categories available on the menu that is displayed.
4. Click the link for a category of interest and review the available photographs.
5. Click on an image of interest within the selected category webpage.
6. Click the Download button on the selected image webpage and save the image.
7. Repeat Steps 5 and 6 for two additional images within the same category.
8. Start the Photos app.
9. Create a photo album with the same name as the category selected in Step 4.
10. Add the three saved pictures to the album.
11. Submit the album in the format required by your instructor.

Extend Your Knowledge

Extend the skills you learned in this module and experiment with new skills. You might need to use Help to complete the assignment.

Using Spotify

Instructions: Use the Spotify webpage to learn more about the Spotify subscription service.

Perform the following steps:

1. Start Microsoft Edge.
2. Type **spotify.com** in the address bar text box and then press ENTER to display the Spotify webpage (Figure 8–79).

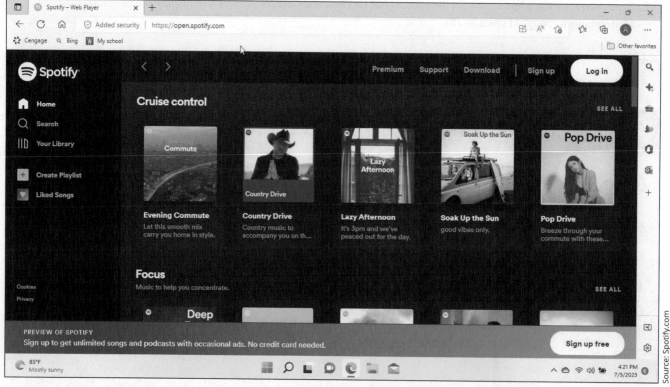

Figure 8–79

3. Open a new document in WordPad and answer the following questions:
   a. What subscription options are available for Spotify?
   b. What are three benefits to the Spotify Premium subscription?
   c. What devices can be used to access content on Spotify?
4. Submit your answers in the format required by your instructor.

Expand Your World

Create a solution that uses cloud or web technologies by learning and investigating on your own from general guidance.

Understanding Creative Commons Licensing

Instructions: Now that you are familiar with the media options that can be used with Windows 11, you will gain an understanding of the licensing options related to the media available on the web. Create a new document in WordPad to gather your results into a brief report.

Perform the following tasks:

1. Using Microsoft Edge, visit the Creative Commons licensing webpage (Figure 8–80) at www.creativecommons.org/licenses and then review the licenses available.

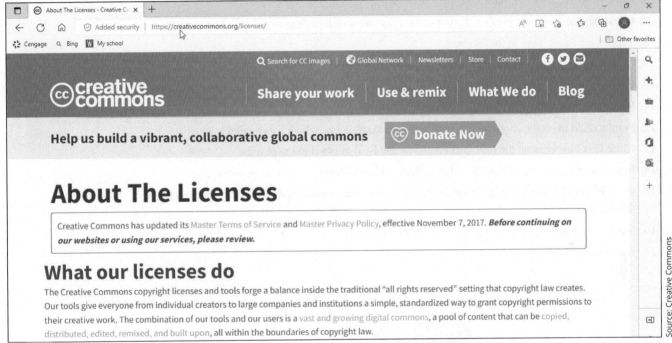

Figure 8–80

2. Review the information provided by Bing at help.bing.microsoft.com/#apex/18/en-us/10006/0 for filtering images by license type.

3. Review the information provided by Google at support.google.com/websearch/answer/29508?hl=en for finding free-to-use images.

4. Perform an image search at www.bing.com/images and review the licensing options on the results webpage.

5. Perform the same image search at images.google.com and review the usage rights options on the results webpage.

6. In a WordPad document, summarize the licensing options available through Creative Commons, noting the ways that these licenses are identified in Bing and Google image search results.

7. Submit the WordPad document in the format requested by your instructor.

In the Labs

Design and implement a solution using creative thinking and problem-solving skills.

Lab 1: Creating a Playlist

Problem: You have collected some of your favorite music in the W11_Mod08_Lab01 Data Files folder. You want to add these songs to a custom playlist for continuous play in the Media Player app.

1. Start the Media Player app.
2. Click Music library in the left pane to display the Music screen.
3. Click the Add folder button on the Music screen to display the Select Folder dialog box.
4. Navigate to the location of the W11_Mod08_Lab01 folder in your Data Files and select the folder.
5. Click the 'Add this folder to Music' button (Select Folder dialog box) to add the folder to the Media Player app.
6. Click Playlists in the left pane to display the Playlists screen.
7. Click the 'Create a new playlist' button in the Playlists screen to display a dialog box to create the playlist.
8. Type   **Jazz Favorites**   in the text box.
9. Click the Create playlist button to add the playlist to the menu.
10. Click Music library in the left pane and then click the Songs tab to display the Songs screen.
11. Right-click Bird in Hand to display the shortcut menu.
12. Point to Add to on the shortcut to display the Add to submenu, which lists available playlists.
13. Click Jazz Favorites on the Add to submenu to add Bird in Hand to the playlist.
14. Repeat steps 11 through 13 for Feel Good Feel, Island Mystery, and Summer Sidewalk.
15. Click Playlists in the left pane and then click Jazz Favorites on the menu to display the new playlist (Figure 8–81).
16. Submit the playlist in a format required by your instructor.
17. Exit Media Player.

Figure 8–81

Lab 2: Sorting Photos into Albums

Problem:　Over the past few years, you have taken several pictures of city scenes stored in the W11_Mod08_Lab02 Data Files folder. You decide to move some of the older photos into albums of nature and city scenes using the Photos app.

1. Start the Photos app.

2. Click the See more button on the toolbar and then click Settings.

3. Click 'Add a folder' in the Sources area on the Settings screen and then add the W11_Mod08_Lab02 folder to your collection.

4. Click the Back button and then click the Albums button on the menu to display the Albums screen.

5. Create a new album named City Scenes by completing the following steps:

   a. Click the New album button on the Albums screen.

   b. Click to select the following images: Airport (12/27/2018), Skyline (7/14/2018), Street view (11/9/2018), and Subway (2/2/2018).

   c. Click the Create button on the toolbar to add the four images to the new album.

   d. Type　**City Scenes**　to replace the selected default title text on the album.

   e. Press ENTER to save the City Scenes album and display the album contents (Figure 8–82).

6. Click the Back button on the title bar to return to the Albums screen.

7. Create a new album named Nature by completing the following steps:

   a. Click the New album button on the Albums screen.

Figure 8–82

   b. Click to select the following images: Bridge (7/14/2018), Leaves (1/13/2018), Waterfall (1/23/2018), and Wildflowers (6/24/2018).

   c. Click the Create button on the toolbar to add the four images to the new album.

   d. Type　**Nature**　to replace the selected default title text on the album.

   e. Press ENTER to save the Nature album and display the album contents.

Continued on next page

8. Click the Back button on the title bar to return to the Albums screen.

9. Submit your albums in a format required by your instructor.

10. Exit the Photos app.

Lab 3: Consider This: Your Turn

Searching the Microsoft Store

Problem: You decided to use the Movies & TV app to manage your existing videos. You now want to find new movies and television shows to add to your digital media collection. You decide to use the Microsoft Store app to locate new media.

Part 1:   Start the Microsoft Store app. Browse the Movies & TV content in the app. Enter at least one movie or television show in the Search text box and then review the results. Use WordPad to create a brief summary of your experience with the Microsoft Store app and then submit the document in the format requested by your instructor.

Part 2:   You explored several features of the Microsoft Store app to complete this assignment. What was the price range for the movies and television shows you located? Was it easy to locate movies and television shows of interest? What are the benefits of using the Search box to locate content?

Understanding Security, Networking, and Utilities

Objectives

After completing this module, you will be able to:

- Configure sign-in options
- Configure family and other user accounts
- Manage Windows Defender Firewall
- Configure User Account Control (UAC) settings
- Protect against computer viruses and malware
- Enable BitLocker drive encryption
- Use the Network and Sharing Center

- Enable Remote Desktop and Remote Assistance connections
- Sync settings across devices
- Use performance tools
- Back up and restore files
- Use System Restore features
- Understand recovery options

Introduction

Users with administrator accounts on Windows devices are responsible for the ongoing functionality of the device. Windows 11 provides a number of administrative tools for maintaining a system that is secure, connected, and reliable (Figure 9–1).

Security features of Windows 11 provide a foundation for the detection and prevention of threats to a computer. Windows Defender Firewall manages access rights for apps with configuration options for both public and private network connections. Windows Security provides core protection against computer viruses and malware. Other features of Windows 11, including User Account Control (UAC), Windows SmartScreen, and BitLocker Drive Encryption, add layers of security to the operating system, apps, and files to reduce the risk of security-related issues on a computer.

The use of devices for communication with other devices across the Internet or in local area networks, both at home and work, presents a variety of networking topics for discussion and management within Windows 11. The Network and Sharing Center provides access to the status of network connections, the capability to connect to wireless networks, and troubleshooting options for connectivity issues. Remote access and remote assistance features ensure that access to the content and help needed in the connected environment is close at hand. Finally, Windows 11 contains features that are focused on the growing number of mobile users.

The reliability of Windows 11 is enhanced by proper maintenance procedures and the use of available tools for managing the necessary maintenance easily. Several performance tools are built into Windows 11 to keep devices running smoothly, and automatic maintenance ensures that certain maintenance activities are performed on a daily schedule. Regardless of how reliable Windows 11 is, the potential for problems still exists. As a result, effective backup and restoration procedures, the System Restore tool, and other recovery options also are discussed in this module.

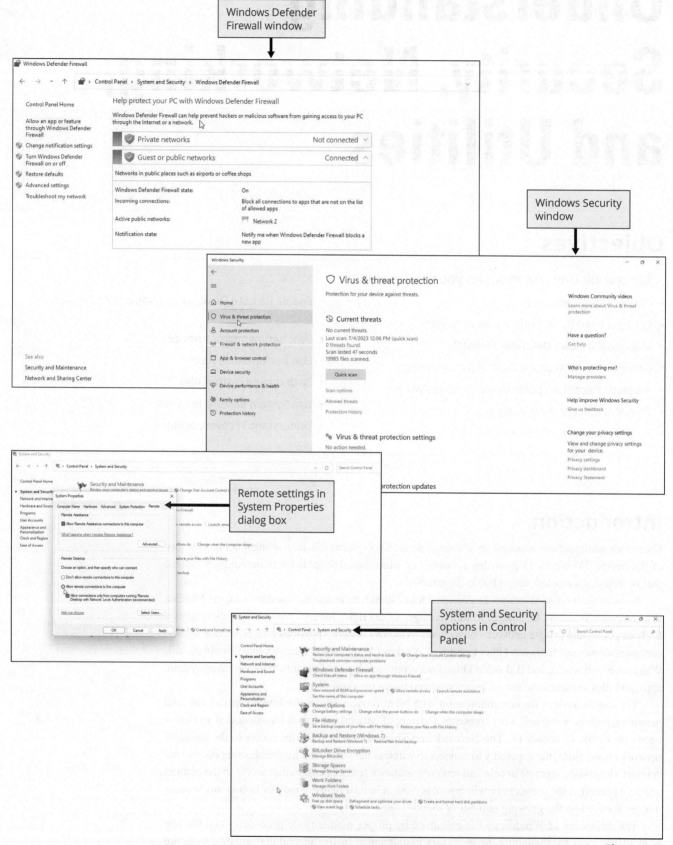

Figure 9–1

Understanding Security

Windows 11 includes improvements in performance, security, malware protection, and system reliability. In addition, a number of updated security features help you accomplish three important goals: to enjoy a computer free from malware, including viruses, worms, spyware, and other potentially unwanted software; to have a safer online experience using Windows 11 apps and websites; and to understand when a computer is vulnerable and how to protect it from external threats.

Malware, short for malicious software, is software that acts without a user's knowledge and deliberately alters the computer's operations. Examples of malware include viruses, worms, and spyware. A **virus** is a potentially damaging computer program that affects, or infects, a computer negatively by altering the way the computer works without the user's knowledge or permission. A virus attaches itself to another program or file so that it can spread from computer to computer, infecting programs and files as it spreads. Viruses can damage computer software, computer hardware, and files. A **worm** is malware that resides in active memory and replicates itself over a network to infect machines, using up the system resources and possibly shutting down the system. A worm copies itself from one computer to another by taking advantage of the features that transport data and information between computers. A worm is dangerous because it has the capability of traveling without being detected and to replicate itself in great volume. For example, if a worm copies itself to every contact in your email address book and then the worm copies itself to the names of all the email addresses of each of your contacts' computers, the effect could result in increased Internet traffic that slows down business networks and the Internet. **Spyware** is a program placed on a computer or mobile device without the user's knowledge that secretly collects information about the user and then communicates the information it collects to some outside source. Spyware monitors the activity that takes place to gather personal information and send it secretly to its creator; it also can be designed to take control of the infected computer.

A **hacker** is someone who accesses a computer or network illegally. A hacker is an individual who uses his or her expertise to gain unauthorized access to a computer with the intention of learning more about the computer or examining the contents of the computer without the owner's permission.

Sign-In Options

Security in Windows 11 begins with the user account. A user account identifies the resources a user can access when working with the computer or mobile device. Different users on the same computer or mobile device may have access to different sets of files, folders, and apps. By default, users are required to sign in when the computer is powered on, restarted, or wakes from sleep.

To secure access to the resources associated with a specific user account, Windows 11 provides several sign-in options, including creating a password using letters and numbers, a picture password, or a PIN (personal identification number). Windows 11 extends the sign-in options with a feature called Windows Hello that works on devices with supported hardware components.

A PIN provides a simpler method for accessing a device, apps, or services but in many ways is more secure than a traditional password. A PIN is local to the device on which it is created. When created on a device, the account is verified and a trust relationship is established for authenticating the user without transmitting the password to an authentication server for future access to resources, apps, or services from that device. A password can be intercepted during transmission or stolen from a server, making it a greater security risk than a PIN that is locally stored and not transmitted for authentication.

To Create a PIN

A PIN commonly is a set of four numbers that can be used in place of passwords to provide an easier way to sign in to your device, apps, and services. For devices configured with Windows Hello, a PIN is used as a backup authentication. **Why?** You want to use a PIN that is easier to remember and enter when accessing apps and services. The following steps create a PIN on your device.

- Display the Start menu.
- Click Settings on the Start menu to start the Settings app.
- Click the Accounts tab in the Settings window to display the Accounts screen.
- Click Sign-in options in the right pane to display the sign-in options for the current account.
- Click 'PIN (Windows Hello)' to display the Set up button in the PIN (Windows Hello) area (Figure 9–2).

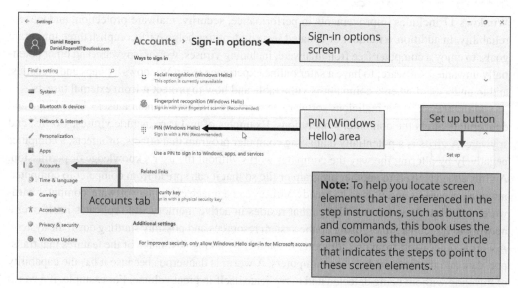

Note: To help you locate screen elements that are referenced in the step instructions, such as buttons and commands, this book uses the same color as the numbered circle that indicates the steps to point to these screen elements.

Figure 9–2

2

- Click the Set up button in the PIN (Windows Hello) area to display the Windows Security dialog box.
- Enter your current account password in the Password text box to verify your Microsoft account (Figure 9–3).

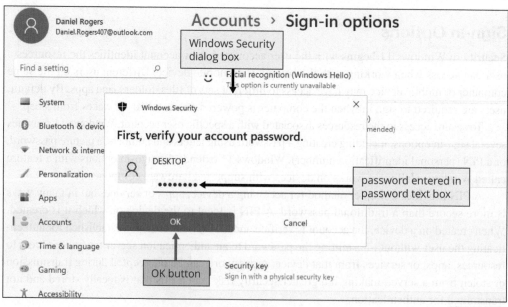

Figure 9–3

3

- Click the OK button to display the Windows Security dialog box.
- Type **1212** in the New PIN text box.
- Type **1212** in the Confirm PIN text box (Figure 9–4).

Q&A Why did my device not show the Confirm PIN dialog box?

If you recently have verified the password for your Microsoft account while making other account changes, the Set up button immediately may display the Windows Security dialog box.

Are the complexity requirements for a PIN similar to those required for a password?

A PIN must be at least four characters in length and typically is limited to numbers; however, administrators can set policies to require or block special characters, uppercase or lowercase characters, and digits. Length, expiration, and history requirements also may be set as part of IT (information technology) management policies.

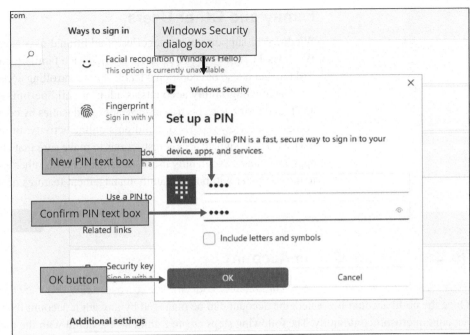

Figure 9–4

- Click OK (Windows Security) to save the PIN and display the sign-on options with updated PIN buttons.

Q&A I have multiple devices running Windows 11. Will the PIN work on all of my devices?

A PIN is tied to the specific device on which it was created. The same PIN value can be used on all of your Windows 11 devices; however, each PIN must be created on the device with which it is used.

To Authenticate with Windows Hello

Windows Hello uses biometric hardware devices to authenticate a user through fingerprint, iris, or facial recognition. A **biometric device** authenticates a person's identity by translating a physical characteristic, such as a fingerprint, into a digital code that is compared with a digital code stored in a computer. Windows Hello requires the creation of a PIN, as was done in the previous steps, to provide an alternative form of authentication if use of the biometric device is not possible. For example, if you cut the finger that is registered with the fingerprint reader device and could not authenticate properly as a result, a PIN would allow you to access the device. Both Windows Hello and a PIN are verified using the Microsoft Passport service, and authentication data is stored locally on the device rather than being transmitted to a server. If you wanted to enable Windows Hello on a device with biometric hardware, you would perform the following steps.

1. Display the Start menu.

2. Click Settings on the Start menu to start the Settings app.

3. Click the Accounts tab in the Settings window to display the Accounts screen.

4. Click Sign-in options in the right pane to display the sign-in options for the current account.

5. Click 'Facial recognition (Windows Hello)' or click 'Fingerprint recognition (Windows Hello)' to display set-up options. If set-up options are not displayed, Windows Hello might not be compatible with your device.

6. Follow the instructions in the Windows Hello area to continue setting up Windows Hello.

Family and Other Users

Windows 11 supports two categories of additional user accounts: Your family and Other users. Windows 11 **family user accounts** provide each family member with his or her own sign-in and desktop, but it also has additional features for controlling access to content for children's accounts.

Designating family accounts as adult or child permits related management tool access for adults and restricts access to websites, apps, and games by content or time limits for children. Adult accounts can view reports of children's online activity, limit how long and when they use their devices, and designate access restrictions to make sure that children avoid inappropriate websites, apps, and games. Nonfamily users should be set up as other users on the computer to permit access to the computer without the family management features or restrictions.

To Create a Child User Account

Why? You have decided to share your computer with children in your family and want to be sure that their experience is safe. Once the child account is created, the account can be managed by any adult account listed in the family for that computer at account.microsoft.com/family. The following steps create a child user account with the name, SC Child.

- Click the Back button to return to the Accounts screen.
- Click 'Family & other users' in the right pane to display the page that allows you to add family accounts to Windows (Figure 9–5).

Q&A What if I do not see the 'Family & other users' option?
You might not be signed in to Windows using an administrator account. Recall that standard user accounts are unable to add accounts to the computer. If you are unable to sign in to the computer with an administrator account, read these steps without performing them.

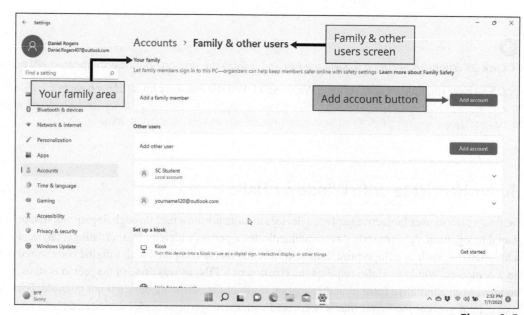

Figure 9–5

2

- Click the Add account button in the Your family area to display the first dialog box in the wizard (Figure 9–6).

Q&A What is a wizard?
A wizard is a step-by-step progression that guides you through a process, usually by presenting a series of dialog boxes or screens. Wizards are used for completion of a lengthy process often associated with the installation of software or custom configurations, such as the creation of the child account in these steps.

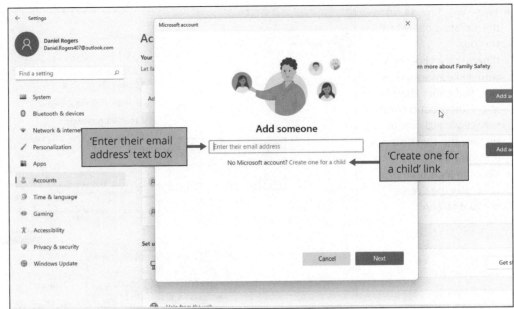

Figure 9–6

3

- Click the 'Create one for a child' link to display the account creation page.
- Type **scchildXXXMMDDYY** in the New email text box replacing XXX with your initials and MMDDYY with the current date (Figure 9–7).
- Click the Next button to display the Create a password screen.

Q&A What if the email address is not available?
Modify the address to something similar that is available.

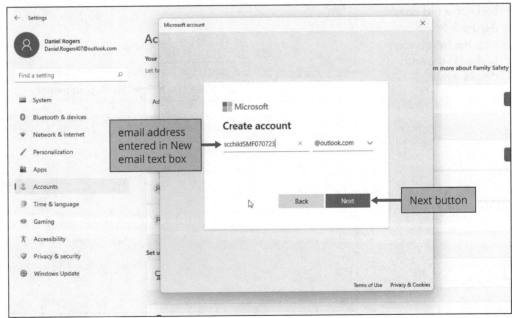

Figure 9–7

- Type **Windows11** in the 'Create a password' text box.
- If necessary, click the 'I would like information, tips, and offers about Microsoft products and services.' check box to remove the check mark (Figure 9–8).
- Click the Next button to display the Create account screen.

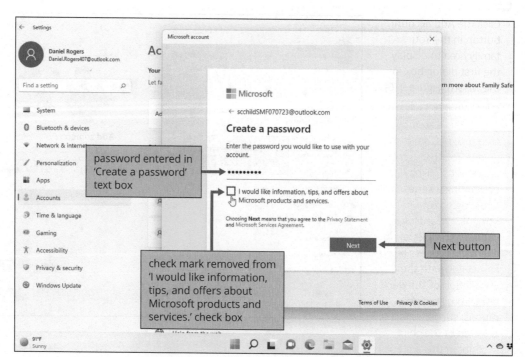

Figure 9–8

- Type **SC** in the First name text box.
- Type **Child** in the Last name text box (Figure 9–9).
- Click the Next button to display the Add details screen.

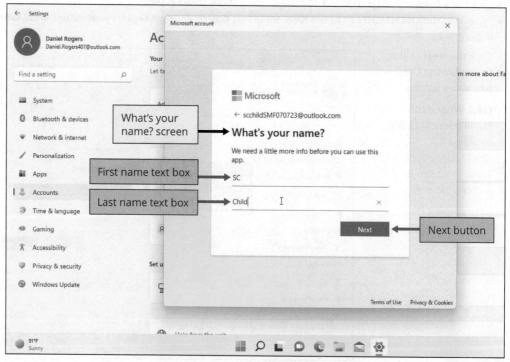

Figure 9–9

6

- If necessary, select United States in the Country/region box.
- Click the Month box and then select July.
- Click the Day box and then select 15.
- Click the Year box and then type **2010** (Figure 9–10).
- Click the Next button to display the Windows Security dialog box.

Q&A I am being asked to reenter my PIN. Why?
Depending on the time it takes to set up the account, you may be asked to verify your Microsoft account by entering your current account PIN before agreeing to the contents of the agreement.

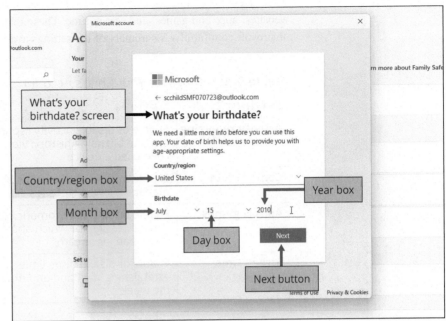

Figure 9–10

7

- Type **1212** in the PIN text box to display the next dialog box in the wizard.
- Click the 'I'm a parent or guardian' button to finish setting up the account (Figure 9–11).
- Click the Continue button to display the Sign in window.
- Sign in with your Microsoft credentials.
- Click the Sign in button to sign into your account.
- If necessary, click the Yes button to stay signed in and display the next step in the wizard.
- Scroll down in the consent form, type your name, and then click the 'Yes, I agree' button to display the next step in the wizard.
- Click the Continue button to create the account.
- Click the Sign out button to save the new account.
- Exit the Settings app.

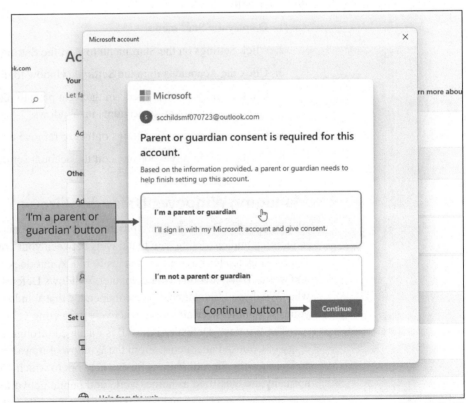

Figure 9–11

To Manage Family Settings

Adult accounts can manage settings for child accounts in the family related to recent activity, websites, apps and games, and screen time. These features are available online at http://account.microsoft.com/family. A summary of the settings available is displayed in Table 9–1.

Table 9–1: Settings for Your Child's Account

Settings Link	Options
Activity reporting	Enable or disable activity reporting, email weekly reports, view website browsing history, view apps and games used, view when a child used a device
Content filters	Enable or disable automatic blocking of inappropriate websites, manage allowed websites list, manage blocked website list
Apps & games	Enable or disable automatic blocking of inappropriate apps and games, set age for which apps, games, and media a child can buy, download, or stream
Screen time	Enable or disable time limits for when a child can use devices, establishing start and end times and daily time limits for each day of the week

If you wanted to manage family settings for a child's account, you would perform the following steps.

1. Display the Start menu.
2. Click Settings on the Start menu to start the Settings app.
3. Click the Accounts tab in the Settings window to display the Accounts screen.
4. Click 'Family & other users' in the right pane to display the screen that allows you to add and manage family accounts in Windows.
5. Click 'Manage family settings online or remove an account' in the Your family area.
6. On the Your family webpage, edit the account settings as desired.

Managing Windows Defender Firewall

Windows Defender Firewall is a program that protects your computer from unauthorized users by monitoring and restricting data that travels between your computer and a network or the Internet. Windows Defender Firewall also helps to block, but does not always prevent, computer viruses and worms from infecting your computer. Windows Defender Firewall automatically is turned on when Windows 11 is started. It is recommended that Windows Defender Firewall remain on unless you have another firewall program actively protecting your computer.

The Windows Defender Firewall is managed through a link in the System and Security category of Control Panel items. From the Windows Firewall window's right pane, you can monitor and manage the firewall settings for any network to which you are connected. Connected networks normally are classified as home, work, and public networks. Home and work networks are considered private networks and have settings that are different from public networks, which are not considered to be as secure.

From the left pane, you can allow programs or features through Windows Defender Firewall, change notification settings, turn off Windows Defender Firewall, restore default settings, adjust advanced settings, and troubleshoot your network. Windows Defender Firewall is set up with the most secure settings by default.

You can adjust Windows Defender Firewall settings as needed. For example, if you have an app or feature that you want to allow to communicate through the firewall, you can allow it using the 'Allow an app or feature through Windows Defender Firewall' link. Caution should be used, because each app or feature allowed through the firewall carries the risk of making a computer less secure; that is, the computer becomes easier to access and more vulnerable to attacks by hackers. The more apps and features you allow, the more vulnerable the computer. To decrease the risk of security problems, allow only those apps or features that are necessary and recognizable, and promptly remove any app or feature that no longer is required.

To Open the Windows Defender Firewall Window

Why? You want to verify the current status of the firewall and access the options for allowing a feature through Windows Defender Firewall. The following steps open the Windows Defender Firewall window from the Control Panel.

- Click the Search button on the taskbar and then type **control panel** in the Search box to display the search results.
- Click the Control Panel Desktop app in the search results to open the Control Panel window. If necessary, maximize the Control Panel window (Figure 9–12).

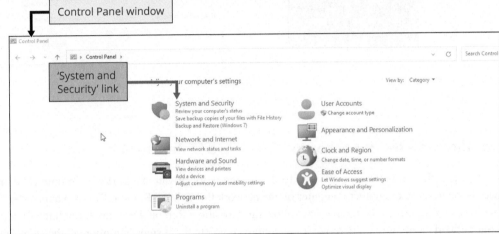

Figure 9–12

Q&A Why does my Control Panel look different?
If you have switched Control Panel views to a setting other than Category view, you may see different options.

- Click the 'System and Security' link to open the System and Security window (Figure 9–13).

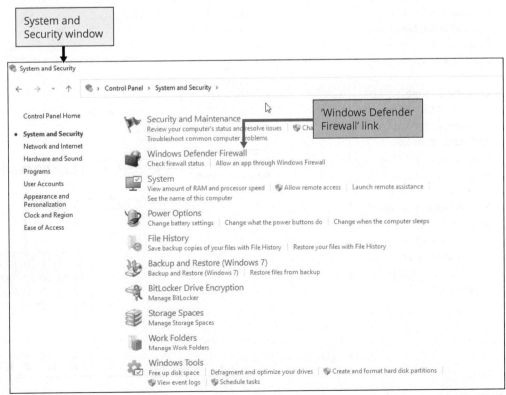

Figure 9–13

3

- Click the 'Windows Defender Firewall' link to open the Windows Defender Firewall window (Figure 9–14).

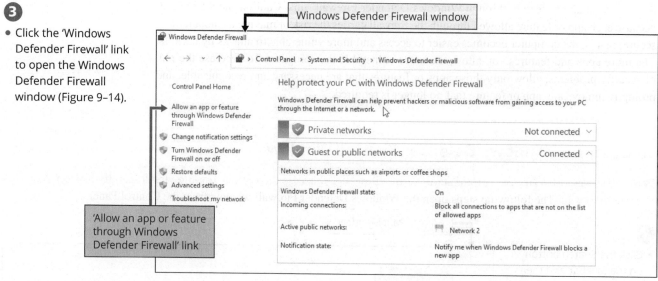

Figure 9–14

To Allow a Feature through Windows Defender Firewall

One feature that sometimes is allowed for home and work private networks is Remote Desktop. This feature allows you to access the desktop of another computer on the network through the Remote Desktop app. **Why?** You want to be able to access the desktop on a remote computer. The following steps allow Remote Desktop through the firewall for private networks only. If your network configuration does not allow you to complete these steps, simply read the steps without performing them.

1

- Click the 'Allow an app or feature through Windows Defender Firewall' link (shown in Figure 9–14) to open the Allowed apps window.
- Click the Change settings button to enable the Allowed apps and features area.
- If necessary, scroll to display the Remote Desktop feature in the Allowed apps and features area.
- Click to select the Private check box for Remote Desktop (Figure 9–15).

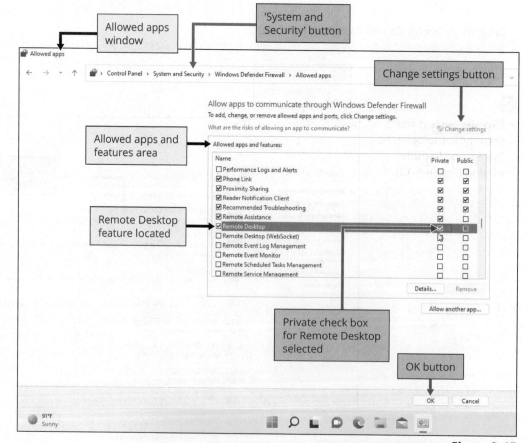

Figure 9–15

- Click OK to accept the changes and return to the Windows Defender Firewall window.

To Disallow a Feature through Windows Defender Firewall

If you later decide that you do not want to allow a program or feature through the Windows Defender Firewall, you should disallow it. The following steps disallow Remote Desktop through the firewall for Private (home/work) networks only.

1 Click the 'Allow an app or feature through Windows Defender Firewall' link to open the Allowed apps window.

2 If necessary, click the Change settings button to access the Allowed apps and features area.

3 If necessary, scroll to display the Remote Desktop feature in the 'Allowed apps and features' list.

4 Click the Private check box for Remote Desktop to remove the check mark.

5 Click OK to accept the changes and return to the Windows Defender Firewall window.

Configuring User Account Control (UAC) Settings

User Account Control (UAC) notifies the user when changes are going to be made to the computer that require administrator-level permission. Changes that require administrator-level permission are installations or configurations that may affect security or settings for other people using the computer. When using an administrator account, the UAC dialog box permits a single-click option to accept or block the change at the time of the notification. When using a standard account, the UAC dialog box requires an administrator password to approve changes. Once administrator account credentials have been provided, the standard account is granted temporary administrative rights for the completion of the process.

To Change UAC Settings

Why? You are concerned that some of the changes you make as an administrator may be potentially harmful and decide that whenever any change is made to Windows settings, you want to receive a UAC notification. The following steps change the UAC setting to always notify you when changes are going to be made to the computer that require administrator-level permission. If your network configuration does not allow you to complete these steps, simply read the steps without performing them.

1

- Click the 'System and Security' button on the address bar to open the System and Security window (Figure 9–16).

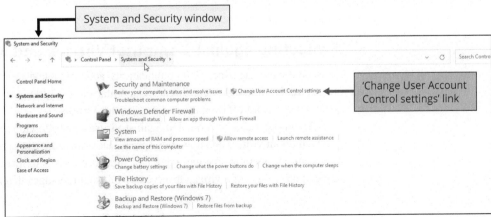

Figure 9–16

- Click the 'Change User Account Control settings' link in the 'Security and Maintenance' area to display the 'User Account Control Settings' window.
- Drag the slider indicator to Always notify at the top of the slider (Figure 9–17).

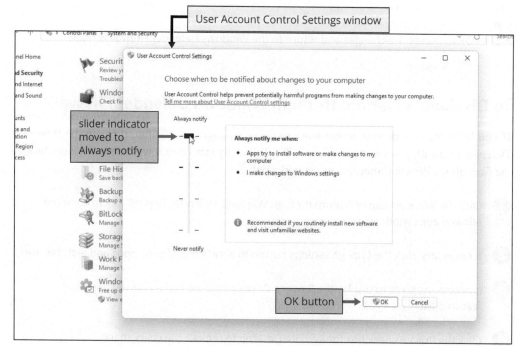

Figure 9–17

- Click OK to accept the changes and display the User Account Control dialog box (Figure 9–18).

- Click the Yes button in the User Account Control dialog box to allow the settings change and return to the System and Security window.
- Close the System and Security window.

Figure 9–18

Protecting against Computer Viruses and Malware

Most computer magazines, daily publications, and even television news channels warn of computer virus threats. Although these threats sound alarming, a little common sense and a good antivirus program can ward off even the most malicious viruses.

A computer can be protected against viruses by following these suggestions. First, educate yourself about viruses and how they spread. Downloading a program from the Internet, accessing a website, or opening an email message can cause a virus to infect your computer. Second, learn the common signs of a virus. Observe any unusual messages that appear on the computer screen, monitor system performance, and watch for missing files and inaccessible hard drives. Third, recognize that programs on removable storage media might contain viruses, and scan all removable storage media before copying or opening files.

Windows Security, which is included in Windows 11, is a program that protects your computer from viruses and malware; you also can install third-party software to protect against viruses and malware. You may decide to install a third-party antivirus program for additional protection or use Windows Security as your primary virus protection. Windows Security helps you stay productive by protecting your computer against pop-ups, slow performance, and security threats caused by spyware and other potentially damaging software. When you scan your computer using Windows Security, it is vital to have the most recent virus definitions. **Definitions** are the files that form a database of all the current virus signatures used by the antivirus software for malware detection. To assist in keeping the definitions up to date, automatically set Windows Update, which installs new definitions as they are released.

To Scan Using Windows Security

Windows Security can notify you when malware attempts to install programs or attempts to change settings on your computer. Windows Security can be set to scan for malware on a regular basis or at any time on demand. **Why?** You suspect that malware has infected your computer and want to perform a manual scan for threats. The following steps scan your computer using Windows Security.

- Click the Search button on the taskbar and then type **Windows Security** in the search box to display the search results (Figure 9–19).

Figure 9–19

- Click the Windows Security search result to open the Windows Security window.
- If necessary, maximize the Windows Security window.
- Click the Virus & threat protection tab in the left pane (Figure 9–20).

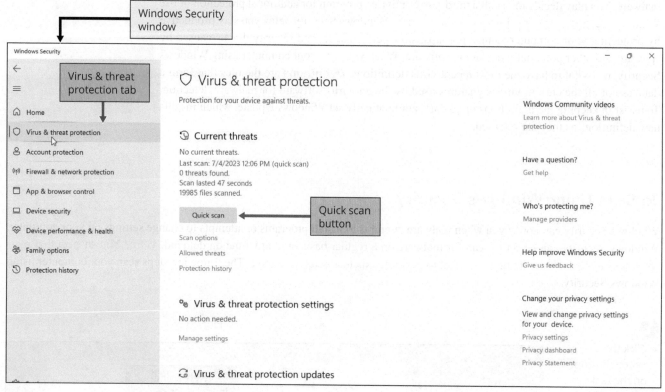

Figure 9–20

- Click the Quick scan button to scan your computer for malware (Figure 9–21).

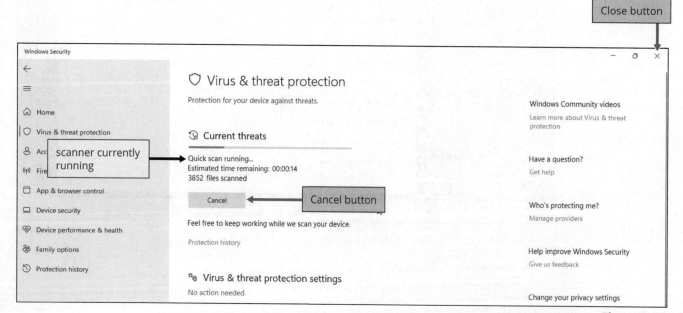

Figure 9–21

4

- Click the Cancel button to stop the Quick scan process.
- Click the Close button to exit the Windows Security app.

Q&A What if Windows Security detects malware?

Based on the settings for Windows Security, threats to your computer may be deleted or quarantined automatically when detected. If Windows Security identifies threats that cannot be resolved automatically, contact an IT professional for additional assistance.

Security and Maintenance

The **Security and Maintenance** tool can help you to manage your computer's security by monitoring the status of several essential security features on your computer, including firewall settings, automatic updating, virus protections, spyware and unwanted software protection, Internet security settings, User Account Control settings, and Network Access Protection.

The right pane, which displays options to let you review messages and resolve problems, contains two expandable sections. The first is the Security section. Clicking the arrow to the right of the Security heading expands the section and displays security features. The On and OK settings mean that the security feature is turned on and working properly. The Off setting means that the security feature is turned off and you should turn it on, if appropriate. For example, if virus protection software if installed on your computer but was temporarily disabled to permit the installation or configuration of a program or hardware device driver, the Off indicator would provide notice that the feature should be turned on when possible. For features that have settings you can change, you will see options for adjusting them.

The second section is the Maintenance section, which allows you to view maintenance features. Similar to the Security section, the On setting means that the maintenance feature is turned on and working, and the Off setting means that the feature is turned off and you should turn it on, if appropriate. The File History feature is turned off by default but may be turned on to save copies of your files on an external drive. If no external drive is present in the system, File History cannot be turned on. Not all maintenance features have the same options. For example, if troubleshooting features are turned on, you will see only the message, No action needed. For some of the features, you also can choose whether you want to monitor the messages that are displayed when an issue arises. If you choose not to monitor a feature, you will see a status of, Currently not monitored. As with the security features, if you can change settings, you will see options for adjusting them.

In the left pane of the Security and Maintenance window are links to Control Panel Home, Change Security and Maintenance settings, Change User Account Control settings, Change Windows SmartScreen settings, and View archived messages. At the bottom of the left pane are links to related areas of the Control Panel that you might want to visit to find and fix problems or enable and configure related features.

To Review a Computer's Reliability and Problem History

The Reliability Monitor generates a report of problem history over time. The report can be viewed in days or weeks and provides an overall stability index on a scale of 1 to 10. Lower index values indicate a less stable environment, and higher index values indicate better overall performance of your computer. The index value is supported by information on application failures, Windows failures, miscellaneous failures, warnings, and information events. Information events are notifications from apps installed on your computer that appear in the Action Center. Each event provides a link to check for a solution, or the option exists to check for solutions to all problems. **Why?** You want to review specific hardware and software problems that have impacted your computer over time. The following steps use the Reliability Monitor to review problem history.

1

- Open the Control Panel window (Figure 9–22).

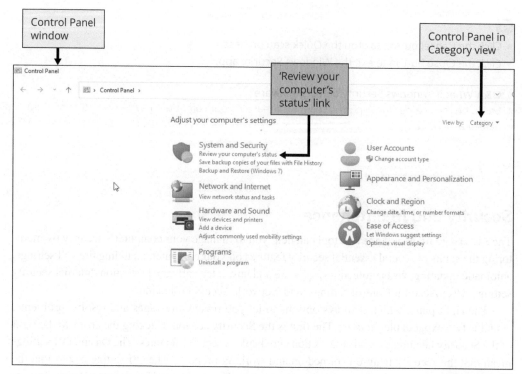

Figure 9–22

2

- Click the 'Review your computer's status' link below the System and Security heading to open the Security and Maintenance window.
- If the Maintenance area is not expanded, click the Maintenance button to expand the Maintenance area (Figure 9–23).

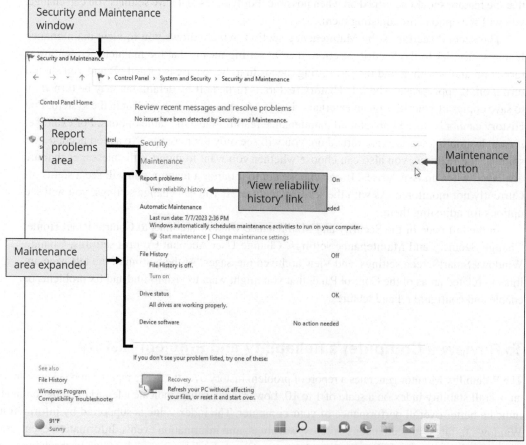

Figure 9–23

- Click the 'View reliability history' link in the Report problems area to display the Reliability Monitor report (Figure 9–24).

Q&A Why would I want to check for solutions to past problems?
Regular updates to the operating system are intended to correct problems that are experienced with the computer. It is possible that one of the recent updates fixed an issue that prevented you from using a particular app or feature in the past and you now can take advantage of the functionality.

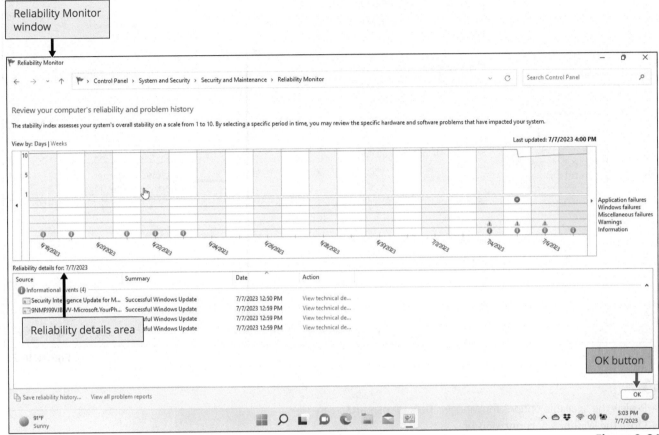

Figure 9–24

- Click OK to return to the Security and Maintenance window.

To Configure Windows Defender SmartScreen Settings

Windows Defender SmartScreen aids in the overall security of your computer by warning you before starting unrecognized apps and opening files downloaded from the Internet. **Why?** Files originating from online sources often are untrusted and may contain malicious code that can cause damage to your computer. You want to ensure that the best option for screening online content is set on your system. The following steps display the Windows Defender SmartScreen options.

- Click the Search button on the taskbar and then type **Windows Security** in the Search box to display the search results.
- Click Windows Security in the search results to open the Windows Security window.

- Click the App & browser control tab in the left pane of the Windows Security window to display the App & browser control settings.
- Click the 'Reputation-based protection settings' link to view the Windows Defender SmartScreen settings (Figure 9–25).

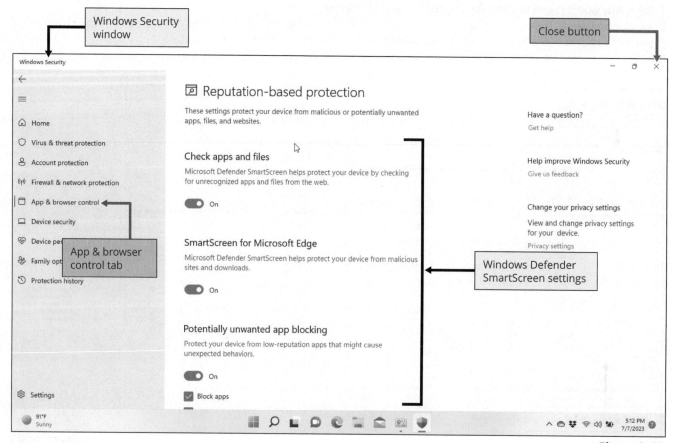

Figure 9–25

2

- Review the available options for Windows Defender SmartScreen.
- Close the Windows Security window.

To Change UAC Settings

Now that you have completed the administrative tasks for which you wanted to ensure UAC notification, you will restore the default UAC notification settings on the computer. The following steps change the UAC setting to notify only when apps try to make changes to the computer (default) option.

1 Click the 'System and Security' button on the address bar to open the System and Security window.

2 Click the 'Change User Account Control settings' link in the Security and Maintenance area to display the User Account Control dialog box.

3 If necessary, click Yes in the User Account Control dialog box to open the User Account Control Settings window.

4 Drag the slider indicator to the 'Notify me only when apps try to make changes to my computer (default)' option (second from the top of the slider).

5 Click OK to accept the changes and display the User Account Control dialog box.

6 Click the Yes button (User Account Control dialog box) to allow the settings change and return to the System and Security window.

7 Close the System and Security window.

BitLocker Drive Encryption

Windows **BitLocker Drive Encryption** is a security feature that encrypts — converts original information into code for security purposes — all data stored on the volume (drive) containing the Windows operating system, which usually is drive C. When built into a computer, a Trusted Platform Module (TPM) is used by BitLocker Drive Encryption to protect the data stored on the volume. A **Trusted Platform Module (TPM)** is a microchip that is built into a computer to store encryption keys that can decrypt the volume for authorized users. In the event that a computer is lost or stolen, the data would remain encrypted without knowledge of the authorized user's credentials. On computers without a TPM, encryption keys can be stored on a USB flash drive that must be presented to unlock the data on the volume.

To Manage BitLocker Drive Encryption   BitLocker Drive Encryption can be enabled or disabled from the Control Panel. When BitLocker Drive Encryption is enabled, the volume is encrypted. Once enabled, BitLocker Drive Encryption can be disabled temporarily, or the drive can be decrypted. Temporarily disabling BitLocker Drive Encryption allows for changes to the TPM or upgrades to the operating system. Decrypting a volume discards any keys and requires a new encryption process to regain the protection. If you wanted to enable or disable the BitLocker Drive Protection you would perform the following steps.

1. Sign in to the computer using an administrator account.
2. Open the Control Panel window. If necessary, switch to Category view.
3. Click the 'System and Security' link to open the System and Security window.
4. Click the 'BitLocker Drive Encryption' link to open the BitLocker Drive Encryption window.

To turn on BitLocker Drive Encryption, you would perform the following steps.

1. Click the 'Turn on BitLocker' link on the operating system volume to display the Choose how to unlock your drive at startup screen.
2. Select one or more of the options for saving the recovery password and then click the Next button to display the Encrypt the selected disk volume screen.
3. Select how much of the drive to encrypt and then click the Next button.
4. Select the encryption mode to use and then click the Next button.
5. Click the Continue button to restart the computer and begin the encryption process.

To temporarily disable BitLocker Drive Encryption, you would perform the following steps.

1. Click the 'Turn Off BitLocker Drive Encryption' link to display the What level of decryption do you want dialog box.
2. Click the 'Disable BitLocker Drive Encryption' link in the What level of decryption do you want dialog box.

To decrypt the volume, you would perform the following steps.

1. Click the 'Turn Off BitLocker Drive Encryption' link to display the What level of decryption do you want dialog box.
2. Click the 'Decrypt the volume' link in the What level of decryption do you want dialog box.

To Encrypt a File

Encrypting File System (EFS) is a feature of Windows 11 that permits storage of files and folders in an encrypted manner to protect them from unwanted access. **Why?** You may have confidential information stored on your computer that is protected by compliance policies and procedures. To avoid potential access to the files by other users on the same device, you decide to create an encrypted folder for storage of sensitive information. **The following steps create and encrypt a folder.**

- Using File Explorer, navigate to the Documents folder.
- Click the New button on the toolbar and then click Folder to create a new folder.
- Type **Confidential** in the new folder's text box and then press enter to assign the name to the new folder.
- Right-click the Confidential folder to display the shortcut menu and then click Properties to display the Confidential Properties dialog box (Figure 9–26).

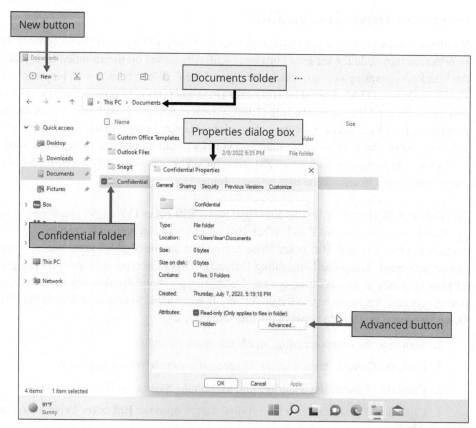

Figure 9–26

- Click the Advanced button to display the Advanced Attributes dialog box.
- Select the 'Encrypt contents to secure data' check box (Figure 9–27).

- Click OK to close the Advanced Attributes dialog box.
- Click OK to close the Confidential Properties dialog box.
- Close the File Explorer window.

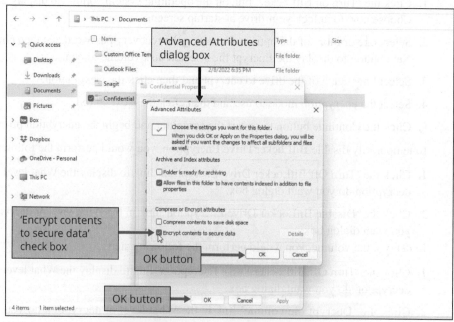

Figure 9–27

Getting Connected

A **network** is a collection of computers and mobile devices connected together, often wirelessly, via communications devices and transmission media. The computers and devices are connected by a communications path, which enables the devices to interact with one another. The advantages of using a network include simplified communications between users, such as email systems, text messaging, video calls, and voice conversations, as well as the capability of easily sharing resources across the network. Shared resources can include hardware (such as printers, scanners, and cameras), data and information (such as files, folders, and databases), Internet connectivity, and programs.

Computers on a network connect to one another using a communications channel. A **communications channel** is the means by which information is passed between two devices. Communications channels include wireless communications (broadcast radio, cellular radio, microwaves, communications satellites, Bluetooth, and infrared) and cable (twisted-pair, coaxial, and fiber-optic). Communications channels are measured in **bandwidth**, which is the amount of data, instructions, and information that can travel over transmission media. The higher the bandwidth, the more data and information the channel can transmit at one time. A wireless network offers the advantage of mobility.

Computer networks can be classified either as local area networks or wide area networks. A **local area network (LAN)** is a network that connects computers and devices in a limited geographical area, such as a home, school computer lab, office building, or closely positioned group of buildings. A LAN enables people in a small geographic area to communicate with one another and to share the computer resources connected to the network. Each device on the network, such as a computer or printer, is referred to as a **node**. Nodes can be connected to the LAN via cables; however, a **wireless LAN (WLAN)** is a LAN that uses no physical wires. Instead of wires or cables, WLANs use wireless media, such as radio waves. A **wide area network (WAN)** is a network that covers a large geographic area (such as a city, country, or the world) using a variety of wired and wireless transmission media. A WAN can be one large network or consist of two or more LANs that are connected together. The Internet is the world's largest WAN.

If you have multiple computers in your home or small office, you can create a home or small office network using Windows 11. The advantages of a home or small office network include sharing a single Internet connection, sharing hardware devices, sharing files and folders, and communicating with others. Three types of networks that are suitable for home or small office use include wireless networks, Ethernet networks, and telephone-line networks.

Understanding Wireless Networks

A wireless network is the easiest type of network to install. Each computer uses a special network adapter that sends wireless signals through the air (Figure 9–28). Any computer located within range that also has a network adapter can send and receive through floors, ceilings, and walls. The distance between devices limits this connection, and the hardware required for the system is relatively inexpensive. Most hardware devices implement the Wi-Fi standard, which was developed by the Wi-Fi Alliance to improve the interoperability of wireless products.

Several companies and industry groups have come together to create standards for wireless networking. The leader is the Wi-Fi Alliance, which certifies the interoperability of Wi-Fi (IEEE 802.11) products. Wi-Fi (IEEE 802.11) products currently offer speeds of more than 1 Gbps (gigabits per second), with that speed increasing as technology advances. The two types of Wi-Fi networks are ad hoc and infrastructure. In an **ad hoc network**, every computer with a wireless network adapter communicates directly with every other device with a wireless network adapter. Although the range varies by manufacturer, ad hoc networks work best when the connecting devices are within 100 feet of one another.

An **infrastructure network** is based on an access point connected to a high-speed Internet connection. An access point functions as a bridge between two different types of networks, such as a wireless network and an Ethernet network. The access point allows for a much greater range

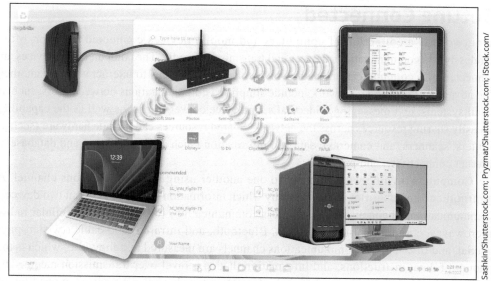

Sashkin/Shutterstock.com; Pryzmat/Shutterstock.com; iStock.com/
adventtr; iStock.com/Chesky_W

Figure 9–28

than an ad hoc network because a computer needs to be within range of the access point and not within range of the other computers. This network is best when connecting more than two computers that are more than 100 feet apart and commonly is used in wireless networks that simultaneously share a single Internet connection.

Some infrastructure networks use a router to share an Internet connection between computers on the network. A **router** is a communications device that connects multiple computers or other routers together and transmits data to its correct destination on a network. Home users typically use routers to connect a cable or DSL modem to a network, allowing several computer users to use the same Internet connection simultaneously. Some network hardware manufacturers combine the access point and router in a device called a wireless router. A **wireless router**, which uses the cellular radio network to provide Internet connections, can function as a bridge between two different types of networks and allows all computers on the network to access the same Internet connection.

Understanding Wired Networks

Wired networks use cables to connect devices together (Figure 9–29). Ethernet is the most popular type of network connection because it is relatively inexpensive and fast. Two types of Ethernet cables exist: **coaxial cable**, which resembles the cable used for televisions and rarely is used, and **unshielded twisted pair (UTP)** cable, which looks like telephone cable but with larger connectors at each end. Category 5 (CAT 5) or Category 6 (CAT 6) UTP cable typically is used for networking. A network based on CAT 5 UTP cable requires an additional piece of hardware, called a **hub**, to which all computers on the network connect.

Another type of wired network is a **Public Switched Telephone Network (PSTN)**. A **telephone-line network** takes advantage of the existing telephone wiring to connect the computers on a network. This technology is supported by a group of industry experts called the Home Phoneline Networking Alliance (HomePNA). The network takes advantage of the unused bandwidth of the telephone lines while still allowing them to be used for telephone conversations. The only equipment necessary for this type of network is a telephone-line network adapter for each computer, as well as a telephone cable long enough to connect each computer to a telephone jack.

A **modem** is used to connect a network to an Internet access provider. Common Internet access providers include cable service providers, phone service providers, and satellite service providers. The modem is connected to the router, which then is used to connect to the nodes on the network. A USB, CAT 5, or CAT 6 cable connects the modem to wired computers. If the network is wireless, the computers connect using wireless network adapters and an access point. Many home networks use a wireless router and support wired and wireless connections (Figure 9–30).

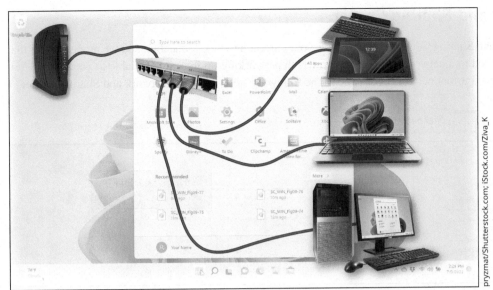

Figure 9–29

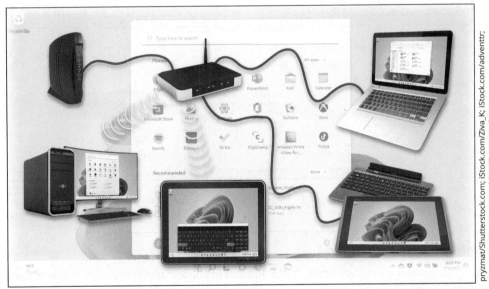

Figure 9–30

Putting It All Together

Each device on a network must have a **network adapter** to connect to the network. Both internal network adapters and external network adapters are available. Most computers are equipped with internal network adapters. And **internal network adapter** plugs in an expansion slot inside the computer. Before purchasing an internal network adapter, check to be sure that the computer has an available slot that can accept the adapter (also called an expansion card). An external network adapter plugs in a port on the system unit. In most cases, external network adapters connect to a USB port.

Using the Network and Sharing Center

Normally when you turn on a computer, Windows automatically detects available networks. You can also set up a connection manually by using the Network and Sharing Center. The Network and Sharing Center is designed to provide you with the tools you need to connect to a network and share information. From the Network and Sharing Center, you can view available connections, connect to a network, manage a network, set up a network, and diagnose and repair network problems.

To Open the Network and Sharing Center

When first opened, the Network and Sharing Center window shows your current network connection and the properties for that connection. If you are not connected to a network, you are shown which networking options are available to you. **Why?** You want to view the properties for your current network connection. The following steps open the Network and Sharing Center.

- Open the Control Panel window.
- Click the 'Network and Internet' link to open the Network and Internet window (Figure 9–31).

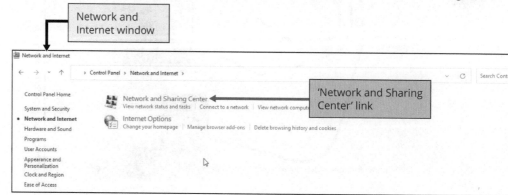

Figure 9–31

- Click the 'Network and Sharing Center' link to open the Network and Sharing Center window (Figure 9–32).

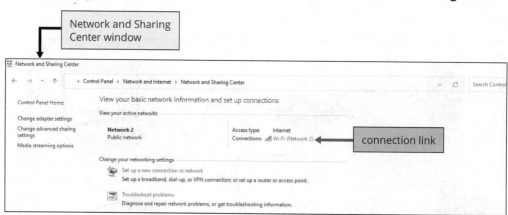

Figure 9–32

Wireless Security Issues

Whether you connect a single computer to the Internet or connect multiple computers on a home or small office network to the Internet, problems can develop if you do not protect computers from external threats. Hackers scan the Internet looking for unprotected computers. When an unprotected computer is found, a hacker can access and damage files on the computer and release harmful computer viruses that can render the computer unusable. A hacker with unauthorized access can steal your personal information, your identity, and company documents or can use your computer as a platform to launch malicious attacks across the Internet.

You can protect computers on a network from hackers, viruses, and other malicious attacks by using a firewall. As discussed previously, a firewall is a security system intended to protect a network from external threats. A firewall commonly is a combination of hardware and/or software that prevents computers on the network from communicating directly with computers that are not on the network and vice versa. Many routers come with integrated firewalls. Windows 11 also contains a built-in firewall, which was discussed earlier in this module.

Wireless networks require careful planning, because they introduce some security concerns that wired networks do not. Because the signal travels through the air, anyone with the proper equipment can intercept the signal. As a result, a wireless network should take extra precautions to prevent unauthorized access. When you purchase a wireless router, it might include a program that allows you to set up security on your wireless network. If the wireless router does not include a program that can set up security, Windows can configure it using the 'Set up a new connection or network' link, accessible from the Network and Sharing Center window.

The key to securing a wireless network successfully is to use a multipronged defense. For best results, use more than one of the following recommended security measures. First, make sure that the wireless router's user name and password are changed from the defaults so that the hacker is unable to use the default user name and password found in the device's documentation (often kept on the manufacturer's website for public access). Second, you can turn on wireless encryption. This can include Wired Equivalent Privacy (WEP), Wi-Fi Protected Access 2 (WPA2), or 802.1X authentication. Encryption protects your data by ensuring that only those with the correct encryption key will be able to understand the information being sent across the network. Third, you can set up the wireless router to not broadcast its **SSID (service set identifier)**, the network name for the wireless router. This makes it more difficult for hackers to detect your router. Next, you can change the SSID from its default setting. The most secure SSIDs are a combination of letters and numbers and do not include any part of your name or location. Finally, you can turn on MAC Address Control so that only devices with authorized MAC (Media Access Control) addresses are allowed to connect. A **MAC address** is an address that uniquely identifies each device that is connected to a network.

To Connect to a Hidden Wireless Network   A **hidden network** is a wireless network that is configured not to broadcast its SSID. When this level of security is in place on the wireless network, the network will not be automatically identified in the list of available connections. If you wanted to connect to a hidden network, you would perform the following steps.

1. Open the Network and Sharing Center window from the Control Panel.

2. Click the 'Set up a new connection or network' link in the Change your networking settings area to display the Set Up a Connection or Network dialog box.

3. Click the 'Manually connect to a wireless network' link in the Choose a connection option list.

4. Click the Next button in the Set Up a Connection or Network dialog box to open the Manually connect to a wireless network screen.

5. Type the SSID of the hidden network in the Network name text box.

6. Click the Security type button to select the security type associated with the hidden network.

7. If necessary, click the Encryption type button to select the encryption type associated with the hidden network.

8. If necessary, type the established security key in the Security Key text box.

9. Optionally click the 'Start this connection automatically' and 'Connect even if the network is not broadcasting' check boxes to select them.

10. Click the Next button on the Manually connect to a wireless network screen to complete the connection to the hidden network.

11. Click the Close button to close the dialog box.

To View the Status of a Connection

You can view the status of the connection from the Network and Sharing Center. The Status window displays the properties of the connection and allows you to adjust the properties of the connection manually, disable the connection, and diagnose problems with the connection. **Why?** You want to view the details of the network to which you are connected. The following steps display the connection status. If you are not connected to a wireless network, simply read the following steps without performing them.

● Click the link next to
the Connections label
(shown in Figure 9-32)
to display the Status
dialog box (Figure 9-33).

● After viewing the
connection status, click
the Close button to
close the dialog box.

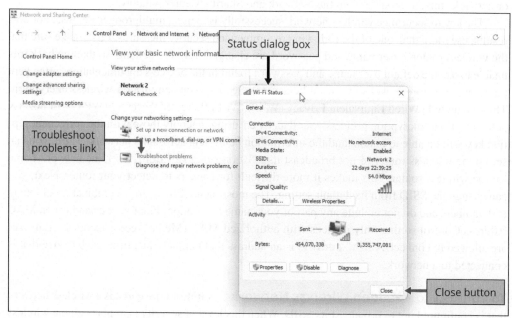

Figure 9-33

To Troubleshoot a Networking Problem

If a network connection is not functioning properly, you can use the Troubleshoot problems link to allow Windows to detect problems and suggest solutions. If Windows cannot determine a solution, a message is displayed. If no problems are detected, Windows also displays an appropriate message. **Why?** You want to troubleshoot your network connection. The following steps use the Troubleshoot problems link to acquire suggestions from Windows about how to fix an Internet connection.

● Click the Troubleshoot
problems link (shown in
Figure 9-33) to display
the Troubleshoot screen
in the Settings app
(Figure 9-34).

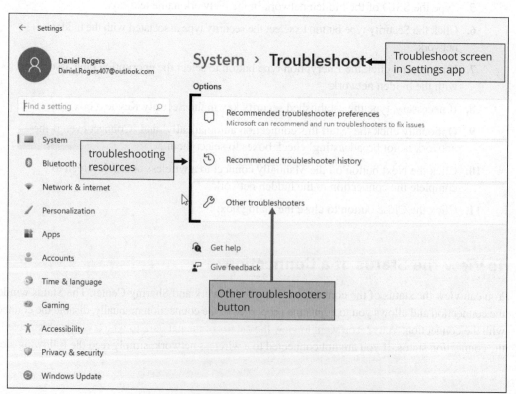

Figure 9-34

②
- Click the Other troubleshooters button to display the Other troubleshooters screen (Figure 9–35).

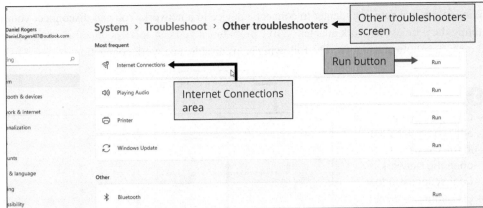

Figure 9–35

③
- Click the Run button in the Internet Connections area to display a list of trouble-shooting options in the Internet Connections dialog box (Figure 9–36).

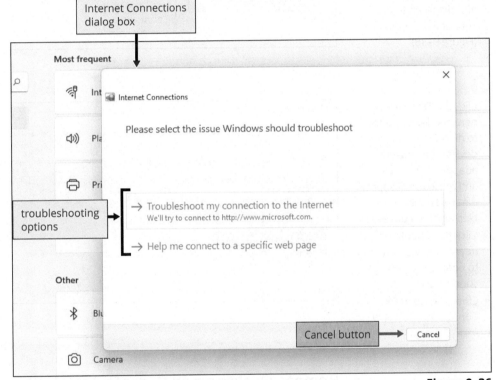

Figure 9–36

④
- Click the Cancel button after viewing the options to close the Internet Connections dialog box.
- Exit the Settings app to return to the Network and Sharing Center window (Figure 9–37).

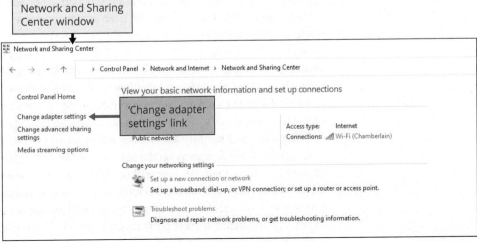

Figure 9–37

To Disable a Network Connection

Windows uses a network adapter to connect a device to a network. You can disconnect your computer from a network by disabling the wireless network adapter. **Why?** Sometimes you can solve connection problems by disabling and then re-enabling the wireless network adapter. The following steps disable a network connection.

- Click the 'Change adapter settings' link in the left pane to open the Network Connections window.
- Click your preferred network connection to select the network and display network connections options (Figure 9–38).

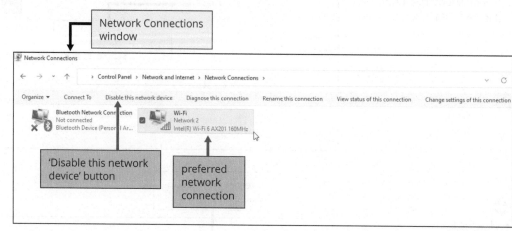

Figure 9–38

- Click the 'Disable this network device' button to disable the network device. The network adapter is unavailable and the icon will appear dimmed until it is enabled again (Figure 9–39).
- Click the 'Enable this network device' button to enable the network connection.
- Close the Network Connections window.

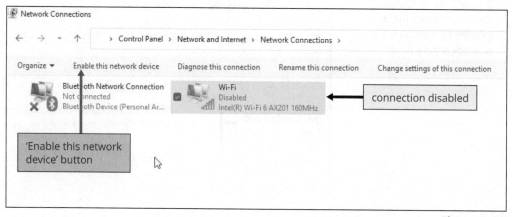

Figure 9–39

Remote Desktop and Remote Assistance

In a networked environment, sometimes it is beneficial or necessary to access the functionality of another computer within your network from another computer or to access a computer in the office while traveling with a laptop. In either of these situations, a Remote Desktop connection provides a solution. **Remote Desktop** is a technology that can be enabled on a Windows computer that allows the computer to be accessed from a remote location. The computer that will be accessed remotely needs to be configured to allow remote connections and set to never go to sleep, so that it is available when a remote connection is required. The Remote Desktop Connection app is used on the local computer to access the remote computer by name or address.

The **Remote Assistance** feature of Windows allows users to request assistance from or provide assistance to other users on the network or Internet. When you send a request for assistance to another person, the other user will be able to see the contents of your computer and be given access to control your computer remotely to provide assistance. You should send requests only to people you trust, and close any open programs or documents that you do not want the other person to see. The assistance request provides only a limited time frame of access to the helper, and the access can be terminated at any time.

To Allow Remote Connections to a Computer

In order to use a computer as a destination for a Remote Desktop Connection, you must first configure the destination computer to allow remote connections and adjust the sleep settings to ensure that the computer is available for access when needed. **Why?** You routinely travel with a laptop computer and need access to files and resources located on a desktop computer in the office. The following steps configure the computer to allow remote connections and adjust the sleep settings to keep the computer awake for access.

- Open the Control Panel window in Category view.
- Click the 'System and Security' link to open the System and Security window (Figure 9–40).

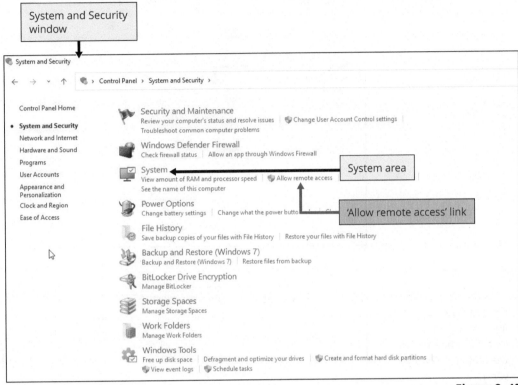

Figure 9–40

- Click the 'Allow remote access' link in the System area to display the Remote tab of the System Properties dialog box.
- In the Remote Desktop area, click to select the 'Allow remote connections to this computer' option button (Figure 9–41).

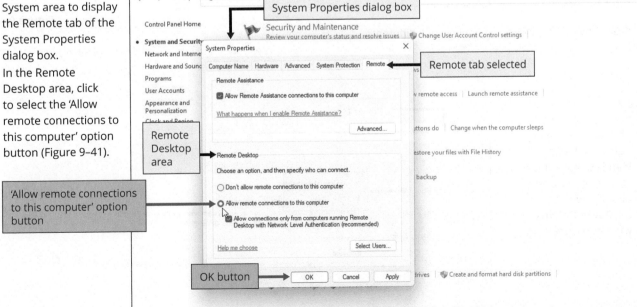

Figure 9–41

● Click OK (System Properties dialog box) to return to the System and Security window (Figure 9–42).

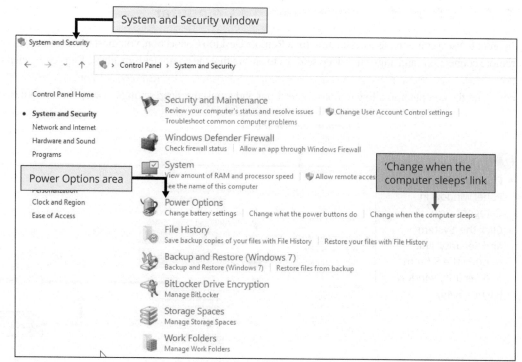

Figure 9–42

● Click the 'Change when the computer sleeps' link in the Power Options area to open the Edit Plan Settings window.

● Click to select the 'Put the computer to sleep' button.

● Click to select the Never option in the list (Figure 9–43).

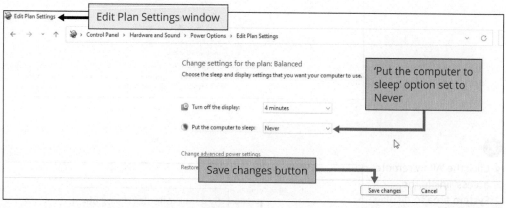

Figure 9–43

Q&A Why do my power plan options look different?
Power plan options may look different depending on the type of computer you are using. For example if you are using a laptop, you might see settings for when the laptop is using its battery and different settings for when the laptop is plugged in to a power source.

● Click the Save changes button in the Edit Plan Settings window to update the sleep option and return to the Power Options window (Figure 9–44).

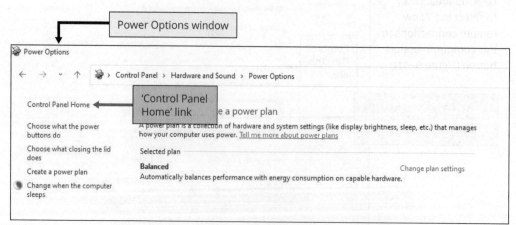

Figure 9–44

To Allow Remote Assistance Invitations to Be Sent from a Computer

Why? You want to be able to request assistance from remote users when you experience technical issues. The following steps configure your computer to allow Remote Assistance invitations to be sent from your computer. If your network settings prevent you from completing these steps, simply read the steps without performing them.

- Click the 'Control Panel Home' link (shown in Figure 9–44) in the left pane to open the Control Panel window.
- Click the 'System and Security' link to open the System and Security window.
- Click the System link to open the System window (Figure 9–45).

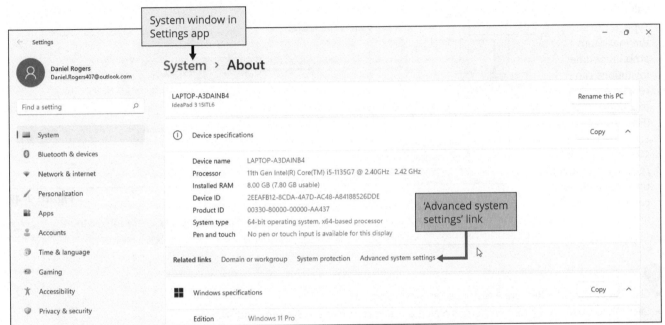

Figure 9–45

- Click the 'Advanced system settings' link in the right pane to display the Advanced tab of the System Properties dialog box.
- Click the Remote tab to display the Remote settings.
- If necessary, click to select the 'Allow Remote Assistance connections to this computer' check box (Figure 9–46).

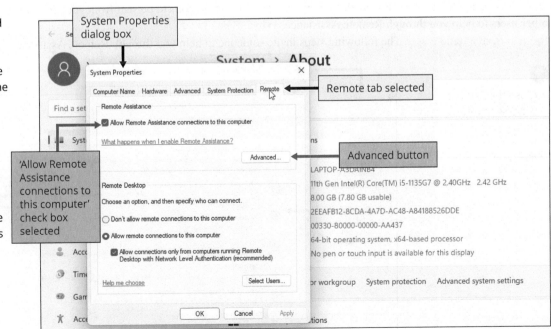

Figure 9–46

- Click the Advanced button to display the Remote Assistance Settings dialog box.
- Click the numeric list in the Invitations area to select the current value.
- Type **2** to set the maximum amount of time invitations can remain open to 2 hours (Figure 9–47).

Q&A Why should I reduce the amount of time the invitations can remain open?

Remote Assistance invitations provide direct access to assistance when needed, but when left open for longer than necessary, they can pose security risks to the computer.

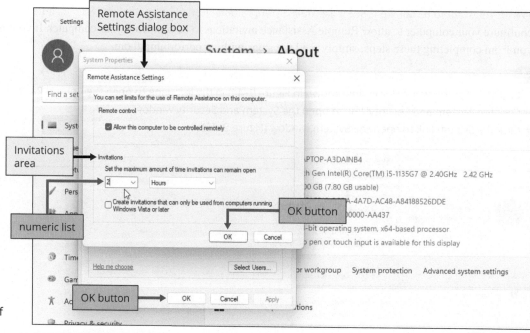

Figure 9–47

- Click OK to close the Remote Assistance Settings dialog box.
- Click OK to close the System Properties dialog box and return to the System window.

To Invite Someone to Help You through Remote Assistance

Once your computer is configured to allow Remote Assistance invitations to be sent from your computer, you are able to invite other users to help you through Remote Assistance. **Why?** When you experience a technical issue, you want to be able to ask for help from a remote user. The following steps invite someone to help you through Remote Assistance.

- Close the Settings window to return to the System and Security window (Figure 9–48).

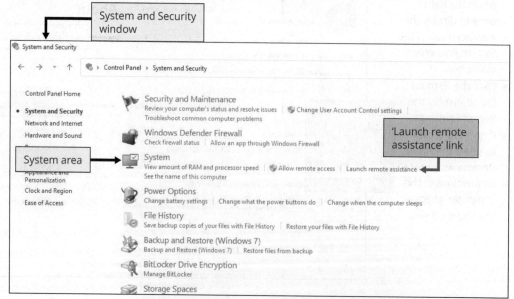

Figure 9–48

2

- Click the 'Launch remote assistance' link in the System area to start the Windows Remote Assistance app (Figure 9–49).

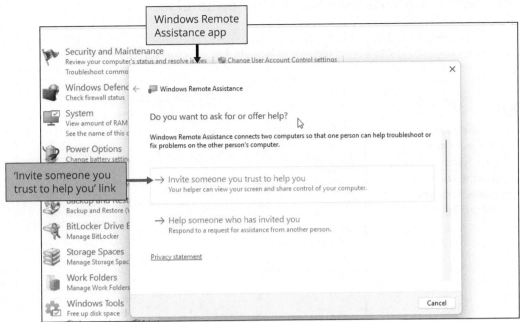

Figure 9–49

3

- Click the 'Invite someone you trust to help you' link to begin the invitation process (Figure 9–50).

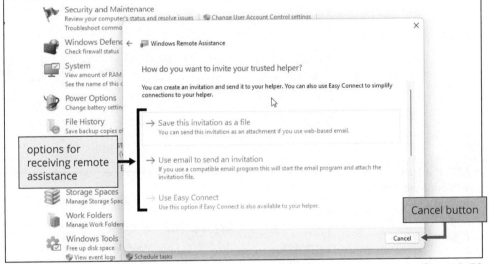

Figure 9–50

4

- Click the Cancel button to exit the Windows Remote Assistance app and return to the System and Security window (Figure 9–51).

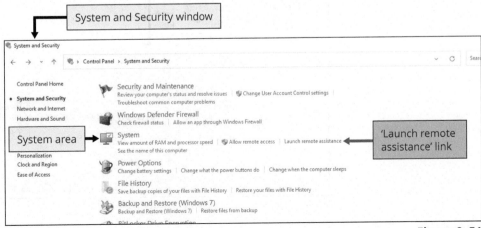

Figure 9–51

To Offer Remote Assistance to Someone Else

Why? As an advanced user on Windows 11, you are asked to provide assistance to others and want to be able to do so remotely from your computer. The following steps offer Remote Assistance to someone else.

- Click the 'Launch remote assistance' link in the System area to open the Windows Remote Assistance window (Figure 9–52).

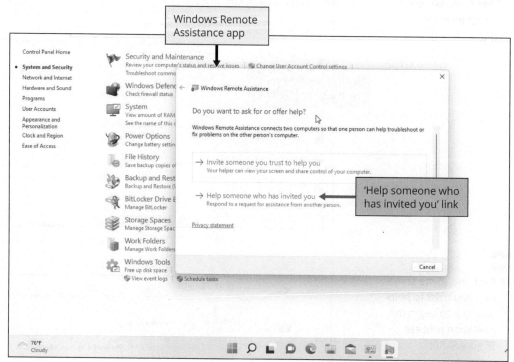

Figure 9–52

- Click the 'Help someone who has invited you' link to begin the process (Figure 9–53).

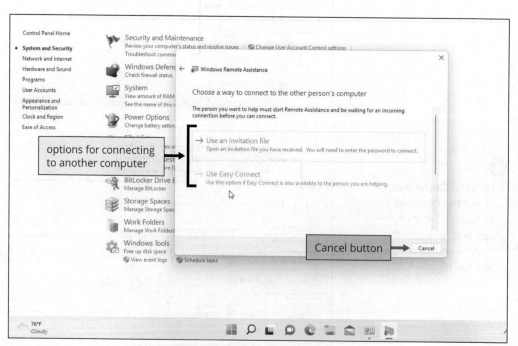

Figure 9–53

• Click the Cancel button to exit the Windows Remote Assistance app.
• Close the System and Security window.

Connecting on the Go

Mobile users often have special needs when using their computers on the go. Many mobile users manage files from multiple devices running Windows 11 and require access to their files from all of the computers and mobile devices, even when they are offline. Windows 11 has several features for keeping files and settings in sync across the various devices.

Work Folders provide a storage location for work files that are accessible from all of your computers and mobile devices. The files are located on the computer or mobile device where you saved the files in Work Folders, on your organization's server, and on any other computer or devices on which you have set up Work Folders. As long as your computer or mobile device is connected to the Internet, you can synchronize the files across the connected devices.

Airplane mode is a setting that provides a quick way to turn off all wireless communications on a computer. Wireless communications affected by airplane mode include Wi-Fi, mobile broadband, Bluetooth, global positioning system (GPS) or global navigation satellite system (GNSS), near field communication (NFC), and all other types of wireless communication.

The **sync settings** feature of Windows 11 keeps track of settings, such as browser settings, passwords, color themes, File Explorer settings, and notification preferences on your devices and applies them to all of your Windows 11 devices associated with your Microsoft account. In order to use sync settings in Windows 11, you need to sign in with your Microsoft account.

To Use Airplane Mode

Why? You are travelling on an airplane that permits the use of electronic devices in airplane mode only. The following steps turn airplane mode on and off.

• Click the Network icon on the taskbar to display the Network menu (Figure 9–54).

Q&A I do not have the Airplane mode button on the Network menu. What should I do?
Airplane mode can be configured from the Network & Internet area in the Settings app. Start the Settings app, click the 'Network & Internet' icon, click the Airplane mode tab, and then click the Airplane mode toggle button to turn it on.

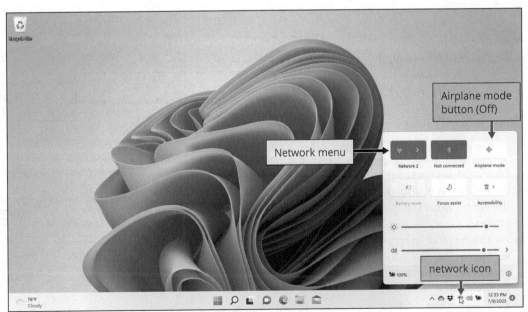

Figure 9–54

- Click the Airplane mode button on the Network menu to turn on airplane mode (Figure 9–55).

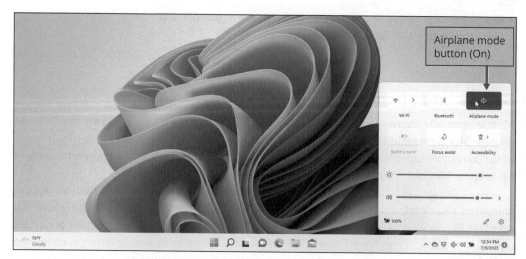

Figure 9–55

- Click the Airplane mode button again to turn off airplane mode off.
- Click outside the Network menu to close it.

Q&A Why did I turn airplane mode off?
Airplane mode disables all network connectivity. This is useful on an airplane, but it eliminates access to network resources and the Internet in daily practice.

Other Ways

1. Start Settings app, click 'Network & Internet' tab, click Airplane mode toggle button in right pane

To Sync Your Settings

Why? As a mobile user, you work with several devices running Windows 11 and want to be sure that certain settings are the same, regardless of the device you are using. The following step configures the sync settings not to synchronize passwords across devices.

❶

- Display the Start menu.
- Click Settings on the Start menu to start the Settings app.
- Click the Accounts tab in the Settings window to display the Accounts screen.
- Click Windows backup in the right pane to display the Windows backup screen.
- Click 'Remember my preferences' in the right pane to display the sync settings for the current account.
- Click the Passwords check box to remove the check mark (Figure 9–56).

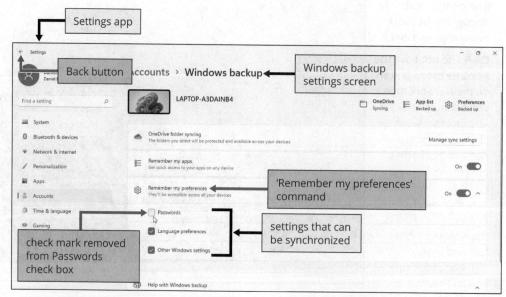

Figure 9–56

Q&A Why would I want to turn off password synchronization?
Storing passwords on single devices presents a level of security risk. Sharing that same set of personal information across multiple devices creates a greater level of risk.

Maintaining Your Computer

It can be frustrating to lose data. Almost everyone has heard a story about someone who lost a file and spent hours trying to recover it. In addition, hard drives fail more often than any other component on a computer. When a hard drive fails, it is extremely difficult to recover the data without obtaining professional help, often at a hefty price.

Even if a hard drive never fails, errors made while using the computer can result in the loss of a file or group of files. If you are not careful when you save a file, you could lose the file by saving a new file with the original file's name or by clicking the wrong button in a dialog box and wiping out the contents of the file accidentally. In either case, you most certainly are going to lose some data. If a hard drive failure occurs, all of the files you have created or saved since the last backup might be gone for good. To avoid the loss of data, you should get into the habit of backing up the data on a regular basis.

Action Center

The **action center** in Windows 11 displays app notifications, quick actions, and tips about Windows. Some of the available quick actions are airplane mode, tablet mode, network connections, and all settings controls. The notifications and quick actions can be enabled or disabled to provide access to the action center items of greatest benefit to the user.

To Display Notification Settings in the Action Center

Why? As you begin using the action center, you want to identify the apps that can display notifications. The following steps display the notification settings for the action center.

1
- Click the System tab in the left pane to open the System window (Figure 9–57).

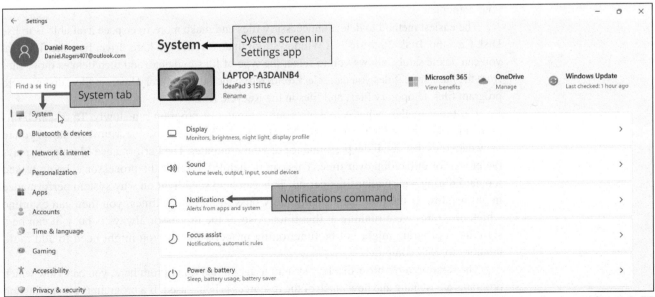

Figure 9–57

2

- Click Notifications in the right pane to display the Notifications options.
- If necessary, scroll to display the Notifications from apps and other senders area, which shows which apps are able to display notifications (Figure 9–58).

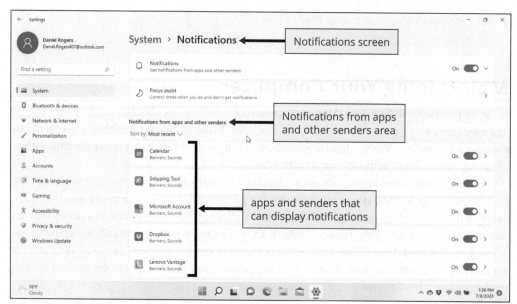

Figure 9–58

Performance Tools

After a long period of usage — and especially after installing programs and saving and deleting files — you might notice changes in your computer's performance. Your computer might not do what it is supposed to do, or it might run slower than usual. These changes mean that your computer is not functioning as it did when Windows 11 was first installed. By performing some system maintenance, you can greatly improve the performance of your computer.

Whenever you start an app, delete a file using the Recycle Bin, view a webpage, or download a file from a website, files are stored on the hard drive. As a result, the hard drive contains many unnecessary files that can reduce the amount of free space. If the free space falls too low for the operating system, error messages might display when you run apps. Removing the unnecessary files and increasing the amount of free space on the hard drive will increase the performance of your computer.

The easiest method to delete unnecessary files and make more free space available is to use Disk Cleanup. **Disk Cleanup** is a Windows tool that searches the hard drive, lists the files that you can delete safely, allows you to select the type of files to delete, and then deletes those files from the hard drive. Files you can select for deletion include temporary Internet files, downloaded program files, temporary files, and files in the Recycle Bin.

It often is unclear what is making your computer or program run slowly. To research this problem, you can use the Performance Monitor tool. The **Performance Monitor** allows you to view data logs that detail the performance of your computer. The Performance Monitor displays the processor utilization over time. This can be helpful to see if the processor is being tasked too hard during a particular time period. This can help shed light on why system performance might be slow. If the processor is extremely busy at particular times, you then can examine which programs were running at that time. Also, if the processor always is busy, it can be a sign that a program might not be functioning properly or that you might need to add more memory to your computer.

The **Resource Monitor** displays system usage in real time. From here, you can view which programs are running and how much of the resources is being used. If a program is consuming too much of a resource, you will be able to identify the program and then attempt to reinstall, repair, or remove the program.

To Start Disk Cleanup

Why? You decide to remove unnecessary files and make more free space available on your computer to improve performance. The following steps start Disk Cleanup.

- Click the Search button on the taskbar and then type **Windows tools** to display the search results (Figure 9–59).

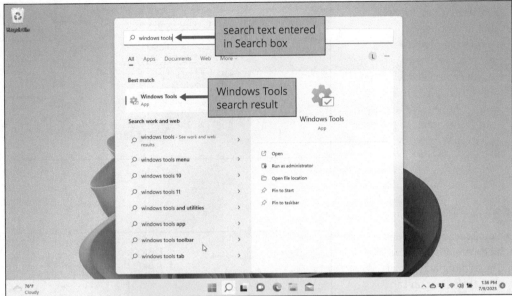

Figure 9–59

- Click the Windows Tools search result to open the Windows Tools window. If necessary, maximize the Windows Tools window (Figure 9–60).

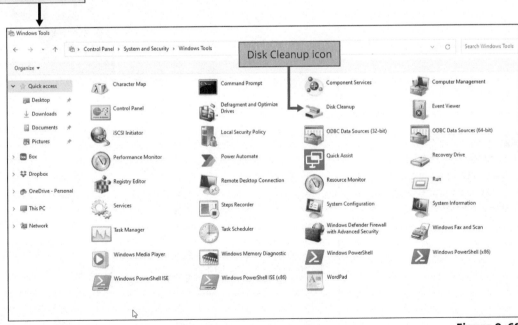

Figure 9–60

3

- Double-click the Disk Cleanup icon in the Windows Tools window to start the Disk Cleanup tool (Figure 9–61).

  Q&A I am prompted to select a drive to clean up. What should I choose?

  If you have multiple hard drives on your computer, you can clean up each with the Disk Cleanup tool. For best alignment with the activity in these steps, choose the drive on which Windows is installed (usually drive C).

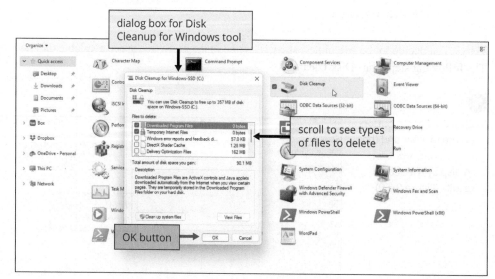

Figure 9–61

4

- Scroll through the Files to delete area to view the additional types of files Disk Cleanup can delete.
- Click OK to display the Disk Cleanup dialog box (Figure 9–62).

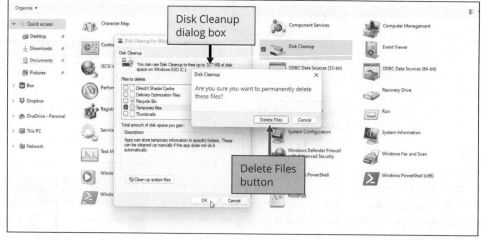

Figure 9–62

5

- Click the Delete Files button to remove the files marked for deletion (Figure 9–63).

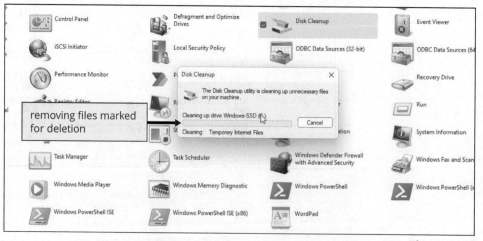

Figure 9–63

6

- The Windows Tools window reappears when Disk Cleanup finishes (Figure 9–64).

Q&A Where did the Disk Cleanup tool go? The tool automatically exits when the cleanup is finished based on your selections.

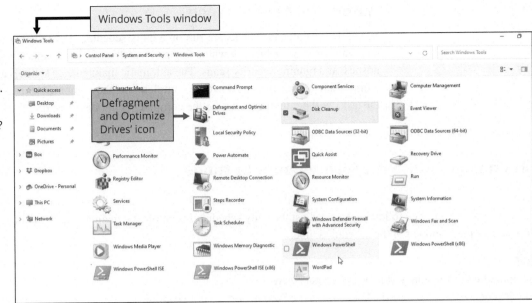

Figure 9–64

To Change the Optimization Schedule and Settings

Why? Due to frequent web browsing requirements of your job, you generate a large number of temporary Internet files and are using Disk Cleanup to delete those files periodically. As a result, you have noticed a large amount of drive fragmentation, despite the weekly scheduled optimization, and you want to increase the frequency to a daily optimization schedule. The following steps change the optimization schedule for the drives on your computer. If network permissions prevent you from changing these settings, simply read the steps without performing them.

1

- Double-click the 'Defragment and Optimize Drives' icon in the Windows Tools window (shown in Figure 9–64) to use the Defragment and Optimize Drives tool.
- Click the Change settings button to display the Optimize Drives dialog box.
- Click to display the Frequency list and then click Daily in the list (Figure 9–65).

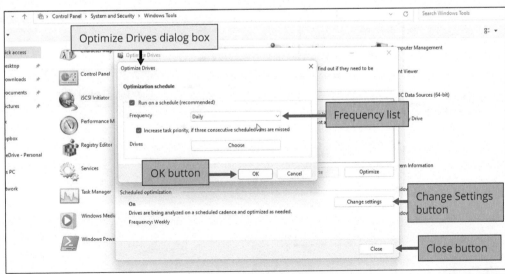

Figure 9–65

2

- Click OK to close the Optimize Drives dialog box in the foreground.
- Click the Close button to exit the Defragment and Optimize Drives tool.
- Close the Windows Tools window.
- Exit the Settings app.

Automatic Maintenance

Scheduled maintenance tasks are run on a daily schedule when the computer is not in use. This automatic process includes downloading and installing software updates, performing system diagnostics, and running security scans. The automatic maintenance settings allow for the selection of a time each day for these tasks to be completed. If the computer is in use at the scheduled time, the tasks will be run the next time the computer is not being used.

To Change Automatic Maintenance Settings

Why? Based on your work schedule, the automatic maintenance tasks are cannot be performed as scheduled because the computer is in use at that time. The following steps adjust the daily schedule for automatic maintenance and allow scheduled maintenance to wake up the computer at the scheduled time.

- Open the Control Panel window in Category view.
- Click the System and Security link to open the System and Security window.
- Click the 'Security and Maintenance' link to open the Security and Maintenance window.
- Click the Maintenance button to expand the Maintenance area (Figure 9–66).

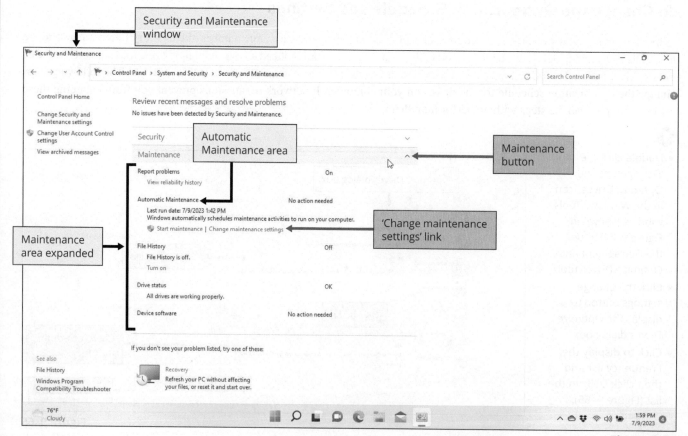

Figure 9–66

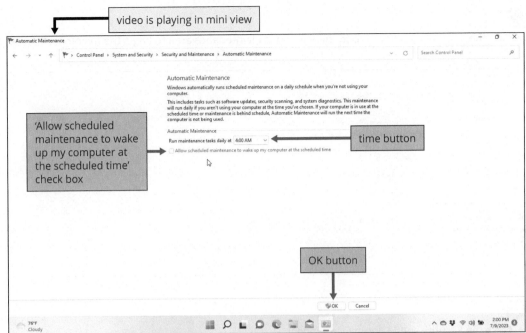

Figure 9-67

- Click the 'Change maintenance settings' link in the Automatic Maintenance area (shown in Figure 9–66) to open the Automatic Maintenance window.
- Click to select the time list and then click to select 4:00 AM in the list.
- If necessary, click to select the 'Allow scheduled maintenance to wake up my computer at the scheduled time' check box (Figure 9–67).

- Click OK to return to the Security and Maintenance window.

To Start Maintenance Manually

Why? You are concerned that so many scheduled maintenance activities have been missed, so you decide to start the maintenance tasks manually. The following steps manually start maintenance on the computer.

- Click the Maintenance button to expand the Maintenance area (Figure 9–68).

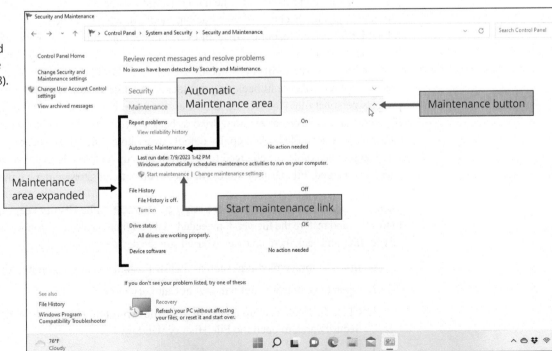

Figure 9-68

- Click the Start maintenance link in the Automatic Maintenance area to begin the maintenance tasks (Figure 9–69).

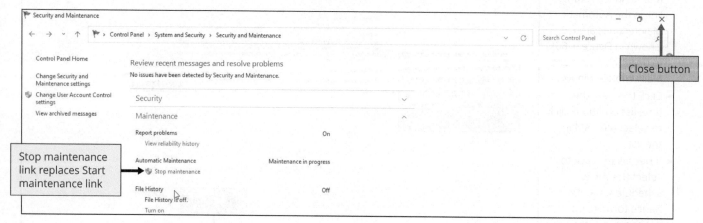

Figure 9–69

- Close the Security and Maintenance window.
- Close the Control Panel window.

Q&A Did the maintenance continue running when I closed the Security and Maintenance window?
Yes. The automatic maintenance runs in the background, so closing the window did not stop the process.

Backing Up and Restoring Files

Although Windows cannot prevent you from losing data on your hard drive, taking proper steps will ensure that you can recover lost data when an accident happens. To protect data on a hard drive, you should use a backup program. A typical backup program copies and then automatically compresses the files and folders from the hard drive into a single file, called a backup file. The backup program stores the backup file on a backup medium, which can be a hard drive, shared network folder, USB flash drive, optical disc, or even another computer on the network. Instead of using a local backup medium, backup files also can be stored on OneDrive using your Microsoft account.

Backing up critical files is something everyone should do. Even with everything stored on OneDrive, you still should back up your local files. File History is a Windows backup tool that protects personal files stored in the Libraries, Desktop, Favorites, OneDrive, and Contacts folders if you set up a network or external drive to back up your files. You can add files to your Library folder if you want a file backed up. By default, every hour, File History scans your local file system for changes and copies the changed files to your backup location. Every time any of your personal files has changed, File History stores the file on an external storage device that you select.

To Back Up a File History to a Storage Device   File History keeps track of file versions to identify and restore the file version needed to its original location. If you wanted to keep a history of your files and back them up to an external storage device, you would perform the following steps.

1. Insert a storage medium, such as a USB flash drive, in your computer.

2. Open the Control Panel window in Category view.

3. Click the 'Save backup copies of your files with File History' link in the System and Security area to open the File History window.

4. Click the Turn on button (File History window) to turn on File History.

To Restore Files from File History   After the files have been saved, you can restore the files created using File History if your original files are lost or deleted. The files are restored to their original location. If you wanted to restore files from File History, you would perform the following steps.

1. If necessary, plug the external device that contains your File History in your computer.
2. Click the 'Restore personal files' link to open the Home - File History window and prepare to restore your files to their original location.
3. Click each file folder and library that you want to restore to its original location.
4. Click the Restore button in the File History window to open the Replace or Skip Files window.
5. Click the appropriate option.

Windows Update

Windows Update helps to protect your computer from viruses, worms, and other security risks. When Windows Update is turned on and the computer is connected to the Internet, Windows periodically checks with Microsoft to find updates for your computer and then automatically downloads them. If the Internet connection is lost while downloading an update, Windows resumes downloading when the Internet connection becomes available.

To Check for Windows Updates

Although Windows Update performs periodic checks for updates, it is possible that an important update has been released but has not been detected yet by your computer. **Why?** After not using your computer for several days, you want to make sure that you download and install any updates that have been released. The following steps check for Windows updates.

1

- Display the Start menu.
- Click Settings to start the Settings app.
- Click the Windows Update tab in the left pane of the Settings window to display the Windows Update screen (Figure 9–70).

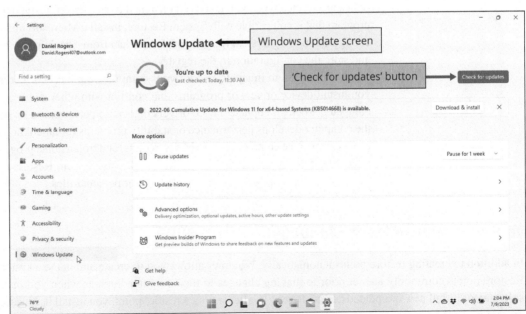

Figure 9–70

- Click the 'Check for updates' button to check for available updates (Figure 9–71).

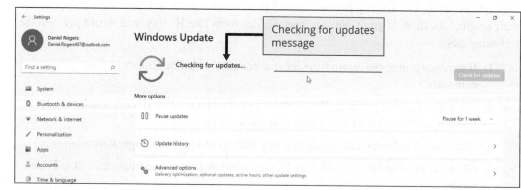

Figure 9–71

- Exit the Settings app.

Q&A Will updating continue after I exit the app?
Yes. Windows Update is a background service, meaning that it continues running even when the app is not actively displayed on the screen.

Using System Restore

Another safeguard for preventing damage to a computer is System Restore. **System Restore** is a tool that tracks changes to the computer and automatically creates a restore point when it detects the beginning of a change. A restore point is a representation of a stored state of the computer. The stored state includes information about personalization settings, installed programs, hardware device configurations, and app settings throughout the operating system. System Restore automatically runs in the background and monitors changes to files, folders, and settings that are essential to the correct operation of the operating system.

System Restore creates an initial restore point when you install or upgrade to Windows 11. At regular intervals, System Restore creates a restore point to capture the current configuration of the computer and stores the configuration in the registry. The registry is the central storage location for all settings related to the Windows operating system, device drivers, and installed apps. Restore points are created when you install an unsigned device driver, install a program using an installer program that is compatible with System Restore, install a Microsoft update or patch, restore a prior configuration using System Restore, or restore data from a backup set created with the backup tool and store the configuration in the registry.

Using a system image to restore your computer can help correct problems that occur when you install device drivers or programs that conflict with other device drivers or programs on the computer, when you update device drivers that cause performance or stability problems, or when the computer develops performance or stability problems for an unknown reason. System Restore cannot protect the computer from viruses, worms, and trojan horse programs. An antivirus program is your best defense against these malicious threats. System Restore does not back up personal files; use the backup features of File History for personal files.

To Set a Restore Point Manually

In addition to creating restore points automatically, Windows allows you to create and name a system restore point manually. Restore points commonly are set prior to making changes to the computer, such as when you install new hardware, install software, or install new or updated device drivers. If, after setting a restore point, you install hardware, software, or device drivers that cause your computer to function improperly, you can reset the computer to the state it was in when you set the restore point. This prevents you from losing personal files (documents, Internet favorites, email messages, and so on) that would have been lost if you needed to reformat the hard drive and reinstall Windows. **Why?** You are preparing to install new software and want to establish a manual restore point. The following steps manually set a restore point with the name, Pre Software Install, and then display the System Restore dialog box.

- Click the Search button on the taskbar and then type **restore** in the search box to display the search results (Figure 9–72).

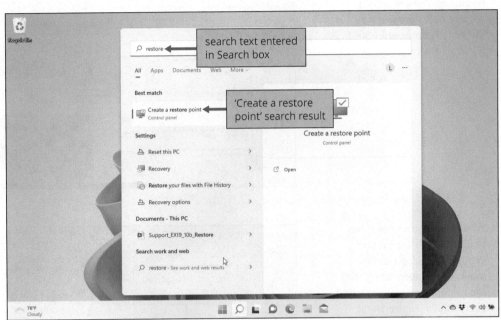

Figure 9–72

- Click the 'Create a restore point' search result to display the System Protection tab in the System Properties dialog box.
- Click the Create button (System Properties dialog box) to display the System Protection dialog box.
- Type **Pre Software Install** in the text box (System Protection dialog box) to name the restore point (Figure 9–73).

Q&A What if the Create button is not enabled?
If the Create button is not enabled, you may need to enable system protection. To do this, click the Configure button (System Properties dialog box), click the 'Turn on system protection' option button (System Protection dialog box), and then click OK.

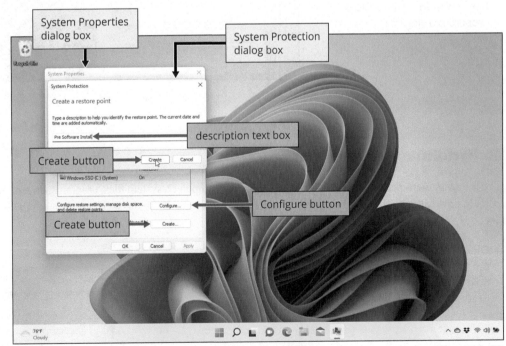

Figure 9–73

- Click the Create button (System Protection dialog box) to create a restore point manually. The Creating a restore point progress indicator becomes animated (Figure 9–74).

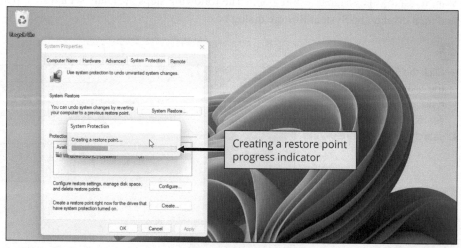

Figure 9–74

- When the restore point has been created, the System Protection dialog box displays a message stating that the restore point was created successfully (Figure 9–75).

- Click the Close button to close the System Protection dialog box and return to the System Properties dialog box.

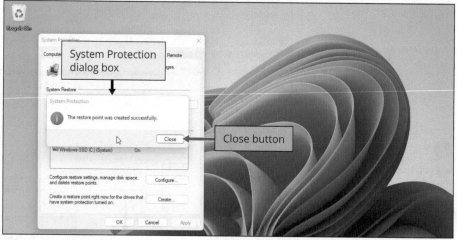

Figure 9–75

To Perform a System Restore

The following steps perform a system restore to return the computer's system files, programs, drivers, and registry settings to an earlier point in time without affecting your personal files. **Why?** After installing the software, your computer began to function improperly.

- Click the System Restore button (System Properties dialog box) to begin the System Restore wizard (Figure 9–76).

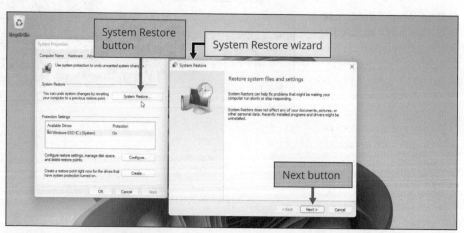

Figure 9–76

- Click the Next button to view a list of restore points (Figure 9-77).

- After viewing the dialog box options, click the Cancel button to (System Restore dialog box) close the dialog box without making changes.
- Click OK to close the System Properties dialog box.

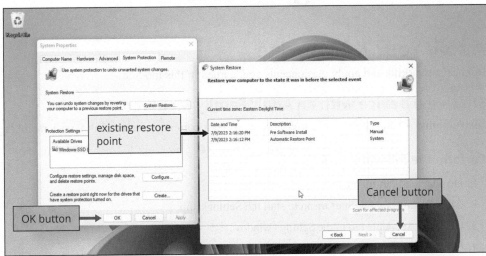

Figure 9-77

Recovery Options

If your computer is experiencing problems, you can reset it. When you **reset** your computer, Windows lets you choose whether to keep your personal files or remove them. It then reinstalls Windows. Another troubleshooting option when your computer is having problems is advanced startup. **Advanced startup** allows you to start up from a device or disc (such as a USB drive or DVD), change your computer's firmware settings, change Windows startup settings, or restore Windows from a system image.

To Reset Your Computer   If a computer is not running optimally, resetting it might help. If you wanted to reset a computer, you would perform the following steps.

1. Display the Start menu.
2. Click Settings on the Start menu to start the Settings app.
3. Click Recovery in the right pane of the System window.
4. Click the Reset PC button in the Recovery options area.
5. Choose an option to begin the reinstallation.

Summary

In this module, you learned how to configure security settings, manage network-related options, and maintain your computer with a variety of utilities. You used sign-in options, configured family accounts, managed the Windows Defender Firewall, configured UAC settings, and explored several features related to security in Windows 11. You explored the Network and Sharing Center, Remote Access, Remote Assistance, and several mobile user tools for getting and staying connected to network resources. Finally, you ran and managed performance, maintenance, and backup and recovery tools included in Windows 11.

Student Assignments

Apply Your Knowledge

Reinforce the skills and apply the concepts you learned in this module.

Sharing a Device with an Adult Family Member

Instructions: You want to add a user account to your computer for an adult family member.

Perform the following tasks:

1. Display the Start menu.
2. Click Settings on the Start menu to start the Settings app.
3. Click the Accounts tab in the Settings window.
4. Click 'Family & other users' in the right pane of the Accounts screen.
5. Click the Add account button in the Add a family member area.
6. Type the family member's email address in the 'Enter their email address' text box.
7. Click the Next button.
8. Click the Confirm (or Continue) button.
9. Click the Close button to exit the wizard.
10. Click the 'Manage family settings online or remove an account' link to view the account.microsoft.com/family website in Microsoft Edge (Figure 9–78).
11. Submit evidence of the family member addition in the format required by your instructor.

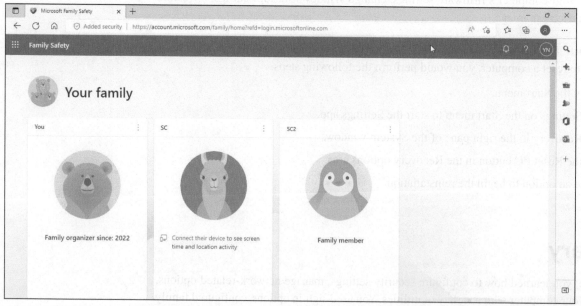

Figure 9–78

Extend Your Knowledge

Extend the skills you learned in this module and experiment with new skills. You might need to use Help to complete the assignment.

Reading Windows Blogs

Instructions: Use the search box to navigate to and review the Windows Blogs page.

Perform the following steps:

1. Start Microsoft Edge.
2. Type **windows blog** in the address bar text box and then press ENTER to display search results.
3. Locate the Windows Blogs page and review the contents (Figure 9–79).

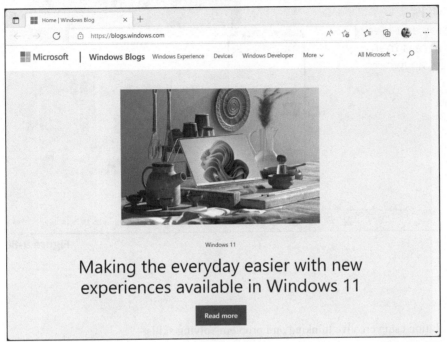

Figure 9–79

4. Open a new document in WordPad and answer the following questions:
   a.   What does the Windows Blogs page contain?
   b.   What are three current postings on the Windows Blogs page?
5. Submit your answers in the format required by your instructor.

Expand Your World

Create a solution that uses cloud or web technologies by learning and investigating on your own from general guidance.

Searching the Web

Instructions: Now that you are familiar with some of the mobile features of Windows 11, you will compare several Microsoft storage technologies to identify the similarities and differences of each.

Perform the following tasks:

1. Using Microsoft Edge, visit https://onedrive.live.com (Figure 9–80).
2. Locate help documentation on OneDrive in Windows 11 to understand the purpose of the tool.
3. Perform a search for additional information on Work Folders.
4. Perform a search for information on Microsoft SharePoint.
5. In a WordPad document, summarize the similarities and differences of the three tools as they relate to storage and mobility.
6. Submit the WordPad document in the format requested by your instructor.

Continued on next page

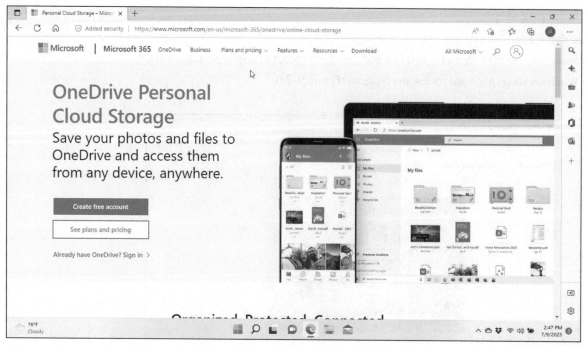

Figure 9–80

In the Labs

Design and implement a solution using creative thinking and problem-solving skills.

Lab 1: Security Inventory

Problem: You have decided to review the security settings used throughout Windows and perform a self-assessment of the features that you could be using to reduce your risk as a user.

Perform the following tasks:

1. Click the Search button on the taskbar and then type   **control panel**   in the Search box to display the search results.
2. Click Control Panel in the search results to open the Control Panel window.
3. Click the 'System and Security' link to open the System and Security window.
4. Click the 'Security and Maintenance' link to open the Security and Maintenance window.
5. Click the Security button to expand the Security area (Figure 9–81).
6. Create a new WordPad document to record your findings.
7. Document and resolve any security problems noted in the Security and Maintenance window. Explain what you did to resolve the issue, if necessary.
8. Document the software identified below the Network firewall heading.
9. Document the software identified below the Virus protection heading.
10. Click the Change settings link in the User Account Control area to open the User Account Control Settings window.
11. Document the current notification level setting.
12. Click the Cancel button to close the User Account Control Settings window.
13. Save and submit the document in the format required by your instructor.

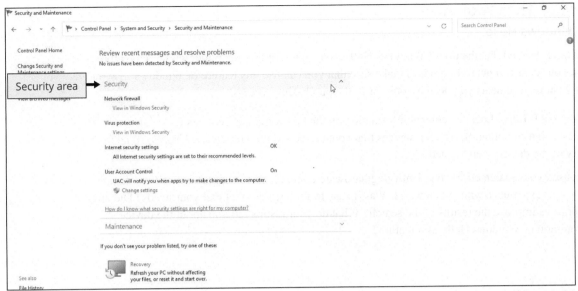

Figure 9–81

Lab 2: Windows Defender Firewall

Problem: You have decided to explore the list of apps and features that are permitted access through the Windows Defender Firewall on your computer. For each app, you will consider the need for its access on either a public or private network.

Perform the following tasks:

1. Click the 'System and Security' link in the Control Panel window.
2. Click the 'Windows Defender Firewall' link to open the Windows Defender Firewall window.
3. Click the 'Allow an app or feature through Windows Defender Firewall' link to open the Allowed apps window (Figure 9–82).
4. Review the list of apps and the current private and public allowances.
5. In a WordPad document, list at least 10 apps and note whether they are allowed through the Windows Defender Firewall on Private or Public networks.
6. Write a brief summary of any changes you would make to the settings for the selected apps.
7. Submit the document in the format required by your instructor.

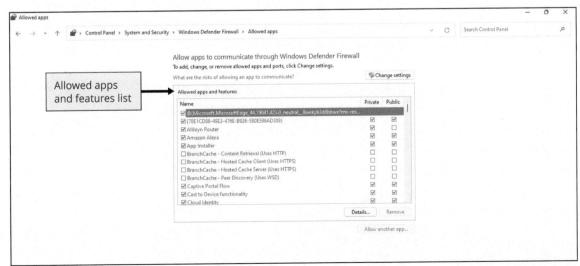

Figure 9–82

Lab 3: Consider This: Your Turn

Researching Windows Hello

Problem: You have decided that the use of Windows Hello as a sign-in option for Windows 11 is a feature that you want on your next computer. In order to make sure that you can use this feature of Windows 11, you want to find out what requirements you need to look for in the purchasing process.

Part 1:   Start Microsoft Edge. Locate technical information on the hardware requirements for using Windows Hello as a sign-in option. Search for devices that contain the required hardware. Use WordPad to create a summary of the devices you located.

Part 2:   You focused your search efforts on identifying hardware components to support a specific software desire relative to your experience with Windows 11. Was it easy to find devices that met your needs? Did any specific search phrases improve the results of the search? What do your results tell you about the device manufacturer's opinion of Windows Hello as a feature?

Index